George John Whyte-Melville

Tilbury Nogo or Passages in the Life of an Unsuccessful Man

George John Whyte-Melville

Tilbury Nogo or Passages in the Life of an Unsuccessful Man

ISBN/EAN: 9783337812607

Printed in Europe, USA, Canada, Australia, Japan

Cover: Foto ©Thomas Meinert / pixelio.de

More available books at **www.hansebooks.com**

TILBURY NOGO;

OR,

PASSAGES IN THE LIFE

OF

AN UNSUCCESSFUL MAN.

BY

WHYTE MELVILLE,

AUTHOR OF "DIGBY GRAND," ETC.

FIFTH EDITION.

LONDON:
CHAPMAN AND HALL, 193, PICCADILLY.
1866.

PREFACE.

Mr. Nogo has been induced to publish the following random sketches, by the favour with which they were received in the pages of the *Sporting Magazine*.

That they are but an unconnected series of scenes and occurrences, usually resulting in his own discomfiture and disappointment, he is obliged in common candour to confess. That a simple relation of such untoward facts may deter others from follies to which they have no inclination, and efforts of which they are physically incapable, is the earnest hope of a disgusted individual, whose only claim to consideration is his invariable prominence as

An Unsuccessful Man.

Munchausen Club,
April 1, 1853.

TILBURY NOGO.

CHAPTER I.

Fortune is Bardolph's foe, and frowns on him.
Henry V.

To fling the billows from the drenched hair,
And laugh from off the lip the audacious brine;
And then to plunge, with wanton spirit, down
Into their green and glassy gulfs.

It is the prevailing cant of the day, to uphold intensity of purpose and force of will as being equal to and commensurate with energy of mind and power of body. Had it but been so, I, Tilbury Nogo, might truly have achieved success; but, alas! like the comforter and consoler of Sempronius, I can only congratulate myself on having deserved it. Before entering upon the thrilling relation of some of my adventures in civilized life, and the detail of my many attempts at distinction and success, it may not be amiss, in these genealogical days, when the landed gentry of this favoured country—from the cotton-lord of yesterday, who has just completed the purchase of his hundred thousand acres, to the sturdy yeoman, who himself tills the profitless soil that barely keeps him from starvation—must all and each be handed down to posterity, with their imaginary ancestors, on the golden page of history, as emblazoned by the ingenious Mr. Burke—it may not be amiss—in fact, it is absolutely essential—that I should commence by specifying how I, T. Nogo, was the only son and heir of Zachary Nogo, Esq., who, in his espousals with the amiable Miss Muff, was blessed with no other issue than the writer of these pages, whose only apology for thus presenting himself to the public is the sincere hope that he may prove as a beacon and a warning to the too ambitious youth of this aspiring age, who often flatter themselves that "to deserve success" is as efficacious as "to command it."

I may here remark that my tendency and attachment to field sports may be attributed to my descent, on my mother's side, from a family who, time out of mind, have been ardently addicted to all out-of-doors pursuits. I have met more Muffs out hunting than in any other assemblage of my fellow-citizens, albeit they are to be found in very sufficient multitudes engaged in graver and more important pursuits.

My father had a great idea of Eton ; and although his death delayed my appearance at that jovial school till I had completed my twelfth year, no sooner was I fairly launched in my teens than I was packed off, *per* stage, to take my chance of arriving at my destination—Eton Coll., Bucks— in company with two other "new fellows," one hat-box, one portmanteau, and one carpet-bag, the latter well stuffed with provision for both body and mind, including a Greek grammar, a mighty cake, a 'Gradus ad Parnassum,' as it is somewhat ambitiously denominated, and a cold plum-pudding.

I have not the face to inflict on my readers the autobiography of an Eton boy; but I must "cry their mercy" for the narration of two anecdotes bearing upon that fatality which has pursued me through life, and which has ever interposed when success was all but in my grasp. Sysiphus was a joke to me ; and, I take it, his task was no pleasant one. Whilst enduring the six-o'clock lessons, long mornings, faggings, and other *agréments* of life in the fourth form, I was induced by the persuasive arguments of a fellow-*scug*, rejoicing in the appropriate name of " Tubbs," to relax my mind and forget my sorrows in the enjoyment of a bath at Cuckoo-weir, the pleasure being increased by its being a drizzling day in October, and the exploit being much enhanced by the certainty of a flogging if caught—or *nailed*, as we termed it—in the fact; that month being, very properly, one of those in which bathing is strictly forbidden. Well, away we went, in the highest of spirits, stripped, sneaked in, ducked, and persuaded ourselves it was delightful; when, in the height of our splashing, holloaing, and enjoyment, we were aware of the tramp of a horse, and the dreaded form of one of the under-masters was seen, cantering his hack slowly along the bank. Tubbs, who could swim like a water-rat, was over to the other side in a second, and on arriving at the shore called (why, I have never been able to understand) " Italy," effected a most successful shirk; whilst poor I, unwilling to be flogged, yet loath to be drowned—for my swimming was only calculated for a short boy, *in* his depth— was forced to emerge, and face the infuriated don.

* * * * * *

It was Tubbs who proposed the lark of going to bathe; but at eleven-o'clock school, next day, it was, "Nogo to stay." I am secure of the sympathy of every old Etonian.

* * * * * *

As years rolled on, and the "scug" of former days rolled out into the well-cravatted stripling in the upper division, so did my ambition—that last infirmity of Nogo's mind— increase proportionately. Our Sculling Sweepstakes was coming on; and, from my proficiency in that particular department of boating, I thought I might fairly calculate on beating the rest of my school fellows. I got a betting-book, ruled it most carefully, and proceeded to enter my wagers on the most approved principle, backing myself heavily with all that would lay against me, but, in my inexperience, omitting to bet against any of the other boys. The consequence was, that I stood to win a large sum in half-crowns and shillings, should I win the sweepstakes, and to lose largely in the same coin, should any other skiff pass the Brocas Clump ahead of mine. Well, the evening came—how well I remember it! The placid river; the level Brocas, with its stately clump standing out against the clear blue sky; the glorious castle; the flag on the round tower, drooping in the summer air—I see it all now. Then the start; the strain against the stretcher; the fever boiling in the veins, till the perspiration, bursting forth, seemed all at once to cool, refresh, and invigorate the quivering frame; then the turn round Lower Hope, the second wind, the rushes gained, and the coming down stream, with a rapturous lead; the holloaing, from the bank, of five hundred fellows, all at the utmost pitch of their lungs, and only subsiding into an occasional scream, when so blown from running along-side the leading skiffs as to admit of no greater vent for the enthusiasm inseparable from a boat-race. "Well sculled, Nogo!" "Go it, Nogo!" "Well sculled, Smith!" "Go along, Brown!" "Well sculled, Robinson!" the latter worthy breaking both his rowlocks, in his animated endeavours to get forward, and being instantly put *hors de combat*. "Well sculled, Nogo!" "Brown will bump him!" "Smith's beat!" "Nogo wins!" "Smith wins!" "Nogo!" "Smith!" "Hurrah! hurrah!" and Smith's skiff shoots by the well-known goal, one boat's length ahead, Nogo second, and the redoubtable Brown a good third.

It almost broke my heart, boy as I was. It was so provoking to have nearly won and landed all my bets. It should have been a lesson; but the elasticity of youth soon brought forgetfulness of the past annoyance, and fresh hopes for the future; and again and again was I forced to admit the truth of the homely proverb that "a miss is as good as a mile." I should have been *sent up*, had it not been for a false quantity in the last of thirty fairly-written long-and-short verses; although I must confess that, prejudiced as I was in their favour, I never could see the merit of the twenty-nine preceding ones. But enough of Eton. "Her praise is hymned by loftier harps than mine;" though, like most old Etonians, notwithstanding all my reverses, my heart still leaps responsive to the well-known cry, "Floreat Etonæ!"

CHAPTER II.

Bard.—Out alas, sir; cozenage, mere cozenage.
Host.—Where be my horses? speak well of them, varletto.
Fal.—I would all the world might be cozened, for I have been cozened.

IT would be superfluous to detail the many good intentions not acted upon, and plans cast aside, which occupied the few years intervening between my removal from Eton, and my entrance upon what is called "life." How I read a little, hunted a little, fished, shot, danced, and drove in the same small proportion; how I matriculated (nothing more) at Oxford; how I thought of going into the army; how I started for the Himalayas, making Paris my first stage, and eventually got no further than that pantomime of a town—returning a wiser, truly, if not a better, man; the old friends who gave me good advice, the young ones who helped me to disregard it, "all these I can forgive and those forget." And I must now introduce myself as Mr. Tilbury Nogo, well dressed, well appointed, and well received; a member of the best clubs; lodging no matter where, within easy distance of the same; and, in short, in the common position of hundreds of other young men about London. I drove a cab, wore lavender-coloured gloves, went everywhere with no particular object, was better supplied with money than brains, by no means good-looking, and decidedly shy.

Such was the individual who turned out of Tattersall's yard one frosty day in February, arm-in-arm with one of that class of acquaintances which the world is pleased ironically to term "a friend," and who is more particularly distinguished by that appellation when he keeps you four-and-twenty hours in the vortex of a quarrel, to extricate you at the end of that time by putting you up to be shot at. Silently we passed the gentleman in the red waistcoat, whose unacknowledged greeting was cordial as ever. That cad is a wonderful official; he has more acquaintances than any man in England, and winter and summer he never wears a coat. Silently we turned our backs upon the triumphant tomfoolery meant to glorify the greatest warrior of the age; and it was not till we caught the keen air blowing on us from the half-frozen Serpentine, that my companion, who had been in deep thought, proceeded to give me the benefit of his reflections.

"Upon my word, I don't think this frost will hold. I wonder, Nogo, why you don't go to Melton."

There was certainly not much in this lucubration; but such as it was, what a number of ideas these few words brought crowding into my brain! Melton, the cream of all winter society: noble earls, jovial M.P.'s, pleasant dandies, good sport, capital dinners, ox-fences, whist, claret, and hard-riding—all jumbled themselves up together in my head, not unaccompanied by certain misgivings that all this might be what is commonly called "too fast" for me; and it was some little time before I replied.

"Melton, eh? Well, I believe it is a very jolly place at this time of year, and—"

"Jolly place! Why, to begin with, it's the only place in the world a man can hunt six days a week from, and it's a bore hunting less. I wonder you didn't go there last year. You know most of the fellows; you've got plenty of money (perhaps he meant *he* had had plenty of *my* money); and you might easily get a few horses together; I'll manage that for you. Why, you've got some to begin upon; and I'll tell you what, my dear fellow, I wouldn't mind letting you have old Congreve and Barabbas for next to nothing, as I want to get rid of all mine."

This was the more kind, as I was well aware of the merits of the animals thus unhesitatingly proffered in the cause of friendship. Congreve was a retired plater, who never having done anything on the turf, was pursuing the same useful career in the hunting-stable; and what with bad legs, bad temper, and a most inconvenient and eccentric way of disposing of his head, was altogether as disagreeable a horse as a man need wish to get rid of. Barabbas, a great white-faced, half-bred brute, whom I did buy, proved himself well worthy of that elegant appellation before I had kept him six weeks.

"Well, you really are very kind," was my reply, "but the fact is, I am not quite sure about the horses I *have* got; and though Phiz, Catamaran, and the old mare are all very well in some countries, and can go quite in front when properly ridden, yet I have my misgivings as to their being good enough for Leicestershire; and then the fences; and then I don't quite know *where* to live there; and, in short, it's not an easy thing to manage, and so I must think it over, &c., &c., &c."

Well, the long and short of it was, that after a *tête-à-tête* dinner at Crockford's, one bottle of dry and three of '25 between the two, I succumbed, made up my mind to go, and that forthwith, and handed over a cheque to my friend for the aforesaid Barabbas, who, I regret to say, became my property from that evening; as for Congreve, though denominated by his owner as an outside good horse, and the best he had ever possessed, Reason sufficiently retained her sway, till we parted, to prevent my having anything to do with *him*.

Next morning the misgivings came stronger than ever; but the die was cast; and when I found the frost was breaking, the wind getting well round to the south-west, my hack looking so sleek and handsome, and London so muddy and disagreeable, I regretted my determination less and less, and even came to think of Barabbas and the cheque of three figures with complacency. I wrote for my horses from the country, ordered some more saddlery, and some top-boots from that prince of the sons of St. Crispin, who, ascertaining that his customer did not intend to hunt at the great emporium of the craft, promised to make him a neat "provincial" pair of boots, and made all my arrangements to "take the field," as the old ladies call it, the following week. I do not know how people feel before a campaign, or on the eve of a revolution—though the latter is now hardly "a sensation,"—but that last week in London was a most feverish one—" fiery expectation's dower "—and the last day I spent in it I quite came to the conclusion that, after all, there is nothing like a town life. But it was too late to retract: the stables were engaged, likewise a swell studgroom, the cavalry had already marched viâ St. Albans, and nothing remained to be done but to take a first-class voucher at Euston Square, buy a Bradshaw, and start.

The journey per rail to Syston was performed, as all such journeys are, without hindrance or excitement of any kind; my fellow-travellers were nothing remarkable, and with the exception of my mistaking one popular M.P. for a friend's stud-groom, and another pleasant-looking, agreeable, sporting gentleman for a dissenting clergyman, the latter supposition being confirmed by the theological knowledge displayed in several expressions with which he garnished his conversation—neither misconception, I am happy to say, leading to my addressing the individual before I had discovered my error—nothing occurred to break the monotony of the London and North-Western line. Sir Francis Head's clever pamphlet, 'Stokers and Pokers,' had not then come out; and the mind was not strained in the endeavour to grasp the magnitude of an undertaking, in which, independent of the expenditure of coke, coal, and capital, the one small item of lunch alone consumes porkers by the thousand, and Banbury cakes by the million—a statistical fact now universally known, thanks to the research of the clever author of that amusing and instructive little work. Syston reached, and a post-chaise with horses in it for Melton duly proclaimed, self, packages, and valet loaded therein and thereon; No. I stowed away in the corner, and abandoned to those reflections, which in my case, inside a carriage, generally resolve themselves into a sound sleep; whilst the post-horses are bobbing and dodging themselves and their short tails through Rearsby, Brooksby, Kirby, and all the byes on the Leicester and Melton road, I may relate a circumstance which is often brought to my mind by the universal affinity there seems to exist between rapid travelling and sound sleep.

A friend of mine, by no means of a wakeful disposition, was summoned to Birmingham—a place he had never before visited—on the most urgent business, one of those cases where delay even of a few hours might be irreparable, and was sure to be attended with the greatest inconvenience. The early train was his only chance; and breaking through all his luxurious habits of late rising, comfortable breakfast, and doze over a cigar until well into the afternoon, behold him up, dressed, and shaved, seated—actually seated, in the worst of humours, in a most comfortable first-class carriage by half-past five A.M. Like all men of late habits, when he did break them he did it effectually; and what with a sleepless night in anticipation of an early start, and the unusual exertion of rising by candlelight, he was as tired when fairly established in the well-cushioned arm-chair of the *coupé* as he ought to have been on his arrival at his destination. Balmy sleep soon shed her influence over the most faithful of her votaries, and deep were the notes in which the sluggard chanted his own lullaby; the sleep of ages, we may suppose, would be but as that of one night—nay, of one hour, or even a few minutes, so mysterious is the agency which " tired Nature's kind restorer " exerts over us; nor is it in the power of mortal to explain, far less control, that influence which bows the eye, relaxes the muscles, and reduces the whole thinking and intellectual man to the level of that which has no life, " sans eyes, sans ears, sans everything "—what is it but a temporary death? But to return to my vigilant friend: small surprise did he betoken at having slept through his journey, when the ringing of bells the shutting off of steam, and all the bustle of a station, brought him back to consciousness. More in accordance with his usual habits would it have been to have remained snoring in that corner till forcibly torn away by guard, stoker, conductor, and porters; but he had a great duty to fulfil, and with the recklessness of a desperate man he fixed his knuckles into his twinkling eyes—those eyes which, on ordinary mornings, the corner of a boot-jack would hardly seem to have power to unclose—and with one mighty shake, and a triumphant exclamation, he grasped his carpet-bag and writing-case, pushed aside the porter who was vainly endeavouring to shut him in, threw back a farewell glance at the train now moving slowly northward, and striding across the platform to a stout man in green, and thrusting his ticket into the hands of the astonished functionary, he emerged into the morning air considerably nearer London than Birmingham; as ere his first impression clothed itself in the half-formed words, " Bless me, how alike all these stations are!" a second glance revealed the very cab that had brought, and the very driver who had overcharged him, whilst around and above him frowned the classic architecture of Euston Square on his astonished gaze. He had jumped out just as the train started, and although his non-appearance at Birmingham was productive of all the anticipated inconvenience, I have heard that when he got back to his own house he went to bed again, and quietly finished his night's, or rather his morning's rest.

Certainly my sleep was not so sound as his, nor was the waking quite so unsatisfactory, as a well-lighted, most comfortable room at the George, with a blazing fire, and that sort of picturesque arrangement of clean table-cloth, glass, and silver, which foretells a well-served dinner, was by no means a bad exchange for the damp cushions and rickety motion of a post-chaise, letting in the draughts of a February afternoon, and cooling the interior till the shivering occupant wonders why a close carriage is supposed to be the warmest, and whether it can be possible that such weather as he feels at his extremities can have anything to do with what we call a thaw.

Everything looked very like hunting certainly; I met the smartest of valets carrying the dirtiest of boots and breeches on the staircase. The waiter informed me of a run they had had that day, but quite in the business-like, unimportant manner that seemed to say such things were of every day occurrence. There were foxes' brushes at the bell-pulls, and the meets of heaven knows how many packs of hounds over the chimney-piece. I quite wondered why a man couldn't hunt eighteen times a week. I am somewhat shy, and as a relief from the agreeable society of the waiter I sent for my groom, hoping to ascertain something about things in general from him, and make my arrangements for the morrow. In he came; such a coat, and such slender supporters! he looked as if he had put his arms through his trousers and his legs in his sleeves. I saw his hat next day, and was surprised no more after that.

"Well, Stubbs, how did you get down? and how are the horses?"

"Horses all well, sir, and most of them fit to go; 'ceptin' two as I had out to-day on the Widmerpool side; and the mare's got a cough, and the hack's been and hit himself, and

Phiz is rather big; I should like to give him a turn afore you ride him, and—"

"Stop," said I, not quite liking the way in which he was running through my stud, and wondering what there would be for me to ride; "stop, I must have something for to-morrow; I see the Belvoir are within reach, and I should like to look at them."

"Beg your pardon, sir, but to-morrow's the Quorn day, in High Leicestershire, so I kept Barabbas and the young one for you to ride to-morrow; ten miles from here, sir, and a very good place. I had the gray out the beginning of the week and he frames remarkably well, never seems to refuse, pulls uncommon hard: but I'll put a bridle on, sir, that'll soon stop, that; and Barabbas will go very well for second horse, and—"

I was forced to interrupt my voluble master of the horse, to beg he would indulge in no vagaries about bridles, as the little experience I have had has convinced me that servants and their masters are apt to differ considerably in their mode of treatment of that most sensitive of all things, a horse's mouth.

"Stop, let me have the hack at the door in time, if he is sound, and—"

"Dinner, sir," said the waiter, which furnished me with a good excuse for getting rid of my attendant, and I stalked into my dressing-room to wash my hands whilst my soup was cooling, with the comfortable reflection that amongst all the horses in my stable, the two I would most particularly rather *not* have ridden for my *début* at such a place as Barkby, were a young one, of whom I knew nothing, except that he pulled hard, and was rising six: and Barabbas, of whom what I did know was by no means enough to give me confidence in a large crowd endeavouring to spoil a quick thing over a stiff country.

CHAPTER III.

A fox-hunt to a foreigner is strange,
And likewise subject to the double danger
Of tumbling first, and having in exchange
Some pleasant jesting at the awkward stranger.

    Mazeppa answered, "Ill betide
    The school wherein I learned to ride."

THE next morning saw me trotting merrily along, after a due study of the map and observation of the sign-posts, on high thoughts intent. I was screwed "up" to the sticking-place, and meant mischief. The morning was as if ordered expressly : there had been a slight frost, but the day was clouding over ; and the wind, though scarcely perceptible, had that keenness which so often accompanies fine scenting weather. I had started early, to avoid the companionship of men with whom I had not yet the honour of being acquainted, and many of whom I did not know even by sight, though their names were familiar to my ear and honoured in my heart. Nimrod's book, 'The Hard Riders of England,' had taught me, as a boy, to look upon "a good man over a country" with a most reverential feeling ; and I had really never quite got over this sort of hero-worship. It would be the height of injustice to deny that many of those whose names my boyhood honoured solely for their well-known success as sportsmen, have been equally distinguished in the more important pursuits of life. Witness the court, the camp, and the bar ; the desert and the ocean, the plains of the Punjaub and the walls of St. Stephen's.

I was a little nervous, certainly, and none the less so for having to ride Gray-friar ; but I was determined to go, and a little more or less of peril made trifling odds. It was a service of danger altogether ; but then the $\kappa\tilde{v}\delta o\varsigma$ if obtained in that country! In short, "Do or die" was the motto—very much the feeling with which a Frenchman goes out hunting. His national vanity makes him think the eyes of all England are upon him, his inborn gallantry impels him to be forward, and his acquired *sang froid* prevents him from disclosing his misgivings. He generally rides unmercifully hard, till in the natural course of events he is stopped by a rattling fall, and is invariably flattered with the somewhat doubtful compliment of having gone so extremely well for a Frenchman; but for all this, I do not think he thoroughly enjoys it. I found my way easily; and cantering pleasantly over sundry most extensive grass-fields, agreed with the noble lord who used to declare riding to covert in Leicestershire beat hunting anywhere else. An early breakfast, not so hearty as it might have been, a free-going hack, and a fine morning are wonderful things for the spirits; and I was delighted with the cheerful "Good mornings" of a farmer or two whom I overtook, and the universal touch of the hat from every countryman I met. A friend of mine used to say, "They always call you My Lord before Christmas; afterwards, lords are so plentiful here that it is no compliment:" and certainly a scarlet coat is duly appreciated in Leicestershire.

"Well, I rode on, and on I rode," as the old Border ballad has it; and after overtaking sundry horses that looked like the impersonation of speed, strength, and gallantry (I am at a loss for a classic simile: the Greeks had not an idea of what a horse should be; look at the heavy-shouldered brutes in the Elgin marbles: no wonder they drove them), I came at last to an open gate, and turning short found myself in company with two or three men in red coats, looking at the neatest pack of hounds in England. "And so they ought to be!" I hear the reader exclaim; well, and so they are: level, powerful, and graceful. What can look more like going than eighteen couple of bitches out of the Quorn Kennels? But hounds are universally voted a bore; so I must close my raptures with the remark that the hounds looked as if they should go the pace, the horses as if they could, and the men as if they would.

After Nimrod's description of a run over Leicestershire, which, written by the best sporting author of the day, was, I believe, touched up by the cleverest reviewer, and illustrated by the most talented artist, it is in vain for an humble pen to attempt to follow in his steps, "*non passibus æquis*," as he himself would have told us, for verily he was *up* in Virgil. Vain, then, would it be for me to attempt to describe, as he did, the "lawless burst," the wicked riding, the "Siberian waste of grass," the cracking rails, the submersion of new coats and gallant souls in the Whissendine, which, it would appear, ought to be regularly dragged during the hunting months; the little bay horse whose untimely stop comes home to the feelings of all "*de te fabula narratur;*" and lastly, the scream, which frighted the village and hall of Cottesmore from its propriety, and must have called forth a responsive yowling from the denizens of its well-known kennel. Neither can I fall back upon a true and particular account of what happened to me individually, in the first person; for I am again "*headed*" by the same author, who describes a most courageous character fighting a young horse through the best part of the best run "that had been seen for three seasons," as the writer himself expresses it in his veracious and autobiographical letter to his friend. My exploits and eventual failures would indeed pale before this worthy's account of "how he rode over young M." (I wonder who *he* was), "how he lost his whip and part of his rear-guard in a bullfinch," how he cleared nine yards with the young one, but lighting in a furrow and on a mole-hill, narrowly escaped the fate of the illustrious Anti-Jacob*ite*, who fell a victim to the architecture of the little gentleman in black velvet; how he was up and at it again; and after many more deeds of daring and sundry mishaps, is eventually reduced to a standstill, the young one being completely beat and minus an eye —an accident not confined to Leicestershire, if we may judge by the number of times the same casualty appears to occur in the neighbourhood of Holborn and other parts of London, "There you go with your eye out" being so common a salutation that it seldom or ever induces the person so kindly warned to turn round and look for the missing luminary.

I can only say we had a run, a right good one. I was carried *well*, and thanks to following those who were of sterner mould than myself, in a most satisfactory place during a greater portion of the time. A fall, with the loss of a stirrup-leather, and a bad turn, chiefly owing to the forbidding appearance of a certain hog-backed stile, extinguished my chance for the remainder; but I came up in time to see a most gallant and straightforward fox properly accounted for and eaten, and went back to Melton wonderfully well satisfied with myself and Gray-friar. Pretty well for a Nogo this, I thought. Besides which, I had met one or two acquaintances, made another by catching his horse, and been cordially and cheerfully invited to dinner by an utter stranger to me, but one of whose hospitality and amiable qualities I had often heard; so that altogether I was what people call well pleased with my day's work, and went to my dressing-room with far different feelings from those which I had experienced in the same locality twenty-four hours before. I was no longer shy of the waiters; I sent for my groom, and *gave* him his orders instead of accepting them from him, somewhat to his astonishment. I felt free of the place; I had actually survived a run in Leicestershire; the fences were not so fearful as I had supposed. People were civil to me; I was going to a pleasant dinner; and, in short, everything was "*couleur de rose.*"

CHAPTER IV.

There was a goodly soupe à la bonne femme,
  Though whence it came from, heaven only knew,
With turbot, for relief of those who cram,
  Relieved by dindon à la parigueux.
There likewise was (the sinner that I am!
  How shall I get this gourmand stanza through?)
Soupe à la beauveau, whose relief was dory,
Relieved itself by pork, for greater glory, &c.

Languidus in cubitum jam se conviva reponit.
HORAT.

I HAVE always admired the sentiments of the late Dr. Kitchener—none the less, perhaps, for the inimitable review of certain of his writings in the 'Recreations of Christopher North;' but though I must needs laugh with honest Kit, I cannot laugh *at* good Dr. Kitchener, whose ideas about dinners were of the most profound and orthodox description. " Seven o'clock is the best part of the day"—how often do we hear this remarked! and in this favoured country, where the majority of us can still get plenty to eat (long may it be so!), it is notorious that nothing can be undertaken or completed without dinner. " Dine, and pass resolutions," as Charles Mathews says. Nobody would dream of passing the resolutions without dining; in fact, there would be no resolutions to pass. The alderman going to a city feast did not pity the mendicant who had tasted no food for four-and-twenty hours: far from it, the heroic feeling of the civic dignitary was that of envy, not commiseration. " Lucky fellow, what an appetite you must have!" was his remark. He could not realize the idea of a man having no dinner to go to; and this feeling, if analyzed, will be found to exist in all classes of the community. What is so popular as eating and drinking, on the stage? Success at the bar can only be obtained by the punctual mastication of "commons." In the army, from the days of Shakspeare downwards, when he says of Henry the Fifth's troops,

> Then give them great meals of beef, and steel, and iron; and they will eat like wolves, and fight like devils,

a good commissariat has ever been esteemed the very foundation of success; and Lord Byron—the poet, of all others, who describes life as it is, and not as it ought to be—calls "the tocsin of the soul," the dinner-bell. I may, therefore, be excused for confessing that I was by no means sorry to find myself, about half-past seven P.M., comfortably settled in a well-proportioned room, eating a capital dinner, drinking excellent wine, waited on by the quietest and most attentive of servants; and though last, not least, enjoying the society of five most agreeable *convives*, the whole effect being heightened by the four red coats and two black, which gave the proper warmth and variety of colouring, and destroyed the usual sombre appearance of an exclusively male party.

Nimrod says, at Melton people never talk about hunting after dinner; and, on this occasion, if the exception prove the rule, he was right. Certainly, the subject was duly canvassed; and the fact of one of the party having been laid up with a sprained ankle, and consequently unable to hunt, though not debarred from the pleasures of society, gives me an opportunity of describing our run, as it was related to him by one well qualified to give an account of everything that was done, of course interspersed with many interruptions and good things said, which must be heard to be appreciated.

Dinner was over, and the first bottle of claret beginning its genial rounds, when the conversation, which had in succession touched upon wine, politics, music, racing, painting, and the topics of the day, was more especially brought round to the subject of hunting by the lame gentleman, thus throwing himself on the mercy of the company:

"Well, now, somebody tell me about the run to-day; for,

except your having found at Barkby, and run for fifty-two minutes, I can get no further intelligence: and this was only from my servant, who told me the day before yesterday there was what he calls 'a splendid hunt'—that they found at Owston Wood, and killed at Launde, which, as I know the distance to be three quarters of a mile, has rather shaken my confidence in his reports of sport."

"Well, I'll tell you," said O—, filling himself a bumper of '34, a vintage of which he had already expressed his decided approval. "We drew all the morning without finding; and had it not been for Barkby Holt to fall back upon, we should have regretted losing so promising-looking a day. However, the Holt is a pretty sure find; and I must say, I, for one, never gave way to despondency about it. They found immediately a brace of foxes. I was standing in the middle ride, and viewed a fellow across, with a tag to his brush like the white flag of a rear-admiral; and, thinks I, he looks like going—I hope they will settle to *him*. Sure enough, though there was a holloa at the upper end, this was the fox they were running; and I had hardly listened for ten seconds when I heard them turning towards me, and presently they crossed close to my horse's feet. Another holloa at the bottom, and down the ride came Ben, blowing for his life; and though his horse put both his feet in a hole, and went end-over-end with him, he never took the horn from his mouth, but kept striving to toot, though his trumpet was stuffed up with dirt. He was with them again directly; and by the time I could get to the end of the wood, the hounds were streaming away over the next field, pointing for Ashby Folville, and with all the appearance of a capital scent. I saw W—, of course, get a start, and I rode two fields to him; and I believe, Mr. Nogo, was of some service to you in saving you a fall."

I bowed my thanks, as the fact is, the young one was so eager that I was forced to let him have his own way; and when my obliging friend holloaed to me, I was going straight for the corner of the field, at a good-sized fence, on the other side of which I afterwards ascertained there was a large, deep pond.

"What a fellow W— is to get a start!" said our host: "he never loses a chance; and what a pace he gets his horses along—he knows so well how to make them gallop!"

I may here be allowed to tell an anecdote of the noble lord alluded to, which, I think, illustrates not only quickness and decision, but a degree of judgment as to pace which must be invaluable in a race. Hounds were running really fast over the finest part of Leicestershire, and were nearly a field ahead of any one. Lord W—, with several others, jumped into a large grass field, at the further end of which, and between them and the hounds, was a strong, black-looking fence, that, on a nearer approach, was found to be impracticable. There was but one place in it, and that was made up of four stiff rails, with a soft green spot to land in, that looked very like a certain fall; and add to this, a large herd of frightened bullocks rushing down towards it. His mind was made up as quickly as his eye glanced towards the place. He had ridden too many races not to know exactly when to "come;" and, conscious he was on a fast one, he "sat down, and set to." It was a capital race. The leading bullock ran remarkably stout; but the noble lord beat him by a length: and although he came heels-over-head in the bog on the further side, that was nothing, and another minute saw him gracefully sailing over the opposite rise, well compensated for a dirty coat by the knowledge that some twenty of his most intimate friends were at that moment fussing, fuming, and swearing behind him, hemmed in by the herd of oxen that effectively stopped up their only egress, and with the comfortable knowledge that, if hounds only went on running as they appeared to be inclined to do, and as they afterwards really did, they would be "nowhere," and not one of them would ever again catch more than a glimpse of Lord W—'s horse's well-squared tail, till all the fun was over—which eventually turned out to be the case.

But to return to the run:

"Nogo, the wine is with you." Having restored the circulation of the fluids, unconsciously impeded by my inattention, O— proceeded. "He had no intention of paying Ashby Folville a visit, but, leaving it on his right, made as straight as a line for Ashby Pasture; and they really went such a trimming pace over the grass, that I began to think twenty minutes would finish the whole thing. However, when we arrived at the wood, it was evident he had no objection to its shelter from being too warm; for into it he went, and out again at the further end, like a shot. I galloped down the outside, keeping the wood on my right, as hard as I could lick, and arrived at the corner just as the hounds came out. Away they flashed, straight across the opposite enclosure, and then up went all their heads at once —much, I confess, to my relief; for, had I not been able to get a pull then, I was beginning to wonder how much longer my horse could live at the pace of an express train. The Baronet, who had gone through with the hounds, had hold of them, in a second, and, casting them short to the left, and down wind, showed that he knew pretty well the nature of the animal, and whereabouts Cream Lodge was. Sure enough, that was his point, for they hit it off immediately; and, notwithstanding one field quite full of sheep, who, in their usual warlike manner, had formed squadrons, and charged right across his line, and another of oxen, they hunted it merrily on, at a good holding pace, nearly up to the gorse. Here, I fancy, he must have been headed from his line; for, with no apparent reason that we could make out, they turned again to the right, leaving the gorse two fields upon the left. I saw rather a good thing happen just at this point. A young man on a neatish-looking, well-bred horse, who had been going uncommonly well, but I suppose had pumped him out in doing so, jumped manfully into a double post-and-rail fence, with the laudable intention of doing it at twice. The ditch, however, between the rails, though dry, was deep, and the further timber looked high and strong; and when '*in*,' like her Majesty's Ministers, the thing was, how to get him 'out.' Off he got, and, sitting on the opposite rail, proceeded to pull manfully at his head. The fish was safely hooked, and the line at its utmost stretch, when crack went the rail on which my friend was leaning for a purchase: at the same moment his horse, who had been making up his mind for a final effort, jumped gallantly at his falling owner, and, knocking him completely over, with one fore-leg through his hat, he dragged him prostrate into the field, only to leave him there with the reins safe in his grasp, but, thanks to a treacherous headstall, nothing else remaining to him of his '*monture.*' Whether he is still in that field, trying to catch the runaway, and singing.

'The last links are broken that bound me to thee,'

I have not since had time to ascertain. The pace improved considerably before we got to the Melton and Leicester road, but not enough to prevent two northern gentlemen, both heavy weights, from jumping a high, strong gate into it; and from our fox having turned down the road we had here another trifling check. By-the-by, I saw a good many fellows looking out for their second horses just about this time; but unless they had been ordered to patrol between Melton and Brooksby, I do not see that there was much reason to expect them. When the hounds hit it off again, and really got their heads down in the grass meadows near the river, away they went faster than ever, straight across the middle of the fields, dashing through those thick fences as if they were paper instead of blackthorn; there was no chance of a pull or even a turn, and the natural consequence was the falls began to get plentiful; I, for one, got a most imperial crowner in what I believe to have been a second ditch; but the fact is, old Golightly was blown, and I had been expecting it for one or two fields. However, they did us a good turn in crossing the river not very far from the bridge, so there was no swimming, or jealousy as to who should be 'in first;' and again turning towards us on the further side enabled us to be on pretty comfortable terms with them." (Once more bells ring, " More claret.") " Well, they never checked again; I don't think I ever remember so gallant a fox. I viewed him travelling across the grass-fields below Hoby, as if he never meant to give in; but he began to run short when we got near Rakedale, and after coursing him up one hedge-row and down another, they fairly ran into him in the open, just one field from Thrussington Wolds; time exactly fifty-six minutes: and the distance with '*the compasses, mind, on the Ordnance map*,' eight miles, from point to point. I think we ought to drink the Baronet's health and his hounds."

This was done justice to, as may be supposed, in a bumper; and the conversation turned upon what L. called the humours of the day.

"Who was that in the brook just after we left Barkby? I never saw such fun. His horse tried to refuse it, and the man forced him; and after sliding six yards at least, in he went overhead."

"Why that was me," said A.; "he is a capital brook-jumper, but a farmer crossed me, and put me out of my stride as I was coming down to it; and being young, and a thorough bred one to boot, he won't bear contradiction, and I was too happy to compound by doing it at two stages."

"Well, you lost no time." said C., "for I saw you at Ashby, and never remarked you were wet."

" How well G. went to-day; what a rattling good horse that is!"

" *Well*, did you ever know him go otherwise? He is the finest rider I ever saw; and no one would suppose he was going out of a canter till they came to gallop alongside of him."

" How well your horse jumped that gate into the Leicester-road, C.!" said L.; " I would not have ridden at it for fifty pounds."

" Oh, yes, you would, my dear fellow: it was not much

of a gate; the taking off was so sound. But he really is a very good horse; I have now hunted him ten seasons, and he has certainly not given me ten falls."

"Not much of a gate?" thought I; "well, I saw it, and it appeared to me at least a foot too high: certainly, these fellows do ride."

"I hope you like Leicestershire, Mr. Nogo," said my neighbour. "That seemed a nice sort of horse you were riding, and appeared to carry you well."

"Like it!" I replied, "I am delighted with it. I never before knew what it was to see a run almost entirely over grass; and although to-day I certainly did not see more than half the run to my satisfaction, I am so pleased that I do not think I shall ever hunt anywhere else."

"Well said, Mr. Nogo," said our host. "Will anybody have any more claret, or shall we go up-stairs? There's whist for those who like it, and weeds if fellows want to smoke."

Not being much of a whist-player, and having done justice to my hospitable landlord's claret, I preferred the latter, and accompanied him to a most luxurious divan; where, ere I had fairly lighted my Havanna and mixed a small modicum of brandy and soda in an enormous tumbler, we were joined by several men whom I had that morning met in the hunting-field, and who had dropped in to smoke one cigar and have a chat before going to bed: amongst others, the gentleman whose horse I had caught in the morning, and who was profuse in his acknowledgments for so trifling a favour. What an evening we had! Songs, good stories, laughter, and that cordial good-humour which so generally influences an assemblage of sportsmen, of whatever rank, the highest as well as the lowest, served to keep the fun alive; two or three sang remarkably well, and everything which admitted of a chorus was most harmoniously appreciated. One song, which actually, I believe, charmed away the whist-players from their game by the manner in which it was sung, in one of the richest and sweetest voices I ever heard an unprofessional gifted with, rang in my ears for months afterwards; it was to the air of "Some love to roam o'er the dark sea foam," and was, in fact, a mere parody on that song, but being devoted to the sport we were all assembled to enjoy, would have been popular, even if sung by a very moderate performer; and delivered as it was, in the sweetest of tones, and with a taste and expression that is seldom met with, no wonder it charmed us all; and I, who had never heard it before, or met with it elsewhere, was naturally more delighted than any one. This must be my excuse for giving, as nearly as I can recollect, the words of the "*chanson;*" should they ever meet the author's eye, he will, I am sure, "*excuse errors,*" when he recollects I was listening "*arrectis auribus,*" under the combined influence of claret, smoke, and the brandy and soda-water before mentioned, and this confession, I trust, will " bear me harmless."

  Some love to ride o'er the flowing tide,
   And dash through the pathless sea;
  But the steed's brave bound, and the opening hound,
   And the rattling burst for me.
  Some track the deer o'er the mountain clear;
   But though weary the stalker's eye,
  Be it mine to speed o'er the grassy mead,
   And ride to a scent breast-high.
      Breast-high, &c.

  There are those that love all the joys to prove,
   That crowd in the mantling bowl;
  Who bow to the nod of the Thracian god,
   And yield him up their soul.
  Some speed the ball through the lamp-lit hall,
   With music and revel free;
  Or woo beauty's glance in the mazy dance,
   But the joys of the chase for me.
      For me, &c.

  When we mount and away at the break of day,
   And we hie to the woodland side;
  How the crash resounds as we cheer our hounds,
   And still at their sterns we ride.

> Then at dewy eve, when our sport we leave,
>   And the board we circle round,
> How each boasts the speed of his fastest steed,
>   And the dash of his favourite hound.
>   His hound, &c.
>
> Then those that will may the bumper fill,
>   Or trace out the dance with glee;
> But the steed's brave bound, and the opening hound,
>   And the rattling burst for me.
>   For me, &c.

When I got back to my room at night, and saw my snowy leathers and well-cleaned boots placed in readiness for the morn, can it be wondered that I went to my couch humming "the steed's brave bound, and the opening hound"? Talking of boots, there is a great deal of countenance in a well-made boot; and a friend of mine always turns his with the toes to the wall during a prolonged frost: he says he cannot bear to see them looking him in the face.

CHAPTER V

> Can honour set a broken leg?
> *Falstaff.*

PLEASANTLY the days rolled on. What with moderate sport in the morning, fine weather, and occasionally the cheering influence of ladies' society in the field, sometimes on horseback, sometimes in pony-carriages, together with the crowd of horsemen, which, besides the coffee-house of the thing, was so convenient to hide in, when the nerves were not quite sufficiently braced, and it was pleasanter to ride amongst a gentlemanlike set of men who opened gates, and knew the country and the bridle-roads, than to go rasping, and bruising, and bustling, and screwing amongst another set of men, fewer in number certainly, and equally gentlemanlike, but who would never allow either that the pace was as good, or the fences as stiff, or the run as satisfactory, as I imagined it in my inexperience to be. Pleasant all this certainly was; and my horses, with the exception of Barabbas, turning out good ones; my cards at whist, which I soon ventured on, being generally favourable, my evenings being spent in eating good dinners in good society, and playing short whist, holding good cards, I began to think that the good things of this world were more attainable than I had formerly supposed, and that I was settling down into a most agreeable mode of life, when, as ill luck—or rather my evil genius, who seldom leaves me alone for long—would have it, I must needs write up to London to ask Segundo to come down and stay a week with me.

Melton, February 12*th,* 18—.

DEAR SEGUNDO,

My horses are pretty sound, and the meets next week are so good, that I am induced to hope that you will do me the favour of coming down and spending a week with me here. I shall be happy to mount you, and hope you will like the stud I have got together. Your old friend Barabbas is looking remarkably well. Pray write a line as soon as possible.

I remain,
My dear Segundo,
Yours very truly,
Alfred Segundo, Esq.   T. NOGO.
(Exact Copy.)

Such was my courteous and civil epistle to my friend, whom I have already introduced to the reader as the original promoter of my expedition into Leicestershire, and the former owner of the calumniated bay horse. When I call him my friend, it must be understood in the most general acceptation of the word, as I never could exactly make out who Segundo was. The style of man, perhaps, will be more easily inferred from his answer to my sober and gentlemanlike invitation.

"I'm there, old boy! Come to the station for me on Sunday, there's a brick! don't be late. Thanks for the mounts. I'll show the nags how to go. Good-bye, old slow-coach.

"Yours (in liquor),
"A. SEGUNDO."

Now I appeal to any disinterested observer whether this was not a most improper letter. I, who hate to be old-fellowed, and patted, and patronized, and slapped on the back, and all that sort of thing, to be called "a brick" and a slow-coach too! (I despise the inuendo about the horses); and then to be ordered to the station like a servant! my blood quite boiled; but there are some men that may do anything they like, and that one always gives in to. Here was Segundo; he smoked my cigars, borrowed my money, dined with me at clubs, was good enough to occupy my stall at the Opera in the summer, and the box I generally secured at the Lyceum in the winter (to the latter he invariably brought a party of both sexes), and all this as if I was the individual obliged, and he the person conferring the favour. But so it always is: of every two persons that associate, one will be the master-mind, or, what describes the imposition still better, will get the upper hand of the other. So it is when boys *go partners at school;* so invariably in the partnership for life of man and wife, and even in the dumb creation. Any man unfortunate enough to be addicted to the amusement of gunning must have observed how if Don and Ponto, pride of their respective kennels, be enlarged together to scare the coveys from a turnip-field, either Don will take the initiative, and go through all the forms of snuffling, staring, galloping backwards and forwards, and then stopping dead short in an instructive and most constrained attitude, whilst Ponto confines himself to a careful imitation of these exciting manœuvres, called by the professionals *backing;* or else *vice versâ,* Ponto becoming fugleman, and Don being content to corroborate him. Yet when either of these sagacious animals meets poor Bang, he immediately assumes the command, and Bang, whose own master would not part with him for untold gold, sinks without a struggle into dummy at once. Thus was I invariably Bang in Segundo's society; yet I could not do without him, and though rather slang, and not the most high-bred fellow in the world, he certainly was an agreeable companion, with a flow of spirits and readiness of humour seldom met with.

My first introduction to him was on the race-course at Lansdown, during one of the Bath meetings, when I was smitten with admiration at the extremely scientific style in which he won a hurdle-race on an inferior-looking screw; I believe it was a match, and put a hundred pounds into his pocket; I afterwards met him at the Red House, where I saw him knocking the pigeons about in so artistical a manner that I was induced to back him to win a sweepstakes, which took five pound out*of mine. There being a difficulty about getting back to London, he kindly undertook to scull me down in a wherry, and being *au fait* at most things, succeeded in landing me safely at Westminster, somewhat alarmed by the voyage and drenched to the skin by the swell we encountered from every passing steamer. Two or three Greenwich dinners, at which I enacted Amphitryon, cemented our acquaintance, and a few weeks saw him as completely installed in my cab and free of my lodgings as if we had been brothers in blood and affection, who had never been separated from our infancy. With all this, I never succeeded in discovering his previous history: whether he had a father and mother; whether he was born a gentleman or a clown, though his appearance hardly favoured the latter supposition; whether he ever *had* any private fortune, or what part of England he originally came from—all these antecedents were to me an impenetrable mystery. I fancy he had seen some service, for he appeared to be well up in most military matters, but certainly not in our army; and though I inclined to think he might have been a Queen of Spain's man, yet his knowledge of German airs and fondness for hock somewhat weakened this theory by the counter-supposition of a campaign with an Austrian hussar regiment—no bad beginning for a man of the world. All my inquiries were parried with a joke, a laugh, a song, or a sell, and I am still as much in the dark as ever. He was a good-looking fellow, spare and muscular; about six feet high; with a most voluminous pair of black curling whiskers, and a quick, searching eye, that nothing could escape. Just the sort of man everybody says is "deuced good-looking," but nobody "a deuced gentleman-like fellow." There was a something—a sort of restlessness, although accompanied with plenty of *sang froid*, that belied the appearance of high birth which his features and figure alone would have given him; and his dress, which partook largely of "the sporting," quite set at rest the question as to whether Mr. Nogo's friend was the sort of person you would be anxious to introduce to your family, and make at once free of your house.

Like the inimitable Daly in 'Gilbert Gurney,' Segundo was a dab at everything, and whether it was boating, cricketing, driving, riding races, fishing (with most people such a pleasant fiction), running, jumping, or swimming, land and water, it was all the same to him; at each and all of these he was as thorough a proficient as if he had studied nothing else. I don't know where he went to school, but certainly they taught many accomplishments to an apt pupil who had the education of Segundo. He could work cross-stitch or play skittles; slang a bargeman or perform creditably on the piano-forte; might have made a comfortable income with the pea and thimble in the palmy days of that exciting amusement; dance, fence, draw caricatures, sing a capital after-dinner song, and conjure better than any one I ever saw, except "the Wizard of the North," that mighty magician, of whom nothing shall ever convince me that he is not in close partnership with another skilful deceiver, who shall be nameless. The latter accomplishment proved a fund of amusement to a party of us returning on one occasion from Doncaster races. We had some miles to go after leaving the train, through a bleak country on a dark night; and a heavy fall of rain made it necessary to perform the rest of our journey in a post-chaise. One of these vehicles we found at the station; but not being "with horses, Lady Clutterbuck," as "Used Up" says, we were obliged to wait till they could be procured from the nearest town. We were not sorry, therefore, to espy a blazing fire in the tap-room of an adjacent pot-house, and to its cheerful warmth we speedily betook ourselves, there to smoke our cigars and enjoy whatever amusement the passing hour might supply. We found the room full of stalwart Yorkshire countrymen, sedulously employed in moistening their sturdy clay, and in the intervals of a warm discussion concerning "t' Moog" and "t' Mare," for it was in Alice Hawthorn's day, watching the progress of a game at "all-fours," which was being played by two of the competitors with as greasy and well-thumbed a pack of cards as the North Riding could supply, but which game, nevertheless, they were pondering over with all the consideration some people think it necessary to bestow on chess. In came Segundo, and after a pleasant interchange of compliments with the rest of the party, down he sat to play the winner at all-fours. I do not understand the principle of this noble game, but from what I could gather he did something with the knave, which they denominated "the jack," that secured his winning every point, and all the wagers being laid in "pots," he had won enough beer before he got up, to have started him at once in a flourishing business as a publican. Much were the Yorkshiremen puzzled at finding one so "far north," as they say; and the more so from his antagonist being not supposed to confine himself entirely to playing on the square. But their astonishment was not destined to end here; for Segundo, shuffling the pack with the true pliancy of finger that betokens a professor of the science of legerdemain, quietly demanded what any one would lay that a particular card being drawn and replaced with the rest, he should without seeing that card or moving from his chair, by one simple sentence cause it to nail itself against the opposite door, some fifteen feet from where he was sitting. The Yorkshiremen looked at one another, and seemed inclined to consider this a slight display of braggadocio, and the investments of the party on the "Moog" having been for the most part favourable, and there being no lack of capital, they seemed to think this a good opportunity to get home after their reverses at all-fours. Well, they laid him crown pieces, and goes of brandy, and pots of beer, and every sort of wager rapidly, and the excitement was beginning to equal that which had accompanied the St. Leger we had just been to see. Segundo shuffled the pack, and proffered it to the patriarch of the parish to draw from—a shrewd, white-haired old man, who during the whole performance never took his keen eye off Segundo's countenance. Warily he drew a card, which they crowded to look at, and which turned out to be the ace of hearts; and cautiously he replaced it in the pack, apparently satisfied that it was impossible the conjuror could have *seen* what it was, at all events. Segundo now shuffled the cards, and begged his nearest neighbour, a giant in a smock-frock, to *cut;* this the giant did with a tremulousness that showed he was not in the habit of patronizing such amusements, the excitement all this time becoming intense. Another shuffle, and our wizard, whose pliancy of voice almost amounted to ventriloquism, began chanting a chorus from a Greek play, that seemed to the astonished rustics to be an incantation coming down the chimney. Θελω λεγειν ατρειδας must have been to their ears as incomprehensible as their own dialect would be to those of the "regius professor;" and then with one prolonged crack, in which each individual card had its share, away went the whole pack skimming across the room, whiz past the head of the astonished patriarch, bang against the wooden door, where they burst like a shell, scattering themselves gracefully around, and leaving the ace of hearts transfixed to the aforesaid partition, with his face to the company, and sticking, actually sticking up there before their astonished gaze!

I never saw people so amazed; I believe they thought us all "*uncanny;*" and although there was a slight reaction in our favour consequent upon Segundo's refusal to take their money, which was honestly proffered in payment of their wagers, I gathered from the old farmer's parting "*bon mot*" what was the general opinion of our friend; for on his taking the reins from the charioteer, who had by this time put horses to the desolate post-chaise, and my impressing on him the necessity of our arriving that night at our destination, "Mind, we must be there by twelve o'clock," I heard the old gentleman mutter to his next neighbour, the timorous giant in the smock-frock, "Moost! aye, sure enough, needs moost when t'devil droives."

The trick, though I believe one of the commonest "on the cards," had evidently then for the first time penetrated into the recesses of the North Riding.

Segundo was as good as his word, and made his appearance on the Sunday following my invitation, as I fully expected he would do. In fact, I have never known an occasion on which he has declined a proffered invitation when anything like good fun or good quarters were likely to be obtained by it. I did not go to the station for him, contenting myself with sending Stubbs and the dog-cart to wait upon him. I afterwards understood from that worthy that he astonished him not a little by taking off successively every article of harness and replacing the whole upon a different system, informing Stubbs at intervals that he knew no more of putting a horse into single harness than a cow did of a pair of breeches, with several other pleasantries of a like nature, more lively than respectful, but which, instead of mortally offending my master of the horse, as I should have supposed they would, only seemed to increase his respect for the strange gentleman.

We dined *téte-à-téte*, but some fellows came in afterwards, and Segundo, who was on his good behaviour, was most agreeable and amusing. I could see he was getting quite popular with the two or three people who joined us for half an hour before going to bed, one of whom invited us both to dinner the following day, and I rather gave myself credit for having asked such an acquaintance down to Melton, and swaggered up to bed pleased with my evening, feeling quite keen about the morrow, and, above all, congratulating myself on my invitation and hospitality. "Let me see—Segundo shall ride Catamount, and I'll have Phiz out first horse, and Barabbas second;" inwardly resolving that, if I could possibly help it, I would not lay my leg over the latter except to ride home upon. Blind mortals that we are! I dreamt that night that I won the Liverpool steeple-chase on a buffalo.

"Forrard, forrard, forrard! too, too, too!" from the noble master; "Get forrard, hounds, get forrard!" from a most varmint-looking whip; whilst Goodall, cap in hand, and boiling with excitement, comes galloping up the ride, just in time to view his fox stealing along over the opposite field, before the ridge hides him from his mortal enemy. He has them out of covert in a twinkling; they settle down, notwithstanding the hurry and uproar, every hound to his fox; and away they go as if there could be no doubt about their being in for a rattler. How well they look with their spotted sides against the bright greensward! somehow the grass always looks a richer green when hounds are running over it. Now they reach the fence: but ere that lucky fellow on the gray horse has crashed into the next field with them, three couple are already through, and before he can again settle into his stride they are scouring away all together fifty yards ahead of him. What a scene it is! Already the line of horsemen is completely broken; some dozen are riding *for themselves*, the rest we have no time to look at. The best rider in England is sailing away, almost alongside the hounds, and by this time appears to skim over the fences in the distance as though they were *straws*. The eleven other "best in Englanders" are riding most wickedly to overhaul him. On the right I see a bay horse very artistically handed over a hog-backed stile with a footboard; the whole being done at a slapping pace. The chestnut of course cannot condescend to follow ("*Oh! no,* mustn't pull a horse out of his stride," is the excuse); and slap he goes at "*the loneliest spot.*" Ah! I thought it was a certainty: up went a very handsome switch-tail, and from the total disappearance on the farther side I fancy he has got "*one.*" Forty thousand miles an hour comes a light weight, who not getting a very good start, and being confident of his horse's pace, is now making up for lost time; he don't seem to know that gate will open. Well jumped, by the powers! I should like to have that horse. That's a thrusting fellow in black; a parson of course; he got deuced well away with them, and though he has had two ox-fences in his line, he is still going close to the hounds, and on most comfortable terms with them. On the left are two thorough-bred ones, apparently racing: watch how like clockwork they rise and fall over the fences alongside each other, whilst hardly a length in the rear comes a fifteen-stone gentleman, making the most of every inch of his ground, and living the pace with the best of them. A little beyond these again, on the left, is a man riding his own line, with the hounds turning towards him, who bids fair, if things go on so, soon to have the best of it. What a clever horse that looks, and how well he jumped the timber under the tree and the double beyond that! There he goes again—ah! safe over with a scramble. By Jove, it's Segundo; no it isn't; yet it is—Segundo and the young one!

Such was my mental soliloquy as I watched what bade fair to be one of the best things of the season from Freeby-wood. We had found instantaneously, and to my unspeakable discomfiture I had ascertained that Phiz was so lame it would be impossible to ride him; there was nothing for it but Barabbas; and what with the delay, and the disgust, and one thing and another, I was reduced to the unenviable position of a looker-on, who, however much he may proverbially "see most of the game," does not in fox-hunting see the only part of the beholding which is supposed to be satisfactory— namely, the hounds; as no credit whatever attaches to the being able to tell your friends, "Here you were down," or

"Here you funked;" from the bare relation of these facts proving of itself that the eye-witness must have been behind, and consequently in a worse place than the sportsman he calumniates. My situation in the road, though humble, was secure; and I am not sure that, mounted as I was, I should have been at all anxious to exchange places even with the foremost horseman. Defend me from riding Barabbas in front of the sort of people before whom one *must* go; no excuse for shirking, no excuse for pulling; hounds running, and your friends *behind* you, with nothing for it but a thick bullfinch, the further side *uncertain*, or four strong bars and a slippery take-off for choice. I know the sort of thing exactly, and therefore was not so very much discontented to find myself trotting along a remarkably sound lane (and to do Barabbas justice, he *is* a good hack), with the laudable intention of seeing as much as I could without unnecessary danger, and, if possible, falling in with those pilots for the "*tailers*," the second horses.

I was never, as the reader has by this time found out, very famous for my luck; and though I trotted to this rising ground and cantered to that, opened a gate here and walked through a gap there, I was unsuccessful either in finding the second horses aforesaid (whose dark mass had often before proved a beacon in my distress), or in making out at all the line of the run. First I went one way and then another, till having wandered about as near as I could guess for an hour, the well-known twang of the horn caught my ear, and ere I had time to turn in the direction of the sound, the whole Field burst upon my sight, standing quietly in the middle of an enclosure some half a mile off; having, as I afterwards found, had a very satisfactory run of five-and-twenty minutes, and killed their fox within two fields of the wood where they found him. Of course I joined them; and having accounted for myself with the usual excuses of bad start, first horse lame, second horse difficult to find, &c., I shared my sandwich and sherry with Segundo, gave him a capital cigar, and disregarding his repeated entreaties that

I would ride the young horse, that he was quite fresh, that Barabbas would be delighted to have his old master on him again, &c., I manfully rode on to see them draw for another fox—some busy devil within me whispering that I really must make an attempt to ride this time; that I had not *gone* a run for a fortnight; that people would think I funked; and, in short, that come what might, I must give Barabbas an opportunity of going if he could, which, I confess, he had never done yet. Then Segundo told me sundry stories how he had ridden him over this fence with *the stag*, and over that bro k with the H. H., and a wonderful place that was measured out larking: more fool he! thought I. So that all this, and the impostor himself carrying me very pleasantly over two or three small fences, going from covert to covert, got my courage up wonderfully; and I determined to shove him along—without, however, expressing my devout wish that there might be no occasion to do so. Alas! if Fortune favours the bold, she is not always so accommodating with the shy. A quicker find than before, and the first half-mile all down hill was extremely trying to my nerves on a heavy-shouldered animal with a bad mouth; but thanks to Segundo's good-nature and quickness, for he piloted me for some time, I got a capital start, and was well with them for two or three fields. "*Vires acquirit eundo*," is wonderfully true about riders, though it may not hold quite so good with their horses; and on my jumping into a large flat meadow with every appearance of a brook in the middle of it, I had not an idea of refusing. Barabbas's blood was up; and the brook being a mild one, I negotiated it so energetically as narrowly to miss jumping on my own horse's back, and annihilating my friend, who had ridden my young one at it a trifle too slow in front of me. It was getting delightful; my sensations were like those of a man in a dream, and I really felt as if I was "doing the trick:" how pleasant to have this six days in the week! On we went, the fences getting rather stiffer; Barabbas much excited, and somewhat blown. A high, strong blackthorn fence in front of me, no a very good take off, and Segundo pulling the young one well together for the weakest place in it, where, behind him as I was, I could spy it was strengthened with a most treacherous rail. Over went the young one; and Segundo, looking back, shouted something, I know not what. I was coming hand over hand towards the fence; I made a desperate effort to collect Barabbas, but I could feel him setting his mouth as if it was cast iron, and in amongst the unsound ground he went like a bull: it stopped our way a little, but not enough to save us, and I have a most vivid recollection of the rail, which on a nearer inspection looked quite strong enough to turn us both over.

* * * * *

The next thing I remember was being bled by candlelight in my room at Melton, where I was gracefully reclining on my back, with a fractured collar-bone and something very like a concussion of the brain; whilst Segundo, who was explaining the circumstances to the doctor and an inquiring friend, finished his apparently exciting history with a few disjointed observations, amongst which my ears were regaled with sentences such as the following: "No fault of the nag's; told him to ride slow at it; worst horseman in England," with something about a child and a donkey, which a second fainting fit prevented my quite catching the meaning of.

Hunting was out of the question for the rest of the season; and after a fortnight of bed at Melton I betook myself to London, where it was a good six weeks before I was sufficiently restored even to be questioned about my accident. However, it is an ill wind that blows nobody any good, and Segundo had the horses to ride till the end of the season, which he seems to have done most gallantly, and, as he wrote me word, with no further casualty than one broken back. I never heard, however, that he could go so well on Barabbas as on any of the others.

CHAPTER VI.

CROCKFORD'S.

Here the blithe youngster, just returned from Spain,
Cuts the light pack, or calls the rattling main ;
The jovial caster's set, and seven's the nick,
Or done a thousand on the coming trick.

BYRON.

"DON'T drink Lady Dowdy's champagne, Nogo. I know where she gets it. Let's go to Crocky's, and have some supper there : this thing's getting a bore," said a voice at my elbow, as I proffered an empty tumbler to be filled with champagne and Seltzer-water by one of Countess Dowdy's officials, in a voluminous white waistcoat ; and turning to my timely monitor, I recognized handsome Jack Raffleton, a young guardsman who had lately been kind enough to patronize me considerably, and whose hospitality at the expense of Government I had repeatedly enjoyed, at his bivouac in St. James's Palace. " Come along, old fellow ! I'll drive you down to St. James's Street. I've kept my cab waiting, and it's past twelve o'clock ; so forward !"

I had just been elected a member of the club alluded to. Alas ! even then had its glories begun to pale. The great financier, who gave his name to that stately pile, had ceased to superintend the phalanx of Fortune's worshippers, though they still hovered round her shrine. His course was almost run, and 'twas whispered that only the talismanic name of Rattan held his mighty spirit in its chains of clay. Had the owner died, the nomination of a first favourite for the Derby must have been void ; and, despite of doctors, Crockford lingered on. The Wednesday came ; and Rattan was nowhere. True, he succumbed to a four-year-old—and *I have* heard that it requires a very good four-year-old to win a Derby ; but the second place was filled, and the third ; and ere Orlando's owner had received the stakes, the earthly career of one of the greatest speculators of modern times was closed for ever. Shortly before these events, I had been elected a member of Crocky's, familiarly so called; but, in the verdancy of my youth and the bashfulness of my inexperience, I had never yet ventured within the precincts of the club, and I was not sorry to make my *début* under the wing of so auspicious a patron as Jack Raffleton, who knew everybody, was hand-and-glove with dukes, earls, legs, millionaires, and spendthrifts, and upon a fixed income of £400 per annum, and a fluctuating one, depending as he said, on public events, meaning Derbies, Legers, Cambridgeshires, &c., contrived to keep his hunters at Melton, and his day and night horse for his cab in London, to say nothing of his " *menus plaisirs* " —I should think no trifle, though, truth to tell, his great friends did pull him through occasionally. He was very popular—could ride " like a bird," and, winning or losing, was always perfectly good-humoured and gentlemanlike—qualifications which, in this wicked world, cover a multitude of sins. Whilst Jack was fumbling for his cigar-case, and shaking out his " gibus," I cast a longing, lingering look behind. I had spent a pleasant evening; and even now, the white shoulder and dark ringlets of her with whom I had danced my last quadrille almost tempted me back to the ball-room. A strain of Jullien's loveliest melody, " Olga," was vibrating on my ear; and nothing but Jack's exclamation, that " that eternal waltz made him sick," and the extreme irritation and impatience of his " night-horse "—an animal that had been twice in harness, and originally drafted from the hunting-stable on account of his violent disposition—induced me to leave the fascinating scene. As we hurried through the hall, we met Lord Dribble-die returning from the cloak-room on his way up-stairs: and as he passed Jack, I saw by the curious vibration of wrist and elbow with which he signalized him, that a perfect understanding reigned between the two, though I was as yet ignorant of the interpretation of this masonic sign. Bang goes the apron of the cab; and the black horse, standing well up on end, throws himself into his collar and dashes off. I can see by the action of Jack's white kids against the dark lining of the carriage, that he is pulling a good one ; and one or two close shaves of a lamp-post and consequent " slews " (as they say in a sledge) in a lateral direction across the next street, help to convince me that, though I am being coached by a workman, it is even betting whether we reach Piccadilly without a smash. However, it does not do to *say* you are afraid ; so I sit still, and talk about Epsom and Ascot, as if I was at ease in my arm-chair. It is a lovely night—the wooden pavement opposite the White Horse Cellar as dry as a bone—and, whisking round the corner where, day and night, stands the Charon of sweepers, with his engaging bow and his red waistcoat, we take a pull at the black horse opposite the old Guards' Club, on the well-worn steps of which, ensigns in white paletots stand smoking their temperate tobacco in the midnight air, and bring him up all standing at the broad portals of our princely pandemonium. Some sitting on the balustrades, some grouped on the flags, some picking their careful way over from White's, are assembled what the *Morning Post* calls "the *élite* of the fashionable world," though the majority of them owe their least claim to distinction to what is called fashion. Lounging round that door are men whose names you will see in every morning paper you may take up—names that the future history of our country shall record on her undying page. Statesmen, warriors, authors, diplomatists, a foreign prince or two, noble lords, and wealthy commoners, mingled with younger brothers, agreeable *roués*, *attachés*, and guardsmen—but all gentlemen, and, with few exceptions, bearing the stamp of gentle birth on their persons and features, assisted by the fact of their being extremely well dressed. It is odd enough, but, considering how little pains he takes about it, an English gentleman is the only animal extant that really looks well dressed in a plain evening costume. A foreigner, if he don't require padding, comes out very creditably in a uniform. Your tailor (the very man whose clothes you wear) passes muster well enough at Richmond or Blackwall; but if I wanted to find out *by his appearance* whether a stranger belonged to what are generally called the upper classes, and was only allowed to judge *by his appearance*, I say, send him up-stairs to dress for dinner, give him ten minutes to do it in, and see what he looks like when he comes down at the end of it!

Following Jack's example, I left my top-coat, or whatever the flimsy sacks are called, with that Simonite, whom Jack took the greatest delight in endeavouring to puzzle. Coat after coat, as he assured me, has he borrowed, to leave in that functionary's care; yet so sure as he came out into the pale light of a summer's morning, on his homeward way, so sure was *that* individual coat forthcoming, and ready to protect his dissipated person. Out of the hundreds of members who nightly left their outward coverings in his charge, he was never known to make a mistake. It was no fault of his, if the wolf was ever disguised in the sheep's clothing. With him, then, I left my paletot, nothing doubting; and, reserving my hat (which I never could understand the comfort of at supper), I followed my leader into the hall, past the weighing machine, whose index never pointed to within a stone of the actual weight, and rushing up the handsome staircase three steps at a time, I found myself in one of the most tastefully furnished drawing-rooms I ever saw—style, Louis Quatorze, and exceedingly well done. Periodicals of all sorts—everything a club generally has; a large mirror over the fireplace; but, like the "Palace of the White Cat," not a soul but our two selves in it. The next room fully explained why; and thither Jack, who was always hungry, hurried me.

I recollect when a five-act comedy, called 'Money,' came out upon the stage (I think I am right in the name, but will not be certain), the scene that, of all others, drew down the greatest amount of applause, was that in which the *dramatis personæ* pair off from the drawing-room to go to dinner, the effect being heightened by the *coup d'œil* of a dining-room, with table laid, servants in attendance, and all the glitter of lights and plate. It was managed as such "*effects*" are only on the stage; and the supper-room at Crockford's forcibly reminded me of this popular scene. There were candelabra, epergnes, vases for fruit, plateaux for everything, and such a supper as Francatelli, with a battery of unknown range, could send up; the only difference between this and the table at Covent Garden being, that the former was surrounded by members busily occupied in discussing the good things eatable and drinkable that were before them, but, as I remarked at the time, all, without an exception, with their hats on. I *have* been told that this was the distinction between Crocky's and "over the way." I believe that in those unapproachable precincts men take off their hats when they go up-stairs; but the sacred rights of the ballot, and the defence of the magic "pill," called by the uninitiated a black-ball, prevent such as me from being able to state, as an eye-witness, the manners and customs of the members of that solemn institution. Why, their very waiter in those days must have been of celestial origin by his father's side, if his likeness to the "heaven-born statesman," and his own diplomatic talents, may warrant the supposition.

But to return to Crocky's. Loud and unceasing was the confusion of tongues, honourable members being engaged in discussing every subject under the sun, in every key, from declamation abusive to whisper confidential. Politics, racing, hunting, wine, women, scandal, music, &c., with a running accompaniment of what Rabelais calls the "cliquetis d'assiettes," and occasionally a protracted rattle as of some small, hard substance violently agitated in a box, concluded by an inexplicable "bang!" composed altogether a *pot-pourri* which nothing in music but Jullien's Row Polka could give the slightest idea of, and which we must despair of being able to convey in sober prose. "Well, I think her singing perfection; but I can't have her acting." "Now, I don't agree with you at all: the acting is lady-like and good, but her voice wants volume." "I **took** 700 to 2 about him to-day; and as for public running—" "I saw you at Richmond; and we know pretty well why you went back in the brougham—eh, old fellow?" "'Pon my soul, I should advise you to buy him: he carried me for five-and-forty minutes, as hard as ever they could go, over the finest part of Leicestershire; and I know Hardup refused two hundred for him." "Didn't quite like the picture—he can't have finished it himself; and then that brown scarf spoils the tone altogether." "Obliged to be at Windsor, or I'd come, only I'm in waiting." "We'll go down by water, and come back in the drag—dine early, for she has to go back to sing." "No division, after all: they are taking 6 to 5 about Ministers over the way. I'll take it, I'll bet it—sure to be beat." "How she dances! By Jove it's the most perfect thing! I like her better than Fanny Elssler in her best days." "Not half a good cook. I stayed with him a fortnight, and lost weight immensely." "Capital shooting. Bought a pack of hounds in Devonshire. Very slow huntsman." "Had a very bad night. Saw him at Rome. Went out with a cardinal All hushed up." "She asked half London. Devilish bad ball. Made our party for Ascot. I'll tell you a good thing about Prince Poskywosky." "Rather you would tell me a good thing about the Derby." *Whisper, whisper.* "Give me some champagne and Seltzer-water." "Raffleton, let's go and look into the next room."

Such was the disjointed conversation that smote on my unsophisticated ear; but claret-cup and Twiss's mixture had brought me to that point at which anything in the shape of a lark is desirable, and accordingly, seeing Jack rise to make a move for the next room, as they called it, I was nothing loath to accompany him into that mysterious apartment. What a contrast with that which we had just left! Imagine a comfortable, well-proportioned room, softly carpeted, well warmed and aired, and lighted so that the glare, shaded from the eyes, was thrown brilliantly upon a green-covered table in the centre; a large screen shutting out the noise of the supper-room, and the irritating tread of footsteps passing and re-passing; a most business-like desk in one corner, behind which is seated a respectable and wealthy-looking individual, of a certain age, who ever and anon hands a neatly-made-up packet of what look like opera-tickets to an attendant minister, proffering a wooden bowl for their reception, and then with a satisfied air appears to make an entry in a sort of ledger before him. But little furniture, and that simple and in good taste: several chairs, many of them empty, placed round the table before mentioned, on whose bright green cloth, soft and smooth as that of a billiard-table, are marked several cabalistic numerals, the words "In," "Out," and sundry lines running round the edges, too well known to the three or four men who are sitting round its surface, and one of whom has got through two princely fortunes in the study of a science to acquire which he is now squandering a third in vain. Two individuals in black preside over the solemnities, both wearing green shades, both armed with small rakes in their hands, and both having apparently no greater knowledge of their mother-tongue than is necessary for the formation of such sentences as "Take on the hand," "Seven out," "Six to five," "In with quatres" (pronounced "*caters*"), "Have a back, sir," "Make your game," "Deuce-ace," &c.; but under whose shades are lynx-like eyes, keen to watch the turning of a die, and brains not to be confounded by the most complicated computation of the odds. Wonderful is the worship of Mammon, and universal his sway, from the penniless *roué*, who plays *avowedly* because he has nothing to lose, to the millionaire who hopes to get his new service of plate for nothing by throwing in a hand: each plays wholly and solely to win money—money alternately the curse and the blessing of a lifetime, but ever sought after as the one thing needful to mortal man. Heed not those who make excuses for the gambler; who say—"Such a one plays, certainly; but he does it for excitement: he does not care for money; he is the most liberal man in the world; he is a capital fellow." I tell you *no such thing*: no man sits down to play with any idea or intention but that of *winning*; the *excitement* is the lust for gold; avarice, avarice is the passion that fills those dens most appropriately called hells; and here, amongst the high-born of the land, alas! the thirst for wealth is still unsatiated, unsatiable. Mammon is an uglier word than Fortune, but they are one and the same idol; and so blinded are their votaries, that it is a well-known fact that several hell-keepers, conscious of the advantages that they themselves enjoy by keeping *the bank* at their own houses, being aware as they must be, better than any one, of the constant pull of the game in their favour as long as they continue only to superintend and furnish the sinews for the struggle; in short, knowing that the bank *must win*—cannot yet resist the temptation of trying their fortune as players at other tables, and placing themselves on an equality *of loss* with the multitude of dupes from whose short-sighted avarice they draw their own resources. But the play-room at Crocky's is hardly the place to moralize, however much it may furnish materials for to-morrow's waking reflections; so let us see how the system works as the ivory representatives of hundreds circulate round the table.

Who is that good-looking fellow, sweeping the dice into the box with his gloved hand, as in the full swing of success he prepares to call his fourth main? Six cool hundreds was he out, when Fortune smiled upon his endeavours, and, regardless of the empty account at Coutts's, the outstanding bills, and the mortgaged patrimony, he "potted it on," when he threw in his first main, as though what he calls "pluck," and his aunt "recklessness," were a negotiable commodity, and would serve to pay his way as well as lawful coin of the realm. Once has he dribbled deuces stealthily over the baize; once has he punted cinques gallantly on the board; once has eleven, mystic link with the magic seven, leapt triumphant from the box; and as he again prepares his skilful cast, the backers spread their accumulating counters where the word "in" points the way to fortune; whilst one pale youth, whose propensity for backing out each player but himself has in this instance cost him nearly the price of his commission, but who prides himself upon his immovability of countenance and temperament, drawls out—" Rather a good caster!" "Page, give me another hundred;" and, with a fresh bowl and another relay of counters, works perseveringly on in his untoward course. But meanwhile the box rattles aloft. " Seven !" shouts the caster, and the green masks echo—" The main is seven." " Make your game, gentlemen." Still the white glove is vibrating aloft, and the lynx-eyes twinkle beneath the green shades of the attendants; one more rattle, and down comes the box with a violence that leaves a semicircular mark indented on the cloth. No seven is there, but an envious five grins at him from the dice. " A five to a seven," says the shade, as the caster spreads his store between the parallel lines in front of him. One voice is heard to say—" What are the odds?" A tyro he, but quickly to be instructed by the brief reply of " Three to two ;" and had he looked at his next neighbour he would have seen two red counters, signifying each one hundred pounds, laid quietly down to be converted into three by one successful cast: the wished-for five comes not, and still delayed is the dreaded seven. All the numerals seem to come up in turn but those on which hope and fear depend. How loud the clock ticks! it jars on the strung nerves of the players as they watch the dice with straining eyes. One turn of the wrist sends a die spinning across the table, which, stopped by the opposite edge, turns up a tray. Now for the tug of war. " If there is one thing I pride myself on, it is dribbling a deuce," says the unmoved caster, in reply to the groom-porter's business-like observation of " tray landed," and laughingly he shakes the still imprisoned die in its cell. Holding the box horizontally, he waves it twice or thrice with a sweeping motion of his wrist, and gently impels the ivory messenger on its important errand. The dice pitches on its corner, rolls over, and lo ! a fatal four stands confessed. " Seven out," says the green shade. Busily work the rakes to gather in the spoil. The pale youth having been scrupulously paid, gathers his winnings towards him, while the defeated caster, declining the courteous offer of "a back," rolls the box on to his nearest neighbour, veiling his chagrin under an affected smile.

I had been so occupied in watching this scene as I stood behind the principal performer, identifying myself with his interests and triumphing in his success, that I never remarked Jack Raffleton, who, having taken a chair on the further side of the table, was now immersed in the chances and changes of the game. Judging by the multiplicity of counters before him, he was winning considerable; but nothing in Jack's handsome face would ever give an observer an idea of what was going on within. Winning or losing, he was coolness itself, and amongst other peculiarities of his temperament, he was never known by his most intimate friends to put himself in a passion. As he himself said, when, meeting him after a certain Derby, I condoled with him on the loss which I knew he had sustained of two thousand—"Yes," was Jack's answer, with his usual cheery laugh; "but, worse than that, I have lost my carriage and my luncheon; been losing my time looking for them; and now, if I can only lose my temper I shall have got rid of everything belonging to me, and start fresh, as an insolvent in a new line." Poor Jack! he was a great friend of mine, and I must be excused if I cannot resist the temptation of relating another anecdote, exemplifying the way in which he could keep his temper under the most ruffling circumstances.

Before he exchanged into the Guards, Jack was a subaltern in a *very crack* Hussar regiment, and, as may be supposed, was a dandy of the first water. Naturally of an affectionate and kind disposition, he was as fond of pets as any old maid that ever kept a parrot; and of all his favourites, two tiny King Charles's spaniels bore the bell. He never walked out without them; they had a seat in his phaëton, and a bed on his writing-table; and it was a joke at mess that the only way to get a "rise" out of Jack was to abuse his long-eared darlings.

One fine summer's day Jack was sauntering leisurely up

the High-street, with his little four-footed friends, as usual, close behind him, when the odour of Midsummer meat from a butcher's shop proved too much temptation for Fan to resist; and, sneaking quietly away, she ensconced herself, in company with a large piece of raw flesh, right under the butcher's dresser. Out of the back shop rushed blue-sleeves in a fury aggravated by the height of the temperature, and with one kick sent poor Fan flying across the street, to where her elaborately dressed master was sauntering quietly along. He heard the piteous howl of his favourite, and saw the stalwart butcher fuming upon his door-step; and one glance explained the whole transaction. But what did Jack?—rush across the street, and annihilate the miscreant who could so ruthlessly treat a dumb animal? No such thing. The highway had been watered, and was inch-deep in mud; Jack's boots were French-polished, and fitted him like a glove: so he gingerly walked on to where a paved crossing enabled him to pass over unsoiled; and, marching down the street again at the same tranquil pace as before, halted immediately opposite the butcher, who was still nursing his wrath in his own doorway.

"I say, butcher," drawled out the dandy, "did you kick my dog? How could you do so? You are very ugly, and enough to frighten any animal to death without mauling it."

Such an address as this was not calculated to soothe irritation; and the butcher, a proper-built fellow of some fourteen stone, intimated his intention of treating the questioner (whose appearance he thoroughly despised) in the same manner that he had served his dumb favourite.

"Oh, you will, will you? Butcher, can you fight?" said Jack, as he buttoned his coat systematically up to the throat; and, drawing on his gloves, stood carelessly in front of his antagonist. "Now, butcher, are you ready?" added the dandy, aggravating his address with a lisp put on for the occasion.

To it went the man of marrow-bones with a will; and, being a stout active fellow, made sure that a few rounds would settle the whole business. And so it did; but not exactly as he anticipated. He had altogether mistaken his customer. Jack, a lathy lengthy man, far heavier than his antagonist had they both been brought into condition, was, besides this, one of the best amateurs in London; and as he kept peppering away with perfect good humour at his adversary, it was evident that what was a mortal struggle to the butcher was merely a "breather" to the swell. After a few unsuccessful rallies, in which the Hussar did not receive a single scratch, a well-planted right-hander in the wind sent the yokel down upon the pavement; where he lay, apparently deaf to the call of time. Ere this a crowd had collected; and the remarks made were, as usual, highly complimentary to the winner.

"Yes," said Jack, in reply to a scientific rat-catcher who was dilating on the issue of the fight—"Yes; I wasted my time sadly upon his dial-plate. Had he been *a baker* instead of *a butcher*, I should have hit him in the *bread-basket* long ago."

So much for Jack's coolness! And as he sat behind his pile of counters (and I saw that he had a sum far exceeding what I knew to be his yearly income, on the table in front of him, depending on the issue of the next main) I could not help regretting that all that nerve, judgment, coolness, and daring should be lavished on such a pursuit as Hazard. Many a good man has rued the hours wasted and the means squandered upon a cubic piece of ivory. Often had I been warned of the fascination of play—often had I been told that the allurements of the demon were irresistible, and that once having given way, once having fallen, there was no retreat; yet, even as I looked, I felt the spell stealing over me, the insidious poison was creeping into my veins, and almost ere I was aware I had seated myself at the table between my friend and a fresh-coloured, good-humoured looking personage who was playing like fury, and prepared to take my first sip of that goblet whose brim sparkles with the keenest excitement—whose dregs, alas! too often drained, are remorse, infamy, it may be suicide.

The heart beat and the hand trembled as I took my bowl with its *modicum* of counters. "Young I was, and sore afraid ;" and a modest *pony* was all I ventured to call for on this, my first essay. The table was pretty full; and I contented myself, until the box should come round to me, with backing "in" or "out," as the whim seized me, in the smallest sums—enough, however, to decrease my store to nearly half its original amount; when my next neighbour, who having called for fresh dice, and selected two with the utmost care only to throw "crabs," with a stifled execration and a pleasing smile rolled the box on to me. Feeling somewhat shy and very nervous, I put £5 on the "in" and called "seven." Up came a ten: two or three more throws, and up came my ten again ; apparently much to the satisfaction of Jack Raffleton and one other man, who had put on "cinques," which, as they said, I had "landed for them." I did not quite understand it; but receiving my winnings with a good grace, allowed them to remain on the table, and again prepared to call "seven." Why was it that the "ins" on each side of the table were immediately filled up ? Why was the disposition to back the caster so unerringly displayed ? Could my verdancy have already peeped out ? Could my generosity to the "table" in having nothing to do with the odds on my previous throw have stamped me at once as a fresh hand, whose proverbial good luck would enable winners to add heap to heap, and losers to "ride home upon the young one ?" I know not ; but I could not help remarking the tendency, and, truth to tell, it served to encourage me wonderfully. "Seven," I called lustily ; and down it came "*a nick*." Still did I leave my winnings untouched ; and again I called the magic number—"Eleven's a nick !" "Bravo !" "A capital caster !" and other laudatory mutterings are heard around. In short, ere I threw out with an unsuccessfully-attempted nine I had attained my *thirteenth* main, to the discomfiture of the bank and the satisfaction of several lords and gentlemen who had speculated on my success. Jack Raffleton won largely ; my fresh-coloured friend enormously; and I myself got up a richer man by £350 in crisp bank-notes than I had sat down. Little did I think how spoonily I had managed my good fortune. I was quite satisfied with my success; and did not disturb myself with the reflection that had my friend Jack, or almost any other man at the table, been indulged with such a run of luck as mine, he would have "broke the bank" to a certainty, and walked off with some three or four thousand pounds as his own share of the spoil.

Up I got, and there was at the same time a general move from the table. Polished attendants offered me every sort of grateful compound to drink, but I felt neither hunger nor thirst; and as I walked home in the cool air of a summer's morning (beautiful *even* in Piccadilly!) and smoked my cigar, in the full flush of triumph, I could not help feeling that I had turned over a fresh page in the book, and like the pleasure-palled despot of the east, I had discovered a new source of happiness. Stay! happiness it could hardly be called: it was excitement—boiling, thrilling excitement. But as I looked on the dappled sky above me, and felt the balmy air of morning breathe upon my cheeks, a purer train of thoughts stole over me; and I felt that the life I was then leading could hardly be called a happy one. Gradually and insensibly long-past scenes came back. I thought of my merry childhood and my mother's care, never to be replaced in after-life; and even then a true friend at my side might have turned me from the career I was pursuing. But no! Jack's merry face, as he rattled by me in a Hansom cab, on his way home to dress for a field-day (sleep, I believe, he never indulged in), broke up my reveries, and I laid my head on my pillow, half pleased, half remorseful at my evening's amusement; and thus ended my first night at Crocky's.

CHAPTER VII.

ASCOT AND ITS CONSEQUENCES.

Falstaff.—Master Shallow, I owe you a thousand pounds.
Shallow.—Ay, marry, Sir John, which I beseech you to let me have home with me.   *   *   *   I beseech you, good Sir John, let me have five hundred of my thousand.
King Henry the Fifth.

CAN anything be more enjoyable than glorious Ascot, in the beautiful weather which our much calumniated climate vouchsafes only to the June meeting on that sunny heath? The three fine days and the thunder-storm, supposed to constitute an English summer, invariably include the "Cup-day;" and, wonderful to say, I have known it so hot during the races as to make the deluge with which they concluded really welcome to the sun-dried sportsmen. To a calculating mind, not immersed in the intricate computation of "the odds," there must be something positively awful in the quantity of soda-water, claret-cup, "Badminton," and other anti-febrile liquids consumed between the Tuesday and Friday of that eventful week which so often determines this knotty point in the speculator's mind—whether, having retrieved the losses that "hit him so hard" at Epsom, he shall proceed, rejoicing in his hazardous career, to woo Fortune during an interminable series of meetings, including Liverpool, Goodwood, and all the gatherings at Newmarket, in the full triumph of success; or whether, adopting the consoling and generally-recognized principle that

      "He who bets, and runs away,
        If he loses, needn't pay,"

he shall take wing, to restore his health and recruit his finances, in the placid recreations of a German watering-place, where, as he cultivates a pair of dirt-coloured moustaches, he may reflect on the close-shaved appearance of his creditors at the Corner, doomed to pay, but *not receive;* an awkward arrangement with a man who considers "no bet can be called so until hedged," and who, like honest Shallow, would be too happy to compound for "five hundred out of his thousand."

But little did I think of all these weighty considerations as I found myself, some five or six weeks after my *début* at Crockford's, which I have already mentioned, inhaling the fragrant atmosphere of a bright June morning on princely Ascot Heath. My costume adapted to the weather, my neck-cloth loose and my boots easy, with a good conscience, and a balance at my banker's, what more could be wanting to youth and health for the rapturous enjoyment of the exciting present? I am bound to confess I experienced an occasional twinge concerning the future, but only as regarded "my book," an appendage with a metallic pencil which I had lately set up, and whose cabalistic page assured me, on reference, that I had better not have backed "Deceiver" at two to one, and "Hidebound" at evens for the "Fernhill," seeing that the former was scratched, and the latter had most unaccountably retreated to the meanest of outside prices. However, I had plenty of other bets on the same event, and with that dubious consolation I made my mind easy.

The most comfortable way of "doing Ascot" is to take a villa somewhere in the neighbourhood, many of which are to be rented during the meeting, at reasonable prices *for a race week*. As Jack Raffleton says, "all enjoyment is cheap at a pound a minute;" and the way he works out his problem is ingenious enough :—" Fewer people have been ruined by fox-hunting than most other sporting pursuits ; *ergo*, a man who hunts saves money. If you calculate the runs you see during a season, you will find a pound a minute rather below the mark in your expenses; *ergo*, a man who lives at that rate must be a most economical personage." On this principle my friend Bloomsbury (a friend of some three weeks' standing—I was introduced to him on a drag at Epsom), Mr. Sharpes (his working partner in a wine concern, whose *locale* I could never distinctly make out), young Plantagenet Cripps (of the eminent firm of "Cripps, Martin, and Co.," whose share in the business appeared to be spending the profits), and myself, agreed to take a small, well-furnished, and picturesque cottage, with French windows, and "*convanient*," as they say in Ireland, to the Heath. Having stored this residence with an excellent commissariat, and an unlimited supply of Bloomsbury's famous '34 (a decoction of hermitage and liquorice), we entered upon our four days' residence with great satisfaction; and, in order to have as little as possible for our money, had agreed to come down the first day, and go back to London on the last. Jack Raffleton was quartered at Windsor; and, having breakfasted with his battalion at the barracks, Plantagenet Cripps and myself had the advantage of getting to the Heath on the outside of a drag, inhabited by a very pleasant lot of Guardsmen, and coached by one of their number, whose predilection for what is termed "fancy driving" was the only drawback to his performance. This arrangement, I confess, originated in the fertile brain of young Cripps, whose adoration for "the military" was unbounded, and whose day-dream, never to be realized, was the achievement of a commission in the Grenadiers; which, for an individual not on *the list*, turned six-and-twenty, and standing an honest five-feet-two in his "brodequine,' seemed a project as unlikely as it would have been inappropriate. Inside the drag, to keep their "collars" and "bosoms' free from dust, were a couple of Yankees, landed only the day before at Portsmouth, and whose knowledge of English scenery and English climate, or, as they termed it, "British clearins" and a "British hoving," was limited to the deep blue sky above us, and the stately vistas of Windsor's magnificent forest.

I was amused at the unblushing manner in which a young ensign, very lately castigated by Dr. Hawtry, was lionizing the Republicans, assuring them, in reply to their many questions concerning our summer and our country, that we called this the "cool" season; that it lasted eight months out of the twelve; and that, with the exception of our manufacturing towns and sea-coasts, the whole of Great Britain consisted of such giant oaks and verdant lawns as were now stretching away on either side of us. On arriving at the course, the younger American—a peculiarly sallow gentleman, with turn-down collars—was most anxious to know why so many carriages containing the fair sex should be ranged on *either side* of the course; his " Cicerone," with the mischievous spirit of a schoolboy, informing him that the aristocracy, gentry, and respectables were placed as near as possible to the Stand, while those facing that edifice were somewhat less particular in their notions of etiquette, and were sufficiently liberal to allow of their acquaintance being made without much unnecessary form or ceremony. A mistake which might have produced such disagreeable consequences was very properly set right, and the wag severely rebuked by a gentlemanlike elderly man, one of the colonels in the regiment, who, however, could not conceal a smile at the conceit which he demolished. After several hair-breadth scapes, and a great deal of getting down on the part of the "militaire," who officiated as "*shoot*," we arrived on the Heath, with the loss of but one bottle of light claret, which, having been broken and absorbed in the contents of a pigeon pie, was voted rather an improvement than otherwise. The first person I met on the course was Jack Raffleton, who had cantered over from the barracks early in the morning, on a most mysterious expedition, to meet a sagacious-looking trainer and a couple of dwarfs, connected in some way with what people call "a *private* trial."

I never had nerve to elbow my way boldly into the ring, and proclaim in a stentorian voice that I would "lay the long odds against Crœsus," or, like the great capitalist of the present day, publish my willingness to "lay against anything," which, to my inexperienced eye, presents the most appalling picture of recklessness; so linking my arm in that of my friend's partner, Mr. Sharpes, I hang on the outskirts of the ring, and am stunned by the ceaseless vociferations,

for which " business " of this description is remarkable.
" I'll lay five ponies to two against Shylock "—" I'll back
the field for a pony "—" Anybody lay against Leviathan ?"
—" I'll lay agin Wrath "—" Six hundred to one against
Woodpecker "—" Can't do it, sir "—" Take five "—" What
about The Crab ?"—" Do it again, Colonel ?"—" What name
shall I put down ?"—" I'll lay against Woodpecker "—" I'll
name two against the field " —" I'll lay ten to one against The
Crab "—" The field for a pony !"—&c., &c. Such is the
Babel-like confusion ringing in my ears; but ere I have
time to marvel at the wonderful hoarseness of " Wrath's "
persevering enemy, a general rush takes place to see the
horses saddled, and we are carried away by the stream. On
looking at my book, I am shocked to find The Crab now at
" ten to one," the horse on whom I stand to win; and I
endeavour in vain to see him stripped and saddled, that I may
gather confidence from his appearance. Twice am I nearly
kicked by the neatest of plates, which are lashed out with
scarcely the warning of one whisk from the thoroughbred
tail. Twice are my toes most painfully trodden on by the
precipitate retreat of the backing crowd. Long ere I have
accomplished my search, the bell rings, the course is cleared,
and I am as ignorant as ever of all concerning The Crab,
except that he is a chestnut, which is hardly a distinction,
seeing that there are four other chestnut horses in the race.
However, Sharpes and I take up a convenient position, and
prepare for the thrilling sight. The horses canter past, some
going remarkably short. I refer to my card, and am gratified
to see The Crab looks racing-like all over, and besides, from
the orange cap, is easily to be distinguished in the ruck.
The noise in the ring is worse than ever, and now, as
Sharpes tells me, is my time " to hedge ;" back I rush to the
congregated speculators, find I cannot wedge my way in,
and determine to stand the shot.

They're off! The flag's down! " There they go !"—
" Redcap leading !" " Woodpecker's coming up !" " My
eyes! how Nat is forcing the running !" " Woodpecker

wins!" "Woodpecker's beat!" "Lord Exeter wins!" "The mare wins!" "Lord Exeter wins!" The mare! the mare!! What a capital race! The thrill is over—delightful while it lasted, though somewhat expensive. I cast a glance at the number up, to make sure, and then with a little simple arithmetic discover that I have lost £75. Never mind; it was a slashing race, won by a head, not a length between the first three. I should have done much worse if Shylock had won; and The Crab ran as honest as the day, and was a good third! so I draw a long breath, like a man who has been bled, and soothe my excited feelings with a tapering cigar.

The next being an unimportant race, and having no bets connected with it, Sharpes and myself, accompanied by Bloomsbury, who had won his money, took the opportunity of inspecting "the humours," not the least amusing part of a race-course, and hunting amongst the carriages and in front of the Stand for our friends and acquaintances. "How are you, Bloomsbury?" "Sharpes, my boy! I'm glad to see you." "Mr. Cotherstone, Mr. Nogo—Mr. Nogo, Mr. Cotherstone;" and with this introduction, and the removal of our respective beavers, we are joined by a gentleman, whom at first sight I took to be a clergyman, but who, notwithstanding his clerical appearance, Bloomsbury afterwards informed me was "far from it." Of the middle stature, close shaved, and got up with the most scrupulous neatness, his whole appearance, though without the slightest pretensions to good looks, was extremely prepossessing. He rejoiced in that prosperous look which white teeth and a fresh complexion invariably produce; and his costume, though not in the least slang—in fact, as I have already said, bordering on the ecclesiastical—had that indefinable something which is always associated in my mind with a good horseman; there was a neatness about his trousers and boots that looked as if *he* *rode* in them, and altogether I should have guessed him to be the rector of some remote parish in the midland counties, whose duties were not sufficiently onerous to prevent his hunting three or four times a week, and sailing away amongst the "best of them."

I quite jumped at his hospitable offer of luncheon in his carriage after the next race, and was picturing to myself the sort of people "Mrs. Cotherstone and my daughter" might be, as he informed us they were on the course, and we should meet them on proceeding to attack his lobster-salad and champagne, when a general rush and separation took place to view the next race, which was a hollow affair, and scarcely created any sensation. Not so the event that came off immediately afterwards, and which gives Ascot its pre-eminence over all other meetings whatever : I allude to the arrival of Royalty to participate in our favourite national sport. The brilliant *cortège*, the well-built carriages and showy horses, the outriders in their scarlet liveries, the *then* master of the buckhounds, whose lengthy, graceful figure, and perfect seat on horseback, combining the *manége* riding of the dragoon with the strength and freedom of the fox-hunter (we beg his pardon—stag-hunter, though we believe the former with him was the earlier creation), obtained its due share of applause. The whole "turn out," so English and gentlemanlike, as well as princely in its appearance ; and then the welcome presence of our fair and gracious Sovereign herself, the most popular Monarch that ever ruled our British realms, with her stalwart consort, and beautiful children—all this together made the heart beat and the eye glisten, as the ear was deafened by the united voices of shouting multitudes. Cheer upon cheer, like the waves of the sea, came rolling onwards, gaining strength and volume as they thundered up the course, till opposite the Grand Stand the enthusiasm was at its height, and Windsor Castle's stately pile itself, towering afar in the silent summer-sky, must have trembled to the echo.

But we proceed to search for the carriage that is to furnish us with sustenance, and on the way thither Sharpes volunteered a little information with regard to our new acquaintance.

There are some people that everybody but oneself seems to

know, and of this class was Mr. Cotherstone. He had been at Cambridge, it appears, and studied for "the bar," but was supposed to have been "rusticated," in consequence of an affair at whist, out of which none of the party came very creditably; after this he seems to have lived upon his wits, and married on the same provision for his future family, and this patrimony had now lasted him for several years. He had a nice house not very far from Ascot, capital wine, two or three first-rate horses, on which he could "go a good one," and everything else, as Sharpes expressed it, "most comfortable," was very popular at all the messes of all the regiments within dining distance, and in short was a "deuced gentlemanlike fellow." All this I extracted as it were on the rack from my informant, Mr. Sharpes being a man of few words, and one who never threw an expression or a chance away.

Declining all offers from dark-eyed gipsy women, and resisting the entreaties for a remembrance of a pecuniary nature from the host of "Paddies" who knew all about us in the hunting-field, and hoped to see "our honors" at Hampton, we charged boldly through "*the sticks*" (at which athletic amusement a noble lord was fast breaking the "bank"); and finding our entertainer's carriage with some difficulty, performed the usual "salaam," and my introduction coming off successfully, were installed without further ceremony, and made free of the sundry good things we had been promised. I found Plantagenet Cripps comfortably settled by the side of Miss Cotherstone; the latter being so taken up with what Plantagenet was pleased to term his *small-talk*, and which certainly was of the smallest description, that she hardly vouchsafed an answer to my introductory bow, and turned herself so completely away that I was forced to be content with the contemplation of her bonnet, through whose transparency I could perceive she rejoiced in long and glossy locks of the raven's hue. But little time had I for anything but Mrs. Cotherstone, a middle-aged lady, with an eye like a hawk, and a "front" coming low down upon her forehead. I am always a little nervous with old ladies, and had no slight difficulty in parrying the host of questions with which I was plied on this occasion. " Been fortunate in your speculations, Mr. Nogo? Come down from London this morning? Choked with dust; beautiful drive through Windsor Forest; and what do you think of Virginia Water? Queen looking uncommonly well, and the dear children. Bore going back to town after the races—makes one so late at dinner."

I here contrived to edge in a word, and had got as far as " Bloomsbury and I have taken a villa," when she broke in again with—" Charming person Mr. Bloomsbury; so gentlemanlike !" (I thought "well!")—"so agreeable! an old friend of ours; had a capital day as yet, won £700. Mr. Cotherstone always so unlucky: only bets in half-crowns, but never wins. Hope we shall become better acquainted, Mr. Nogo; trust you will come and dine with us before you leave Ascot. Have some more lobster-salad?— thank you—champagne—." And with this running fire we passed the time till the father of the family made his appearance, linked arm-in-arm with Bloomsbury, and looking, with all his calmness, uncommonly like a man who, however much he might have been *losing* in half-crowns during the morning, had evidently been *winning* in hundreds.

This arrival made a slight diversion in my favour; Bloomsbury immediately taking the elder lady off my hands, and entering upon a brisk and chatty flirtation with his old friend. I remarked Bloomsbury's wig was exactly the colour of Mrs. Cotherstone's. I suspect they both patronized one of those advertising emporiums which profess to supply "mustachios, whiskers, eyebrows, and," above all, " that grand desideratum, a fine head of hair!" The patriarch of the family, who looked twenty years younger than his fatter half, had some mysterious information to convey to Cripps, for which purpose he took that diminutive dandy aside for a long conversation, in which the words " broke down," " coughing," and " not worth a row of gingerbread," were more than once overheard. All these arrangements left me a clear field with the young lady; and champagne, under a midsummer's sun, having pretty well overcome my natural timidity of disposition, I assumed the vacant seat by her side, and proceeded to go ahead. As the bright eyes which I now saw for the first time had a good deal of influence on my movements during the ensuing season, I may be allowed to indulge in a faint sketch of their seductive owner.

Kate Cotherstone was a young lady peculiarly adapted by nature to the part which I learnt, in time, she had been sedulously instructed to perform. With a short and neat figure, that looked enchanting on horseback, she combined a most piquante and joyous expression of countenance, set off by beautiful teeth, in a rather large mouth, jet black hair always "done" to perfection, and a fresh healthy colour without being "*blowsy.*" Her eyes, of a very light gray, and with a cunning and malicious expression, were her worst feature; but then such long black eyelashes and arching eyebrows would have made amends for a squint itself. She rejoiced in such a foot and ankle as our native soil does not often produce; and, need I add, that she could dance *too well* for a lady. Young Sabretasche, of the —th Hussars, swears he once waltzed with her for five-and-thirty minutes; and, as that polished young warrior expresses it, she was not "half-beat at the finish." Her other accomplishments I may sum up in a few words. I have seldom met any one who could ride so well, play and sing better, or draw half such good caricatures; she always held a capital hand at whist, which she played most judiciously; and I have known her, in the free and nautical regions of Cowes, to inhale the pleasing narcotic of a mild cigar!

My recollections of that heavenly day at Ascot are one whirl of blue sky, racing, shouting, champagne, and Kate Cotherstone. I was fairly *hooked* before I had sat with her for half an hour. We voted the open carriage the only place to see the races from; we pored together over my book, whose figures my fair adviser appeared perfectly to comprehend; we rushed headlong into a half-sovereign lottery, which Mrs. C.

won, as she said, "quite providentially;" we arranged a ride to Virginia Water on the worst day's racing, and a pic-nic in the forest for the following week. Once I descended from my perch, and proceeded boldly into the ring to back "Here-I-go-with-my-tail-on," because *she* thought it such a *darling* name; on which occasion I lost "a pony" to Papa, which it afterwards occurred to me I might have done as easily from the carriage. Then I wagered a pair of gloves with my enslaver; and, losing of course, had to request the *loan* of one of the pretty little white kids, that clung so lovingly to that tapering hand, that "I might make no mistake about the size." Under the most sacred promises of a speedy restitution, this was at last granted; and I was in the act of placing the late-won treasure next my heart, *inside* my waistcoat, when the effect of my chivalrous and devoted action was much spoilt by the consciousness that I was watched by Bloomsbury and Co., Plantagenet Cripps (confound him), and Jack Raffleton, who was to dine with us—the whole four excusing this disgraceful *espionage* by the pretence that they were waiting to accompany me home to our villa, the races being over. Heavens, so they were! I blushed up to the rim of my white hat, crammed *the glove* into my coat pocket, bid Miss Cotherstone a most confused "Good morning," stammered out an unintelligible acceptance of Mamma's hospitable invitation to "dine with them to-morrow not later than a quarter before eight;" and joining my quizzing associates, was much discomfited by Jack's very disagreeable remark, that "Nogo's hit very hard; got it just under the wing, and likely to prove a bad case!"

CHAPTER VIII.

ASCOT AND ITS CONSEQUENCES.

Benedick.—Suffer love. A good epithet!
  I do suffer love indeed, for I love thee against my will.
Much Ado about Nothing.

OUR dinner-party at the villa, as we called it *par excellence*, consisted of Bloomsbury, Sharpes, Cripps, and myself, with the addition of Jack Raffleton, whose good humour and good spirits enlivened us considerably. Many a sly hit and inuendo were pointed at my devoted head, and the most sacred feelings of my bosom (all arisen since morning) appeared to these worldly spirits only to furnish an endless subject for bad puns and impertinent remarks.

"Nogo! let's go to the Windsor ball to-morrow night; there's always a good ball during Ascot week. All the First will be there, and we shall have some fun," said Bloomsbury, heating an already much inflamed countenance with a third bumper of his own most execrable champagne. Why is it that a wine-merchant should always think it necessary to consume his wares in such profusion? The sorcerer imbibes not the philtre of his own compounding, and the apothecary most religiously eschews the mixture he has himself made up. "Besides," added Bloomsbury, smacking his great lips with a relish that could hardly be feigned, "we shall have all the people who live about here, and Mrs. Cotherstone made me promise to bring some dancing men."

"Nogo! a glass of wine!" "Nogo! your good health!" "Nogo! *you'll go!*"—the latter from Jack Raffleton—burst upon my tingling ears. I blushed. How could I help it? I swore I hated balls, and never danced—did not think 1 should go. Heaven forgive me! I had promised *her* that very afternoon that nothing earthly should prevent my being at the ball and claiming her hand for the very first waltz.

In short I was over head and ears in love; and the whole of that glorious June evening, despite of a most elaborate dinner, despite of the rallying of my companions, despite of the many bumpers of claret, so grateful to the throat parched and fevered with the excitement of a day's racing in that tropical weather—despite of all, I sat as one entranced. I saw, heard, felt nothing but Kate Cotherstone. I ate strawberries; but their fragrance only reminded me of winding paths through gardens of roses, and I thought of the bliss of an evening stroll with Kate Cotherstone. The ruby wine sparkled in my thin crystal goblet, and bore my spirit on its blushing wave to the clustering vineyards of sunny France, the joyous region of Bordeaux (an imaginary district, which, if truth must be told, the innocent liquor before me had never visited), and I thought what a paradise it would be with Kate Cotherstone!

Heedless of the chat and merriment of my companions, I looked through the French windows, thrown open down to the ground to catch the faintest sigh of the summer's evening breeze; I gazed on the sloping lawn, the darkening woods, the last faint blush of sunset fading into that indescribable clear transparent hue, which of all the gems of earth the opal alone can strive to imitate; and I thought of Kate Cotherstone. How I treasured up every syllable we had interchanged during the day! how I twisted and tortured every word she had uttered, to discover some hidden meaning of approbation or encouragement. How I thought of what she *might* have said, and what I *ought* to have said!—how I speculated on the possibility of her affections being disengaged; and made the boldest resolution of declaring my attachment, and distancing all competitors! In short, the ideas and improbabilities that succeeded each other through my brain can only be conceived by those whose youthful fancies have been, like mine, the sport of a wayward and uncontrolled imagination. I was a fool; I think I knew it, and yet I was a happy one. The evening wore on; the last, positively the last of a series, every one of which had in turn been called "just another bottle," had been drained. Midnight approached, and coffee and candles made their joint appearance, when a suggestion from Sharpes, I believe the first he made that evening, with regard to broiled bones, produced a simultaneous demand for the backgammon board, not for the purpose of indulging in that innocent recreation of the elderly, but in order to bring into play quite a different sort of "bones" from those for which Sharpes had asked.

"A little chicken?" said Jack Raffleton, parodying the lines of Lady Mary Wortley Montagu—

> "And when the dull hours of the public are past,
> We meet with champagne and *some chicken* at last."

"Chicken, by all means," shouted Cripps.

"What do you say to 'Vingt-John'?" hiccuped Bloomsbury, overcome, like some Bacchanalian wizard, by the spirit he had himself conjured up.

"Not enough for a round game," was the unanimous reply; and chicken-hazard was voted the only pastime for the small hours of morning. We sat down to play accordingly; and a glorious summer sun had already risen for two hours when I sought my couch, jaded and headachy under the combined influence of noise, excitement, and cigar-smoke. The never-ceasing rattle and bang of the dice-box, as it circulated with varying fortune from hand to hand in our small party, might have deafened less sensitive ears than mine: and the paltry gain of "a pony" was hardly an equivalent for a feverish night and seedy morning.

Let me pass over the following day's racing and the usual repetition of betting, luncheon, gain and loss—like all repetitions, somewhat flat, stale, and most decidedly unprofitable. The gloss of novelty soon wears off; and excitement must be kept continually increasing, or it ceases to deserve the name. The horses ran or were pulled, the odds were laid or were taken, the people shouted, and the sun shone, but it was all a blank to me. What was Ascot and its glories—what was champagne and lobster-salad? There was no Kate Cotherstone, and I loathed the smiling summer's day. There was her father, however, the Rev. Mr. Cotherstone, as I could hardly help calling him—he looked so like a clergyman. There he was, clean, fresh, and healthy as usual, making innumerable entries in a large betting-book, with unvarying urbanity. Some intuitive knowledge of racing he must certainly have possessed. When he laid against Don Cæsar de Bazan, down went that herring-shaped animal to zero; when he took the odds about the "Odalisque colt," up came the nameless flyer to "par." And he assured me with an unblushing countenance that he was "merely booking a few trifling bets for a friend"—making a small fortune for the best friend he ever had, would have been nearer the mark. I stammered out an inquiry after his daughter, and my heart leaped when he told me she was "only keeping fresh for the ball." Ah! that ball! How I looked forward to it; and how glad I was when a general move from the course enabled me to get home to dress for a dinner at the Cavalry Barracks, previous to the anticipated gaieties of the evening!

Any man not in love must have enjoyed the merriment, fun, and good-humour which reigned paramount at the mess of our military entertainers. The party was certainly numerous; but all the material belonging to a mess is calculated for any number of visitors, and confusion is banished from the arrangements of the dinner-table as sedulously as from the evolutions of the field. No other description of entertainment is so generally agreeable as a mess dinner; there is all the variety of a large party without its formality —all the ease of a family circle without its occasional dullness. Of course our conversation turned much upon racing, as was natural in a party gathered together for the enjoyment of that sport; but literature, painting, and music, with an occasional dash of the old staple subject of fox-hunting, or perhaps I should rather say riding across a country, had each their turn; and had I not been so anxious to get in good time to the ball, I should have been loath to leave such excellent claret, and so many agreeable companions. Resisting many kind invitations to stay and smoke "a capital cigar," I got nervously into the fly which I had ordered to be in readiness for me, and proceeded to the ball-room in a state of comparative lunacy.

To the observing mind a country ball presents many more objects for study and examination than does the regular stereotyped pattern which makes a London party; there are more peculiarities to be admired, more individuality in the characters, and certainly, towards the close of the evening, more enjoyment and freedom, to make up for the greater stiffness and formality with which these rural gaieties invariably commence. The musicians, too, are of quite a different species from their brother-followers of Orpheus in the metropolis; they go to sleep more readily, appear to enjoy more tranquil slumbers, and when in that state play with a correctness that is quite surprising. I have remarked that the harp is an instrument which yields its sweetest tones to the touch of a performer more than half asleep; and the minstrel who evokes its ringing sounds, with closed eyes and drooping head, only wakes when startled by the sudden cessation of his noisy companions during the pause that gives the fair waltzer breath to begin a fresh round of hard labour to the stunning accompaniment of the Row Polka.

I was one of the first arrivals, and had ample time, whilst drawing on my kid gloves, to observe the desolate appearance of an unfilled ball-room, with the musicians huddled up in their corner, and the only fellow-sufferers of my undue punctuality crowding round the empty fire-place, which doubtless they would have done had there been a blaze to roast an ox, though the thermometer the whole of that day must have marked 80 in the shade.

Never greyhound, straining in the slips, watched more eagerly than did I for the engrossing pursuit I had in view. As with longing eyes I gazed upon the doorway, I had an opportunity of remarking the oddities of the several strange-looking individuals who made an early appearance on the scene—men in quaintly-constructed garments, bearing the freshest gloss of novelty, with coats too tight and gloves a world too wide, waistcoats of gorgeous rainbow hues, and "continuations" which "Herr Cahan," of Anaxyridian fame, would have swooned to contemplate. Truth to tell, their fair companions had not so disfigured themselves, although I distinctly perceived an unsightly opening in the ball-dress of one damsel, at that critical place where the graceful folds of a descending skirt spring from the tightest portion of a lady's figure. Later in the evening, as we watched the gentle *figurante*, still "all agape," through the mazy evolutions of a quadrille, Shabrac of the Life Guards whispered to me that he thought her "tail was devilish badly set on." However, many of the rustic beauties, despite the want of a London dressmaker, and the inconvenience of one maid amongst five sisters, were really very lovely; and I could not help thinking that, if the *coiffures* were less glossy, and the gloves and satin shoes less shapely, than those I had been accustomed to admire in corresponding scenes in the metropolis, still the blooming roses and sparkling eyes of these rural *débutantes* were a pleasing exchange for the pale, wan hues and listless languor of a London girl.

But the room gets more and more crowded, and the polka generates its accustomed fray. Pre-occupied as I am, I cannot help being amused as I watch the motley crowd. Couples of all sorts and sizes; dancers of every style, from young Graceless of the Guards, and Miss Wideawake, swimming smoothly round in masterly *abandon* (she is ten years older than her partner, and Jack Raffleton says he'll bet five to two she hooks him), from that high-bred, easy-looking couple, to their next neighbours—a very badly-dressed gentleman, in a profuse perspiration, with a countenance like the "dancing faun," who, furious with haste, and regardless of time and tune, is hustling that fat, fair, dowdy damsel along at a pace it needs no prophet to tell must be too good to last. See, they bump against yon elderly young lady in yellow, who, with projecting shoulder-blades, and all her remaining hair piled in wondrous superstructure on the top of her venerable head, is cautiously steering through the intricacies of the dance her unfledged partner, a small, slight youth, just promoted to his first tail-coat. In vain—all motherly though the care she takes of him be, she shall not save him from his fate. He is knocked ruthlessly out of her hands by the "dancing faun;" and the aggressor, tripping over one of his own enormous feet, *ricochets* back amongst the crowd of dancers, and, with a bump that makes the sitting *chaperones* nod again, comes headlong to the floor, dragging with him, in his precipitate discomfiture, his poor, pale, panting partner. Miss Wideawake looks up at young Graceless with *such a* smile. Poor boy! hereafter shall those haunting eyes look through you in many a morning dream in your lonely barrack-room. The music stops for an instant, but soon resumes the exhilarating air; and as I turn my head from the prostrate couple, I see that Mrs. and Miss Cotherstone have just made their appearance in the doorway. Need I dwell on our greeting? Need I dwell on our first dance? I never was much of a waltzer, at the best of times; but Kate's *deux-temps* was the most perfect thing that ever twinkled round a floor, and she "put me along," as Jack Raffleton afterwards described it, "in the best form going." How the minutes flew! how soon the *Valse d'Amour*—that dreamy, heavenly melody—came to its close! "Did not Miss Cotherstone find it very hot? Would she not like some tea?" "Thank you; if you please," with a glance that went through me; and I could almost fancy a slight, nearly imperceptible pressure of the arm I was so pleased to offer. All flirtations, I suppose, are the same—like "cockamaroo," or any other game adapted only for two people, however engrossing they may be to the players, they are somewhat dull to the lookers-on, and will not bear repetition at all. The whole of that night I was like a man in a dream. Once she made me very angry by leaving me planted with mamma, whilst she not only waltzed, but likewise retired to a sort of "cooling room," with Le Beau of the "Tenth," a good-looking, flashy sort of fellow, that I did not at all fancy. But how could I bear any malice, when, on her return to the maternal wing about which I was still hovering, she gave me a rosebud out of her bouquet, and asked me if I understood "the language of flowers?" Not I; but I thought I knew what that meant in any language. Dear, dear! notwithstanding all that is gone and past, I have got that withered rosebud still.

I must confess that I deserved some remuneration for being left alone with Mrs. C. Her morning volubility, at all times most formidable, was now increased to a perfect torrent of small-talk, and accompanied by a slight hesitation and thickness of speech, which the uncharitable might attribute to "her medical man recommending port wine." Besides, her appearance in a ball-room was, to say the least of it, somewhat marked; as a stout, florid lady, in a red velvet dress and gorgeous jewellery, adorned with a very rubicund face, and further decorated by an exceedingly low front, and equally high turban, can scarcely hope in these days to escape observation—and such was the *tout ensemble* of Mrs. Cotherstone.

Many and reiterated were the injunctions that I should not forget to dine with them on the morrow. "Mr. Cotherstone will be *so* happy to see you," said the hospitable lady; "and I am sure you will like our little house so much. No pretension, Mr. Nogo. As I say to Mr. C., says I, don't let's have pretension, but everything conformable—I mean comfortable. Mr. C. would have been here to-night, but he never goes to balls—don't like sitting up so late. He's a quiet, domestic man, my husband, Mr. Nogo" (I happen to know he was at that moment playing *roulette* next door)—"'early to bed and early to rise;' and what a blessing *that* is! As I say to Kate— Kate, says I, if ever you marry (you'll excuse a mother's feelings, Mr. Nogo), marry a domestic man, Kate: for what says the poet? I forget at this moment what he does say; but I dare say you remember, Mr. Nogo, and so—Thank you; a little port-wine negus, if you please." And all this I endured for the sake of Kate Cotherstone, and thought myself richly rewarded when cloaking and shawling-time arrived, and as I enveloped her lovely form in the softest cashmere, and gave her my arm to conduct her to the carriage, she whispered her "Good night!" in those thrilling accents which none knew better how to modulate. "We shall be *sure* to meet to-morrow —Oh, yes, I have got the gloves, and will never, *never* part with them."

A happier man than I never smoked a cigar, as, driving back through the perfume-laden air of a June midnight, I listened to the nightingale warbling in the deep, dark glades of Windsor's stately forest, and looked upward at the benignant moon shedding her silver radiance over all the summer night.

The following evening found me stepping out of my fly at Mr. Cotherstone's door, at a quarter to eight punctually. Another day's racing was concluded; and in my new character of a domestic man, which I had now resolved to adopt, I had carefully eschewed the betting-ring and all its vicissitudes. Besides a ten-pound note on "The Cup," I had not risked a shilling all day; and I rather congratulated myself on this decided improvement in my moral character. "What will not woman's sweet influence bring out?" I thought, as I drove up to Mr. Cotherstone's door, through a sort of half-shrubbery and half-garden, studded with evergreens and fragrant with roses. Nothing could be prettier than the house and grounds—the former a long, low building, standing so white and level on its smoothly-shaven lawn, with French windows opening in every direction on the well-kept flower-garden, now in all its midsummer beauty, from whence winding gravel-walks, with heavy borders of box, allured you into the picturesque and luxuriant shrubberies, whose dwarfish proportions formed a pleasing contrast, shut in as they were by the noble oaks of Windsor Forest, which completed the picture. There was no smell of dinner in the hall as I entered; and a respectably rotund servant out of livery divested me of my paletot, whilst a foreign-looking individual —probably the valet—hovered about to assist him. On the right of a tasteful staircase, with carved oak balustrades, a door was thrown widely open; and "Mr. Nogo!" shouted in a stentorian voice by my fat friend, ushered me into the drawing-rooms and the presence of my enslaver. I was the latest arrival; and, as everything was done in *that* house in the most agreeable manner, I had hardly time to shake hands with Mr. and Mrs. Cotherstone, and exchange glances with their daughter, when dinner was announced, and the party pairing rapidly off, foiled me in a plan I had meditated for securing the society of my ladye-love, so that I found myself bringing up the rear, in the post of honour, with my flourishing hostess, who seemed to take exclusive possession of me, and treat me at once like a son.

It was not until seated at a well-appointed round table, in a brilliantly-lighted and extremely pretty dining-room, that I had time to look about me and reconnoitre the party I had been asked to meet. We were eight in all; and, with the exception of myself, the guests appeared to be intimately acquainted with each other. On my left was a dashing-looking lady, certainly not very young, but showing the remains of great beauty, with a pair of piercing black eyes, whose brilliancy was enhanced by a judicious touch of rouge towards the cheek-bone, and to whom I was introduced as Mrs. O'Cleverly; her husband—a dark, forbidding-looking man, who was called "Major,"—being nearly opposite. Kate was nearer Papa; and my view of her was somewhat obscured by the curly brown head and stupendous whiskers, mustachios, &c., of a Count Favoris, an extremely good-looking foreigner, who paid her, I thought, much unnecessary attention, and who doubtless would have been still more agreeable, as well as intelligible, had he spoken the English language less entirely from ear. Next to him came my friend Sharpes, who had been obliged to be in London all that day, and had stopped to dinner with Mr. Cotherstone on his way back to our joint abode. A place had been laid for Mr. MacBullion, of Discount-villas, Regent's-park, and the Stock Exchange, whose name it struck me I had heard somewhere; but he never made his appearance. Dinner progressed prosperously. Mrs. O'Cleverly and I became great friends; and her husband drank "woine" with me, in a strong Irish accent, with the greatest condescension. This ceremony—finding, I presume, the liquor to his taste—he repeated more than once. The champagne being excellent (certainly not from the firm of Bloomsbury, Sharpes, and Co.), we all soon became on the most sociable terms; and the deference with which I was treated by my agreeable entertainer and his guests, and to which, in the company of Jack Raffleton and my own friends, I was totally unaccustomed, was as pleasing as it was unexpected. Cotherstone was a most agreeable man, with a fund of small-talk and anecdote which was invaluable at a dinner-party. Then the whole thing was so exceedingly well done, and the discipline of the servants was so perfect, that not the slightest mistake or *contretemps* of any kind could occur to spoil the effect of the performance. I believe Mrs. Cotherstone deserved the credit of drilling the domestics, and was fond of the occupation. In after-days, when a great deal that had before been inexplicable was made clear to me, Jack Raffleton told me an anecdote that strongly exemplified the quaint good-humour of my former host. He and Jack were sitting after breakfast in the library, immersed in the computation of a money transaction in which they were jointly engaged, when the footman, in putting coals on the fire, by some unlucky movement brought down fender and fire-irons with an alarum that might have wakened the dead. Jack is not a nervous fellow; but he assured me that the crash was such, he could not repress the oath that rose to his lips. Not so the master of the house. Looking up from the paper on which he was engaged, with the utmost coolness, and keeping his finger on it to mark his place, he thus addressed the astonished domestic: "It is lucky for you, my friend, that your *mistress* was not in the room, or she would have fetched you such a kick in the rear of your person as you would have remembered to the last day of your life;" and without further remark resumed the abstruse calculations which had been so rudely interrupted. But dinner was at length over. The ladies departed to the drawing-room; the claret was done ample justice to; coffee was announced in the "other room;" and, as we entered the tasteful drawing-room, our ears were greeted by the harmonious notes of the pianoforte, and our eyes indulged with all the usual arrangements of a properly set-out *écarté*-table.

CHAPTER IX.

Ophelia.—What means this, my lord?
Hamlet.—Marry, this is miching mallecho; it means mischief.
Ophelia.—Belike, this show imports the argument of *the play.*

HAD I been possessed of the shrewdness of him who had so much method in his madness, the haunted Dane, or even of poor Ophelia, Hamlet's ill-starred love, I might have suspected that all the show before me in Cotherstone's *bijou* of a drawing-room imported the argument of very high play indeed, and that sort of play in which the blind goddess was likely to dispense no equal favours; but youth is naturally unsuspicious: forbid it, heaven, that it should be otherwise! My objection to the rising generation is, that they *know too much;* and an Etonian of the present day, in all matters of "nobbling," is able and willing to get the best of his grandfather. Accordingly, I sipped my coffee, and made eyes at Kate Cotherstone, without the slightest feeling of insecurity, and thought myself superlatively happy when I had manœuvred my person into a vacant chair by her side, to watch her taper fingers plying a mysterious vocation, which ladies denominate "crochet," and the bands of her glossy raven hair throwing off the light with all the sparkle and polish of Count Favoris' jetty boots. I am at a loss for any other simile that would equally convey the idea of intense blackness. We were undisturbed in our delightful *tête-à-tête;* for mamma, reclining in an exceedingly recumbent attitude, on the easiest of all easy chairs, looking like an impersonation of midsummer, and fanning furiously with an instrument formed from some tropical bird's wing, was plying the silent Sharpes with ceaseless questions as to a late bit of London scandal, whilst Mrs. O'Cleverly, looking over a piece of new music, with an amused expression of malice in her large black eyes, was watching the impenetrable countenance of the laconic Sharpes, and listening to the quaint answers with which he put off his talkative hostess. Cotherstone was helping Count Favoris to understand the Major's account of an animal he possessed. "A well-lept horse, bedad," and with which it was impossible to make out what the excited owner wished to do, as he declared at one moment that nothing should "injuice" him to sell so "accomplished a hunter," and at the next, that the Count should have him for "a hondred pounds, aqual to fourteen stone ;" all which confused particulars his well-bred landlord was translating out of pure Milesian into the colder languages of England and France.

But Count Favoris finishes his coffee, and asks "Madame Clevare," as he dubs her, for "some song," and she sings what they all call "that beautiful Spanish thing" on the guitar. I do not understand the words, which appear to me to be a repetition of "cachecho, cachecho, cachecho," with a strong thump on the unoffending instrument, and a sound like a hiccup at the end of each stanza; but I applaud as vigorously as the rest, and venture a whisper to Kate that Mrs. O'Cleverly makes dreadful faces when she sings, upon which she calls me "a satirical creature," and vows she is "getting quite afraid of me," on which I think of saying something tender ; but, having nothing ready-coined, I am compelled to hold my tongue. Then Mrs. Cotherstone, who being stout is consequently sentimental, asks for "When we two parted, in silence and tears." Which melancholy ditty is really well sung by our guitar-playing *prima donna*, and we are all more or less affected by it, Kate looking down at the point of her little satin shoe with an air of becoming dejection that makes her prettier than ever. Then we talk about new music and the opera, and Count Favoris comes out wonderfully, for he is hand-and-glove with the professionals, and dines early with Lablache, and tells us how "the thunderer" rests his score against a claret bottle (an empty one, you may be sure), and hums through the whole of his part, in those magnificent tones, during his repast, nor leaves out whole scenes, nor substitutes a waggish remark in French, for Donizetti's elaborate conceptions, as is sometimes the case on the stage, when the "maestro" is lazy. And the Count, who is a perfect musician, and endowed with a deep rich voice and exquisite taste, needs little pressing to sing us some beautiful old *romans* of Berenger's school, and concludes with a Bacchanalian air of more modern date, graced with a constant repetition of the monosyllable "hein," but sang with infinite zest and spirit; and Kate, who has got a little cold, and is hoarse, is at length prevailed upon "to favour us."

In vain had mamma requested "dear Kate" to give us that pretty thing in the "Reine de Cypre," or her favourite air from the "Fille du Regiment." The young lady persisted in her cold and her refusal, till I said, "I had wished so to hear her sing." "Well, if *you* wish it, Mr. Nogo, I'll try;" and she forthwith marched to the pianoforte, and warbled forth the "Blind Man's Bride," till I thought I should have cried. She really sang well, and with a degree of expression such as I have seldom heard. I sat with my eyes riveted on her countenance; and when she came to the "refrain," "True love can ne'er forget; dearest, I love thee yet," and looked at me with those piercing eyes that seemed to gaze into my very soul, what wonder that I quite made up my own mind as to who should be the future Mrs. Nogo? But sentiment must have an end, and perhaps is put to flight by nothing more effectually than that most practical of all games, whist.

Cotherstone rings the bell; green tables are put out; lamps, with green shades, are placed upon them. Cards, counters, &c., are displayed in workmanlike profusion, and we commence the ceremony of "cutting-in," the Major and Count Favoris at one table, against Mrs. O'Cleverly and our host. They play what they call "the regular stakes—pounds and fives," and enter upon their game in that business-like manner with which the real whist-player pursues his profession. The other quartette, consisting of Sharpes, the two remaining ladies, and myself, form a lighter game, in which the stakes are lower and the conversation allowed to proceed, and I have the delight of Kate Cotherstone for a partner. We played an agreeable rubber, to which nobody seemed to pay much attention; but it struck me at the time, although I am but an indifferent performer, that my partner never *made a mistake.* Whatever the card that Hoyle would have recommended, that was the card that leapt from her graceful hand. And when, in the changes of the game, she and her mother sat opposite each other, and entered upon the tug of war against Sharpes and myself, they cleaned us out most handsomely, considering the light stakes for which we were contending, and as that silent individual briefly remarked, as he rose from the table, "Good cards—well played; I lose eight pounds seven and sixpence."

But the other table is broken up, and enter tray with sandwiches and sherry, and a servant to announce Major O'Cleverly's carriage; but Mrs. O'Cleverly must go home alone, as the Major means to stay and "smoke a cigar with Jack-me-boy," meaning Mr. Cotherstone; and the lady is put into the carriage, and carefully packed up by the host and Count Favoris, who looks as if he would like very much to attend her during her drive. And we give hand-candlesticks to the others, send them to bed, and adjourn to Mr. Cotherstone's sanctuary, where hot water, all kinds of liquids, cigars, and actually *another card table* awaits us. Soon is the steaming comfort compounded, and the fragrant smoke-wreath rises from the well-stored produce of the Havanna, and we interchange our ideas upon men and things, under these combined influences, as if we had all known one another for years.

After a cigar or two, the conversation turns upon whist;

good and bad players—the chances and changes of the game—Major A., Hoyle, &c. Favoris hovers, like an unquiet spirit, round the table; and the Major, in exemplifying some knotty point connected with the concluded rubber, discovers that the cards he is dealing are arranged for *écarté*.

"A foine game, sir! Me brother Cornaylius is the best player now in England."

The upshot of all this is, that I, Tilbury Nogo, understanding the science of the game in the sort of way that nine out of every ten unsophisticated English gentlemen do *mis*understand it, and, moreover, dazzled and excited by the combined influence of claret, music, wax-lights, and bright eyes—to say nothing of cigars, and wonderful whisky-punch, compounded by mine host—sit recklessly down, to pit my unfledged strength, a willing pigeon, against Count Auguste Anatole Jean Louise Favoris, of Burlington-street, London, and the Bois de Boulogne (for aught I know), Paris. I win the first three games off, and scouting the moderate stakes at which we commenced, I boldly accede to the Count's proposal of a pony on the game, and fifty on the rubber, betting on the points *ad libitum*.

Of all tempting games that have ruined their thousands of votaries, none, perhaps, with the exception of hazard, has done its work more effectually than *écarté*. It is a trial of skill between man and man, and, as such, brings into play all the feelings of self-love and vanity that have their stronghold in the human breast. Then there is a sufficient degree of chance in the changes of the game to lure on the blind worshipper of Fortune, with the fascinating hope of a run of luck or an unlooked for "coup." Add to this the unlimited nature of stakes, depending on the will of two reckless and desperate gamesters, and the facility of doubling to recover a loss, allowed and perhaps encouraged by the more confident and fortunate player, and it is not to be wondered at that the money lost and won at such a game as this is to be reckoned by tens and hundreds of thousands.

The Count was a most agreeable person to play with, even

to a loser. As he smoked his cigar, and displayed his white hands and glittering rings to the greatest advantage, he seemed utterly careless of the issue of those cards which he fingered so adroitly. Always ready to propose, or to allow of his adversary proposing; always accommodating as to the amount of stakes, and regardless of his reverses, he prattled on in his broken English, interrupted only by an occasional scrap from some French song, as though it were a matter of perfect indifference whether he lost or won his hundreds on the game to me, and his ponies and fifties to Mr. Cotherstone or the Major, both of whom backed me now and then, although the latter, on two or three occasions, booked heavy bets against my success, all of which, I regret to say, I lost to him. This is a sort of specimen of the pastime, towards half-past three o'clock in the morning:

Mr. Nogo (much excited and dishevelled): "I propose—"

The Count: "Ver g-o-o-o-o-d; how manies?"

Mr. Nogo, looking at his score, now at three, the Count having marked but one in this game: "Four."

The Count deals them, and, helping himself, observes: "I mark ze king."

Mr. Nogo, having already lost about four hundred, declines to bet any odds, and the game proceeds, the Count winning the odd trick, which makes the antagonists even.

It is now my deal, and I turn up a diamond. We play our hands rapidly, and I lose the odd trick, but account for it by what my adversary calls a "stupid mistake." I cut to him, and compare the scores. Mine is but three. I have two to get to win. The Count only requires one; and it is his deal. He bets me two to one. Something prompts me to take it. I feel confident of winning. "Done," I say, "in hundreds. Would you like to back him, Cotherstone? or the Major?" "Yes." They both back him to the tune of fifty pounds a-piece, to give me *my revenge*. The Count deals, sneezing violently, and making much use of an exquisitely-perfumed handkerchief, and turns up a grinning king. My capital melts, like snow before the sunbeam.

Reckless and annoyed, I persist in going on. Cotherstone good-naturedly endeavours to dissuade me. " You are out of luck, Nogo," he says : " take my advice, and shut up for tonight." The Major thinks I play a very "foine game; careless, bedad, but uncommon like me brother Cornaylius." And, ere I have concluded my evening's amusement, I deliver to the Frenchman a cheque on my London bankers, Flint, Golding, and Co., payable to self or bearer the sum of thirteen hundred and fifty pounds, in consideration of which, the accommodating "bearer," pulling out a note-case quaintly embroidered in green and gold, liquidates a balance of a couple of hundreds, which I lose to the Hibernian Major and the smooth Mr. Cotherstone.

Is it credible that, as I drove home, far from dwelling on my losses, or having my eyes opened through the medium of my pockets, my thoughts dwelt on nothing but the image of my charming Kate, and the ride I had arranged to take with her the following afternoon, in Windsor Forest? Nor was it till I had nearly arrived that I remembered I had to bring Sharpes home to our joint abode. That wily gentleman had, however, preferred a moonlight walk of a few miles, to the expensive pursuit in which I had been engaged.

My servant dispelled the most delightful dream that was ever dreamt by infatuated youth in love, in liquor, or in debt, by bringing in hot water, and cold water, and soda water, and all the necessaries of a dissipated gentleman's toilet, about half-past eleven on the following morning, accompanied by the announcement that Captain Raffleton had ridden over from the barracks, and wished to see me, if I was up. A quarter of an hour sufficed for the use of bath, razors, and soda-water bottle ; and, as I enrolled my glowing frame in the softest of dressing-gowns, Jack's merry face showed itself at my door; and, throwing himself into an easy chair, he questioned me, as I went on with my toilet, on the proceedings of the last few days, and my intentions for the future. " Have a care, Nogo," said he, when I mentioned that afternoon's intended ride with Miss Cotherstone as a reason for my not being able to take an oar with a party of his brother-officers, on a boating excursion up the river—"Have a care, old fellow, about these Cotherstones. I know very little of them; but what I do know is rather shady. You may depend upon it this is a regular plant, and these people are making a dead set at you for what they can get. As for the girl, I don't believe there's a wickeder little devil out; and I know that she went on with that unfortunate Cripps till she made him a greater fool than nature had already done to her hand. Old Cotherstone's a regular sharper; and I was told this morning at breakfast, by a man very likely to know, that his wife was Lord Loosebrough's housekeeper, or something worse."

"I must really beg, Raffleton," I rejoined, in my most stately manner, and in a towering passion at hearing my beloved and her belongings spoken of in such a tone, "that you will be good enough to recollect you are abusing people who are personal friends of my own; and as for anything that may be said of them at your mess-table, I think I know the amount of slander and nonsense that is talked at such gatherings too well, to give a word of credence to anything of the kind; and I allow no man to abuse my associates, more especially a young lady who—"

Here Jack burst out laughing, and finished my sentence for me in most disrespectful terms. "Who has cooked your goose for you, you mean, old fellow. Well, I am sure I do not wish to offend you, or any of your *friends* of two days' standing; but I hear you dined there last night, and I am only curious to know something about your party, and who was there, and what you did."

"Well, in the first place, there were Mr. and Mrs. Cotherstone."

"Hem!" says Jack. "Papa and mamma-in-law to-be, and the *fiancée* in muslin 'temptation,' with her Sunday face on: of *them* I say nothing!"

"Count Favoris—a very agreeable, gentlemanlike fellow, belonging to some legation."

"Sharper of the first water. Exposed at Bath, under another name, for cheating at *écarté*, and kicked out of Cheltenham by 'Bruising Bill,' of the — Lancers, for bringing false dice to a private party. I know all about him."

"Mr. Sharpes, who lost seven pound to Mrs. Cotherstone, at whist."

"A shrewd, sensible fellow. He keeps that humbug Bloomsbury's business together. Clever old woman that, to win *his* money."

"Major and Mrs. O'Cleverly;" I added. "He seems a fine specimen of a real Irish gentleman; and she is still a very handsome woman."

"A ruined horse-dealer, now principal partner in Macer's gambling-house; and a broken-down actress, who married him under false pretences. My dear fellow, what a nest of sharpers you have got amongst! Now tell me honestly, had you any play, or did they keep you in ignorance of their practices, so as not to land their fish before he was thoroughly gorged?"

"Why, we played, certainly. I had a turn at *écarté* with the Count."

"And he won of you—?"

"Thirteen hundred and fifty altogether amongst the party. Rather a facer, my dear Raffleton; but I assure you it was all on the square."

Shall I ever forget the expression of Jack's handsome features when I came out with this disclosure? The prolonged whistle with which he found it necessary to give vent to his astonishment spoke volumes for the healthy action of his lungs, as did the concern betrayed upon his open brow for the goodness of his heart. Long and earnestly he argued with me upon my folly in what he was pleased to term being robbed with my eyes open. Warmly he expostulated with me on my infatuation for Kate Cotherstone, and unceasingly did he beg of me to break off all my engagements with this dangerous family, to leave for London immediately, and to abjure for ever the fatal and alluring passion for high play in which I had lately indulged.

" I have been an infernal fool myself," said Jack, becoming quite eloquent upon the subject, "but that is no reason why I should not endeavour to dissuade others from practices of which I know too well the folly and the end. Look here, Nogo; I am now a subaltern in the Guards, with some few hundreds a year besides my pay, and all the tastes and pursuits of a man who can draw for thousands; the consequence is, I never have a shilling that I can honestly call my own. I am hampered and distressed by bills and creditors, and driven to do things that, by Jove, I am perfectly ashamed of. And all this is owing to my passion for play. Had I not been a gambler, Nogo, I might have done anything. I might have commanded a regiment of cavalry by this time. I might have earned honour and distinction in those glorious campaigns in India. I might have married;" and here poor Jack's voice faltered—" I might have married the nicest girl in England. And what am I now?"

" Why," said I sedulously brushing away at my grinders, with my mouth full of tooth-powder, " your position is a very good one, and you lead a very pleasant life, Jack. You go where you like, and everybody is glad to see you. You do what you like, and nobody dreams of objecting to any of your proceedings. I have always considered you the most enviable fellow I know."

" All very well," resumed my military Mentor, coming out in a new light as a moral philosopher. " All very well. But happy as I seem to you, and good as are my spirits when you see me in society, there are moments of my existence bitter and miserable as remorse can make them. You have always heard of Jack Raffleton as a good-humoured, careless rattle, but little troubled with either money or brains, and thoughtless as that butterfly at your window. But it was not always so. There was a time when I had energy, ambition, and honest pride; when I had something to live for, and a motive for exertion. Put into a cavalry regiment as a fatherless boy of sixteen, I had all those hopes of advancement, all that thirst for distinction, too seldom felt but by those who have never known disappointment, but which, nevertheless, are the surest guides that lead to honour and renown. I was passionately fond of my profession; and as, step by step, I watched my name working its way upward in the Army List, I burned only for an opportunity of showing that I was capable of winning for myself a name and character in the service. I had a moderate income, enough for all my wishes, and in those days I *never played*. It would have broken my mother's heart to be told her son was a gambler, and she was spared that trial. Alas! she died when I was twenty; and I sometimes think that had it not been so, her influence might have saved me from many of the follies and vices of my manhood; Heaven only knows! I had then another and even a dearer tie that should have kept me out of evil; but I was doomed. *Poor*, POOR Ellen! We were to have been married as soon as I should have obtained my troop; and my idea then was to exchange into a regiment in India, and take her out with me to a climate more likely to agree with her than the colder temperature of her native land. I was rising rapidly to the top of the Lieutenants; and with a thorough knowledge of my duty, good health, a good conscience, and my union with Ellen to look forward to, I WAS happy. Well, I could ride pretty well then; in fact, I can slip over a country now as quickly as my neighbours; and, in an evil hour, I entered old Brunette, a famous mare I had, for a great regimental steeple-chase. I backed her heavily, and won easily, landing four hundred on the event. From that day I date my ruin. Ellen heard of my triumphs, and wrote to congratulate me, poor girl! at the same time she warned me of the danger of getting into habits of betting and play. I do not mean to say I became a gambler all at once; but the excitement of speculation, and the success which at first I met with, begetting hopes of improving my income, and so bettering the position of Ellen and myself, drew me gradually, but securely. into the net from which I am now warning you. It were a long story to tell you how I lost at length the greater part of my fortune, how I strove desperately to regain what I had so madly parted with, how I became more and more deeply involved, till the obtaining my troop was hopeless, and it seemed impossible to entertain an idea of marrying. Poor Ellen! the suspense and misery she endured on my account were too much for a frame already enfeebled by a consumptive tendency, and she died at nineteen of a decline." Jack's face was deadly pale as he added, after a pause of fearful distress:—"I have never cared a farthing for a woman since, and never shall. After this, I became, as you may suppose, entirely reckless. A death-vacancy in the regiment, and a run of luck, set me on my legs again, and since then I have been what you see me. I live, as I told you, from hand to mouth. I have had all my worldly goods, horses, carriages, and furniture quivering upon the turn of a die, and this repeatedly. Some day it must go against me, and I shall pay up, but I shall walk out a beggar. As you say, people are glad to see me, and ask me to their houses, to shoot their pheasants, ride their horses, drink their wine, and abuse their cook: but Lord A. only invites me because he knows I am going on to Lord B., and Lord B.'s hearty and hospitable welcome depends upon the fact of my arriving from Lord A.'s. Which of them, if I had not a house to my head or a coat to my back, would give me half a crown to keep me from starving? Believe me, my dear Nogo, mine is a false, and consequently an unhappy position, and I warn you not to tread in my footsteps. Your hack is at the door; take your ride with this new flame, flirt as much as you like, but do not commit yourself with the young lady; and, whatever you do, beware how you sit down to play with her papa."

CHAPTER X.

No—vain, alas! the endeavour
From bonds so sweet to sever:
Poor Wisdom's chance
Against a glance
Is now as weak as ever!
T. MOORE.

Cassio.—Not to-night, good Iago. I have very poor and unhappy brains for drinking. I could well wish courtesy would invent some other custom of entertainment. *Othello.*

"I SUPPOSE I can trust her with you, Mr. Nogo," said the anxious mother, as Kate and I walked our fretting horses away from Mr. Cotherstone's door. Kate looked charming in her riding-habit, and sat upon her horse with an ease and grace all her own. The weather was delightful; there was no groom to mar the happiness of our *tête-à-tête;* and of all the glades in verdant England for love-making, commend me to those that twine in leafy beauty round Virginia Water. But with all this, I was restless and disquieted. Jack's conversation with me in the morning had, to a certain extent, opened my eyes; I was not sufficiently infatuated to rush blindly into destruction, and I began to have that most unpleasant of all misgivings—a suspicion that I had made a confounded fool of myself. My fair companion, although in the highest glee when we started, although at first she rallied me, not without an object, on my very uncomplimentary lowness of spirits, soon saw with a woman's quickness that there was something wrong; and our ride, which I at least had looked forward to with such anticipations of delight, was fast verging into a rather dull *tête-à-tête;* when, at a turn in one of those grassy avenues, we came upon a galloping party of young Guardsmen, laughing, chatting, and smoking, enjoying their afternoon ride, and talking over the running of the different "favourites" at the late meeting. I blushed up to my eyes at the collision, more particularly as I detected certain exchange of glances among the party, that to my sensitive mind seemed to betoken no great respect for the character of my companion or the "common sense" of her devoted attendant. Kate, who seemed to know the whole clique, behaved with admirable self-possession and *sang froid;* but I could *not* stand the free-and-easy manner with which she was greeted by young Fitz-Arthur and Captain Clare, nor the extremely good understanding that seemed to reign between my charge for the time being, and the military in general. Wider and wider were my eyes being opened; and such conversation as the following gave me more and more an insight into the character of Miss Cotherstone.

Ensign Fitz-Arthur (an attenuated youth of seventeen, who looked as if he lived upon "sardines," and sat up all night—as indeed was the case): "I *am* rejoiced to see you again, Miss Cotherstone. I hope you have recovered the ball. I sent the gloves; but I have kept the bouquet: I give you my honour I slept with it next my heart."

All this in an audible voice, to my unspeakable discomfiture.

Miss C.: "You silly boy! you know you sat up playing chicken-hazard till parade."

Captain Clare: "So he did, Miss Cotherstone—not so devoted as I am: I walked in the park the whole night after the ball, and thought over our polka—nothing like the devotion of a middle-aged man."

Clare was one of the handsomest fellows in London, and I began to get into a cold perspiration.

"Well, Captain Clare," was the guarded reply of the well-drilled young lady, "if none of my admirers were more devoted than you are, I should indeed be badly off; you forgot all about the waltz we were engaged for. Mr. Nogo, we had better canter on, or we shall hardly be in time to dress for our early dinner." And bringing her horse well up to his bit, she started him at once into a hand-gallop, which soon took us out of sight of our military friends. This was entirely a volunteer on the part of Kate; and the casual mention of an *early* dinner, which was never served till past eight o'clock, was only a *ruse* to get away from a party who, however agreeable they might severally be in their proper places, as pleasant "flirting-blocks"—to use her own expression—were decidedly *de trop* in a *tête-à-tête* ride with the gentleman on whom she had thoroughly made up her mind she would bestow the honour of her hand. Many a glance was cast at me from beneath those black eyelashes, and many a hint given and opening afforded for an explanation which must have ended, as all such explanations do, in a shower of tears and a declaration of attachment; but I was not to be caught. I was sulky and immoveable; and when I took Kate off her horse at her own door, and rode my hack home, to dress for the dinner to which I was engaged at her father's, we were upon more distant terms; and I felt "safer in my shoes" than at any previous period of our acquaintance. The fact is, my suspicions were fairly aroused: like all individuals not gifted with a superabundance of brains, my bump of caution was largely developed; a beautiful arrangement of Nature, which may be generally remarked in those who have not the ready-wit nor intellectual energy to get out of a scrape—it is but fair that these slower coaches should possess an instinct which prevents their getting into one. And so was it with me. From my boyhood I had a horror of deep water, even after I had learned to swim; I used to think it far safer, and just as pleasant, to float upon a surface, to the bottom of which I could at any time place my feet; and I have ever been subject to misgivings when the magnitude of an undertaking on which I have once embarked has been fairly set before me.

"Good gracious," I thought, as I made my dinner toilet— a time during which the most reckless of mankind has no means of escaping from his reflections—" what a nice mess I shall be in if I marry this girl, and find out, after all, I have been imposed upon! if I take her down into 'my own county,' and find people won't visit her! and still worse, that she does not care a farthing for me, and has perhaps entertained throughout a real attachment for Captain Clare, or Count Favoris, or some scapegrace who is fast on his way to 'the Bench!' And then the mother! Cotherstone is well enough, *if he is honest;* but conceive Mrs. C. for a mother-in-law! No, it will not do. I shall dine with them to-day, and after that gradually break off the acquaintance"— and with this doughty resolution I took the now well-known road to Cotherstone's villa.

Kate was late for dinner; but she came down before the soup was off, looking like an angel who had been weeping over man's fallen lot—an angel, be it understood, extremely well-dressed, and far, very far different in figure from those whose proportions we are used to see so miserably curtailed in the creations of the sculptor. But weeping she had certainly been, and the swollen eyelids gave a softness of expression to her countenance that I had never seen before. I felt getting worse again.

"We have nobody to meet you, Mr. Nogo," said Mrs. Cotherstone; "we treat you quite like one of the family. I asked Kate, says I, Kate, are you sure Mr. Nogo won't find it stupid being here in the family way? I mean," added the matron, picking herself up, "nobody but ourselves. And Kate, you said you were sure he would like it better, and you knew his tastes—didn't you?" Calling my attention to that ingenious young lady, who, with a faint blush upon her gentle brow, was looking sorrowfully down into her soup-plate.

I muttered something about "delighted" and "much pleasanter," and so on, but all in vain to stop the torrent of Mrs. Cotherstone's eloquence; till her husband, who was really an agreeable man, came to the rescue, with a few words of well-bred quiet welcome, and a glass of dry champagne, fit, as the nursery-song expresses it, "to set before a king."

Everything in his establishment was as well done for our small party of four as it could have been had mine host been entertaining a company of princes of the blood. The dinner consisted of just the right number of dishes, dressed to perfection; the servants waited noiselessly as spirits; the *épergne* was decorated with the rarest flowers, most tastefully disposed; the decanters sparkled with the raciest and most curious of wines; and Mr. Cotherstone seemed determined that none of these good things, particularly the latter, should be lost upon his guest. " Nogo, have you tasted that sparkling Moselle ?"—" Nogo, have another glass of the dry champagne." —" Nogo, I can recommend that old sherry :"—till my brain began to reel with its effects, to do justice to all these hospitable challenges, and by the time I had finished my share of a magnum of 25, preparatory to coffee, ladies, and the drawing-room, I felt wound up to that pitch which is equally prepared for all pursuits and contingencies, "from pitch-and-toss to manslaughter," " from rat-catching to the use of the globes."

With a flushed countenance and unsteady step I entered the drawing-room, to find it deserted: Papa calling to me from the rear, "that he was going to his own room to write a letter, which must be sent off the first thing to-morrow morning—to ring for coffee when I wanted it—and that he would join me in half an hour." I have said the drawing-room was empty; but out of the drawing-room a door opened into the pretty little conservatory, with its lamps and flowers: and out of the conservatory the cooling night-breeze tempted me through another open door into the silvery moonlight, shedding its soft rays over towering shrub and smoothly-shaven lawn. The flutter of a white dress, flitting slowly down the gravel walk, soon attracted my attention and my footsteps. Mamma was gone to bed with a headache—Papa was safe for at least half an hour over his letter. The field was all her own. Now or never was the time. Young, romantic, and flushed with wine, I was in for a moonlight stroll alone with Kate Cotherstone.

It was truly a dangerous situation, and one from which few men on the sunny side of what people call the "prime of life" (an epoch always placed five years beyond the age of the individual making use of the term) would have escaped scathless; but I was not daring enough to be an utter fool: the instinctive caution of my nature had taken fright, and notwithstanding the claret, notwithstanding the fascinations of scenery, moonlight, flowers, perfume, and white muslin, the warnings of Jack Raffleton were never present so vividly to my mind as when, putting her arm within mine, on the plea of fatigue, Kate walked me quietly away in an opposite direction from the house, and half playfully, though with a mournful accent on her melodious tones, warbled forth a fragment of Tommy Moore's harmonious ballad, "Fly to the desert, fly with me." Verily, Mr. Moore, you have a great deal to answer for; and hard must be the heart that can resist your thrilling numbers dropping from "the lips that we love;" but that hardness of heart was mine, and when, after one turn round the garden, during which a stoic might have envied my callousness, we returned to the realities of lamplight and the drawing-room, I had a bitter sort of satisfaction in feeling that Kate could make nothing of me. I caught one glimpse of her countenance as we entered the conservatory, when she thought she was unobserved, and on those exquisite features I read an expression of contempt, hatred, and bitter spite, that made me shudder as I gazed: the curl on that beautiful lip would have made the fortune of a painter who had undertaken to depict Mephistophiles; and almost worse than all was the instantaneous change that came over her when she perceived she was watched. I could not have believed the "human face divine" was able so rapidly to alter its whole appearance, and wreathe itself so suddenly in smiles. Once or twice during our walk my heart had melted within me, and I had nearly fallen a victim to the spells of the enchantress; but I had gathered more than usual firmness from the wine I had drunk, and I strenuously resisted her blandishments, and the impulse of my own heart; but now the mask had fallen off, and I re-entered the drawing-room completely sobered by my conflicting feelings, and with every faculty sharpened by the contemplation of the danger I had escaped. Cotherstone's good-humoured matter-of-fact countenance, and carefully-ironed white neckcloth, recalled me more quickly than anything to the material world; and ere I had drunk my coffee, I was again lulled into security by the quiet ease with which he led the conversation, amusing and quaint as usual, as he discussed the every-day topics of *our world*, and the coolness and *sang froid* with which Kate joined in our discourse, as though nothing had happened, and the cherished schemes of the last fortnight had not melted away like an air-bubble during that fatal evening. " Kate, let us have a little music ;" and she glided away to the pianoforte with a readiness and good-humour that was perfectly enchanting.

I am very susceptible to the influence of music; and in my then excited state, I felt half-maddened by the silver tones of that voice which I knew not yet whether I most loved or hated; and the consummate skill with which she modulated the tones of her instrument, now dreamy and soothing as the evening breeze, now startling and inspiriting as the trumpet-blast, roused my feelings to the uttermost, and I longed for some vent to the excitement that was boiling within. The tempter was close at my elbow. " Nogo, what do you say to a pool at *écarté*, you, and I, and Kate ? or if she will go on playing to us, we can have our quiet '*parti*,' and listen to her performance the while." There is an old Latin adage, often quoted, about which a good deal of money has been lost, as it is not to be found in any author of earlier or later date, but of the truth of which, nevertheless, there can be little doubt—and thus runs the aphorism, " *Quem Deus vult perdere prius dementat.*" And certainly, if Kate had set her heart upon my ruin, she had adopted the preparatory step of bidding me take leave of my senses, or I should never have dreamt of easing my mind by contending single-handed in any game of skill with my accomplished host.

The table was wheeled down within a yard or two of the pianoforte, the wax-lights on which threw a strong glare upon my "hand," as I took my seat in obedience to Cotherstone's courteous gesture, with my back to Kate, who, as usual, expressed her interest in my success. Shuffling the cards with a careless remark about "moderate stakes," mine adversary drew his chair to the opposite side of the table, and we entered upon the tug of war to the accompaniment of a rare and beautiful symphony, exquisitely performed by our fair musician; and the ever-varying strains of which, now fading with a "dying fall" into almost imperceptible melody, now returning in fuller tones, and thrilling like some well-remembered voice upon the ear, required indeed the skill of a thorough and accomplished musician. I am thus particular in specifying the exact position of the parties and the circumstantial details of that memorable evening, as it was on this occasion I first discovered the extent of dishonesty and dishonour practised by a man holding by such means the position of a gentleman, and to whose course of fraud and swindling I had voluntarily exposed myself.

The game progressed and the stakes increased. Blind, reckless, and infatuated, for some time I rushed wildly into the excitement of the hour. Stakes were doubled and trebled with a carelessness of consequences that was perfectly frightful. Nothing could exceed the quiet courtesy of mine host, except, perhaps, the readiness which he showed in complying with my insane and reiterated proposals for higher stakes—always higher stakes—and still fortune went against me, and the anticipated run of success—the change of luck—that "will-o'-the-wisp" ever present to the gamester's mental vision—still fleeted on before and still eluded my disappointed grasp. At length came a reaction. The amount of my losses was dreadful to contemplate, and the effect upon my previous state of excitement was sedative in proportion to the magnitude of my difficulties: the continued run of ill-luck that had dogged me ever since I sat down to play was startling even to an inexperienced practitioner like myself; I never *had a chance.* If I held a bad hand Cotherstone would not allow me to propose; if a good one, he seemed to possess a magical insight into the value of every one of my court cards; and I derived the least benefit possible from those very smiles of Fortune which she was so niggard in bestowing. And ever, as my strategy was foiled, my cards out-trumped, and my tricks taken, would the pealing notes of that glorious symphony ring upon mine ear, like the sweet yet mocking laugh of some alluring spirit exulting over the ruin to which it beckoned. I know not what may be the effect of wine combined with intense excitement upon the nerves of others; but with me, after a certain point, it has ever had a positively *sobering* tendency. There is a period at which, after the exhaustion of the spirits by their previous hilarity, the mind, fatigued and overstrung, sinks into the opposite extreme: if the excitement be still kept up, then, as in the case of the habitual drunkard, a state of helpless despondency will ensue; and such a course, if persevered in, will inevitably lead to that gloomiest of all the phases of insanity —" delirium tremens." But this is only the doom of those who, day after day, and month after month, devote themselves to the pernicious use of alcohol: and such victims are, fortunately, becoming more and more rare.

To return to my own sensations:—On the evening in question, the excitement I had gone through, both as to my better and worse feelings, had completely counteracted the effect of those potations which had at first enhanced its power; and by the time Cotherstone and I had concluded our third rubber, my brain was sobered, my faculties sharpened, and my nerves braced to an extent which enabled me to discover the ingenious and well-planned fraud of which I was the victim. It flashed upon me suddenly that Kate's symphony was ever loudest when my hand was most miserably poor; and upon such occasions it invariably happened that her father denied me the privilege of improving my position by what is called "proposing"—a course which, as I was not disposed to pursue it with regard to his daughter, he took care I should derive no benefit from in my struggle with himself. I then reflected that Kate, from her position behind me, and that of her wax candles on the pianoforte, could see distinctly into my hand, and that in all probability so accomplished a young lady was as good a judge of *écarté* as she was of whist. No sooner did this suspicion cross my mind, than, disregarding the playing of my cards, I devoted myself entirely to watching the proceedings of my antagonist and his accomplice. Ere long I had abundant proof to satisfy my own mind as to the disadvantages under which I had that evening been fleeced of a small fortune. I remarked that Cotherstone never once *looked* in the direction of, or exchanged a single glance with his daughter. He had a fine ear, and doubtless that was quite sufficient to guide him in his movements.

Once I shifted my chair in such a manner that my cards were entirely hid from Miss Cotherstone's view, and on that occasion the liquid treble and resounding bass were steady and unvaried as a funeral march; but on a fresh game commencing, and my continuing in the same cautious position, the young lady left her seat for the ostensible purpose of fetching some more music, and as she passed behind me, deliberately and searchingly she scanned the cards in my hand, which for once were most favourable. Need I add, that when she resumed her place at the pianoforte, the waltz of Weber, which she commenced with such unrivalled skill, died away in its second bar into a faint and fitful melody, like the music of a dream!

I was now convinced: but how to proceed? Determined not to sit still and be robbed with my eyes open, I was yet extremely averse, more particularly in the presence of a woman, to what is called "a row;" and my uncertainty how to act, and the difficulty—I had almost said "delicacy"—of my position, made me so absent and "*distrait*," that it was impossible Cotherstone should fail to remark the alteration and embarrassment of my manner.

"Nogo," said he, in his usual frank, good-humoured manner, "you are bored with this; let us leave off. And Kate!" added the paternal hypocrite, without a blush on his open countenance, "play us something lively, instead of that confounded thing you have been hammering at all night."

My half-inaudible and absent answer was not remarked; for Kate, dashing off a brilliant conclusion, shut the pianoforte, and, lighting a candle, retired for the night, leaving me with her father, in a state of painful indecision as to how I should act.

"Well, Nogo," said he, as soon as the door closed upon her retreating form, "I wish we had not played quite so high. I see you lose more than eighteen hundred; but of course, my dear fellow, you need not trouble yourself about an immediate payment, if it is any inconvenience to you. I only play, as you know, for amusement; and, therefore, whether you pay me now or two months hence little matters, or if you like to give me a bill for the amount——"

"Mr. Cotherstone," I replied, in a voice almost inarticulate with a mixed feeling of anger, annoyance, and a certain degree of apprehension for the probable consequences of such a demonstration, whilst my whole frame shook and my lips trembled with the violence of my agitation, "I distinctly refuse to pay you one farthing of the money I have lost tonight, and out of which I have been swindled—yes, sir, most disgracefully swindled!—by an ingenious combination between your daughter and yourself."

I saw him look up for an instant with a guilty, startled expression, as I delivered this home-thrust, that convinced me more and more of the truth of my suspicions. His cheek grew perfectly livid, and his nostril dilated, with an expression that changed his whole countenance, and which even then brought forcibly to my recollection the glance his daughter threw at me that evening, in the conservatory. There was the same fiendish expression of malice and re-

H

venge disfiguring the shapely feature; the same scornful sneer on the well-cut lip, that betokened pain and disappointment, curbed and kept down by the strong will within. There was, if I may so call it, a family likeness of evil between father and daughter; nor did the well-schooled man of the world more readily recover his equanimity and usual bearing than she—that heartless girl—had previously done under parallel circumstances, when *her* schemes of enrichment and aggrandisement were foiled by the clearsightedness of her victim. But Mr. Cotherstone had only one course to pursue; and Bayard might have taken a lesson in chivalry from the temperate bearing, the firm manner, and high tone adopted by this most consummate of knaves.

"I am at a loss to account for your extraordinary behaviour, Mr. Nogo," was his quiet and gentlemanlike reply. "I should be sorry to believe that I had sat down to play with a gentleman in a state of intoxication—the only excuse I can think of for your conduct. You will allow me to ring for your carriage; and I trust that to-morrow you will see the propriety of making an ample apology. In justice to myself, however, I must insist upon the trifling sum we have been discussing being immediately paid over; and I am sure in your cooler moments you will see the absolute necessity of such a proceeding."

And with these words, he bowed me out in a state of complete distraction, staggered by his coolness, alarmed at what I had entailed upon myself, and with no very clear perception, except that advice and assistance must immediately be sought from Jack Raffleton, and from him alone.

CHAPTER XI.

Sir Toby.—He is knight, dubbed with unhacked rapier, and on carpet consideration; but he is a devil in private brawl. Souls and bodies hath he divorced three; and his incensement at this moment is so implacable that satisfaction can be none, but by pangs of death and sepulchre. Hob-nob is his word, give't or take't—
Sir And.—Plague on't, I'll not meddle with him.
Twelfth-Night; or, What you will.

I DO not set up for the character of having more nerve than my neighbours; and I can conceive no anticipations, except perhaps those of a gentleman engaged to be hanged, more disagreeable than the forebodings which darken the existence of a quiet steady-going man, who for the first time in his life finds he has got a duel upon his hands. When I left Cotherstone's house on the night of our *fracas*, it was evident to me that, come what might, the thing could only have one conclusion. If I steadily persevered in my resolution of refusing to pay, mine adversary would of course take such steps as should make it imperative on me to call him out. If, on the other hand, I accepted the unpalatable alternative of " booking up," I was not at all satisfied that the language I had made use of would not be sufficient to provoke a man in Cotherstone's ambiguous position to the immediate use of fire-arms at a short distance; and view it whichever way I would, one thing was clear—the business must end in a fight. With this soothing lullaby, I sought my pillow; and feverish was the rest, and disturbed the dreams, that hovered over my couch. Now I was Gustavus, of dancing memory, threading the lively " galop " with my fascinating Kate, through the conservatory, out into the garden, round the shrubberies, while Mrs. C. beat time, and nodded with a mother's pride in the graceful pair. Anon, Papa, in the guise of the jealous Ankerstrom, rises from the Ha-ha, with a long rifle-barrelled pistol in his hand, and Kate, flying into the house, disappears with an *eldritch* shriek. Then the scene changes, and I am driving with Jack Raffleton to witness a private trial, from which we both expect great things. It is early morning as we arrive upon the Downs; and the sun, just peeping above the horizon, throws his slanting beams over as fair a scene as merry England can produce. The lark is rising into the deep blue sky, marbled here and there with light and fleecy clouds; and never, I think, was the world so beautiful—never was life so enjoyable. I get up to ride the trial!—such are the inconsistencies of a dream—but the animal I bestride is rooted to the ground. "Give it him!" says Jack, as he puts a pistol into my hand. John Scott assumes the form of Mr. Cotherstone, and Alfred Day shoots suddenly up into a truculent-looking gentleman, six feet high. I find myself placed within arm's length of my antagonist, and in a frantic attempt to cock my pistol, the hammer of which no power seems able to displace, I awake! with that heavy feeling of oppression which makes us conscious of misfortune, ere our faculties have shaken off the influence of sleep sufficiently to perceive the whole extent of the troubles in which we are involved. It was later than I should have thought; and hurrying my toilet, I ordered my hack, and galloped off to the barracks at Windsor, to gather counsel and assistance from my friend Jack Raffleton. That gallant defender of his country was in the act of sitting down to a late and luxurious breakfast, after the fatigues of a "marching-order field-day" in the park, when I was ushered into his presence in the mess-room. Jack saw by my countenance that the mission with which I was charged was of no pleasant nature; but as several brother-officers were present, it was not a time for explanation, and I accepted, though with no great appetite, the cordial invitation to join these joyous spirits in their merry repast. Fun, good-humour, and "*chaff*" were paramount as ever; and although in low spirits myself, and by no means in a frame of mind to make the companionship of a lot of devil-may-care fellows any more acceptable than the profuse breakfast which tempted my unwilling palate, I could not help envying my companions their hilarity, and thinking within myself, "What a jolly life these fellows lead!" The repast, interminable as I thought it, at length came to an end, and over a weed in Jack's barrack-room I explained to him the scrape I had got into, and asked his advice as to how I was to act.

"Why," said Jack, to whom, as an oracle in these matters, I listened with undivided attention, "we have nothing to do but to keep quiet: you have distinctly refused to pay, and have, besides, given Cotherstone a pretty good piece of your mind. If he takes no further notice, well and good; though, from my knowledge of the man, I think such a chance extremely improbable. He is a fighting sort of fellow, confound him! and I recollect his 'parading' Brampton of the Bays, about a disputed bet at Newmarket: everybody said Brampton was right, but he had to pay, notwithstanding; and Cotherstone, not satisfied with receiving his money, must stand upon his character, forsooth! and have a shot at him, besides."

"How did it end?" I inquired, somewhat aghast to hear of these strong fighting inclinations.

"Cotherstone shot him in the wrist," was the reply: the ball took off the lock of his pistol, and ran up his arm to the elbow. The whole thing was badly managed by the seconds: however, it was hushed up, and made all right. But I'll tell you how we must act. It will never do for you to be out of the way should a message arrive. We will drive back to your villa together; stay there all the afternoon, and have an early dinner with a bottle of light claret,"—Jack settled it all as if it was a picnic—"and then if anybody calls we shall be ready for them, and I should hope, with a little good diplomacy, it will not be necessary to come to extreme measures."

With this consolatory remark, Jack ordered his dog-cart, and sending my horse back by his servant, we drove together through the glorious summer noon, striving to converse on indifferent subjects; but, as far as one of us was concerned, I can answer for the effort being most unsuccessful. Why did Windsor Forest look more beau 'ful, bathed as it was in that flood of sunshine, than it had ever looked before? Why had the hum of insects, the song of birds, the towering elms, the stately oaks, the massive shade of the deep woodland glades, a charm that, to my unawakened feelings, had never previously existed? Could it be that life, in all its beauty, all its capacity for enjoyment, *that* life of which the sunny summer noon was so suggestive a type, had never been really appreciated, until the probability of its being hazarded, the possibility of losing it, had startled me into the consciousness of its innumerable blessings and delights? Certainly I found myself becoming more and more keenly alive to the pleasures of existence, and contemplating with more and more disgust the disagreeable necessity to which I was reduced. Gradually I tasked my memory to recall in long and ghastly array all the traditions of duelling that I had ever read or heard of—how a certain English gentleman, of undaunted courage and unerring aim, had been insulted by a French Count, celebrated as a bully by preference and a duellist by profession; how he retaliated by pulling the Frenchman's nose, and thus, placing himself in the position of the challenged, obtained the option of weapons, and chose pistols as placing him more upon a par with his antagonist than the small-sword; how they fought at "the Barrier," as it is called, beginning at twenty-five paces, how, ere one step was completed, both the pistols had been discharged, the Englishman being the least moment in advance, and shooting his adversary through the heart, at the same instant that the Count's ball grazed his forehead—the fact of receiving a bullet in the "pericardium" only disturbing the Frenchman's aim to that extent. How, upon another frightful occasion, at one of these sanguinary "*barrier*" duels, the younger combatant of the two, the hope and stay as he was the representative of his family, having failed in bringing down his antagonist at a long shot, was forced by the rules of the "*duello*," and the exigencies of "*honour*," to walk coolly up, with his discharged pistol in his hand, to be murdered in cold blood at the white handkerchief, placed on the ground half-way between the principals; how his adversary—a fiend in human form—laid his hand upon the youth's person, to feel the exact spot where his heart beat, and pressing the muzzle of his weapon against that wellspring of vitality, immolated him then and there with the words—" I pity your poor mother!" How, in later days, men had been shot dead in duels, such as the customs of society made inevitable, and the survivors rendered amenable to the laws of their country, on the capital charge; how, the option between being shot and hanged was by no means agreeable; and how it was very possible that the events of the next four-and-twenty hours might give me my choice of either catastrophe. In short, by the time we drove up to the door of my villa, and my servant informed me "that a gentleman was waiting to see me in the drawing-room," I had worked myself up into a state of nervousness and agitation, the least calculated to get me well through the business upon which I concluded the gentleman "had called."

An interview of half an hour with Major O'Cleverly, who turned out to be my visitor, did not serve, as may be supposed, to tranquillize my nerves. As my prophetic soul had already taught me, the Major had called on the part of Mr. Cotherstone, and was the bearer of a proposition, to which I felt it quite impossible to accede. I was to pay over the eighteen hundred immediately, as a proof of the most satisfactory nature that I had no accusation to make as to the manner in which it was won; I was to apologize for my intemperate behaviour the previous night, laying the blame on the quantity of wine I had drunk, acted upon by the excitement of high play, " and thus," concluded the Major, drawing himself up to his full height, with a bland smile, "having made the '*amaunde honorable*' customary amongst gentlemen, me friend Mr. Cotherstone will be happy to look over this most unfortunate '*fracaw*,' and will be ready and willing—Bedad! he's a good fellow, Cotherstone!—to shake hands with yerself, Mr. Nogo, and say no more about it." I summoned up all my dignity to reply with becoming pomposity to the Milesian ambassador; and the upshot of it was, that I referred him for all further particulars to my friend Captain Raffleton, at that moment waiting in the next room. I thought this announcement rather staggered the Major, and I must do him the justice to say, that throughout the whole proceedings he was decidedly against warlike measures, if they could possibly be avoided; and no doubt it would have suited the purpose of himself and his confederate better could they have succeeded in fleecing their pigeon quietly, as they had one and all been before the public quite often enough to make such a display by no means desirable.

Jack's interview with the Major soon came to a conclusion, my friend adopting a very high tone—distinctly refusing, on my part, to pay the money, or withdraw the charge of cheating at play, which I had made against Mr. Cotherstone, and expressing a perfect readiness on the part of himself and his friend to abide the issue of the ordeal of single combat, the preliminaries of which were duly settled in my drawing-room during the Major's visit—time and place arranged, and even a jocose allusion, on O'Cleverly's part, to trains and steamboats, which might allow of the survivor's escaping to the Continent. Jack's reasons for this decided line of conduct were sensible enough in their way, though I could not help thinking that, like all men engaged as seconds in a duel, he did not quite see the "last appeal" in so important a light as it appeared to his principal.

"I do not think," said he, as he walked up and down the lawn after the Major's departure, "that these fellows will come to the scratch at last: depend upon it, they do not mean fighting. Their object, of course, is to get the money, and they are trying to bully you into paying; but we must be firm with them, and after all, if worst comes to the worst, we 'can wink and hold out iron' as well as they can—by-the-bye, can you shoot any, Nogo?"

I was forced to confess that my pistol practice was by no means first-rate, and that, in fact, I had no idea of the weapon whatever; had certainly never loaded one; and very much doubted if I had even "let one off." It was accordingly agreed upon, that, if we heard nothing further from "the enemy" before four o'clock that afternoon, we should consider such silence tantamount to a declaration of war, and prepare accordingly, Jack binding himself to give me correct instructions, as to the most authentic manner of holding, levelling, and discharging my pistol, with all and sundry niceties and arrangements peculiar to the "duello."

What a long afternoon it was! I thought the shadows on that shaven lawn would never lengthen: I could settle to nothing: the uncertainty of my position was worrying and annoying to a degree. I would have given anything to have had the matter brought to a conclusion one way or the other, even if that way was to produce the dreaded encounter. I quite longed to take my ground, and fight it out like a man. I wandered in and out of the house like some unquiet spirit; smoked half a cigar, then threw it away; glanced listlessly over the newspaper; even went to the stables to look at my solitary hack, and found myself wondering when I should ride him again, and unconsciously quoting "the Arab's farewell to his steed." Three o'clock had struck, and the last hour of suspense was drawing on towards its close. At four we were to consider ourselves "booked," and to make all our preparations accordingly. Jack was even then upstairs, arranging his pistols, and humming a whole opera through as he proceeded with his task, and I was wondering where I should be this time to-morrow, and whether the sun would be shining as brightly, and the birds warbling as gaily, though I might be blind to sunshine and deaf to song, when the train of my reflections was interrupted by the tramp of a horse cantering up the grass ride that led to the stables; and ere I had time to conjecture whether this was "the Major," with some pacific proposal or a chance visitor from the barracks, unconscious of our dilemmas and ravenous for luncheon, Kate Cotherstone galloped into the stable-yard, pale and dishevelled with the speed at which she had been riding, and lovelier than ever in her agitation and distress.

Ere I had recovered from my astonishment at her sudden appearance, she had jumped off her horse, put her arm within mine, and trembling all over like an aspen-leaf, had walked me through the French windows into the cool and half-darkened drawing-room, where she explained to me in broken sentences the object of her unusual visit. As far as I could make out—for Kate's nervousness, too evidently not assumed, made her at times rather incoherent—she had heard our voices raised as if in anger, when her father and I parted the previous night; she saw in the morning, by Cotherstone's manner, that something was wrong; and when the Major arrived, at so unusual an hour as nine o'clock, evidently in consequence of a summons from his friend, she felt satisfied from her previous experience in such matters that something serious was about to take place. Brought up in a school not over-fastidious as to its ideas of honour, the young lady had small scruple in listening at her papa's door, and making herself mistress of the conversation going on within, from which she learnt the whole particulars of our disagreement, and the contemplated duel. She was obliged to pretend to be ignorant of everything till the time approached for her usual afternoon ride, when, dismissing her groom, and concealing her intentions from every one, she had galloped over to my villa, in a state of mind not to be described.

"And promise me, Mr. Nogo—promise me, I beseech you, that you will not allow this frightful business to end in a duel. Heavens! it is too horrible! Any sacrifice would be preferable. My poor father—a man twice your age; you never could lift your hand against him. If ever you cared for me—and there was a time—" said Kate, looking lovely beyond conception, and not acting now, "There was a time that you said my word should always be your law—if ever you cared for me, I entreat you not to fight with papa! Promise me that you will agree to a reconciliation, and the whole thing may be hushed up. What will people say to my riding over here alone ? I have sacrificed my character—surely you can make the comparatively trifling sacrifice of foregoing this dreadful alternative !"

What could I do ? Here was a young, handsome girl, one to whom I had certainly for a time been much attached, pleading with me for the sake of her father; using all the advantages of her beauty, her position, and her distress; employing all the arguments and sophistry that fall so persuasively from woman's lips, to induce me to forego this infernal duel, for which I had myself the smallest possible inclination—what could any man do? Of course I gave way, and promised her all and everything she required. She was, for once, honest in her purpose: there was no mistaking the daughter's eagerness and anxiety on the father's behalf for anything but truth, and I flattered myself I saw more into Kate's character, and liked her better, if I *loved* her less, during that painful half-hour, than in our acquaintance and flirtations for weeks previously. The upshot of it was, that I put the young lady again upon her horse, after administering all the restoratives in my power—outward applications of eau de-Cologne, and inward consolation in the shape of a glass of brown sherry—happy in my assured promise, that come what might, no power on earth should induce me to harm a hair of her father's head, and pledging my honour as a gentleman that no effort should be wanting on my part to avoid the proposed rencontre, and I then walked back into the house to relate all that had taken place to Jack Raffleton, who had discreetly remained up-stairs during the whole time of Kate's visit. We talked it over again and again, but we could make nothing of it : as Jack said, I had now succeeded in entangling the whole affair in such a manner that it required a wiser head than his to set things straight.

" In the first place," argued my indignant friend, " we have an Irishman to negotiate with ; then we have 'a leg' to deal with, whom we must either pay eighteen hundred, or fight. He is utterly reckless, and can shoot like blazes ! But that is neither here nor there. Then I have a principal to act for who has never been concerned in an affair of this kind before, and who consequently depends or should depend wholly and solely on my experience. And lastly, just as I have screwed him up, and brought him to the scratch, a meddling little devil in ringlets comes poking her nose in, to make a mess of everything; and my friend, whose honour imperatively requires that he should go out and be shot at, the first thing to-morrow morning, pledges *his honour* that he will do nothing of the kind; and I am expected to reconcile all these impossibilities and contradictions. By Jove! it's enough to provoke a saint! I'll tell you what, Nogo—fight *you must*. I can't help what you have promised: the Major and I settled this morning, that unless certain terms were agreed to, there was only one course. You are now in my hands: it is my duty to see you through this without loss of character; and, by heavens! fight *you shall!*"

Mine was the weaker mind—the more yielding spirit—and again I gave way. The events of that afternoon almost made me doubt my own free agency. I seemed to be a shuttlecock, bandied to and fro between Jack, the Major, and Kate; and the only privilege of self-will that I reserved to myself was a determination to shoot in any direction but that of Mr. Cotherstone, thereby redeeming my promise to his daughter, and careless whether, by such a course, I might or might not endanger the safety of his second with a stray bullet. Ere Jack's remonstrances were completed, and I had come to this conclusion, the hour for our quiet little dinner had arrived; and just as we were sitting down, who should make his appearance, to add to the inconveniences of the day, but Captain Clare, accompanied, as usual, by young Fitz-Arthur. We could not do less than ask them to join us in our early meal; and the pair, who had been on horseback all day, concocting some robbery, which they called "a good thing," were too happy to anticipate their usual dinner-hour, and do justice to our hospitality. The bottle of light claret, which Jack had so fondly anticipated, very soon multiplied itself into half a dozen. The new arrivals were both particularly agreeable men; Jack himself, especially when he had anything on his hands, was one of the pleasantest fellows in England; and there I sat in that cheerful room, with its open windows and its lovely view, enjoying myself to the utmost. Ay, incredible as it may appear, of all the merry gatherings it has been my luck to attend, that was the one at which my spirits were most buoyant, and my laughter wildest and most hilarious—to which I look back with a sense of the keenest, the most thrilling enjoyment. Could it have been that the uncertainty —nay, the settled gloom—that made the future too forbidding to contemplate, enhanced beyond price the charm of the tangible present? Was it that the consciousness of peril and distress, of which two of my companions could form no idea, gave to me, in that separate existence which they were unable to appreciate, a superiority that in such society I had never felt before? Was it that something within told me the resolution I had formed for Kate's sake was generous, and true, and worthy of the days of chivalry? or was it merely the sense of impending danger that had so bracing and exhilarating an effect? I cannot tell. Probably Damocles, who sat down to dinner every day with a sword suspended over his head by a single hair, might be able to analyze my sensations and explain my feelings. But the reaction came. Our guests were bound for London by an evening train; and as they lit their cigars, and mounted their horses to depart, the sun was still above the horizon; and oh, how beautiful was the world, in the mellow lustre of that calm June evening! How could we, reprobates as we were, dare to insult the majesty of nature, by the pursuit on which we entered, as soon as our guests had disappeared, and the coast was clear? We had now no time to lose in our preparations; and the deep blue sky, serene in its holiness, looked down upon the premeditated guilt of two mortals, perfecting themselves by practice to destroy the life of a fellow-creature. With an accuracy that nothing but long experience could have attained, Jack had paced out the established twelve yards, from the trunk of a giant elm that shaded the lawn of our abode. A large sheet of white paper served as an excellent target; and, placed at duelling distance, I commenced my first lesson in the use of the pistol. Twelve paces is no very great interval between two gentlemen with arms in their hands; but to those who have never made the attempt, it is extraordinary how often an object, the size of a man, may be missed, even at that range, by an inexperienced practitioner. Certainly my nerves were not in the best shooting trim, and the way in which I had been spending the last four-and-twenty hours was not likely to be conducive to accuracy of eye or steadiness of hand; and I blazed away some half-dozen times without the slightest effect upon my gigantic antagonist, whose gnarled and knotted trunk remained scatheless as before. At last I hit him, though about ten feet from the ground; and Jack, out of patience with my repeated failures and slow progress, exclaimed, " This will never do ! I'll set the hair-triggers, Nogo; and mind what you are about with them. Above all, be steady." The hair-triggers were accordingly set. The pistols, as Jack assured me, were true as rifles; and, certainly, the mechanism of the locks, and the manner in which these fine triggers went off at the slightest conceivable touch, was curious in the extreme. I took one out of his hands, and, bringing the sight to bear with all the accuracy I could command, succeeded in planting a bullet well into the sheet of white paper, then doing duty as an antagonist. " Bravo, Nogo!" said Jack; " this is what you required !" and, with a smile, he handed me the remaining weapon, prepared, as before, to go off at the very lightest touch. I had just taken it into my hands, with some remark eulogistic of its properties, when " bang!" I was startled by a sudden explosion right under my face, that made me leap three feet from the ground. The next moment I felt a thrill in one of my arms, as though suddenly seared with a red-hot iron. I was conscious of every pulsation in my brain, beating with a sound like the stroke of a church-clock. I heard Jack's voice, thick and indistinct as the shouts of a multitude. The giant elm and the evening sky were swimming before my eyes; the short, mossy turf, to which I seemed suddenly so close, was heaving around me. I grasped it with the clutch of a drowning man. Of that last effort I have the most vivid recollection—but I can remember no more.

*   *   *   *   *

CHAPTER XII.

And they will learn you by rote where services were done—who came off bravely, who was shot, who disfigured—and this they can perfectly in the phrase of war; but you must learn to know such slanders of the age, or else you may be marvellously mistook.

Henry V.

Now Lord be thanked for my good amends.

Taming of the Shrew.

PEOPLE may talk of the blessings of health, and doubtless without health there can be but little enjoyment in any pleasure which life can bestow; but of all delightful sensations commend me to those of what medical men call "convalescence," when every hour brings fresh proof of returning strength, and every function of Nature is alone busied in the one great object of "getting well." The sturdy labourer, whose frame and appearance are the very types of "rude health," might have envied the soundness of my sleep and the keenness of my appetite during the fortnight or three weeks which restored to me the use of the arm I had myself so provokingly injured. In an airy and cheerful lodging, in a quiet street not very far from the Park, with all the new novels to read, with all my acquaintances delighted to while away an idle hour in my society, with the most agreeable of doctors, who persisted in looking upon me as a hero who after several exchanges of shot had at length been taken unwillingly off the ground with an injury that nothing but his own skill could have healed, I found the confinement to one room and the regimen required of a patient anything but tedious or disagreeable.

Jack Raffleton, who had been kindness itself after the accident, and who perseveringly cursed his own stupidity in ever trusting "such a muff as Nogo with hair-triggers," had arranged my "affair" with Cotherstone with a tact peculiarly his own. Pay I certainly did, but not to any very large amount; and as the musical sharper was compelled to leave England on business of his own, at very short notice—in fact, was in that pleasant predicament which the Yankees call "a fix," having made Tattersall's too hot to hold him, and got into some stock-jobbing scrape into the bargain—a compromise was effected, by which, in consideration of certain "value received," nothing more was to be said, on either side, as to his ingenious method of playing *écarté*, or my non-appearance at our matutinal trysting-place.

The worst of it was the manner in which those infernal Sunday papers got hold, as usual, of the wrong end of the story; and as each had its own absurd version, of course from the very best authority, my leisure was amused with paragraphs such as the following:—

"A hostile meeting is stated to have taken place between a well-known sporting character and a young and fashionable millionaire (?). The parties met on Tumble-down Common, and we regret to say that both were severely wounded. Two military gentlemen officiated as seconds. Of course until a judicial investigation has taken place, more especially as one of the combatants is in immediate danger, it would be premature to give the names of these offenders against the law."

"We have to record a *rencontre* of a hostile nature which has taken place between Mr. T-l-b-r-y N-g-o and J. C-th-st-ne, Esq. The *causa teterrima belli* is said to have been the attentions paid by the former gentleman to the fascinating and beautiful daughter of the latter. Mr. N-g-o was attended on the ground by the Hon. Capt. R-ff-t-n, and the well-known Major O'C-v-r-ly officiated for Mr. C-th-st-ne. Both gentlemen fired in the air!"

"The duello again! Another of these unmanly and un-English performances has again taken place, in the vicinity of Ascot, and on the very ground immortalized by the game and never-to-be-forgotten struggle between 'The British Buster' and 'Turner's Black.' Our readers need hardly be reminded that exhausted Nature gave way, and the 'Buster' ceased to breathe after fighting the unprecedented number of 157 rounds! And now two assassins have desecrated this hallowed spot; and instead of settling their differences by ' peeling ' and ' to it like men, have had recourse to the cowardly pistol as an arbiter of their quarrel. England! indeed thy glory hath departed; and our upper classes have themselves to thank for hastening thy decay."

Such were a few of the versions furnished by these caterers for the amusement of the public. The *Illuminated Gazette* presented its readers with an exceedingly well-composed tableau, in which were portraits of the two belligerents, their seconds, and Kate Cotherstone in the distance. The great daily organ of public opinion itself found room to insert a couple of lines, in which the whole business was disposed of under the heading " Determined Suicide by a Gentleman :" and as far as my unfortunate accident was concerned, this was perhaps nearer the truth than any of them. But the *Morning Muffineer*, that chronicle of the fashionable world, was more mysterious, and yet more diffuse, than all the rest of its contemporaries put together. First of all it had heard of "a rumoured *fracas* in the higher circles, involving unpleasant disclosures, and ending in a personal collision." Then, " it was whispered that the elopement of a young lady in the vicinity of Windsor had led to a hostile encounter between the gay Lothario and offended parent, in which the latter was severely wounded." After this, " it was informed that the late ' affair ' between two well-known sporting gentlemen, had its origin in certain play transactions to a large amount: the younger belligerent lies dangerously wounded at his house in town." Lastly, it stated boldly that it "was happy to hear Mr. Nogo was rapidly recovering from the effects of his wound, and that amputation was fortunately unnecessary. Mr., Mrs., and Miss Cotherstone have taken their departure for the continent."

With all these paragraphs, and with all the different stories told by my different friends, each knowing his own version "for a fact," I was quite a hero during the nine days that elapsed, before some fresher "wonder" called off the attention of the gossiping and the idle. I began to think at last that I was in truth the champion they took me for; and although I could not quite persuade myself that I had actually received Cotherstone's fire, I took all the credit of having screwed my courage up to fighting pitch, and was firmly persuaded that I should have gone through the affair with as much coolness and determination as everybody seemed to think I had, more particularly as Jack Raffleton himself declared, "Nogo showed a great deal more pluck than he should have expected—but nervous, confoundedly nervous."

My little doctor, as well, added largely to this hallucination; nothing would persuade him that the wound to which he applied so much surgical skill was the effect of accident; and although, like other well-principled men, he abhorred duelling in the abstract, still he could not divest himself of a certain degree of interest and admiration when brought into personal contact with a man whom he believed to have "stood fire" unflinchingly. How often we see this amongst mankind!

I am afraid more of us are cowards at heart than we would fain believe, as it is only to the principle of cowardice that we can attribute a blind admiration of that which is in itself wrong, merely because accompanied by a personal risk that we dare not ourselves incur. Woman is supposed to be most susceptible to the fascination of courage from her own deficiency in that quality; and it must be something of woman's weakness in our hearts that makes us gaze with approbation, which amounts almost to envy, at the prize-fighter or the steeple-chase rider, Van Amburgh in his cage, or Mr. Green in his parachute.

Doctor Dotterell was besides, like many who belong to the graver professions, devoted in theory to those field sports from which in practice he was debarred by his business; and if there was one thing the Doctor was really proud of, it was

a certain black cob, the image of himself, which he drove
with the careful and sedulous air of a daily coachman working
a heavy load for a long distance over a bad road. His gloves
and hat betokened "the Jehu"—the rest of his "get up" was
strictly professional; but the Doctor at heart preferred *Bell's
Life* to all the pharmacopœia, and looked forward to his
week's partridge-shooting with his cousin in September, more
than to all the rest of the year put together. Now he had
taken it into his head that his patient, Mr. Nogo, was a
sportsman of the very highest calibre; an infatuation first
suggested by my admiration of the black cob—a really clever,
serviceable little animal. And a few words which I happened to drop alluding to Leicestershire, Scotland, and other
sporting localities, served to confirm him in this opinion, to
a degree which was inexpressibly ludicrous, when, as was
often the case, he asked my opinion upon some matter of
elephant-shooting or tiger-hunting, of which I knew as much
as the man in the moon.

"Regular exercise, Mr. Nogo," he would say—"regular
exercise will soon set us on our legs again, when once the
injury to the 'biceps' is sufficiently restored to admit of personal exertion. To a man like yourself, devoted to the
sports of the field, and accustomed to negotiate the ox-fences
of Leicestershire, and to breathe your lungs in the pure air,
and up the steep hills of the Highlands, I need not insist on
the necessity of vigorous muscular exertion. I am myself
always in better health when partridge-shooting with my
cousin in Berkshire, and Mrs. Dotterell declares I am never
so well as when I come home fagged and tired after ranging
the stubbles with dog and gun. We must provide some
substitute, Mr. Nogo, even in London, for this kind of severe
exercise; and if I might venture to recommend a little fenc-
ing, or even —ahem— sparring, whilst you remain in town, I
think I may stake my professional reputation that you will
acknowledge the benefit of my advice." Such was ever the
burden of the good little doctor's song; and I verily believe
that in his own heart he was firmly persuaded that if a man

could only remain in a state of profuse perspiration in the open air, during twelve hours out of the twenty-four, he would live for ever.

After the worthy Esculapius had taken his final departure, and I had for the last time indulged myself by watching the knowing manner in which he patted the black cob, glanced over the "tackle," as he called the harness appertaining to his one-horse chaise, shook his beaver into its place on his little round head, drew on his gloves, and squared his elbows, preparatory to turning the corner into the next street, where another patient resided, I bethought myself seriously of following his advice; and feeling that my arm was now as strong as ever, and that a sedentary life with an increasing appetite had brought about the usual effect of making all my waistcoats too tight, I resolved on putting myself into the hands of some professor of self-defence, who whilst he knocked me about for his amusement, and worked me into a state of complete exhaustion for my improvement in condition as for his own benefit in pocket, should teach me that noble science, so useful at Vauxhall or Cremorne when the ambitious snob, or slightly inebriated "gent," vapouring about "punching heads," or in his vinous courage too abruptly coming to conclusions with a graduate in the art, finds perchance that he has unwittingly "caught a Tartar." Besides, I was now considered, amongst my friends and acquaintance, "a determined sort of fellow," "a man of undoubted pluck," "as game as a pebble, and stands no nonsense;" and it would be quite in keeping with this sort of character, that I should be able, if necessary, to vindicate my reputation in a chance row, or hand-to-hand conflict with some too "bumptious" adversary of the baser sort.

Accordingly, after a consultation with several of my young associates, beardless Guardsmen, and fast clerks in public offices—but one and all appearing to know everything that was to be learnt in London, and never to be at a loss— it was decided that I should immediately enter upon a course of tuition from the hands, or rather the knuckles, of no less a person than "The Muff of the Minories" himself. This was indeed a cause for self-gratulation, "The Muff" being acknowledged as the best glove-fighter of the day. His career in the ring had been, as he himself allowed, unfortunate. Out of five appearances, two battles had gone against him, as he said, by gross partiality on the part of the referee, his enemies declaring that each event was what is familiarly denominated "a cross." Of the third contest in which this hero was engaged, it is only necessary to say, that he was deprived of the laurels which he considered his due, by going down ignominiously, without a blow; as in the fourth he himself purposely delivered a foul stroke on the body of his antagonist. An opportunity, however, again offered itself for wiping away the stain of previous defeats, and the fancy invested largely on "The Muff," in his great match for 100 sovs. a-side, with the "Slasher of St. Giles." Money was posted, articles entered into, a referee agreed upon, time and place named, and for once the battle was fought upon the square. Fortune favours the brave. "The Slasher," though of smaller proportions and lighter build, beat his man out of time in the first ten minutes; and from that hour "The Muff" bade adieu to the Prize Ring, and devoted himself to the infinitely more agreeable and lucrative pursuit of knocking gentlemen about in their own private apartments. Of his personal appearance I need only state that he was a low, deep-chested, powerful man, very much let down in the shoulders, which gave him an appearance of being smaller in every way than he really was; and rejoicing in what is appropriately termed "a fighting nob," namely, a villanous-looking countenance, with deep-set twinkling eyes, projecting lips, and a broken nose.

Such was the worthy that, much to my servant's astonishment, made his appearance in my lodgings immediately after breakfast, one sweltering morning in July, and suggesting "beer" as his favourite refreshment in reply to my hospitable inquiries, pulled his extremely short hair, as he offered his "sarvice" to me ere he buried his unprepossessing physiognomy in the grateful pewter. This ceremony concluded, the professor calmly expectorated on my French carpet, and expressed his readiness to commence the lesson, premising that as his was the only method of teaching the art of boxing, it would be as well were I at once to dismiss from my mind, and endeavour totally to forget all my previous knowledge on the subject, to me by no means a difficult task.

"Most of 'em teaches nothink," argued "The Muff;" "but I teaches this—to keep the 'ands allays ready to 'stop' and to 'return,' and above all, never to parry a blow with your 'ead."

I was by this time placed "in position," and the latter self-evident maxim being enforced by a lightning rap, which made my eyes water and my nose swell, served to convince me that my present attitude of self-defence was one in which every portion of my frame was most utterly helpless. Do what I would, turn which way I might, the professor's glove struck, true as clock-work, exactly between my eyes; and as the lesson proceeded, so did my firm conviction that nature had never intended me for a bruiser, and that art would never succeed in making me one. Did "The Muff" generously devote his ugly face as a target to my blows, encouraging me to "'it out! let it come from the shoulder," and reassuring me with the faithful promise that there should be "no reprisals," a sharp electric pain in my elbow-joint warned me that all my strenuous exertions were "lost in air," and the forbidding object at which I aimed was still untouched. Did I summon up all my fortitude and resolution to parry the adversary's rapid blow, even if I succeeded in escaping the first half of what he called his "one, two," the latter was as certain to come in "flush" on mouth or nose, as it was to confuse and utterly bewilder all my ideas; and thankful was I indeed when the lesson came to a conclusion, which it did at the same time as the beer; "The Muff of the Minories" taking his departure with a kind promise that he would be with me at the same hour regularly, "Tuesdays, Thursdays, and Saturdays," and leaving with me two tickets for a sparring benefit, for which I paid him the sum of ten shillings, and an odour of violent exercise, which open doors and windows seemed unable to alleviate.

According to promise, these lessons of chamber practice were day after day repeated; and by dint of constant pommelling, I did certainly in time obtain sufficient quickness to guard my own face, at least from the assaults of my instructor, to whose method I was getting accustomed. A hard hitter I should never have become, nor will all the painstaking in the world give a man that facility of "letting out," which depends, like swift bowling or long throwing at cricket, entirely upon natural formation; but I began to be able to "spar" in a sort of way, and from feeling tolerably at home "with the gloves," foolishly imagined that I should prove a dangerous "customer" in a real fight.

The primary object, however, for which I had engaged "The Muff's" services was now gained—my health and strength were thoroughly re-established, my muscles enlarged, and my weight decreased.

The vigorous exercise of my mornings made a ride in the park quite unnecessary in a salubrious point of view, and I began to take up a strong *penchant* for driving. My phaeton horses were well-bitted, quiet, and perfect as animals could be; and emboldened by the success with which I steered them through the crowded streets of London, I bethought me that it was a pity to waste so much good coachmanship upon a pair, and that I, as well as others, might aspire to the honours of "a drag" and "a team." Besides, a coach would be so useful to my friends; for since my scrape with Kate Cotherstone, I lived entirely amongst a "man" set. I could take my party to races, to Richmond, and to Greenwich; and now that I had set up as a sporting character, it would be the very thing to have fellows talking about "Nogo's coach," and Nogo's charioteering talents. The idea once broached was not long in being carried out.

Of all people in the world, who should call on me, one morning, as I was thinking over my scheme, but Segundo?

—the very man to put me in the way of doing that which I was now so ambitious to effect. Poor fellow! he looked thin and careworn, and was more seedy in his dress and appearance than formerly; in fact, his object in seeing me was to request some pecuniary assistance, which, small as it was, I unhesitatingly offered. As we warmed in conversation, and talked over old times, his ancient swagger and quaint fun began to peep out; but he was still mysterious as ever as to what he had been doing, or where living since I saw him last; all I could gather was that he had been abroad, and, notwithstanding all his talents and pursuits, had been at times wofully "hard-up." He jumped at the notion of a drag; in fact, as he said, it was quite in his line. "The very thing, Nogo. I saw this morning a capital coach, to be sold for a mere song. She is as good as new, dark-green picked out with red; the man she belongs to is in hiding, but I know where he is, and you can have her for half nothing, money down. I saw you driving two bay horses yesterday, in the park, that would make perfect wheelers; and we can pick up a couple of leaders on Monday, at Tattersall's (at least you can send your groom to do so,—I shall not be able to go there for a week or two), for five-and-twenty pounds a-piece. Capital! I'll go and buy the coach directly." And without more ado, away marched my friend, looking more himself, now that he had got something to arrange, than he had done during the whole time we sat together.

The coach was soon bought; a very handsome chestnut with a game leg, and a little grey mare, were purchased at Tattersall's for no large sum, as leaders; and after a few early lessons round the parks, with Segundo on the box as my Mentor (in fact he did me the favour of breakfasting, dining, and living with me altogether), I thought myself as capable of taking my team and my load down to a convivial Greenwich dinner-party as any one of the knights of the whip that start weekly from the Crown and Sceptre or the Trafalgar.

The morning rehearsals having proceeded so favourably, a performance in public was soon decided on; and ten days' notice enabled me to secure a sufficiently numerous coachload of swells to grace my drag on its downward journey to Greenwich, there to eat turtle, flounders, and white-bait, and drink bad wine, at my expense. Sunday, I am ashamed to say, was the day chosen for our demonstration; nor do I understand why, amongst all the days of the week, that should be the one invariably set apart for the noisiest and most convivial gathering afforded by the hebdomadal list of engagements which decorates the chimney-piece of a man about town.

However, Sunday came, and with it my well-appointed drag, and really neat-looking team. We were to take our departure from Limmer's—that unceremonious hostelry, whose doors, like those of another much-thronged locality, stand open "night and day." In fact, so careless are its inhabitants of times and seasons, that I well remember one of its most constant frequenters giving as a reason for his preference, that he could not enjoy the same comfort elsewhere, of never knowing what o'clock it was. "I sleep," he said, "till I feel inclined to get up. My bed-room *always* requires candles; and when I come down and order breakfast after the rest of the world have dined, the waiter looks as little surprised as if ten o'clock at night was the usual time for every one to begin the day." From this accommodating "Liberty Hall" we started accordingly. And Segundo, who sat by me on the box, had indeed done his best to get together a very agreeable and merry party. All that were in difficulties, all that were in debt, seemed to congregate upon the roof of my coach; and such an array of curling whiskers, trim moustaches, well-brushed hats, and choice spirits, I have seldom seen even on that much-affected road.

We left a volume of smoke behind us that would not have shamed a goods-train on the London and North-Western; for lips ringing with jest, fun, and repartee were graced with regalias, the shortest of which must have averaged eighteen nches. We called, according to promise, for Lord Loosefish, at his lodgings in Bond-street, and proceeded thence boldly down St. James's-street, recklessly braving the ordeal of the bay-window at White's. Confound that chestnut leader! how short he went upon the stones! I knew, as well as if I heard it, that some splenetic dandy, in that crowded morning-room, was good-naturedly remarking to a brother-cynic—"Look here, Jim," or "Cis," or "Bo," or whatever the familiar abbreviation might be—"look at that team of cripples!" And the worst of it was, I dared not hit him—I mean the chestnut—till we were safe down the hill. However, I paid him off when we turned the corner into Pall-mall, and with such good will, that I caught the end of my thong in the grey mare's splinter-bar. This set her a-kicking; and had not Segundo jumped down and put us right with wonderful dexterity, I might never have got farther than the Carlton Club.

London, on a Sunday, is not overcrowded with vehicles; and we got on swimmingly till we arrived at Westminster Bridge. Here, a trifling and momentary indecision on my part got us jammed in between two omnibuses, a hired barouche, and an extremely impertinent Hansom cab. The knot, however, at length untied itself; and, thanks to Segundo's advice and injunction, "Now go on, Nogo—now a little to the right—don't let this fellow cut in!" we cleared the metropolis triumphantly, and bowled up to the door of the Trafalgar without any further impediment or hindrance.

I have but a misty recollection of the dinner, since, notwithstanding the predominant idea in my mind, that I must keep sober to drive my party back to town, the clatter of plates, the confusion of tongues, the constant challenges to slake a throat on fire from devilled white-bait, the fun and merriment, to say nothing of cigars and singing, were enough to confuse a stronger brain than mine. Notwithstanding my endeavours to the contrary; notwithstanding that my contribution to the amusements of the company was confined to applauding and "encoring" their songs—songs of which "love was the theme," the material, however, far outstripping the ideal; notwithstanding my resolution to avoid "mixing my liquors," and my stedfast adherence to champagne and sherry, I cannot but think I must have been a little exhilarated, possibly by the turtle, inasmuch as I have reason to believe that upon several different occasions I invited the whole party to dine with me again on that day week, in the same locality—a sentiment received with shouts of applause, and carried without a dissentient voice.

The dinner being mine, the bill—that bitter ingredient in the cup of pleasure—was upon this occasion dispensed with; and the midnight hour was rapidly approaching, when Segundo whispered to me to come and look after the drag, as it was time to be off. My absence was the immediate signal for loud shouts of applause: I presume my friends were again drinking my health; and if I might judge by their shrieks of laughter, the toast was accompanied by some very humorous observations.

With supernatural gravity, I walked down-stairs, and, guided by its two lamps glaring fiercely through the surrounding darkness, I found my drag, to which Segundo, sober as a judge (which I must do him the justice to say he always was, whatever quantity of wine he swallowed), and two rather incoherent ostlers, were busily harnessing my impatient team. " You're no use here, Nogo," said he, with his usual abruptness. " Go and get some soda-water, and try to coach us home steadily. I'll sit on the box with you." No more satisfactory reply occurring to me at the moment, I indistinctly stated that "it was all right," and meandered my way through the darkness back again towards the house, to administer the sedative Segundo recommended.

I never knew exactly how it happened, but all at once I found myself engaged in a lively discussion with a sort of half-ostler half horse-dealer-looking fellow, who accused me violently of having shoved against "his missis," as he called her, and gave me a good deal of friendly advice as to supporting my claim to be considered a gentleman by behaving "as sich." What I had done to raise his ire, I could not guess; but, casting my eyes over his corporeal proportions as well as the darkness would allow, it occurred to me that now was the time to put in practice all the advantages of that science which "The Muff of the Minories" had so sedulously taught me, and, assuming a strikingly-imposing attitude, I threatened to stand no more nonsense, but to punch my antagonist's head. Not a word did the little man reply; but, ere I could well distinguish his features in the darkness, I received " one " between the eyes, and another in the waistcoat, that made a flash vivid as the lightning start from the one spot, whilst all the breath in my body seemed to take an instant departure from the other. It was in vain to "spar," and "feint," and "guard, and try to "counter:" the little man might have no science, but, confound him! he could fight like a good one; and, after the most disagreeable five minutes I ever recollect to have spent, Segundo came to my assistance, to find me breathless, bleeding, and dishevelled —very angry, but inwardly resolved never again to "box without the muffle;" my active antagonist taking to his heels, with this pithy remark: " There's more of 'em coming, I make no doubt; but I've sarved that one out, at any rate— blow me!"

Much was the condolence I received from my friends; nor, in my account of the transaction, did I think it necessary to state that my adversary was, to the best of my knowledge, untouched: on the contrary, I left it to be inferred that we had both given and taken severe punishment; that I knew the "party" as a low "fighting man," but that I should have paid him off handsomely, had he not run away; and finally, swore that my revenge was only put off to a more convenient season.

Despite of Segundo's remonstrances, I expressed my determination, mauled as I was, to drive back to town, incited thereto by sundry audible expressions of encouragement and approbation, to the effect that I was a "rare good plucked one," "game to the back-bone," &c.; and, lighting a fresh cigar, which smarted uncommonly against my cut and swollen lip, I took hold of the team, bid my charge "sit tight," and were soon rolling rapidly through the darkness, with the lights of Greenwich far in our rear.

It is wonderful—nay, providential—that more accidents do not happen at night to those aspiring spirits who love to drive after dinner. Certainly, horses go freer and pleasanter in the cool night-air, run more up to their bits, and consequently are less liable to get into scrapes; but many a Jehu, I fear, gets upon his box to guide the more rational animal home, whose own legs would hardly convey him safe across Piccadilly. How far I might have walked without holding on, it is impossible to say; but I sat behind my free-going team with all the confidence of a Peyton in days gone by. My horses, inspirited by the cool breeze, and cheered by the melodious tones chaunting in chorus behind them, shook their harness, and rattled away merrily, as if they too had dined on white-bait and champagne. Segundo, I could see, kept a watchful eye upon the leaders, and was ready, at an instant's notice, to take the reins; but I laughed at him for his nervousness, and, for a time, all went prosperously as could be.

"Pride goes before a fall." I was just congratulating myself on my triumphant *début* as a coachman, and Segundo had relaxed his attention sufficiently to turn round and get a light from the man behind him, when bang! ere I could pull them up, or pull them off, or pull them anywhere, my leaders ran slap into the ill-omened cart of an early fishmonger, or a belated baker; and, ere I could scarce tell what had happened, my wheelers were on to him, my pole was threatening him with instant impalement, and harness, horses, baker, and cart were all mixed up in a state of terrific confusion, that to this day it makes me shudder to think of. Segundo and the load were down in an instant; the baker, or whatever he was, behaved like a trump; but the smash was irremediable, and we returned ignominiously to town with an humble pair.

I may remark that the grey mare—an animal of an irritable disposition—kicked herself clear of everything; and the chestnut horse's game leg was from that day "gamer" than ever.

CHAPTER XIII.

Man, being reasonable, must get drunk:
   The best of life is but intoxication.
Glory—the grape—love—war: in these are sunk
   The hopes of all men, and of every nation;
Without their sap, how leafless were the trunk
   Of life's strange tree, so fruitful on occasion!
But to return—Get very drunk; and when
   You wake with headache, you shall see what then.

A GREENWICH dinner—comprising as it does every variety of eatable and drinkable capable of being consumed by that omnivorous animal, man—followed by a sharp and breathless set-to, in which the individual lately replenished has indubitably come by the worst, is not by any means fair usage of a digestion which has already been taxed beyond its powers by the numerous and successive entertainments of a London season. It has been the opinion of many deep and experienced medical men, borne out by the example of the brute species, and corroborated by the natural tendency to slumber so apt to steal over those who have dined "not wisely, but too well," that the process of digestion goes on best in a state of perfect repose, and that all extra-expenditure of vigour, whether of mind or body, unfairly deprives the stomach of that energy which can alone enable it to cope with the mighty task of reducing and arranging its various contents into an orderly and health-restoring whole.

"Throw your feet on a chair," says good Dr. Kitchener, "to the end that all your powers may be concentrated upon that one important organ."

"Drink a bottle of port, with deliberation and gusto, in

the society of some agreeable and long-appreciated friend," says another valetudinarian and *bon-vivant*.

"Bring me a cigar and the bill," exclaims the very bagman, to whom time is of the utmost importance, and yet who seduces himself with the black, acrid cabbage-leaf that wreathes its foul yellow vapour around his shining physiognomy, into the belief that he is soothing his nerves, and assisting his digestion, with the pause of contemplation and repose that serves to consume that truly British cigar.

Not a labourer but smokes his pipe in peace after his much-relished and much-required meal. Not a sailor, miner, hillman, or operative, but devotes a few spare minutes of his valuable time to that species of rumination which he catches instinctively from the very cattle who chew their cud so composedly and contentedly in the fields. But one and all seem agreed that during the important period which follows a heavy and hearty meal, any strong muscular exertion of the body, any violent emotion of the mind, is as prejudicial as it is disagreeable. Of all things, then, a combat "*à l'outrance*" with the naked fists, combining as it does the ungovernable passions of emulation, anger, and fear, with the very severest description of bodily exercise, must be the worst conceivable desert for a sumptuous dinner; and if mere authority were necessary to prove that, according to the Scotch proverb, slightly altered, "It's ill *fighting* between a fu' man and a fasting," I need only quote the well-known advice of that fine old veteran, whose high principle and judicious practice shed a lustre upon the annals of the prize-ring, in the days when true British pluck and sterling British honesty regulated that institution—the undaunted and unconquerable Jackson:—"You gentlemen," the old champion would observe, with a grim smile, "you gentlemen generally get into all your rows after dinner—the worst possible time, either for giving or taking punishment. You drink a fair share of wine after eating a large and indigestible meal; and you come across some blackguard, with whom you enter into an altercation, that is pretty sure to end in a fight. 'Well,' you think, 'now is the time to find out whether the science that Jackson has taken such pains to teach me is of any use, or whether he is an old humbug after all!' and you take your coat off, and get your hands up. Now, mark me! the blackguard dined at one o'clock, and beyond half a pint of beer and a couple of whiffs from his pipe, he has had nothing since. The consequence is, he is empty and in good wind, as you soon discover, when after the first three rounds he comes up fresh and handy, whilst you are hitting out all abroad, blown and confused. The enemy is two stone lighter than yourself, and shorter in the arms; and although his practice may have been greater, he has not had your advantage of scientific tuition; and yet, much to your surprise, you are getting the worst of it. Shall I tell you what to do? If you find you cannot polish him off in one more round, there is a last resource—a manœuvre I have never yet known to fail, and which I strongly recommend you to put in practice immediately: *you give his friend a guinea to take him away!*"

Would that I could transfer to paper the inimitable humour with which the old hero used to come to the moral of his tale—a moral borne out in many a street-row and chance encounter, where the gentleman, with all his courage roused, and his chivalrous feelings excited by some unbearable piece of insolence or aggression on the part of an inferior, has found himself most provokingly worsted in his endeavours to inflict a well-merited punishment, by the very state of things old Jackson so graphically described; or even should his superior pluck carry him through, and enable him to obtain a hard-won victory, it is mortifying to find that, although he may remain master of the field, and enjoy the empty glories of a triumph, he has sustained a mauling which will compel him to keep his room for a fortnight, whilst his defeated antagonist, after a brief and unaccustomed ablution, and a " pull at the pump," is as fresh and well again as ever. I could certainly boast of no victory in my short and sharp skirmish with the unknown pugilist, outside the Trafalgar Hotel, at

Greenwich; but I felt for several days the effects of his quick, vigorous style of hitting; nor would a pair of black eyes, and a somewhat swollen nasal organ, allow of my taking my accustomed rides and drives in the park, doing the attentive in morning calls upon my fair friends, or otherwise resuming my previous habits, and frequenting my usual haunts.

Besides these outward injuries and inglorious scars, I felt decided inward symptoms of having been living too fast, and should most assuredly have called in the professional assistance of my friend Dr. Dotterell, but for the feeling that I could not bear to lower my personal character for prowess in the eyes of that sporting little medico, by disclosing to him the marks of the encounter in which I had been so ignominiously worsted. I determined, therefore, to wait till my physiognomy had recovered its wonted sleek appearance before applying to the doctor for advice and prescription.

In the mean time, as I was again a prisoner to my chamber during the day, my lodgings became, as before, the resort of divers "fine young English gentlemen" of "the looser sort"—pupils and imitators of my friend Segundo, who, like their worthy preceptor, were good enough to consider my house and worldly goods their own, sharing amongst themselves, with a degree of social generosity to me quite incomprehensible, *my* horses, *my* carriages, *my* cigars, liqueurs, gloves, sticks, canes, umbrellas, and opera tickets, with other trifles of a like nature, generally supposed to be provided by a gentleman for his own individual comfort and delectation. Such scenes as the following were of constant occurrence:—Segundo, who was now living in a spare room of mine, originally intended to hold nothing cooler than a bath, but now devoted to the service of one whose *sang froid* Wenham Lake could not equal, is seated in *my* rocking-chair (the especial resort of its own master when he wishes to be thoroughly comfortable); *clad* in one of *my* dressing-gowns, and smoking a long cherry-stick pipe, which I have procured at his especial desire, and keep continually supplied with the choicest and most fragrant

K

tobacco for his use, with his feet on the breakfast-table, and his head in a Greek cap, quaintly embroidered for me in other days by the delicate fingers of Kate Cotherstone. With one of *my* shooting-jackets on his shoulders, and one of *my* large regalias between his lips, reclines Lord Loosefish— a young nobleman who does me the honour of bestowing on me a large portion of his spare time, and who finds himself less annoyed and importuned by duns at my lodgings than his own. Frank Racer, who does not smoke, is looking out of window with his hat on, and moistening the toothpick which he consumes so greedily with occasional applications to a large liqueur-bottle, rapidly waning under his attentions. Two other young gentlemen, both enveloped in fragrant clouds, and known respectively by the cognomens of " Nobs " and " The Bouncer," are playing backgammon with much unnecessary vivacity, and enhancing the effects of that sufficiently noisy game by several highly reprehensible execrations, levelled at their alternate good or bad success, as the fickle goddess now showers her favours upon the triumphant " Nobs," now smiles propitious on the energetic " Bouncer." Need I specify that I love " a quiet morning!" and that neither my health nor my habits empower me to live thus constantly in the midst of noise and excitement?

" Can you let me have the cab to-day, Nogo?" says the silent Mr. Facer, and without waiting for an answer, rings the bell to order my vehicle at his own time, leaving me in uncertainty as to when he means to come back, or whether he will come back at all—the latter consummation being one to which, if I thought it likely to take place, I feel that I could sacrifice the horse, harness, cab-boy, and carriage, without a shadow of regret.

The servant comes in, and Segundo orders "the phaeton at three!" without so much as looking at its ostensible owner; whilst Loosefish drawls out—

" By-the-bye, Nogo, can you let me have a hack to-day? I want to ride down to Wimbledon in the course of the afternoon!"

And this series of arrangements having pretty well emptied my stable, Messrs. "Nobs" and "Bouncer," finding their choice of locomotion now remains between grinding their French boots upon the hot pavement, or chartering one of Her Majesty's Hansoms by the disbursement of Her Majesty's coin, kindly volunteer to stay and keep me company during the afternoon, adding, "We can finish our match at backgammon; and as these weeds are 'none so dusty,' I dare say we shall make it out very well till dinner-time, if Nogo will send for some beer!"

Such was a sample of one of my "mornings at home;" and had it not been that the approach of twilight enabled me to go out without fear of remark, I do believe these kind friends would have dined, and sat up with me during the greater portion of the night. Things, however, came to a crisis at last; and a dinner at the lodgings tenanted by Loosefish was the last of a series of Bacchanalian festivities at which I was able to attend. Although I have no doubt that this hereditary legislator—son and heir to the Earl of Dungeness, with whom he had quarrelled, and who, having nothing to leave, had thought it correct to go through the form of disinheriting his reprobate successor—although I have no doubt that from the many calls upon his purse, entailed by his rank and position, coupled with the inconvenient fact of his having nothing in possession, Loosefish was more uncomfortably hard-up than any other of his impoverished companions, he was the only one of the set who seemed to think it necessary to repay my attentions and hospitality, morning receptions, and afternoon rides and drives, by an invitation to dinner. Such invitation he continually pressed me to accept; and at length, partly because I had no other engagement, partly because I was curious to see how the war was carried on by a young nobleman residing in London, without money and without credit, I promised to be with him and to partake of his hospitality at the orthodox hour of a quarter before eight. Segundo, of course, was to be one of the party; and at the appointed time I drove that worthy in my cab to No. —,

Jermyn-street, the temporary residence and much-besieged citadel of the Right Honourable Viscount Loosefish.

As we rattled up to the door, I was somewhat disconcerted, though I cannot say surprised, to find that we had alighted in the midst of an energetic altercation, carried on between a fat, flabby individual, apparently a tradesman, accompanied by a less enterprising friend and presumed fellow-sufferer, who kept much in the background, and a respectable, sedate-looking personage, who I concluded was the young nobleman's servant, and who was denying the fact of his master being visible, and dexterously inferring that he was "not at home," with a degree of consummate art that nothing but long practice could have enabled him to acquire.

"Not at home!" fumed the fat man, "not at home, ain't he? why I see a gentleman with my own eyes a-goin' up the stairs! It ain't no use a-leaving my account; nor I ain't a-goin' to be put upon, any longer. I must see his Lordship myself, I tell ye."

"Quite impossible, Mr. Thrimbles, I do assure you," replied the courteous and unmoved domestic; "to-morrow morning, after breakfast, Mr. Thrimbles. My Lord is always at home till three."

"Not a bit of it!" shouted the enraged Thrimbles. "Now's yer time, Meekes; come on! we'll see him ourselves, and give 'un a piece of our mind."

And whilst the well-drilled valet and factotum of the beleaguered nobleman was ushering us into the tiny lobby that led to a narrow staircase, which he motioned us to ascend, the energetic Thrimbles and the valiant Meekes, carrying the doorway by a *coup de main*, found themselves in possession of the body of the place. So ill-timed an interruption, so unexpected an addition to his dinner-party, would doubtless have been very disagreeable both to an entertainer and his guests; nor did I see any way of averting so inconvenient a rencontre as that which seemed now about to take place between the long-suffering tradesmen and their oft-reminded customer. But it was here that Segundo showed that rapid grasp of mind, that instantaneous decision of action, which Napoleon called "*coup d'œil*" in his marshals, but which my less-assuming friend dignified with the humbler title of being "up to trap." Walking pompously into the hall, as if he had no connexion with myself, the last arrival— a deception assisted by the fact of his having stayed behind to give some orders to the cab-boy—and assuming a grave and imposing demeanour, considerably enhanced by the white neckcloth and suit of sable which were his constant evening wear, he addressed the astonished servant in a tone of mournful inquiry, the meaning of which I gave that quick-witted functionary the greatest credit for catching so instantaneously.

"I trust his Lordship has not suffered in health from this sudden and unexpected shock?" began Segundo, in a loud important voice, "and that so untimely a bereavement will not preclude him from entering upon a few matters of business imperative on the successor to such a fine estate as that of the late Earl?" he continued, drawing from his coat a huge pocket-book filled with papers and memoranda.

I saw the two invading tradesmen start and change colour, whilst Segundo followed up his advantage.

"Very sad thing, sir!" he said, turning to me as if he had never set eyes on me before; "yesterday, in the prime of life—only seized at six o'clock last evening—full habit— gout towards the head—Sir Joseph could do nothing for him —all over in three hours—in the midst of life, sir!—very fine property, and the young Earl succeeds to everything. Excuse me, sir, for detaining you: as the legal adviser of the family it is absolutely necessary that I should have five minutes' private conversation with his Lordship."

And with these words Segundo passed the irresolute Meekes and the astounded Thrimbles on the stairs; and taking up a position on the landing-place above them, began to examine his papers with a most business-like air. I saw Meekes nudge Thrimbles, and I heard Thrimbles whisper to Meekes. At last the former, who had all along taken on himself the office of spokesman, began to stammer out his apologies to Segundo for being present at such a season of mourning, the only word that was intelligible being something about "his account."

"Your account, my good man!" said Segundo, taking his bill from him with an air of stately condescension, whilst he extended the other hand for a long paper document proffered by Meekes, "Your account had better be delivered to me, that it may be at once filed with the other claims against the estate. Regularity, I need hardly inform a tradesman—regularity, sir, is the soul of business; and when other matters of greater importance have been settled, your trifling account (here poor Thrimbles winced, whilst the face of Meekes became several inches longer) shall receive proper attention. Good morning!"

And the door closed upon Messrs. Thrimbles and Meekes, hastening home under the impression that they would not only obtain immediate payment for those claims which they had begun to consider hopeless, but would likewise enjoy the future custom and patronage of the Earl of Dungeness, in return for the liberality and credit which they had extended towards Lord Loosefish.

"Not badly done! was it, Nogo?" said the pseudo man of business, as we followed the now relieved domestic up the narrow staircase. "If I had had a little more notice, I could have seen my way better, and got a pony apiece out of those two fellows, on account. Confound them! they would have been just as well pleased to lend their money to a fellow that was rolling in riches, as they are to send in their cursed bills to a poor devil like Loosefish, who they know can't pay them. I wish I had got something out of them, the rascals! It would have served them right for their impudence, in coming so near dinner-time."

"A fellow-feeling makes us wondrous kind!" thought I, as I listened to Segundo's philippic against these unfortunate tradesmen, who, however inopportune might be their visit, had, after all, only come to seek for what was really and justly their due. But much as I pitied their coming disappointment, I could not refuse my tribute of admiration to the quick-witted auxiliary who had rid us of their inopportune presence—a feeling in which I am convinced I was joined by my Lord's sedate domestic; who, however, was so well drilled in his vocation, that albeit far more accustomed to those vigorous attacks than to such a rapid and unexpected rescue, he did not suffer his countenance to betray the slightest discomfiture or surprise, as he ushered us into the small but convenient apartment in which the banquet was about to be set forth. A low, but well-proportioned chamber, littered with prints, casts, sketches, and other works of curiosity or art, mingled with the usual quantity of miscellaneous articles that collect themselves insensibly in the domicile of every bachelor, was adorned by a round table, covered with a snowy cloth, and prepared to receive the eight guests who, including ourselves, were now lounging about the room. A large bouquet of flowers, fresh that morning from Covent Garden, adorned the centre of the board; whilst around the pure alabaster vase which supported them, glittered a profusion of very curious and beautiful plate, soon destined, as our host volunteered to inform us, "to be cut up into half-crowns." Claret-decanters of quaint device and antique shape reared their fantastic forms on a sideboard; whilst at convenient distances on the table we were about to occupy, peeped forth the taper, graceful necks of the dark champagne bottles, cooling luxuriously in that icy embrace which the broad Atlantic had been traversed to procure. Two dumb-waiters of elaborate carving and ingenious structure supplied the place of servants, none of whom, with the exception of my Lord's factotum, were permitted to enter the room; thereby combining, as Segundo remarked, the ease and piquancy of a pic-nic with the comfort and refinement of an elaborate *cuisine*. Jermyn-street, be it remembered, is not very far from certain clubs, whose cookery has been pronounced the nearest approach to perfection yet realized by *the science*, and it may be that such commodious vicinity might account for the very capital dinner which rapidly made its appearance, and of which the component parts, from turtle to "*caviare*," were blended with a skill and subtlety for which we gave Loosefish probably more credit than he deserved. The guests were varied and racy as the entertainment: none of your stereotyped dandies; none of your exalted and not very amusing personages who constitute what people facetiously call "good society," and whose immovable dulness would assuredly render them respectable in *any sphere*. Loosefish could command as many of these as he chose when he was what schoolboys call "at home;" which was probably the reason he studiously avoided all such correct companions, when able to select his own associates. What a curious thing this same "good society" is! like a gilt cage hung up in the window, the birds that are out are dying to get in; the birds that are in are dying to get out. Mr. Snobbes would give his ears to be asked to dine with the Duke of Ditchwater! and who shall measure the amount of metaphorical dirt which Snobbes will consume to arrive at that almost hopeless glorification? But ask the Marquis of Mortmain the pleasantest day he spent last week. Was it the dreary dinner-party he was forced to attend with his ducal cousin at Ditchwater House? Was it the prandial solemnity at which, as a privy councillor, he assisted in the halls of his Sovereign? None of these was it, Mr. Snobbes —none of these! but there was a certain breakfast at Richmond—a certain dinner at Greenwich, to neither of which did rank or respectability offer an *entrée*, but of each of which the gay Marquis confided to his toady, who told his valet, who informed my hairdresser, who related the fact to me, "that he never had enjoyed anything so much in the whole course of his life." And in this there is a moral, Mr. Snobbes, if you could but see it: there is wholesome advice, if you would but take it. Not you! you will go on, year after year, season after season, wasting your time, impoverishing your substance, and destroying your spirits—and all to get amongst a set of people with whom you would find yourself not a bit more amused, and not one half so comfortable, as you used to be when you were contented to enjoy the unassuming festivities of those of your own rank and condition in the world, when Burke was a sealed book, and the Queen's drawing-room as inaccessible as Kamschatka; when you lunched with Dobbes, and dined with Figgins; nor found the venison one whit less fat, the champagne one particle worse iced, because partaken of in social good-fellowship with your old chums and associates, Smith, Brown, Jones, and Robinson.

But in the mean time, the feast is progressing in Jermyn-street; and as the wine disappears down thirsty throats, and mounts into reckless and mercurial brains the various characters of the different *convives* come out, like the colours of some old picture when submitted to the revivifying touch of an artistic connoisseur. Most of them were in difficulties— all of them were in debt. There was young Graceless, of the Foot Guards, and Sabretache, of the Dragoons, each of whom might probably last another six months; after which, the sales of their respective commissions would enable them to get abroad for an additional twelvemonth, and then there would be nothing left but their liabilities. No wonder they enjoyed the present with such gusto. Then there was our entertainer himself, who, having spent all he had at New-market and Crockford's, and borrowed all he could from the Jews, was now fain to support a precarious existence upon these very uncertain resources, and lived every day of his life as if there was no to-morrow. Next to him sat an actor, whose convivial talents alone prevented his being one of the brightest ornaments of the British stage; and a painter, who might have vied with Apelles, could he have imparted to his canvas the brilliant colouring with which he adorned his anecdotes. Segundo had known this worthy intimately at Rome; and their joint recollections were more amusing than edifying. The former was the quietest of the party, it being an essential characteristic of the man to be always equally collected and calm, in the noisiest revelry as in the most painful vicissitudes of his chequered and exciting career. There was something about Segundo that nobody was able quite to make out; and he might have been soldier, sailor, courier, conspirator, or pirate, so intimately did he seem acquainted with all the more stirring scenes, all the darker phases of life on the continent. Our party was completed by a pale, haggard youth, whose handsome features appeared wasted with dissipation, and on whose brow, young as it was, care had too evidently imprinted her unsparing seal. Loosefish whispered to me that he was the "cleverest fellow of the lot;" and when I marked the occasional flash of brilliance that darted from his hazel eye, I could easily believe that the spirit within was of the brightest and the keenest. He had been in the army; at the University; had studied for the bar; stood for a seat in Parliament; been married and divorced; and spent two fortunes—all before he was six-and-twenty. And there he was—a ruined man in credit and character, earning with his pen sufficient funds to take him to the gaming-table, where, as he played high and recklessly, he was occasionally an enormous winner; when he immediately entered upon his habitual course of dissipation, nor a line did he write till a run of bad luck or a continuance of revelry had again reduced him to the dread of actual starvation. But apart from his moral worth—of which, perhaps, the less I say the better—never was it my lot to cross my legs under the mahogany with so agreeable a companion. Fun, anecdote, jest, and repartee, came ringing from his lips in an uninterrupted stream of merriment and good humour. He could mimic, he could conjure, he could play on a knife, ventriloquize, sing—ay, and write his own songs, to boot; and I laughed till I cried, and my sides ached, at the quaint buffooneries and humorous fancies of my melancholy-looking acquaintance. I wonder whether he was laughing at *me!* but I took a great fancy to this accomplished individual, and we struck up a firm alliance, long before the dessert made its appearance. He encouraged me to "punish Loosefish's champagne," as he called it; and the punishment, which I repeatedly administered, I soon found to produce its usual effects. The outlines of my various companions became slightly indistinct; their voices came sweetly, but unconnectedly, like the music of gushing waters, upon my ears; and I have a vague recollection of making myself extremely agreeable and relating a curious anecdote, much applauded by my friend the dissipated author, of which I forgot the proper names at the commencement, and of which, hastening over such trifling omissions, and coming rather abruptly to the conclusion, I was dismayed to find that I had likewise forgotten the point. It must, however, have been a capital story in itself, if I may judge by the roars of laughter with which it was received by my auditors. The fun became gradually but surely faster and more furious; and I could perceive that our host's excellent wine was beginning to tell upon all but the seasoned brain and firm organization of Segundo. "A song! a song!" was soon vociferated in every key; and Loosefish, looking round the table, quickly fixed his eye upon the young author, and called upon him for "a chant." The verses with which he replied to the invitation, and which were of his own composing, struck my fancy so much in my then vinous state, that I endeavoured to scribble them down in my betting-book, on a blank leaf, between a total of certain disbursements at Goodwood, and a combination of probable loss on the St. Leger; and, deciphering them with much difficulty the following morning, I found their Bacchanalian tendency to be, as nearly as possible, the following:

A WORD FOR CHAMPAGNE.

I sigh not for woman, I court not her charms—
 The long-waving tresses, the melting dark eye—
For the sting of the adder still lurks in her arms,
 And falsehood is wafted with each burning sigh.
Such pleasure is poisoned, such ecstacy pain—
Forget her! remembrance shall fade in champagne!

For the bright-headed bumper shall sparkle as well,
　Though Cupid be cruel, and Venus be coy;
And the blood of the grape gushes up with a spell
　That years shall not deaden, nor care shall alloy.
It thrills through the life-blood, it mounts to the brain—
Then crown the tall goblet once more with champagne!

The miser may gloat o'er his coffers of gold;
　The merchant may balance investment and sale;
The land-holder swell with delight to behold
　How his acres are yellowing far o'er the vale:
But mine be the riches that blush on that plain
Where the vintage of Sillery teems with champagne!

Rejoiced is the sage when his labours are crowned,
　And the chaplets of laurel his temples adorn—
When pure gems of science are scattered around
　A name still undying to ages unborn;
But benumbed are his senses, and weary his brain—
Let him quaff at the fountain which foams with champagne!

Ambition is noble, they tell ye—to sway
　The fate of an empire, a nation to rule;
To be flattered and worshipped, the god of a day,
　And then learn to cringe in adversity's school.
But vexed is the spirit, the labour is vain;
And the crest-fallen statesman flies back to champagne!

Then give me champagne! and contentment be mine!
　Women, wealth, and ambition—I cast them away.
My garlanded forehead let vine-leaves entwine!
　And life shall to me be one long summer's day,
With the tears of the clustering grape for its rain,
And its sunshine—the bright golden floods of champagne!

"Bravo!" "Bravo!" "More champagne!" was the chorus to such appropriate sentiments; and more champagne, accordingly, poured forth its exhilarating floods—not the less intoxicating from the previous magnums of claret, and bottles of curious old sherry, that had found their way down our insatiable throats. I have but a vague recollection of the after-events of the night. It appears to me that scarcely two minutes had elapsed since the fresh supply of Sillery was called for, ere I found myself with Loosefish and Segundo, smoking a cigar, with my hat on. Was I in the street? or could it be Loosefish's other room? I have a faint idea of an anchovy-toast, and a distinct recollection of a certain board of green cloth, a man with a rake, brandy and soda-water, a multiplicity of wax candles, and my anger with Segundo for not allowing me to play—suddenly converted into a superhuman effort to wind up my watch carefully, which failed! Twelve o'clock the following day brought back returning consciousness, accompanied with yellow looks and a beating brain, which, failing to recover in the usual twenty-four hours that obliterate the effects of a debauch, apprehensions of a bilious fever soon brought Doctor Dotterell to my couch; and the ominous shake of his sporting little head, as he felt my pulse and looked at my tongue, reduced me at once to a state of the most passive obedience.

"This cannot go on, Mr. Nogo," said the dapper little man: "we must get you out of town, sir. Fine constitution sapped. Athletic frame reduced. Muscular energy enervated. Get you on your legs, Mr. Nogo, as soon as we can; and then I must advise—I must beg, sir—nay, I must insist upon your leaving London, and recruiting your organization with quiet and country air!"

And the Doctor slapped his hat on his head, and stumped down-stairs with the self-sacrificing air of a medical Cato. Ill as I was, I got out of bed, and crawled to the window, to see him start the black pony, and round the corner, with squared elbows and careful coachmanship, that might have piloted Mr. Batty's gilded chariot, with its team of twelve horses, all on end!

CHAPTER XIV.

The ancient Persians taught three useful things:
To ride—to draw the bow—to speak the truth!
Such was the mode of Cyrus—best of kings—
A mode adopted since by modern youth:
Bows have they—generally with two strings!
Horses they ride without remorse or ruth:
At speaking truth perhaps they're not so clever;
But draw the long-bow better now than ever!
Don Juan.

———— and taught his novice hand
To aim the forked bolt; while he stood trembling,
Scared at the sound, and dazzled with its brightness.
GRAY's *Agrippina.*

LONDON in the season is doubtless a very delightful place; and while the frame is vigorous, and the nerves unshaken, there is more enjoyment within the grasp of the votary of pleasure in the metropolis, than elsewhere. But let sorrow cast her shadow over the giddy trifler; let sickness poison the source of every gratification, which he has quaffed so eagerly; or let "*ennui*"—the certain offspring of false excitement—cloud his satiated mind, and paralyze his enfeebled energies, lo! a sudden change comes over him who erewhile seemed as if he could only exist in Pall-Mall, and, like a child flying back to its mother's quiet smile, when surfeited with the caresses and indulgences of a birthday, he betakes himself for rest and refreshment to the inexhaustible stores of rural Nature; and weary, dejected, disgusted though he be, her legitimate amusements and invigorating pursuits soon renovate his flagging spirits and drooping frame—soon bring back the bloom of health to his cheek, the lustre of contentment to his eye.

So was it with me. After a season of gaiety and adventure

sufficient to undermine the constitution of any man who was neither a philosopher nor a Hercules, I felt so completely "done up" with over-exertion and over-excitement, that Doctor Dotterell found little difficulty in persuading his alarmed patient to subscribe willingly to his fiat, delivered by the leech in his most oracular tone.

" Country air, Mr. Nogo, is now the *sine quâ non*: tonics I have tried, and, as you must perceive, ineffectually. I have studied your constitution, Mr. Nogo, which is in many respects like my own. You require exercise: you require amusement—hem! and you are benefited by generous living (let me look at your tongue). You are, like myself, devoted to the sports of the field—not an uncommon taste among men of our organic vigour (the doctor weighed eight stone and a-half, and was weak in proportion), who are formed for the ruder and more perilous occupations of life—(allow me to feel your pulse)—and it is my opinion, sir—I speak it advisedly—that you must immediately leave town. Science has done her best for you: *I* have taken care of that; and we must now trust for a perfect cure to Nature—Nature, sir, without whom the whole pharmacopœia is but a fiddle without strings!"

I was much of the little doctor's opinion as to the pharmacopœia—whatever that imposing word may signify—and lost no time in writing to my old friend and schoolfellow, "Joe Baggs," as we called him at Eton—now the Rev. Josiah Bagshot, incumbent of Wilton Cowslips, in the diocese of Bath and Wells—proposing that I should immediately pay him a long-promised visit at his quiet retreat in that most beautiful of all the beautiful localities adorning the west of England. It is needless to say that the *ci-devant* Etonian's acceptance of my offer was cordial, as his previous invitation had been hospitable; and if I thought Dotterell was right in ordering me out of town, whilst my lungs were still oppressed by the smoke-laden atmosphere of London, how much more was I convinced of his skill and judgment when I awoke to the delightful consciousness of restored health and returning spirits, in the pretty bedroom of my friend's snug parsonage, on the morning after my arrival! The stillness, the utter repose, so grateful after the turmoil and constant noise inseparable from the existence of streets, amounted to perfect luxury; and as I lay awake, whilst my well-drilled servant was putting out my things with the stealthiness of a midnight conspirator, and watched the sunbeams streaming through my closed window-shutters, I felt a lightness of heart—a boyish gaiety, to which I had been a stranger for months: and when I did prevail on myself to get out of bed, it was with a frolicsome bound, such as had planted me on the floor of my tiny dormitory at Eton, in years long since gone by, when a whole-holiday rose—as in those days it seemed always to rise—in cloudless magnificence; or better still, when the golden sunlight, bathing in floods of beauty the College turrets and Mother Angelo's chesnuts, ushered in the long-looked-for, heartily-welcomed, glorious Fourth of June! I am neither above nor below the weakness of being acted upon by such extraneous circumstances as fine weather and lovely scenery; and when I opened my window, and looked over my friend Joe's ornamental garden, his rich and leafy orchard, his sloping paddock, with its huge old trees, and its cows grazing as they only graze when the thermometer stands at 70 in the shade, to the unequalled view beyond, it was with a thrill of delight as keen, as delicious as could have been experienced by a Poussin or a Claude Lorraine. Hill and dale, wood and water, the neighbouring forest, and the distant hills, all that could constitute beauty, all that could delight the eye—there they were, heaped together in lavish magnificence: the golden stubbles studded with the shocks of late-reaped corn; the smiling meadows throwing out in crisp relief those gigantic elms, that towered into the sunshine; the broad river glancing like a sheet of burnished silver; the sweeping masses of wood, black as midnight, in their depths, from the contrast of light and shade; and the distant horizon blending with the sky in that sunny haze, which to me always realizes the idea of Fairy-land. What a gorgeous panorama to feed the vision of contemplative man, whilst he was shaving! But Joe's voice, as he inspects his now-fading roses—for alas! ere the prime of summer mellows into autumn, the fairest flower is doomed to droop and die—Joe's full and manly voice admonishes me that tub and toilette must be proceeded with, for that "Breakfast will be ready in a quarter of an hour!" So whilst I am getting on with this necessary duty, and the clerical landholder walks as far as his orchard and his cows, let me devote a few lines to describing the person and position of my old schoolfellow and present host.

"Joe," then, as his friends still call him—or the Rev. Mr. Bagshot, as he is entitled by the rest of the world—is a man basking in that enviable period of life which the young anticipate as the completion of their prime, and the old look back to as the flower of their youth. Joe Bagshot is thirty if he is a day: and a more comely and athletic specimen of the Anglo-Saxon race it would be difficult to find in a summer-day's journey. Five feet eleven in his stocking-soles; fourteen stone without offal—for severe exercise prevents the good-humoured parson from getting fat; with a rosy countenance, beaming with benevolence; a merry blue eye, and curling light-brown hair—it is no wonder that he is as great a favourite with the fair sex for his engaging appearance, as he is respected by the rougher portion of humanity for his bodily vigour and aptitude to all kinds of sports and exercises. Cricket, quoits, foot-ball, and wrestling—at these, the indigenous amusements of the country, he has not an equal in his parish. To walk a mile; to run a hundred yards; to leap, swim, or lift weights, he might be safely backed against most professionals; but many of these talents being decidedly unclerical, Joe is sedulous to conceal. For instance, although the best sparrer of his day at Cambridge, I recollect that the topic of self-defence being on one occasion brought forward at a numerous dinner-party which he attended, my friend was the only person in the room who had

L

not a word to say upon the subject; nor was it until the gloves were actually produced, and, *nolens volens*, Joe was compelled to put them on with the biggest man present, that it was discovered that the parson was the only practitioner of the lot to be depended on in a veritable set-to. How curious it is that so many of these athletic men, so many stalwart frames, gifted with extraordinary facility for all games and field-sports, and consequently imbued with a strong attachment for such pursuits, should have chosen the church for their profession! Who shall appreciate the sacrifice which, with scarcely an exception, they make, one and all, for conscience-sake, in giving up these their favourite pleasures, rather than furnish one censorious individual with occasion to say that there is aught in their conduct unbecoming a Christian minister? Joe could ride like a bird; but he gave up hunting the instant he discovered the slightest objection on the part of his parishioners; and in the kindred sports of fishing and shooting he only allowed himself such occasional relaxation as could not be construed by the most uncharitable into neglect of his professional duties. As a boy, at Eton, "Joe Bags," as we called him, always promised to be a sportsman. Besides his rowing and cricket-playing proficiency, he was celebrated for his partiality to such live stock as terriers, rabbits, ferrets, &c.; in fact, he prided himself greatly on the performances of the latter pets, as to their efforts he owed much of his well-known fame in rat-hunting. His exploits as a shot were necessarily tainted with the misdemeanour of poaching; and despite of watchers and gamekeepers, many a fat pheasant and savoury hare from the adjoining manors of Stoke and Thames Ditton—nay, occasionally from the august preserves of royalty itself—graced the stealthily-cooked breakfast of the daring Etonian. Doubtless, had he been driven to it, he might have emulated the feat of a certain sportsman* since distinguished in the coverts of Norfolk, as over the plains of Leicestershire, who, when pursued by two royal keepers, and driven down to the flooded

* The well-known William Coke.

Thames, plunged boldly into the wintry torrent, and reached the opposite shore much exhausted truly, and considerably nearer Staines than his starting-point, but having swam the whole distance with the hare, for which he had risked so much, still in his mouth!—a rare instance of pluck and determination in a boy, and to those who know what the Thames is, in November, opposite Datchet, an exploit seldom if ever surpassed. Joe was just the fellow to have accomplished this or any other dare-devil feat, although, like the *preux chevalier* of olden times, the "lamb among ladies, and lion among lances," he was gentle and almost womanly in his love for gardening, music, sketching, and such softer pursuits; and I have often been amused to watch the brawny hand that could floor a bargeman, delicately manipulating the light and shade of a water-colour, tying up a carnation, setting a rose, or executing some complicated passage on the violin. But my toilette is ere this concluded, and descending the staircase I find Joe—who, it is needless to specify, is a bachelor—presiding over his comfortable breakfast-table, drawn close to the open French window, which connects us with the lawn, the roses, and the glorious sunshine "out-of-doors."

"Another cup of tea, Joe, and a slice of that ham: I find the country air works wonders upon a London appetite!"

But alas! everything must have a conclusion, and breakfast cannot last for ever, though protracted by the luxurious concomitants of fresh fish, new-laid eggs, late strawberries, and Devonshire cream.

"One weed, Nogo?" said mine host, "a look at the garden; a run for the pointers; and we will settle our plans for the day. I cannot tell you how glad I was to get your letter, old fellow! to say you were coming here."

And, lighting two huge regalias from a wax candle brought in for that purpose (it is only by attending to trifles such as these that real comfort can be obtained), we stepped out upon the smooth-shaven lawn; and as we walked up and down shady walks and trim parterres, now basking in the summer sunshine, now inhaling the perfume of roses, pinks, honeysuckles, and sweet-brier, we enjoyed to the utmost that greatest of all luxuries—the after-breakfast cigar. Two couple of rare pointers were released for our inspection; and as they gambolled here and there, and traversed the home-meadow, in wild enjoyment of their liberty, my friend proceeded to detail to me the series of amusements and gaieties which he had provided for my especial delight.

"There is an archery-meeting to-day at Castle Bowshot, and a cricket-match to-morrow at Ripley Down. Then we have the otter-hounds coming for a week's hunting in the Slug; and a gathering of all the rank, beauty, and fashion of our county, for the Race meeting at Weatherley; besides which, I can give you some capital fishing, and, next week, undeniable partridge-shooting; and when we have nothing better to do——"

"Stop, my good fellow!" said I. "One at a time, and it will last the longer. Here have you provided a bill of fare that it will take at least a month to get through!"

"So much the better," was the reply. "Now that we have got you down into the west, we don't let you off again in a hurry, I promise you. But if you would like to patronize the archery-meeting, I'll order the trap round *instanter;* for Castle Bowshot is a good eleven miles from here, and up or down hill every yard of the way."

Accordingly, before I had time slightly to humanize my costume, and Joe had donned, as professionally bound, a stiff white cravat, over whose well-starched folds his whiskers clustered in unclerical profusion, the aforesaid trap made its appearance at the door, and proved to be an exceedingly well-hung and neatly-painted dog-cart, drawn by a clever short-legged brown horse, with all the appearance of a capital heavy-weight hunter, as indeed, in my friend's hunting days he had often proved himself, but whose trotting qualities I had yet to discover. The harness was plain and workman-like, fitting, of course, to a nicety; and the whole thing had the unmistakeable air of appertaining to a sportsman; whilst a white great-coat on the driving-seat, and the name of the

"Rev. Josiah Bagshot, Wilton Cowslips," painted in letters an inch long on the back of the vehicle, proclaimed at once the ownership of the whole turn-out.

A glass of home-brewed ale, clear as amber, and I am afraid to say how strong, another cigar, and we are bowling merrily along, discoursing as we go, now of the pace and action of the brown horse, now of the ever-changing, ever-beautiful landscape through which we are passing, now of the disgraceful state of the road, whilst ever and anon we digress into conjecture as to the people we are about to meet, and the anticipated humours of the coming gathering.

"Mr. and Mrs. Shaftoe are what is called 'people of the old school,'" said my cicerone, as he drew the lash gently across the brown horse's quarters, and made the eleven miles in the hour an honest twelve—" that is to say, he rises at six, goes round his farm before breakfast, and drinks a bottle of port every day of his life after dinner; whilst she takes care of the poor, wears black mittens, and hopes 'your room was comfortable' when you come down in the morning. But they make their place very pleasant to stay at; and I assure you there are many worse billets in the west than Castle Bowshot. The old couple have no children of their own, but take forcible possession of all the young people in the neighbourhood, and are never so happy as when they are arranging a ball, a pic-nic, or a 'breakfast' for their favourites. The great let-off, however, is their autumn archery-meeting, which comprises all the other gaieties put together, and finishes with an out-of-doors dinner, and a dance. Only take care of your heart, Nogo! this is a dangerous place for a 'soft one;' and our west-country ladies are celebrated for their witchery—particularly the widows! I should say, now, Mrs. Montague Forbes was the sort of woman to knock you over, to a certainty."

Ere I could inquire into the peculiar dangers likely to be encountered from an introduction to Mrs. Montague Forbes, we had arrived at the lodge-gates, which admitted us into a magnificent avenue of Spanish chesnuts, leading directly up to the castle. Long ere we reached its hospitable portal, we could discern, by the white tents which dotted the lawn, and the occasional strains of music wafted to our ears upon the summer air, that a *fête champêtre*, upon a large scale, was going on in the magnificent pleasure-grounds, filled with that motley and highly respectable assemblage which landed proprietors somewhat pompously designate as "the county people." As we drove up to the door, we were welcomed by Mr. Shaftoe in person—a venerable and fine-looking old man, erect as one of his own arrows, and bearing unmistakeable proofs of having been very handsome in his youth He still stuck to powder and knee-breeches; but had it not been for this peculiarity, he might well have passed off for a younger man, by a dozen years at least, than the parish register avowed him to be.

"Delighted to see you, Mr. Bagshot!" said the courtly old gentleman—"delighted to see you, sir! and your friend, Mr. Nogo—charmed to make your acquaintance, sir, and proud to welcome you to Castle Bowshot. You will find luncheon in the library; after which, I hope to have the pleasure of presenting you to Mrs. Shaftoe and my guests."

Declining the offer of refreshment, our only chance between such a breakfast as the parsonage had furnished, and an early dinner, we proceeded forthwith to the scene of gaiety, presided over by Mrs. Shaftoe—a stately but good-humoured old lady, who received Bagshot with affectionate warmth, and myself with dignified courtesy. Leaving the former to make the agreeable to the several circles amongst which he appeared a prime favourite, I moved through the crowd, according to my custom, remarking, as I lounged about and contemplated the scene without interruption, on the manners and customs of the English in the nineteenth century, so facetiously set forth by the inimitable Mr. Punch.

How different from the practice of archery in the present day must have been the use of the long-bow, in what are jocosely called "the good old times," when every man who was not a thief appears to have been a thief-taker, and when security and comfort, as we understand the words, were unknown ; when

"Bold Robin Hood was a forester good,"

and kept the whole of the North Countrie alive, and the "Sheriff of Nottinghame"—apparently a highly unpopular functionary—in a constant state of apprehension with his vagaries and eccentricities ; when his outlawed band of merry men—unlike the goodly " foresters of Arden," whose " wardmote" at the present day is a term synonymous with a gathering of all that is kindly and sociable—ranged the wilds of our midland counties, much in the predicament of the Bedouin Arab, " whose hand is against every man, and every man's hand against him!" This is not a climate nor a country to live all the year round

"Under the greenwood tree ;"

witness the pic-nics every one of us can remember attending even in the month of June ; and, despite of the " butt of malvoisie " and " pasty of the doe," despite of ancient saw and time-renowned ballad, despite of antiquarian romance and black-letter enthusiasm—ay, despite of the glowing page of " Ivanhoe " itself—we cannot picture to ourselves the band of shivering spoilers—albeit clothed from top to toe in " Lincoln green "—other than a very woe-begone assemblage, when the second four-and-twenty hours of seasonable rain had rendered their leafy canopy like an alpaca umbrella, or a continuous shower-bath ; and an easterly wind, as it shook the dripping branches, and crept coldly to his very marrow, had blanched the cheek of Will Scarlett, or, whistling through his limp and saturated garments, made even Little John himself look small.

But there are other and stirring recollections associated with the bow, besides these predatory exploits of the Middle Ages. We are taken insensibly back to the triumphant days of Cressy and Agincourt, when the " cloth-yard shaft," with a stout English heart behind it, seems to have done yeoman's service, and stemmed the foeman's overwhelming charge, much in the same manner as the uncompromising bayonet of later date, when backed by the same sterling stuff. We glory with the victorious archers, as their hissing volley, rattling like a hailstorm on their panoply, breaks the advancing chivalry of France ; and the cheering war-cry, " St. George for merry England !" rings upon our ears whilst we behold the tossing fleur-de-lis borne backwards on the tide of defeat. Or we heave a sigh for the brave, the devoted, the gentle, and the loyal, who formed with their bodies a corpsebuilt bulwark around their dead sovereign on Flodden's field, where the gallant King of Scotland held his state as warlike monarch should when overcome by odds—stretched upon his shield, his face to heaven, and surrounded by his prostrate knights and nobles, overwhelmed, repulsed, defeated, but all unconquered still—a sacred rampart, immortalized by Aytoun in his soul-stirring lament :

> " Every stone a Scottish body,
> Every step a corpse in mail ;
> And behind it lay our monarch,
> Clenching still his shivered sword—
> By his side Montrose and Athol,
> At his feet a southern lord."

Well may Scotland rue the gray-goose shaft that thinned her serried ranks, and laid her stoutest warriors low—a man-at-arms for every missile. Perchance when we have dried the tear that falls for Flodden, we may moralize with good *Justice Shallow*, on the uncertainty of life and the Grim Archer, whose quarry sooner or later we must all of us become. " And is old Double dead ? See ! see ! he drew a good bow—and dead ! he shot a fine shoot—John of Gaunt loved him well, and betted much money on his head !" and yet this veteran toxopholite, though he could "clap'i' the clout at fourscore, and carry you a forehand shaft, a fourteen and fourteen and a half," must go the way of all flesh as surely as the prime buck that he loved to strike in season. And then the train of my ideas having once arrived at Shakspeare, the mighty magician bears me off upon the wings of fancy to the golden days of Good Queen Bess, and the image of Falstaff; the reality of Sir Walter Raleigh, the progress to Coventry, and the pageantry at Kenilworth, drive from my mind all disagreeable ideas of archers, archery, war, flesh-wounds and slaughter, till unpleasantly reminded by my precarious position that I am still a denizen of this present world, though not likely to continue so, if I persevere in such close proximity to the target as my day-dream has lured me to, unperceived—Whiz! an arrow sticks six inches into the ground within finger's length of my patent leather boot. Whiz! comes another in its erratic course, threatening me with the possibility of the Red King's fate, and shaving my white hat so closely as to give me a very clear notion of the sensations entertained by that pomiferous youth who, as heir of entail to the celebrated Swiss sportsman, William Tell, so manfully stood up to the paternal shot. A ringing laugh from the lips of the fair Diana, who has well-nigh sacrificed an unwary stranger, brings me completely to myself; and as Bagshot rushes forward, and, drawing me out of the line of fire, presents me to the dangerous charmer, I return a few unmeaning compliments, which will not bear repeating, to the apologies poured forth by Mrs. Montague Forbes—for Mrs. Montague Forbes it is—who so nearly "hit the white," though not exactly in the manner described by the old chroniclers of archery. As their practice never approaches a much greater degree of accuracy than what may be termed "the roving range," I presume it is the extremely picturesque and becoming dress assumed by its votaries that makes this such a favourite exercise with the fair sex. Certainly Mrs. Montague Forbes was got-up to admiration; and her fine rounded figure, large blue eyes, and waving golden locks, were set off to great advantage by the close green tunic, and Spanish hat and feathers, which seemed to be the uniform of the competitors for the silver arrow. I have reason to know the lady in question was at that time turned of forty; but whatever attractions she might have lost by the unavoidable fading of youthful bloom, were fully made up by that experience with which a woman of a certain age prepares with deeper craft, as she exhibits with greater skill the restorative auxiliaries of the toilette. Really, on that bright sunny lawn, with its fine old oaks, and its distant view, its crowds of well-dressed people, bevies of lovely girls, and groups of handsome matrons—with all to attract and fascinate the eye—there was no object present, animate or inanimate, that received a greater share of spontaneous attention than did the much-admired widow, Mrs. Montague Forbes. Thanks to the good character with which it appears Bagshot had already furnished his friend, I soon found myself in high favour with the lively widow, who did not disdain, when the contest for the great prize had terminated in her triumph, to instruct me with her own fair hands in the use of the *lethal* weapon.

After she had received the compliments and congratulations of the party, earned by her comparative superiority over her fair competitors, with whom the attitude appeared the great point, the further direction of the shaft being a matter of secondary importance; and after a burst of triumphal music, celebrating the victory with an air compounded of " See the conqu'ring hero !" and the prophetic intimation that " This day a stag must die !" the most ambitious professors of archery amongst the gentlemen proceeded to compete for *their* prize—an old illuminated volume, treating of all the mysteries connected with The Bow; whilst the uninitiated, thronging round two other targets placed within easy distance, disported themselves with what may be not unjustly termed *discursive* shooting. Amongst these humbler individuals I now took my place, to be instructed by Mrs. Montague Forbes in the *arcana* of the craft; and though sorely distracted by the manifold charms of my monitress—charms that the different positions in which she herself placed me, gave me full opportunities of appreciating—I made very fair progress for a first lesson, actually hitting the outer rim of the target no less than twice, and once narrowly escaping the fate of the " struck eagle," who "winged the shaft that quivered in his heart," by transfixing my plaid trousers, and grazing the cuticle of my thigh, in an ill-advised attempt to combine accuracy of aim with an easy and graceful deportment. Little did I dream that a dart was even then working its silent way to my heart—there to inflict an insidious wound, to which torn "continuations" and an excoriated surface were indeed a joke!

Shooting, flirting, laughing, and talking, went on by turns, till the afternoon sun, throwing the long shadows of the giant elms across the lawn warned us that dinner-time was approaching; and need I say that Mrs. Montague Forbes did me the honour of accepting my arm to conduct her to the tent, where we were to rough it, as best we might, on white soup, cold chickens, lobster-salad, and iced champagne, not forgetting strawberries and cream? Of all auxiliaries to flirtation, commend me to that sort of impromptu dinner-arrangement comprising the piquancy and ease of a picnic with the luxuries and comforts of a well regulated establishment. You have the fresh green turf under your feet; but in case of rain, which spoils hot dishes, you have a good canvas covering over your head: you need not sit with your feet in a puddle; and a cane-bottomed chair is a pleasanter resting place than a piece of spongy moss on a three-cornered block of stone. The port wine has not flooded the salad, nor has anyone spilt the salt and forgotten the corkscrew: so you have nothing to do but to eat, drink, and make yourself agreeable.

"Another wing, Mrs. Forbes, after your exertions with the bow? Let me give you a little more champagne; and won't you *venture* on another slice of tongue?"

Diana works away like a good one, repaying my assiduities with a shower of smiles. We are getting on very comfortably, and the tongues of the guests becoming momentarily more loosened—the men pledging each other with increasing cordiality, and pretty faces waxing a trifle flushed—entirely in consequence of having been all day in the open air, of course!

Just as we are at the merriest, the clatter of knife-handles against the table produces a general silence, only broken by the voices of one or two prosers, who are somewhat slow in finishing their sentences—good line-hunters, as we say of hounds, and not to be done out of their share of the sport.

Mr. Shaftoe rises, and, backed up by continuous applause, proposes the health of the "fair toxopholite who has that day carried off the silver arrow!" coupling with it the name of the successful male archer, who is consequently nailed for a speech in reply.

Mrs. Forbes smiles and blushes, apparently having both these weapons quite at command; whilst after a vast deal of hesitation and delay, Mr. Quivering rises to return thanks, in a state of extreme confusion. I am convinced that if he —a first-class man at Oxford—had only known what was expected of him, he would have shot in any direction rather than at the target on that fatal day. However, there is no escape, and up he gets: "Honour—happiness—distinguished party—hospitable landlord—fair archers—surrounded by a galaxy of beauty (great applause)—healthy recreation, and graceful pursuit!" Here the orator warms with his subject, and involves himself in a complicated treatise on the antiquity of the bow; the training of Cyrus; the Parthians' flying warfare—with an attempted quotation from Horace, coughed down *instanter* by the ladies; the weapon of Apollo; the delight of the spotless Diana; and the retreat of the "Ten Thousand"—where he suddenly recollects himself, and abruptly breaks off, with a general good health, and a bumper of champagne, when he sits down, blushing hugely, amidst the congratulations of his friends, and sundry exclamations of "Bravo, Quivering!" "fine scholar!" "deep research!" "modest delivery! "capital speech!"

An over-dressed young man, evidently a swell in these parts, now rises, and in general terms proposes the health of the ladies, on which those charmers take their departure, and diving like a retriever under the table-cloth, I bring up and present to Mrs. Montague Forbes in rapid succession a laced pocket-handkerchief, a pair of white kid gloves, a small *bouquet*, a clasp bracelet, and a French fan—all which articles I presume must have been lost but for my exertions.

We drink a little more wine, and Bagshot introduces me to sundry "capital fellows," by all of whom I am most graciously received. Just as we are beginning to think of the charms of a cigar on such an evening, we are summoned to the ball-room, there to meet the ladies again, who have taken advantage of the mysterious *interim* to "do up" their hair, exchange confidential secrets with their particular friends, and have a little tea. Judging from the welcome smile with which she greeted me, I should say Mrs. Montague Forbes was not a favourite with ladies; and I have often remarked that the good opinion entertained of a woman by her own sex is generally in an inverse ratio to her popularity with ours. Be that as it may, to my mind she was infinitely the most agreeable person in the room; and after a night of music, waltzing, flirting, and philandering, such as I have seldom encountered, the early streaks of dawn greeted our aching eyes, as Joe and I climbed into the dog-cart for our homeward journey; and the pretty parsonage was smiling in the full light of a glorious summer sun, ere we sought our respective couches, cordially agreeing that we had spent a delightful day. What may have been the nature of my friend's visions, I am at a loss to state; but I can safely aver, with all regard to truth, that I dreamt that morning of Mrs. Montague Forbes!

CHAPTER XV.

> The evaporation of a joyous day
>   Is like the last glass of champagne, without
> The foam which made its virgin bumper gay;
>   Or like a system, coupled with a doubt;
> Or like a soda-bottle, when its spray
>   Has sparkled, and let half its spirit out;
> Or like a billow, left by storms behind,
> Without the animation of the wind.
> *Don Juan.*

> Oh, monstrous!—eleven buckram men.
> *K. Henry IV.*

MONSTROUS indeed. It might be difficult in the days of chivalry to recognize one's dearest friend, when, like a lobster in its shell, he appeared armed *cap-à-pie* for the encounter. But what shall we say of eleven stout elderly gentlemen, lapped in leather and swathed in cork, their natural rotundity increased tenfold by their voluminous defences, and their jolly faces crimsoned from the effects of such a costume, under a midsummer sun; but one and all gallantly bent upon achieving "a score," in defiance of the present terrific system of round bowling, which places cricket on a par with the tilts and tournaments of the middle ages? Such was the array that greeted my eyes, on our arrival at Ripley Down, the day after the Castle Bowshot Archery Meeting; a day ushered in with such tropical sunshine as England can rarely boast, and to be made memorable by a contest for supremacy between the Ripley eleven and twenty-two of the surrounding district; the whole thirty-three comprising, I verily believe, every cricket-player within fifty miles. Need I say that Bagshot, the pride of the "Upper Shooting Fields," in his Eton days, was the very Achilles of the Ripley champions? or that his eagerness to be in time for the fray deprived me of sundry hours of necessary repose, and forced me to dispose of my breakfast in that uncomfortable manner which we condemn in the equine species under the term "bolting their food"? It seemed as if I had only just left the brown horse and the dog-cart, when I found myself again "taking the road" in that locomotive vehicle, my jaded spirits and London pallor contrasting most unfavourably with Joe's rosy face and jovial tones, as he descanted upon the anticipated triumphs to be won by bat and ball. Why is it that to some, and those too often the very temperaments most susceptible of its enjoyments, the exhilaration of a gala-day should be invariably followed by a corresponding depression of spirits and incapacity for exertion? Is my frame weaker, or are my nerves more susceptible than my neighbours', that I should never fail to be the victim of this distressing reaction? I know not. But here I was, as usual, dull and weary in proportion to my yesterday's enjoyment; whilst Bagshot, who had drunk infinitely more champagne, and smoked twice as many cigars on his way home, looked fresh and rosy as a child—not a line in his beaming, good-humoured countenance, not a shade on his frank, open brow. I could not help complimenting him on his superiority of organization, when I found that, like all people who live entirely in the country, he had formed a most exaggerated idea of London dissipation; and actually looked up to me as a man of iron frame, for sustaining as I did the pleasures of a fashionable life.

"Very few men could stand it as you do," said the unsophisticated parson. "I have heard of you, Nogo—dancing, and sitting up, and Crockford's, and all that: it would kill me in a fortnight," added the clerical Hercules: "and I am only too thankful that my lot is cast in this quiet nook of the country, where I can enjoy the out-of-door life that I am so fond of, and have no temptation to late hours and smart company."

And thus we chatted on, beguiling the way with remarks

on our previous day's amusement, and the different West-country notabilities whose acquaintance I had made; nor did Mrs. Montague Forbes obtain less than her due share of our attention, Bagshot declaring her to be "a very charming person, and just in the prime of life;" to which I gave a tacit assent, not the less cordial for its confinement to my own bosom.

But a long steep hill, which must have been interminable had the brown horse been less well-bred, brings us at last to the "Down," where a large tent, surrounded by rows of benches, and sundry spectral figures flitting about in white flannel, announce that the cricket-match is about to be holden. Already have several vehicles deposited their alluring loads; and pretty faces, peeping from under pink, blue, and white parasols, lavish glances of welcome on Joe, and curiosity on his companion. Here and there a gracious damsel, recognizing the partner of last night, bestows a nod that seems to court further acquaintance; and it is evident to me that Mr. Tilbury Nogo is not half the man in Kensington Gardens or the Park that he promises to be on Ripley Down.

The eleven, or rather *nine* of them, gather round Joe, as he descends from his dog-cart; while the confusion of tongues and elongation of faces proclaim that some dire catastrophe has taken place, and that, in the oratorical words of Mr. Quivering, whom I recognize with difficulty in his panoply, "this will prove a disastrous day for Ripley." I whisper an inquiry to a short-legged gentleman—in flannel, of course, with a red silk handkerchief bound round his head, whose name I afterwards discovered to be Swaddles—and the truth bursts upon me volubly.

"Trimmer is absent! Trimmer has written to say he can't come! Trimmer has been tampered with by the twenty-two! It's disgraceful!—it's too bad!—it's beyond a joke! The only man who can stop Trundle's bowling. The only bat in England that really knows how to 'hit to the leg.' It's absurd to say his wife is taken ill. (Mrs. Trimmer has already had twelve children, and this is her thirteenth confinement.) He might have gone back after the match; it's only nineteen miles across country. He's used us shamefully. Never forget it!"

And the tide of indignation sets in violently against the uxorious absentee; Mr. Swaddles, in particular, becoming ludicrously excited.

"We must make up our number," says the latter gentleman, apparently much inclined to quarrel with somebody; "how is it to be done? I ask you, how is it to be done?"

And he glances fiercely round on the devoted band, whose blank visages promise no solution of the inquiry. At length taking Bagshot aside, he enters into a whispered conference, in which such expressions as these force themselves upon my startled ear:—"He used to play, when at Eton." "Hunting man, did you say? Of course he can bat." "Good shot I dare say; don't doubt he can bowl. Light, active figure— sure to be able to run." And the pleasant conviction obtrudes itself on my mind that I am about to be selected as a further victim to the terrific bowling of the insatiate Trundle. Sure enough Mr. Swaddles, who has constituted himself a dictator in the present crisis, marches up to me with short, determined strides, and informs me, as if I had no voice at all in the matter, that they have "chosen me into their eleven, and they have no doubt I shall prove a most efficient aid, and worth a dozen of the degraded Trimmer; who," adds Mr. Swaddles, with a parting growl at the deserter, "ought never to have been elected a member of the club at all."

Vanity! ambition! the defect of the bravest, the infirmity of the noblest; much have ye to answer for. From the submersion of a Narcissus to the Moscow of a Napoleon—still, sister-failings! have ye lured mankind to their downfall; and now would nothing satisfy either or both of you but to lead the unfortunate Tilbury Nogo a willing victim to your delusive altar? Weary, jaded, and unwell, I was in the very worst possible condition for the manly game I was about to join : added to which, I cannot conceal from myself that I am of a nervous temperament; and such, I need not say, is the organization least adapted to encounter "round bowling." Besides, I had not touched a bat since I left Eton : and yet, despite of all these drawbacks and deficiencies, I could not resist the temptation of appearing before that crowded assemblage as one of the heroes of the day. Bright eyes were to look approval of my deeds, fair hands would lend their gentle plaudits to a successful " swipe " or a scientific " block ;" and casting all personal terror to the winds, I took my place amongst the staunch supporters, destined to uphold the cricketing fame of Ripley.

In this unjust and unsatisfactory world, I have often thought that the amount of glory which we obtain is most unfairly disproportioned to the mental suffering we undergo in its acquisition. Bodily peril is to one man a decidedly agreeable sensation, whilst in another it produces a degree of what schoolboys denominate " funk," which amounts to positive agony. Leonidas and his Spartans, looking forward to a hot supper with Pluto—" the three who kept the bridge so well, in the brave days of old," opposed to the swelling masses of the Tuscan army—Cœur de Lion in the desert—or the Hero of Houguemont at Waterloo—were doubtless, one and all, men of that glorious organization which woos danger as its bride, and kindles like a chafing war-horse at the clash of steel ; but we cannot allow such spirits as these the credit claimed as due to his personal valour, by a well-known character at Quatre-Bras, who, comparing his own coolness with that of the men under his command, when their apparent insensibility to danger called forth the admiring encomiums of a brother-officer, argued that he alone deserved praise for his gallantry, " because," said he, " those fellows don't care how much they are peppered ; whilst *I* stay here, although *I am most devilishly afraid !*"

In the same way, to compare small things with great, it is all very well for men like my friend Bagshot, of Herculean mould and corresponding activity, skilled besides in all the stratagems of the game, to jest and laugh at balls delivered with catapultic energy, or skimming the sward about the height of your knees with a velocity that threatens to take a leg clean off without the ceremony of amputation. By the way, I can only account for the excellent fight the wooden-legged pensioners at Greenwich make annually against their one-armed antagonists by their utter disregard, during the existing low price of timber, for such vicious " shooters " as these. But though Bagshot, Quivering (for, to give him his due, like most hard-reading men, he was a first-rate cricketer), and one or two others, might look upon all this as sport, it really threatened to be death to me ; and I claim accordingly my due share of applause for thus boldly standing in the gap occasioned by the non-appearance of the much-abused Mr. Trimmer. I think Swaddles was not very comfortable, but he carried off his feelings with a nervous fuss and swagger which effectually concealed any unmanly apprehensions lurking at his heart; nor did the extreme caution which he manifested during the after-progress of the game warrant his entertaining any great degree of alarm for his personal safety. But in the mean time the moment for opening the lists is rapidly approaching. Already has the ceremony of " pitching the wickets " been gone through. Fortune has decided by the augury of a tossing half-crown that Ripley shall go in first; and as Bagshot, the champion of its eleven, places himself in an attitude of defence at his wicket, and " takes guard " from his opposite colleague, the redoubtable Trundle bares his nervous arm, and spinning the ball playfully betwixt finger and thumb, scans with wary eye, that takes all in at a glance, the stalwart batsman, the " inner stump," on which he meditates his attack, and the intervening sward, true and level as the surface of a billiard-table. The twenty-two hover round with a vigilance that would appear to leave no loop-hole for a single score. The umpires are placed like the seconds in a duel, where the peril they undergo may impress upon their minds the responsibility of their situation. The gentleman who "keeps the score " takes up a position in the tent, out of the line of fire, and where he can command the beer, and is liberally supplied with blacklead pencils, one of which he wears continually in his mouth. Everything is in readiness, and the hush of expectation, broken only by the silver tones of Mrs. Montague Forbes, pervades the assembly. Like the chivalric "*laissez aller,*" from the mailed marshal of the lists, that set hearts beating and eyes straining in the olden time, the word " Play!" enunciated in tones hoarse with emotion from the lips of the umpire, rouses the players into simultaneous action, and places the spectators on the tiptoe of expectation. Every scout is on the alert, and the fielding promises to be excellent. My friend Joe stretches his athletic frame over his bat, as he crouches to the ground like a tiger about to spring, then rising suddenly erect, poises the polished weapon towards his antagonists, ere he resumes his attitude of calm and self-possessed defiance; the wicket-keeper behind him, gloved to the elbow and padded to the waist, stooping towards the stumps, and watching, all eye, the motions of the bowler, seems to anticipate the triumph of his vigilance and activity. Trundel creeps back a few paces, starts suddenly forward with a lightning-like sweep of his long sinewy arm, and ere the baffled sight can follow his spinning missile, a dull, heavy sound, and Joe's collected attitude—fit study for a sculptor—announce that the well-directed ball, speeding straight and true to the bail of the "leg stump," has been quickly and scientifically stopped. The first " over " causes a general change of places amongst the field; nor has the scorer yet had cause to dull the point of his extremely well-cut pencil; and it is now Quivering's turn to stand up to the reckless bowling of a brawny blacksmith, celebrated for the rapidity rather than the accuracy with which he delivers his ball. Two "byes" and one "wide ball" remind the first-class man of his merry school-days, and with increasing confidence he makes a brilliant hit " to the leg," and " goes for a three." The fielders run, and holloa: "Now! now!" resounds over the plain; the lookers-on applaud; the scorer refreshes himself with a pull at the beer, which is his way of rendering homage to an illustrious feat; and the discomfited blacksmith, shaking his head, prepares an astounding "shooter" for Bagshot, who is this time opposed to him. Straight and rapid comes the ball, rising at that inconvenient distance which tempts an inconsiderate "swipe," withheld ere delivered by the doubting batman, who is then too late to "block," and finds his bails scattered, and himself sacrificed by his own indecision. Not so my friend Joe: stepping boldly out, he met the deceiving globe when just upon the rise, and lending the full swing of his brawny shoulders to the stroke, far above the astonished heads of the open-mouthed fielders—far beyond the remotest "fag," placed upon the outskirts as an especial compliment to his prowess—cleaving the blue heaven, and bounding over the emerald sward—he sent it for a "sixer," even into the very tent where the fairer portion of our company had gathered, in gorgeous assembly, for shelter from the noonday sun. Amidst the shaking of petticoats by their laughing owners, as if to assure themselves and the breathless scout who rushes headlong into their presence that they have not involuntarily secreted the indispensable article, amidst peals of mirth and shouts of applause from the delighted multitude, amidst uproarious congratulations from the side that is "in," and frantic recrimination from the side that is "out," the cry of "Lost ball!" ratifies the six that have been already run, at the same moment that the missing treasure is discovered, snugly ensconced in the folds of Mr. Swaddle's brown frock-coat, incautiously laid aside in the back of the tent; and to reach which hiding-place it had broken two ginger-beer bottles, and gone through the best part of a raised pie in its tumultuous career. But triumphs such as these fall to the lot of mortals only in sparing numbers, few and far between; nor was Bagshot totally invincible, any more than Achilles. Although he saw Quivering out, and after him witnessed the defeat and discomfiture of no less than four of his colleagues, his own downfall was rapidly approaching. Flushed with the success of a score now counted by decimals—intoxicated by the lavish applause of the ladies, no less than the thrilling excitement of the game, my friend began to play on a wild though brilliant system, and, after sundry effective and extraordinary hits, was at length "caught out," in an ambitious effort at immortality, by a youth of sixteen, the very humblest of the twenty-two, then making his first appearance in public as a match-player, but whose success on this occasion stamped him a cricketer for life.

The score by this time looks well, and the beer is waning rapidly, but we have already got through most of our good men; and although I have kept modestly in the back-ground, there is a murmur of "Mr. Nogo!"—"Mr. Nogo!"—"Where is Mr. Nogo?"—that summons me to the breach: I shall have to encounter the blacksmith, who has just disposed of my predecessor with a crashing ball that has shivered his outer stump into a dozen pieces; and whilst a fresh wicket is being put up wherewith to glut this athletic savage, I arm myself for the fray. Invulnerable leggings, tied by a multiplicity of white strings, defend my lower extremities, whilst I plunge my trembling hands into leather gloves, the damp and clammy interior of which convinces me that I am not the only person whose courage, like that of Bob Acres, has oozed out at the palms of his hands, notwithstanding the confidence supposed to be inspired by knuckle-preservers of tough India-rubber. Thus accoutred, I walk up to my post, and my diseased fancy metamorphoses the good-humoured smile on the bowler's countenance into a glare of demoniacal triumph at his victim. Absurd as it is, I feel confoundedly nervous; and none the less so for the consciousness that Mrs. Montague Forbes is looking on. The blacksmith measures me with his eye, and I feel that the dreadful moment has arrived. "Play!" a dark object comes whizzing towards me, apparently in a direct line for my head. Involuntarily I shut my eyes, and with an energy borrowed from despair scoop wildly with my bat somewhere in the direction of the wicket-keeper. I have yet to learn how

I escaped decapitation; but, on recovering my senses, I found my wicket was still untouched, and a welcome "over" gave me a little breathing-time, and an opportunity of observing the demeanour of my colleague under similar trying circumstances. He is a round-about little man, of some fifty or sixty summers, with short, sturdy legs, and a bald head, glistening like polished ivory in the sun. He stands gallantly up to his bat as if nothing could ever knock him down; and, though time and good living may have told somewhat upon the flexibility of his muscles, he is evidently a master of the craft. Right and left he "swipes out" over the plain, and gives the fielders little time to fall asleep. Then to see him run! his honest face crimson with excitement, his stout thick arms tossing wildly about his person, and his spherical proportions impelled forwards upon those short, twinkling legs as though by some supernatural agency, he reminded me of the lines applied to a corpulent sportsman devoted to the chase, once right-well known in "the shires"—

"For beef on the rib no Leicestershire bullock was rounder;
 A wonderful weight at a wonderful rate—he flew like a sixty-four pounder."

Gathering confidence from the prowess of this modern Daniel Lambert, I, too, endeavour to keep my eyes open; and, thanks to my favouring stars, actually succeed in obtaining a run. Great applause from the spectators, and a white handkerchief waves from within the tent that can belong to no other than Mrs. Montague Forbes. The blood of the Nogos swells in my veins, and again I nerve myself to do or die. The blacksmith looks wicked, and delivers a straight one. I dash boldly at it, and, striking wildly over the revolving object, am sensible of an electric shock just below the knee-pan, at the same moment that my bails fly upwards; and, despite of bodily pain and mental agitation, I am disagreeably conscious of being "bowled out." Probably no man has ever yet succeeded in the often-attempted feat of walking away from his his wickets, under defeat, with an unconcerned air. It is amusing to observe the diffcrent conduct of different individuals during this trying ordeal, and to remark upon countenances of every hue, and features of all shapes, the selfsame constrained and ghastly smile vainly assumed to conceal intense mortification. Although writhing with pain (for a cricket-ball meeting an angular portion of the human frame at the rate of forty miles an hour is by no means a pleasurable sensation to the subject), the annoyance of failure in the presence of so many spectators, and the plaudits which greeted my downfall like every other event in the game, were infinitely more disagreeable than the actual infliction of corporeal agony. "Keen were my pangs, but keener far to feel" that Mrs. Montague Forbes should be looking on with her laughing blue eyes and her saucy smile, doubtless recognizing in the clumsy cricketer that unsuccessful marksman whom yesterday she had taken such pains to instruct in the use of the bow.

Ere I could limp up to the tent to receive with feigned good humour the ironical compliments of my disheartened colleagues upon my modest score of "one," only surpassed by that of the irascible Swaddles, "whose timbers," to use the language of the *Ripley Watchman and Cricketers' Chronicle*, "were scattered to the tune of a round o," I discovered that the increasing pain in my leg would render my further assistance, in the way of fielding and second innings, totally unavailable to the contending eleven; and that I should be compelled, for that day at least, to remain an inactive spectator of the manly sports, which, truth to tell, I had no longer any strong inclination to join. My new acquaintances were full of sympathy and assistance; arms were proffered to assist me to a resting-place, cushions procured on which to stretch my wounded limb, and declarations rife on all sides that I "had played very pluckily, and although evidently out of practice, should have been a most valuable auxiliary in another innings." But the last of the Ripley eleven has been now disposed of, and the ball is triumphantly ascending from each of the twenty-two in turn, who are as eager to touch its brown surface as though some mystic virtue lay hidden in that worn and tightly-stitched leather. The devoted band, now reduced to ten, prepare for the arduous duties of fielding. Swaddles votes for going to lunch; but the idea is scouted by his eager comrades, and the proposer infinitely disgusted by being placed at a point technically called "long leg," and which will probably entail on his short legs an infinity of violent exercise. This arrangement is consequent upon my defalcation, and the victim scowls angrily upon my mutilated form as he struts sulkily off to the post assigned him, leaving me, like another Ivanhoe, to be tended by a fair "sympathizer," who varies her exclamations and remarks upon the strife without by expressions of concern and pity for the sufferer within.

> "Oh woman! in our hours of ease
> Uncertain, coy, and hard to please;
> When pain and anguish wring the brow,
> A ministering angel thou,"

says the bard, and so say I; at least, so I said cordially on that sunny afternoon, as reclining at ease in the shady quiet tent, waited on by fair and gentle hands, soothed by the sympathy of sweet Mrs. Montague Forbes (whose first husband, the late Mr. F., had been a sad invalid), I learned from the energetic conversation going on around me how the contest went, and, without even the trouble of looking, was made aware of the changes and vicissitudes of this all-important match. To complete her entire subjugation of my indolent nature, the artful widow herself proposed that I should light a cigar—"they all liked the smell *so* much in the open air;" and Mrs. Montague herself had once smoked " a whiff at one of her brother's, and it did not make her the *least* ill!" So I lay back upon my couch; and as I watched the fumes of my fragrant regalia wreathing into the summer air, I realized to myself the advantage of the position enjoyed by the Grand Turk, who, I have been given to understand, spends the greater part of his existence in the charming society of his wives, varied only by the equally intellectual pleasures of his hookah.

But the match goes on, and the fair spectators, generally in superlatives, exclaim upon its incidents and events.

"Gracious!" says one, clasping her hands, "that duck, Swaddles, has caught the blacksmith out! How charming! How delightful! How heavenly! I'm so glad! Fanny, ain't you?"

"How beautifully Mr. Quivering bowls," is the response of that artless damsel, who is supposed to entertain a lurking predilection for the attenuated scholar. "I'm sure Ripley *must* win; and think of their only having ten against the others' twenty-two! So noble, isn't it?"

"Let me put this cushion a little more under your shoulder, Mr. Nogo," says my enchantress, with a smile that makes me forget the match, the blacksmith, the rapidly-stiffening joint and probable lameness to come—all and everything, save those sunny ringlets and that peach-like cheek. I feel as I used to do about Kate Cotherstone, and, as I had since thought, I should never feel again. The moments flew in a blissful dream of bright eyes, mellow sunshine, balmy breezes, and soft tones—all these blended charms combining to produce that delightful languor which can only be experienced in the enjoyment of bodily repose accompanied by such accessories.

What cared I that Ripley won in a second innings with five wickets to go down? that Bagshot played as never mortal played before? that Swaddles (I quote once more from the *Ripley Watchman*) "again retired from his wicket without troubling the *scorer*?" or that the exhausted players were to adjourn to an *impromptu* dinner in the very tent where I was now luxuriating—except in so far as the latter arrangement promised to interrupt my delightful *tête-à-tête* with the widow?

The shouters shouted; the band played; Joe Bagshot, in consideration of his making sixty-eight off his own bat, was carried round the ground on the shoulders of his confederates; the cloth was laid, the ale broached, and the dinner ready; but instead of being stunned by toasts, overwhelmed by hurraing, and stifled by tobacco-smoke, I was lolling comfortably in an open barouche in the moonlight, and set down by Mrs. Montague Forbes at the door of Joe's parsonage, after a drive such as seldom falls to the lot of a maimed and unsuccessful cricketer in this work-a-day world.

CHAPTER XVI.

Bring forth the horse! The horse was brought.
In truth, he was a noble steed,
Who looked as though the speed of thought
Were in his limbs; but he was wild—
Wild as the wild deer—and untaught;
With spur and bridle undefiled.
Away! away! my breath was gone;
I saw not where he hurried on.
Mazeppa.

Whoever casts to compass wightie prize,
And thinks to throw out thundering words of threat,
Let poure in lavish cup—and thriftie bittes of meat.
SPENSER'S *Œclogues.*

THERE is a depth of philosophy in the oracular wisdom of the immortal Mr. Weller which can only be equalled by the pithy brevity of his remarks, striking from their truth to the mind of the superficial observer, as they are calculated to awaken the most profound reflections in the attentive student of human nature. Not the least instructive of his apophthegms are those in which, inspired by the affection of a father as by the prophetic wisdom of a sage, he warns his son "Samivel" against the alluring blandishments of that unsparing enemy of the masculine species which he denominates "the widder." Forgetting, in the magnitude of his object, such petty arithmetical details as to how many ordinary women a widow is equal in "point of attraction," he adjures his darling boy, in tones choked with emotion, to avoid that pitiless class, affirming that, although with maid or wife there may be a chance of escape for the unwary victim, at no time and no season is he safe with a widow!

If such was the case with a sexagenarian Jehu of Mr. Weller's physical and mental constitution, what could possess me to trust myself for a moonlight drive with such a syren as Mrs. Montague Forbes, armed as she was, not only with her own peculiar charms and attractions, managed with the natural coquetry that had grown with her from her cradle, but likewise doubly and trebly fortified with that dangerous experience which had been acquired in the subjugation of the late Mr. Forbes, and was afterwards brought to perfection by an unsparing career of universal conquest over the male creation? How could I escape? Many an act of folly have I performed in my chequered life: but, with one great exception I probably never did so foolish a thing as volunteering to ride her brother's famous horse "Saraband" for the Hurricane Handicap, during the ensuing Weatherley Races. Nothing but my adoration for my companion, which was now becoming perfectly insurmountable, could have made me forget that neither by nature nor education was I fitted for the task of controlling a violent six-year-old plater through two tempestuous miles of unbridled confusion, amidst a throng of "gentlemen riders," all probably, like myself, very much at the mercy of the infuriated animals they bestrode. Besides, though not likely long to continue so, I was even then a cripple, in consequence of my ill-advised cricketing exhibition; and that alone should have been warning sufficient not again to run myself into uncalled-for peril, a prey to that thirst for display which had already involved me in so many annoyances. However, I offered to do it; and when I bade farewell to the enslaver, and kissed the fair hand that had volunteered to work me a jockey-cap, gorgeous in her brother's colours, it was too late to retreat. My dreams that night were a confused and chaotic "jumble" of racing-leathers and muslin "aggravations," long ringlets, snaffle bridles, ambition, misgiving, repentance, and apprehension. But "truth came with waking, as light comes with day;" and when I looked out from my bedroom-window on the little Paradise around me, and saw Joe, as usual, busy amongst his roses, need I be ashamed to confess that the feeling uppermost in my mind was, "I wish I was well out of it!"

There was no escape. When I descended to breakfast, the first object that greeted my eyes was a note in an unknown handwriting, sealed with a fox's head, and an ominous "*floreat scientia*," which, on being opened, corroborated with its short and pithy contents my surmises as to its authorship. I give it verbatim, as a despatch concise, peremptory, and to the point:

"Topthorne Lodge, August the ——

"DEAR SIR,—Understanding from my sister that you have kindly consented to ride my horse Saraband for the Weatherley Handicap, I now write to apprise you that the weights are out, and he will carry 10st. 7lb. The race comes off on Wednesday week, so you will have plenty of time for preparation. Saraband is doing good work; but you will excuse my mentioning, even to your experience, that it would be advisable for his rider to be in tolerable wind, as the horse at times shows a little temper! and is an extremely hard puller!!

"I remain, dear sir, very truly yours,

"JOHN TOPTHORNE."

Pleasant, certainly! Then, as soon as my leg was well enough, I should have the satisfaction of living like a hermit and working like a galley-slave, to reduce my "too, too solid flesh" to such attenuated proportions as a bad-tempered weed was capable of carrying; and all because, forsooth, Mrs. Montague Forbes happened to have been born a Miss Topthorne, and Mr. Tilbury Nogo was ambitious of acquiring more than his natural share of fame as a sportsman. Bagshot was delighted. I cannot think why, but he, like the rest of them, seemed to have imbibed the idea that I was a second Osbaldeston in the saddle, and firmly believed that the *experience* for which 'Squire Topthorne gave me credit could not fail to win a triumph, in which he as my host and anticipated trainer, would obtain a reflective share. I had been introduced to Mr. Topthorne, the day before, at the cricket-match. He was a great card in this part of the world, being master of that old-established pack of fox-hounds which from time immemorial had hunted the Pippingdon country, conferring upon their supporters a right to wear that uniform which, resplendent with a *green* lining and a *black* collar— startling additions to the brilliancy of a red coat—and further adorned with a stupendous button, displaying on its convex surface a fox rampant, surrounded with the letters "R.A.P. F.H.C.," or "Royal and Ancient Pippingdon Fox Hunting Club," is so generally known and admired in the ball-rooms of the west. Besides this he was a short, stout, peremptory man, with grey hair and bushy red whiskers, and, altogether, not the sort of person to be trifled with. So, trusting to my lucky stars, and secretly hoping that riding a race might, after all, be a matter of no such very overwhelming difficulty, I wrote the M.F.H. a civil note, begging him to call at the Parsonage on the first convenient opportunity, and prepared, by going into severe training, to reduce the unnecessary "adipose" matter which was now beginning so comfortably to clothe my frame.

Let me not dwell upon the miseries of that eternal week's training! if Bagshot had been going to ride in his own ponderous person, he could not have taken more pains to lessen the load which Saraband was destined to carry. Directly the sun peeped above the horizon, Joe would knock at my door, and insist on my immediately accompanying him for the diurnal walk. Two pair of flannel "pettiloons," as people call them now, thick winter-trousers, a couple of waistcoats, and every great-coat in the house, are not the articles you would choose for a costume in the dog-days. Then that infernal hill, of which I could just see the top, with its solitary fir-trees, from my window! To those firs it was an honest three miles, if it was a yard; and to those firs and back, it was my miserable fate to trudge every morning before breakfast, and that not at the easy pace which the load of old clothes on my person would have rendered warrantable, but at the utmost stretch of "heel-and-toe" going I could command, alongside of one of the best amateur pedestrians in England, and not even allowed the unspeakable relief of breaking ever and anon into an occasional "jog." Early rising, with such a waste as this upon the system, would make an anchorite hungry; and when I returned, ravenous for breakfast, what was my repast? A cup of hot tea, and a roll between the blankets, to exude whatever small quantity of vigour might still remain in the system. By the time I felt utterly sapless, I was allowed to dress and eat two slices of dry toast, after which—my only comfort in this period of purgatory—Joe had not the heart to deny me a cigar. An underdone mutton-chop, and some toast and water, at three, made another walk in the afternoon sun absolutely indispensable; and this penance was prolonged to perhaps eleven or twelve miles. Imagine a man in the position of a gentleman toddling along for bare life, enveloped in swaddling-clothes, and streaming from every pore; and conceive his meeting a lady of his acquaintance when in such a predicament! I did; and although I shirked Mrs. Montague Forbes's carriage with the rapidity of an Eton boy when he sees a "master" in the forbidding regions of "up town," I am convinced that not only did that lady recognize the ludicrous pedestrian, but her coachman and footman likewise participated in the joke, as they enjoyed the spectacle ere I had time to conceal myself behind the nearest thicket. No supper, and a glass of hot gin and water—the only liquid I really detest—concluded each of these never-to-be-forgotten days; and Joe with a praiseworthy anxiety for my success, and distrust of my forbearance, not only saw me to my room at night, but carefully put away and locked up everything eatable and drinkable that the house contained. In addition to this severity of training, my friend further proposed that, in order the more to confirm my powers of resistance, and strengthen my frame and lungs, I should put on "the gloves" with himself in a daily bout at what enthusiasts term the "science of self-defence;" but this, with a lively recollection of my studies in that art under "The Muff of the Minories," I resolutely and peremptorily declined. Well, "time and the hour wear through the roughest day;" and although a week of such preparation may appear to be spun out beyond four times its usual length, yet, submissive in this one respect to the immutable laws of nature, it comes to an end at last. Nor is the self-denying athlete without his reward. When I looked in the glass, on the eventful morn that ushered in the Weatherley Races, I beheld the reflection of a clearer and healthier, albeit pallid and attenuated, countenance, than I had ever before recognized as my own property whilst submitting to the diurnal discomfort of shaving; and, though much reduced in size and weight, I felt infinitely more vigorous than I had ever conceived it possible to become on short allowance and toast and water. My limbs had never before felt so strong, in proportion to my frame, when the system had been "kept up," as the doctors say, on beefsteaks and port wine ; and whether it was the temperate life I had been leading, or the sporting appearance of my racing gear laid out upon the sofa, or, more probably still, the rainbow-like cap worked by the fair hands of Mrs. Montague, and sent the previous evening, with her kind regards, and such a pink note! I know not, but my nerves felt braced to encounter the unruly propensities of a dozen Sarabands, and, for one short hour, I felt man enough to have ridden—ay, even for the Liverpool Steeple Chase itself!

Irreproachable leathers, cut out by Hammond, and made, as far as the different configuration of our lower limbs would admit, in imitation of those worn by Mr. Mason, of steeplechase notoriety; boots of a texture that scarce outweighed the silk stockings beneath, and a pliancy that would not have encumbered an opera-dancer ; a snowy neckcloth, fastened by a gigantic pin representing "the memorable start for the

Derby of '44," and protected by an outer handkerchief of the sportsman's bird's-eye ; a silken vesture, of hues to which the flamingo's wing were a colourless daub ; the whole enveloped in a loose white great-coat and surmounted by a shaved hat, with a narrow brim—presented a *tout ensemble* that I rather flatter myself was not to be outdone on Weatherley race-course ; and when Joe drove me on to that Olympic plain, he himself confessed that, if Saraband only looked as "like winning" as his jockey, the odds in his favour were, to use his own clerical metaphor, "a deanery to a deaconship."

"A lovely day for our triumph, Mr. Nogo," said the winning voice of Mrs. Montague Forbes, as we brought the dog-cart to an anchor alongside of her well-appointed barouche ; and ere I could reply in suitable terms to the fair instigator of my present undertaking, and express my thanks for the cap she had worked for me, I was interrupted by the rough tones of her brother Topthorne, as he rode a short, square cob, the very image of himself, hastily up to the carriage—

"All right as to weight, Nogo ? Look very pale !" (Confound him !) " Here, jump on this mare ! I want to show you the course. There's an awkward turn at the gravel-pit corner, and that is the way Saraband always goes home after galloping ; so I think you had better be prepared for it."

And before I knew very well where I was, I found myself seated on a great, lumbering, lop-eared bay mare, evidently belonging to the Pippingdon establishment, as what is termed "one of the men's horses," with an enormous head, and her tail tucked close into her quarters, as if she was only waiting for a dirty place to kick till she got rid of her burthen—a consummation which her absence of "mouth" made me sensible she was quite capable of effecting whenever she should think proper ; and ere I had time to reflect upon the inconveniences of such a downfall at such a time, I was galloping for bare life after the sturdy little cob and its energetic rider, to inspect the dangerous corner which led so temptingly to Saraband's wished-for home.

"Look here, Mr. Nogo," said the laconic Topthorne, as he pulled the cob up with a jerk, and wiped his brows with a yellow pocket-handkerchief: "Mind that post! that's where he'll try to bolt. There's the horse—looks well in his clothing, don't he? It's a pity you couldn't have ridden him one or two gallops; only, with *your practice*, it wasn't necessary. Now listen to me. I'm a man of few words: *if you can hold him*, you wait upon the others till you get past this turn; don't let him run you against that post: then get up to your horses, take a pull at him, and *come* like blazes! If he don't win, it's your fault."

All this was Greek to me; but it was getting so disagreeable that I began to feel desperate. What with *this* turn and *that* post, and the chance, if not certainty, of the brute bolting, and then *coming* like blazes, which I presumed meant *going* like lightning; and, after all, that it should be *my fault* if I did not succeed in steering this accursed animal safely home, in advance of his competitors! Had I not felt that SHE was a Miss Topthorne, I should have been quite angry: as it was, I answered, sulkily enough, "that it was an awkward, ugly sort of course (the view, I may remark, commanded half a dozen counties, and was one of the finest in England); but I dared say was good enough for *platers ;* and if Saraband was 'worth a row of gingerbread,' he ought to win in the company he was likely to meet." This uncourteous reply, I found, elevated me at once twenty per cent. in the estimation of my companion; and as we rode back to the carriages, to gain a position for the first race, he listened to my remarks with deferential attention. For one brief and delightful half-hour I forgot my miseries, I disregarded my apprehensions, I shut my eyes to my fate; for was I not sitting by sweet Mrs. Montague Forbes, in the delicious sunshine; exchanging those *nothings* which may mean so much, especially with a widow, and reciprocating what Moore calls "the twopenny-post of the eyes;" whilst my companion gazed upward into my face with that expression of hero-worship which we may imagine Thais to have directed towards Alexander? What was it to us that the Two-year-old Stake brought *one* to the post, and ended in a miserable " walk-over?"—that the Farmers' Plate " for horses *bonâ fide* the property of yeomen holding land within the district hunted by the Pippingdon hounds, and ridden by their owners," after three false starts and two sworn cases of " crossing," terminated in a wrangle ; the decision of which by Mr. Topthorne, as the only steward present, gave such universal dissatisfaction as eventually to lead to the total dis-memberment of the Pippingdon Hunt ? Small care had we of such trifles as these, for were we not all-in-all to each other ? and did not the widow's hand tremble in mine, as she lent a gentle pressure, and bade me " Come back to luncheon after winning my race ?" Come back indeed ! how could I tell I might not be *carried* back?˚ There was a white gate, that looked the very thing, when taken off its hinges, to sustain the mutilated form of a hapless equestrian ; and had I not read and heard of such catastrophes, till my very blood ran cold ? However, it is too late now ! Top-thorne summons me from the carriage, and, as he casts his eye towards the heavens, suggests the propriety of getting "the Hurricane Handicap" over before the thunder-storm, which is obviously brewing, and which my pre-occupation has prevented my perceiving; and I am torn from the com-fortable barouche and its gentle owner, to consign my person to the miseries of a five-pound saddle and the tender mercies of the impatient Saraband.

" What horse is that, kicking so violently in his clothing, and enlarging with every lash the circle of his admirers?"

" That be 'Squire Topthorne's," is the consolatory reply of the rustic to whom I had addressed the unconscious interro-gatory.

" This way, Nogo," says the hurrying owner, as the first heavy drops of rain plash upon my ungloved hands ; " come and get weighed before the storm."

And, utterly incapable of resistance, I follow my conductor into the narrow weighing-house, where a fellow-sufferer is even now "going to scale," with straightened legs and upturned toes, as he swings betwixt earth and heaven, his whip between his teeth, and nursing on his lap a confused mass of girths, saddle-flaps, snaffles, martingale, and stirrup-irons. Good heavens! it is Segundo! And I feel for a moment as if my chances of success were increased tenfold by the presence of my knowing friend. Alas! I forget that with such an antagonist I cannot hope to win. Short and hurried are our mutual greetings and inquiries; for the Clerk of the Course, a sporting hairdresser from Weatherley, is waxing impatient of the many delays occasioned by gentlemen's utter ignorance of their probable weight. I have only time to ascertain that Segundo has just arrived from London, for the purpose of riding Colonel Crowther's "Stopgap;" and when he casually mentions that he has backed the old screw for "a pony," I feel that *my* chance is indeed out. How I envy my former instructor's coolness, as, after weighing like a man whose whole life had been spent in doing nothing else, he swaggered off to superintend in person the saddling of the docile "Stopgap!" He never saw the horse before; yet, when he bounded lightly on his back, the animal bent his neck and played cheerfully with his bit, as though he recognized a master's hand, and cantered up the course with a long easy swing that argued volumes in favour of Segundo's judgment.

In the mean time I find myself divested of the white greatcoat, and furnished in lieu thereof with a saddle and stirrup-irons, of much the same pattern as those which caparisoned the rocking-horse of my juvenile days. I swing dizzily in the scale, and, thanks to Joe's judicious training, I am right to a pound.

"Make haste, if you please, sir," says the Clerk of the Course, with a pen in his mouth, and a red book, like a tax-gatherer's, in his hand; "for there are three more gentlemen-riders to weigh."

And as I leave the weighing-house, in the custody of Squire Topthorne, I catch a glimpse of my fellow-sufferers. A stout yeoman, who has entered his own half-bred bay; a nondescript elderly man, that looks like a veterinary surgeon out of practice, and presents the anomaly of long grey hair streaming from under a black velvet jockey-cap, and whose qualification to ride as a gentleman consists in his subscribing five pounds a year to the Pippingdon Hunt; and a tall, lanky youth, who, if not now in a funk, must be at all times an individual of unnaturally pallid complexion, complete the field about to contend for the Great Hurricane Handicap.

I walk up the course like a man in a dream—a peal of thunder is growling round the horizon, but I hear it not—the rain has set in, as only summer rain can; and a silk jacket, however gorgeous in colour, is but a poor protection for a wasted frame; yet I heed it not. Topthorne is descanting volubly upon the strategy by which I am to win the race; but his pithy sentences fall unheeded on my ear. One object alone rivets all my attention—one group of struggling figures have a morbid fascination for mine eye :—a chesnut horse is plunging wildly forward, with a cloth about his head; whilst a trainer, a groom, and a boy, are vainly endeavouring to saddle the refractory brute. That horse is Saraband; and on that saddle am I destined to embark! Topthorne's conversation seems to flow on, in an unconnected string of sentences, about "coming," and "going," and "waiting," and "staying," and "hugging the posts," and "living the distance," and, above all, not "disappointing the horse." How I wish I could disappoint him!—but it is too late now. The confused hum of voices plays soothingly on my ear, as I approach the spot where the chesnut horse is fidgetting; and, with that appreciation of trifles peculiar to moments of intense excitement, I remark a small piece of orange-peel on the turf, and wonder how much bigger it would require to be to throw a horse down. An iron gripe seizes me by the ankle—Topthorne's face is turned upward, towards mine—an elastic pair of shoulders lengthen themselves out in front of me—I am conscious that my reins are knotted extremely short, that my mainstay, the trainer, has abandoned me to my own devices, and I feel that I am face to face with my fate. Great is my surprise to discover that the dreaded Saraband requires an immense deal of kicking along to induce him to extend himself in his preparatory canter, and that the infuriated horse who must be saddled blindfold and ridden by an equestrian Hercules may turn out the veriest slug after all.

What is it but a beautiful arrangement of Nature, proving the reciprocal fitness which exists between the biped and the brute, that causes a man, however nervous he may have previously been, to feel, when once settled in the saddle, a degree of courage rising within him proportionate to the occasion? Though Saraband gave me a taste of his eccentricities as he wheeled round to come up the course, and pulled and tore disagreeably enough directly his head was turned in the direction of his own stable, I felt so much more at home on him than I expected, that the reaction from a state of positive alarm to one of comparative confidence enabled me to take notice of all that was going on, and to scan, though with an inexperienced eye, the different competitors for the race.

Segundo, who was good enough to compliment me on my sporting appearance as we rode together to the starting-post, was the only one that appeared dangerous; the farmer's horse was evidently fat, and looked, what he was, a good average hunter; the Vet's narrow, fiddle-headed weed was obviously over-trained; and the pale youth, though mounted on a racing-looking animal in excellent condition, was notoriously a muff of the first water. I had a sort of impression on my mind that Topthorne had told me my horse was more speedy than lasting, and I determined to take advantage of Segundo's knowledge and experience to wait upon him throughout the race and win at the finish, if I could—a wise resolution, and one to which the only objection was the difficulty of carrying it out. What a business it was to start us!

The hairdresser had a good idea of how it ought to be done, and strutted about with his red flag in his hand in a most imposing manner; but the team he had to deal with were obstreperous to a degree, and it would have required a far more practised hand than the man of curling-irons to insure to each his fair chance. First, the Vet would get too far forward, and had to be cautioned, not to say rebuked : then the farmer's horse dodged right across the pale young gentleman, who stared about him in utter helplessness.

In the mean time Saraband backs out of the turmoil, and, standing bolt upright on his hind legs, is with difficulty persuaded to re-enter the undisciplined ranks. When this is accomplished, a fresh disturbance breaks out with the bay. And, just at the moment when we are most hopelessly at sixes and sevens, the hairdresser loses all patience—the flag drops—Saraband bounds forward into the air—my cap flies from my head—every man for himself—the devil take the hindmost—and we are off!

CHAPTER XVII.

I prithee go and get me some repast,
I care not what, so it be wholesome food—
Why then the beef, and let the mustard rest.
Taming of the Shrew.

Why need my tongue the issue tell?
We ran our course—my charger fell.
Marmion.

" I don't care—I can't help thinking you made too much use of the old horse. I begged of you upon no account to *come* till the finish; and hang me! if you didn't make strong running the whole way round!"

Such was the expostulation addressed to me by the disappointed owner of the beaten " Saraband," as we sat in juxtaposition at the ordinary table, and waited sulkily for our dinner on the afternoon of the race. As in its kitchen arrangements the "Green Dragon" at Weatherley was like the "Green Dragon" everywhere else—profuse in its promises, and lavish in its bill of fare, but provokingly dilatory in the production of those dishes it set forth so vauntingly—I cannot better employ the interval which elapsed between our sitting down to a long table, covered for an ordinary of some twenty or thirty guests, the majority of whom were even now impatiently beginning upon dry bread, and the welcome appearance of the first tureen of mock-turtle, borne by a perspiring waiter in Berlin gloves, than by describing the proceedings of that eventful day, which led to the ungracious remark from Squire Topthorne recorded above.

The instant the flag was dropped I have already said Saraband started away with a bound, like that of a stricken deer; and for a few awful moments I felt utterly powerless to control or even guide the tearing brute. With the small muscular strength I naturally possessed reduced by inanition; with knotted reins, shortened stirrups, and a saddle the size of a dessert-plate, all my preconceived notions as to horsemanship, all the practice I had acquired in the hunting-field, were utterly unavailable. Pulled over his withers by his awkward "boring" ways; only saved from being unhorsed by the comparative smoothness of a thorough-bred one's stride; dizzy from the terrific rapidity of the pace, I was confused and helpless as a child. Luckily for me, however, the course for the first half-mile was perfectly straight, nearly as deep as Knavesmire at all seasons of the year, and considerably on the rise—this it was that preserved me from destruction. Saraband, at no time a stout horse, was perfectly amenable to reason before he reached the first turn, and the ill-judged pace at which I had been going had left the others far in the rear. Though weakened by my training, I had the advantage of being in good wind; and as my horse dropped to my hand, and became every stride less uncontrollable, the delightful thought flashed across my mind that I might win after all! I tried to nurse him; I tried to steady him; but in vain: if I wished to decrease the pace, he wasted his powers in the air: if I got fast hold of his head, down it went between his knees, pulling me over his shoulders, and grating my unprotected knuckles most painfully against the buckles of his breastplate. There was nothing for it but to run the race through from end to end; and even whilst I thus determined, the awkward gravel-pit corner came in view; and here it was that Joe Bagshot proved himself a trusty friend. As we neared the dreaded turn, I felt by the uncomfortable manner in which Saraband was going that he meditated some awful act of insubordination: and when within half a dozen strides of the well-known post, he got his head in the air till I saw the white streak down his nose, and swerving violently across the course, bore me "*nolens volens*" in the direction of the dangerous gravel-pits. I had just given myself up, when Joe's stalwart form, waving a voluminous red pocket-handkerchief in the brute's face, sent him back with a bound into the proper direction. The posts were a long way apart; and although I shaved the next one with my knee as we resumed our career, it was on the right side, and I was never actually off the course. It was "touch and go," and nothing but a firm reliance on my stirrup-leathers, and the strong hold I had of his head, saved me from a rattling fall. But in the mean time the other horses were overhauling us, our swerve had lost us several strides, and as I reached the distance-post, Colonel Crowther's Stopgap showed his ugly head at my girths. Soon he was alongside of me; Segundo sitting motionless, as if in an arm-chair. My blood was up, and I flogged with energy, and would fain have spurred as well. I thought I did; but an after examination of Saraband's sides convinced me that, with the exception of one ill-directed thrust, which reached his shoulder! my kicking and sprawling were wasted upon empty air. Well, I ran a good second, everybody said. I *finished* beautifully: and a good-natured remark of Segundo's, to whom they all looked up as an authority, "that no man in England could have ridden that awkward brute better!" stamped me at once as a jockey of the highest order. It was a triumph, though a defeat. Joe Bagshot congratulated me on having *so nearly won*. Mrs. Montague Forbes showered her sweetest smiles, as I did justice to her lobster-salad. I presented Saraband's groom with a sovereign, and everybody was satisfied except the owner, who, having made up his mind that his horse must win, could only find consolation in such muttered compliments as the following, which I unwittingly overheard—

"All nonsense! run the horse's head off—these dandies all alike—think they know better than anyone else—he's a puppy, and my sister's a fool!"

Man is a gregarious animal, and as such it is natural for him to feed in the society of his fellow creatures: but although I am far from denying in theory the propriety of such sociable arrangement, I cannot but confess that in practice an overcrowded ordinary is to me the most disagreeable method of discussing my daily sustenance. Nor was that at which Squire Topthorne presided, as principal steward of the Weatherley Races, any exception to the generality of these gatherings. After waiting forty minutes for dinner, it is hard to have your soup as cold as if the repast had been that length of time waiting for *you;* and as mock-turtle loses much of its natural merit by being chilled, so is inferior sherry—" such as the Spanish nobles drink"—not improved by being poured out lukewarm into a cloudy glass. A waiter, though he enjoys the nearest approach to ubiquity of any known animal, save the Irishman's bird, cannot multiply himself sufficiently to attend to the wants of some twenty guests; nor does the ostler's assistant, albeit clad for the nonce in a tail-coat and coloured neck cloth, effectually remedy this deficiency of attendance. True, the female servants of the establishment render all the aid in their power on the further side of the door; whilst now and then she whose colour is freshest, and ribbons of the gayest hue, may be tempted over the threshold by one of the fortunate occupiers of the lower end of the table : but such an apparition is only additionally aggravating to us dignitaries at the top, whose turbot must be eaten without the lobster-sauce, which, however, reaches the scene of action in time to supply the place of that missing mustard for which we call in vain with our boiled beef. Then do what you will, you cannot help eating in a hurry, consequent upon the crowd, noise, and confusion around you; which reminds you irresistibly, if you are old enough to remember them, of the coaching dinners in days gone by. The consequence is that your digestion, if not your appetite, is perfectly satisfied by the time the square little pieces of strong cheese make their appearance : and when the cloth is drawn, and the president's hammer proclaims that the season for toasts has arrived, for once contrary to the laws of Nature, and the whole practice of your lifetime, you feel thankful that "dinner is over at last!"

Strong thumps from Mr. Topthorne's hammer, and his stentorian voice shouting to the vice-president, " Mr. Scrubley —' The Queen!' " produce an immediate demand on the part of the guests for those " vanities " with which it is their practice to moisten their after-dinner clay. Strong red port appears to be the beverage most affected by the members of the Pippington Hunt; whilst their previous experience of its excellence during dinner makes the orders for sherry less numerous than usual amongst the company. The pallid young gentleman of the morning, now enjoying a far healthier bloom (who, I may remark, contrived to get distanced in the race), orders claret; whilst the jolly yeoman, game to the last, and incited thereto by his veterinarian competitor, shouts lustily for a bottle of champagne, and pays for it on the spot in a multiplicity of half-crowns. Brandy and water is not without its votaries at the lower end of the table; whilst Mr. Scrubley, hair-dresser of the town of Weatherley, Clerk of the Course, Vice-president of the Racing Club, and Secretary to the Pippington Hunt, carries a highly popular motion in favour of a huge bowl of punch. The members of the fox-hunting establishment, whom I observed to apply themselves most religiously to port, were one and all conspicuous for their ruddy countenances and portly persons; so concluding their beverage could not possibly be unwholesome, I hastened to follow their jovial example, thereby winning an approving nod from the president, who seemed to be much of old Doctor Johnson's opinion, as regarded fluids— "Claret is all very well for boys; port for men; but he who aspires to be a hero, sir (smiling), should drink brandy!" The usual toasts having been got through, and the company in a pleasing vein of jovial liberality, a certain red book, bearing the appearance of a ledger, made its appearance, and was handed from one to the other with ominous rapidity. No one seemed much inclined to master its contents, till an adventurous individual, warmed with wine, and recollecting that a twelvemonth would elapse ere he should be called upon to pay, handsomely headed the list as a subscriber to the handicap for the ensuing year, and thus purchased a nomination not likely to be particularly useful to a man who, as he himself told us, "never had kept race-horses, and never would." Example is contagious: and ere long the column was half filled, Mr. Nogo's name, I am sorry to say, imprudently appearing amongst the other sporting subscribers. Segundo likewise, much to my surprise, favoured them with his signature; but afterwards explained to me that his autograph was all he thought necessary to bestow; and that having some few acres in that part of the country, he considered it due to his station to give them at least *a claim* upon one of their landed proprietors! As the decanters waned, caution and shyness rapidly gave place to magnificence and bravado. Phantom steeple-chases, of incalculable "entries," over impracticable lines, were sketched with a spirit and enthusiasm that made it a thousand pities they should never arrive at maturity, and disclose to an astonished country the unheard-of clippers, of which each man seemed to have at least one in his stable. Matches over Weatherley racecourse, for half-bred horses, to run distances varying from two to four miles, with the rigorous stipulation that they should be "half-forfeit" and "owners up," were discussed in unlimited profusion, though I did not remark that many of these challenges were entered in those fatal pages from which there was no withdrawal, that reposed under the especial care of Mr. Scrubley. (Why is it—I may here ask in parenthesis—why is it that when gentlemen, unconnected with the turf, are prompted by their worse angels to make matches, involving the contest of horses of unknown pedigree, they will always select the longest distance and the severest course for the massacre of their favourites? It is, I believe, generally conceded at Newmarket, that one mile, if the pace be good enough, is distance sufficient to try the merits of an Eclipse, with all the advantages of such preparation as Newmarket trainers can bestow; but I am at a loss to conceive upon what principle the squire's coachman should be unable to contend with the doctor's Welsh galloway unless that distance be increased fourfold.) Nor was the Babel-like confusion, incidental to a large and convivial party— all talking and betting at once--the only entertainment furnished for our evening's amusement. Orpheus vindicated his power over these modern Centaurs; and amidst wreaths of smoke from the unfailing cigars, the very rafters shook to jocund glee and stentorian chorus. The champagne-drinking yeoman, in a fine mellow voice, indulged us with "The Brown Bowl;" Topthorne gave us "Tally-ho the Hounds, Sir!" and Scrubley—the accomplished Scrubley—led the time-honoured catch, that preserves the deathless fame of "Molly, the charming maid, that carried the milking-pail!" Dickens's cobbler gives the most unanswerable reason for dining early—"I finds I gets on better at supper when I does!" and, like him, we discovered ere long that a hurried dinner at six, succeeded by a protracted sitting and "a wet evening," was an admirable preparation for a hot supper. "Broiled bones, devilled gizzard, anchovy-toasts, and red herrings fried in gin (the latter an inspiration of Segundo's, and by him denominated "Hussar Broth!") are wonderful auxiliaries to that thirst which the same authority declares to be the normal condition of man; and by the time it is quenched with bottled porter, pale ale, and "brandy and soda," all sublunary matters assume a rosy hue of contented joviality, and " We won't go home till morning!" springs unbidden to the sleepless Bacchanalian's lips. But there appears to be a great disturbance going on at the bottom of the table; and through the din of voices the reiterated assurances of the jolly yeoman rise triumphant over the storm. " Do it!" he exclaims, his broad face purple with excitement, his sturdy figure waving to and fro as he grasps his neighbour's chair, and his eyes glaring through the cigar-smoke like the lamps of the down-train in a fog.

"I'll bet two to one he does it, without a balk or a refusal! Two to one! who'll take it—pounds, ponies or hundreds?"

"What is it?" "I'll take it!" "I'll lay it!" resound through the room; and ere I can gather from my neighbour Topthorne, who waxes more laconic as he gets drunk, " that the fool wants to jump his horse over the dining-room table," a space has been cleared away by the applauding crowd, and a slipping, staggering step, like the approach of a ghost in a farce, is heard ascending the wooden stairs. Sure enough the jolly yeoman has backed his famous bay hunter " Shamrock," that day so unsuccessful for the " Hurricane Handicap," to walk up-stairs (fortunately the steps are broad and few) to carry twelve stone over the " social board " as it stands, with its glittering array of lights, glasses, jugs, and punch-bowls; to walk down again into his own stable, without giving his rider a fall; and eat a quartern of oats and a double-handful of beans as if nothing had happened. The latter part of the wager is not much speculated on; but the principal feat of clearing the mahogany creates a vast amount of conversation; and ere I have recovered my astonishment at such an unheard-of proposition, sufficiently to form an opinion of its feasibility, a clothed head makes its appearance at the door, and, amidst shouts of wonder and applause, in walks " Shamrock," hooded and " done-up" for his rest, looking no whit more surprised than those wonderfully-educated animals which nightly astonish the play-goers "over the water" at Astley's Amphitheatre. Although not "broke to the drawing-room," he betrays but little alarm at being stripped; and as he cocks his ears, and turns his sagacious head round to his excited master, who is busy saddling him, I cannot help thinking how very much the soberest and most sensible of the party is the unreasoning animal. By the time he is fully caparisoned, however, a difficulty arises as to the terms of the wager. Shamrock is to carry twelve stone, and his owner, besides being incomparably too drunk to ride, must weigh at least thirteen, after all the eatables and drinkables he has been stowing away so diligently—not that he cares a farthing! but the sharp old veterinarian, who has been eagerly watching the horse, seems to scent "a good thing," and will not hear of his throwing away a chance. This old man, although he has been eating, drinking, and smoking incessantly since six o'clock, is now as sober as when he sat down; and walking quietly up to Segundo, he whispers a few words in his ear, which produce an electrical effect on my friend, ever wide-awake when there is what he calls "anything to be done." The fact is, the horse has performed the same feat before in his presence; he has ascertained that the animal is not much frightened, and his shrewd eyes twinkle with anticipated triumph as he whispers to Segundo—

"You sit quiet on him, sir, and give him his head! *he* knows how to do it: and (*sotto voce*) you back him for a trifle with Mr. Nogo, or the Squire!"

Segundo, who values his neck as little as any other of his remaining possessions, bounds on him in a moment, having previously laid out a few "fives," to make it worth his while: the crowd draw back to give him a fair "offer," as they say in Ireland, at his fence, and everything is prepared for the feat, when, "fierce as ten Furies, terrible as Hell," the landlady of the Green Dragon—herself a host and hostess, all in one — bounces into the room, and stalking up to the astonished Topthorne, now more than half asleep, confronts him then and there on his presidential throne, and pours upon his devoted head the pent-up torrent of her wrath—

"Gentlemen, indeed! and call yourselves gentlemen, who are ignorant to behave as such! which has never before taken place in the Green Dragon and Commercial Posting-House—for a brute *h*animal to be taken like a Christian out of his warm bed—and you, Mr. Topthorne, the father of a family, as ought to be a respectable man, and a magistrate likewise—to sit there and stare at a lone woman like a block of wood, and never to say good or bad, which is unbecoming your station and all your stations; for to decent mirth I never have, and never will object, which is what we all lives by; but to be bringing your racehorses and your quadrupeds up two pair of stairs, into a respectable woman's principal dining-room, thirty feet long, with a bay-window and mahogany dining-tables, and the filth and the mess of it, is what I will not abide if there's justice to be had for rich or poor!"

And here an opportune flood of tears, and an attack of what medical gentlemen term "hysteria"—a formidable malady when seizing a stout elderly lady, of some sixteen stone, and enhanced in its awful symptoms by a festive costume, such as that borne by the interesting sufferer—put a stop to the volubility of her abuse: and entrusting her to the care of the veterinary surgeon, as the most eligible substitute for a regular practitioner, we proceeded with the business in hand, which the unfortunate landlady, notwithstanding all her protestations, was compelled to witness. The steed was mounted, the room cleared, and the word given. Segundo sat as still as a statue upon the docile animal; and Shamrock, trotting up to the unusual fence, cleared it like a deer, then stood quietly in the middle of the room, snorting as though to express his surprise at the vagaries of us bipeds, and pawing the unyielding floor, as much as to inquire if we had any more orders ere he might go quietly back to bed.

The landlady had in the mean time been somewhat mollified by the attentions of so many gentlemen, all eager to deprecate her indignation; and as, like most of her sex, who, to use her own words, "cotton to be led, but can't abear to be driven," she was a regular trump if you only knew how to manage her the right way, she quickly forgot her previous ire, in her unqualified admiration of the dangerous feat; and walking up to Shamrock's head, patted his smooth satin neck, amidst rounds of uproarious applause. We drank her health then and there; and the whole thing must have gone off in the most triumphant manner, had not this last bumper, in addition to the many which I had already quaffed, prompted me to undertake in my own person the most dangerous part of the performance, which was to ride the horse down-stairs again on his way to his own apartments, and which portion of the equestrian feat, as it was not comprehended in the bets pending thereon, Segundo had positively declined to perform. Here, I thought, was an opportunity of out-Heroding Herod, and distancing even him who had instructed me in all such deeds of daring. Accordingly, much to the amusement of the drunken throng, and the re-awakened horror of the landlady, I mounted the impatient Shamrock on his homeward journey, and accompanied by the good wishes of Topthorne, who was unable to leave his chair, and guided by the two most drunken gentlemen of the party, bearing each a silver candelabrum, with its load of wax-lights swaying to and fro in their unsteady hands, I reached the top of the staircase without injury, and commenced my perilous descent. A cat on the ice, who has been shod by the mischief of the rising generation with a complete set of inverted walnut-shells, is about as vivid an emblem of alarm and insecurity as can well be exhibited; but I doubt if the action of Grimalkin herself, under these uncomfortable circumstances, is more uncertain than was that of the cautious Shamrock in his precarious journey.

The first landing-place we reached triumphantly; and we

were now directly opposite the bar-window, which opened on the stairs, and through which, the sash being up, a very pretty attendant, with corkscrew ringlets, was watching the performances. Ambitious of distinguishing myself in the eyes of this Hebe, and demonstrating the thorough understanding which, under all circumstances, exists between the good horseman and his steed, I ventured most incautiously to hurry the careful pace at which Shamrock was so sagaciously toiling down-stairs. A hind foot slipped; a loud snort announced that the horse was thoroughly terrified; he lost his footing and his presence of mind at one and the same time; with a wild plunge forward he knocked down the leading torch-bearer, and we were enveloped in comparative darkness. I heard a scream of terror, and the crashing of wood-work—probably the banisters, as I found myself describing a "parabola" over my horse's head into the obscure; and although my fall was broken by its fair denizen and the whole interior furniture and economy of that snuggery which is denominated the bar, I was carried to bed sufficiently confused to be utterly unconscious of the devastation which accompanied my downfall.

The bill which I had next morning to pay gives me a vivid idea of the general smash created by my unexpected visit into this portion of the premises watched over by the Green Dragon. A gentleman flying head-foremost through an open window into the arms of a pretty barmaid, and *with* her bringing to the ground a half-dozen of sherry, a case of liqueur-bottles, a set of tea-things, a large fire-screen, a cold apple-tart, and several jars of hot pickles, is lucky if he escape as I did, with a contused shoulder, a pair of black eyes (not quite such pretty ones as the barmaid's), and a swinging long bill to liquidate for this unceremonious method of being "called to the bar."

CHAPTER XVIII.

Give me mine angle. We'll to the river. There,
My music playing far off, I will betray
Tawny-finned fishes : my bended hook shall pierce
Their slimy jaws : and as I draw them up,
I'll think them every one an Antony,
And say, Ah, ah! you're caught.
Antony and Cleopatra.

LET it not be supposed by the reader, to whom I have so openly confessed my many follies and vagaries, that my whole life, as a quiet invalid, on a visit to a country clergyman for the restoration of his health, was nothing but a series of such morning adventures and midnight freaks as those I have recorded in connection with my *début* as a "gentleman rider." Other and more contemplative pursuits served to fill up my leisure hours; and whilst Bagshot was engaged with his clerical duties, which no temptation could ever induce him to neglect, I had abundant opportunities for the restoration of my health and improvement of my intellect in his grounds and library. A book in the open air, whether it be a Dissertation on the Specific Gravity of Fluids, or the last number of *Punch*, is infinitely more agreeable than the same volume perused in an arm-chair; and many a delicious hour did I enjoy, reclining at my ease in Joe's delightful garden, basking in the sunshine, or dozing in the shade, inhaling the fragrance of his roses, fanned by the breeze that stole over his new-mown hay (a *second* crop, of which the owner was justly proud), and lulled by the hum of what Dr. Watts piously denominates the "busy bee," but with whom I never can help sympathizing as a thorough idler like myself. All this, with the page of instruction spread open on my knee—too often disregarded, in my intense enjoyment of the surrounding atmosphere—made a paradise of indolence, to which the addition of a "real foreign cigar" left nothing to be desired —not even the "black eyes" which, according to Tommy Moore, in conjunction with "lemonade," constitute the Persian's idea of a future heaven. Nor were these orbs, albeit of languishing blue instead of sparkling black, very far distant from the bower I so constantly frequented. From the parsonage to Topthorne Lodge was but three miles as the crow flies; and at Topthorne Lodge, need I say, Mrs. Montague Forbes was staying with her bachelor brother, on a prolonged visit? Between the two houses, and within easy reach of either, lay a broad and picturesque sheet of water, called Cowslip Mere, beneath the sedgy banks of which the gigantic pike loved to doze away the dreamy hours of noon, whilst the lake's unruffled surface bore punt and pleasure-boat noiselessly above his haunts. Here did l acquire my only knowledge of the Waltonian science; and here, under the tuition of mine accomplished host, did I progress rapidly in the contemplative art of trolling. But was the shark in miniature—the scaly monster of the hideous jaw—the only attraction that lured me to these golden waters? Was it a pure admiration for Nature, or an unalloyed love of sport, that led me to inclose my person in duck continuations, turned-down collars, a straw hat, and a tailless jacket—a costume which it is advisable for gentlemen to abandon when turned of thirty—or had I truly "other fish to fry?" Was there another bait, to which I was the unsuspecting gudgeon? Even so. Antony—"broad-fronted Antony"—despised not to dress the hooks of his "serpent of old Nile;" the "first gentleman in England" had his Virginia Water, nor are we to suppose that he was destitute of some fair minister to carry his landing net; the "monks of old" were anglers to a man, as the site of every ruined abbey and monastery vouches for, with its neighbour, the trout-stream—and, although inveterate bachelors, they were anything but callous to the charms of the other sex, "if ancient tales say true, nor wrong these holy men;" and with such worthy examples before our eyes, it is not too much to say that "fishing and flirting" may be coupled together with as much justice as any other two unconnected pursuits. Behold me, then, embarked on the crystal surface of Cowslip Mere! the waters glistening in the sun like burnished gold, the summer breeze sighing in the woods that fringe the lake, the wood-pigeon ever and anon pouring his plaintive note from their cool, shady depths, the plash of oars falling drowsily on the ear, and the low, sweet, pleading voice of Mrs. Montague Forbes completing the spell that pervades the whole enchanting scene. Our craft is a roomy, broad-bottomed punt, warranted not to upset with any amount of romping, and, if pace be no object, sufficiently handy to be guided (I can hardly say propelled) by two short, sturdy oars,

"Youth at the prow, and Pleasure at the helm."

Our crew consists of the syren aforesaid, her brother the Squire (who, not without grumbling, takes his share of the locomotive labour), Joe Bagshot, and myself. Four rods, supplied with all the mechanism of multiplying reels, patent lines, and ill-fated natural bait, are sticking out in every direction, for the entrapping of some unwary fish; whilst the spare paraphernalia which encumber the bottom of the boat would lead you to suppose that a war of extermination had been declared against the cold-blooded denizens of the deep. Need I add that, in such society, a well-filled hamper, containing cold pie, hard-boiled eggs, and bottled porter, was not forgotten? The Squire is toiling at the oars, and his broad face (never of the palest) is now in hue like the setting sun. Mrs. Montague Forbes, reclining in a graceful attitude upon the "well" which contains the living, but doomed, gudgeons preserved for "bait," is shading her handsome face with a gorgeous parasol, and doing the agreeable most diligently to my unworthy self, who am lying with my face to heaven, and my straw hat protecting my eyes, in a state of indolent satisfaction, having left my rod and line to trail over the stern, and take its chance of any erratic fish that may accidentally fancy the treacherous morsel it offers. But of no such idleness is Joe guilty. Ever keen in all matters of sport, from ratcatching upwards, he is now standing like a Colossus in the bows of our boat (if bows those can be called, which need only proceed in a contrary direction to become the stern); and dexterously does he fling out the glittering bait, with as much energy and precision as that of the fly-fisher, who directs to an inch the gaudy imitation, which I have always marvelled should be taken for a real insect by the hungriest of trout.

"Under the bank, Joe," grunts the labouring Squire. "Just where those weeds are parted, I had hold of a monster yesterday; but I did not give him time to gorge."

Whirr goes the line, strong enough to hold a crocodile, and in flops the bait at the exact spot designated. Ere the circling eddy has widened into repose, the reel is rapidly spinning off its coils; and, though he scorns to complain, I am sure it is burning Joe's nervous fingers as it slides through his grasp. Out comes Topthorne's watch, for he is punctilious to a degree in all matters of this kind; and he imposes on us an ominous silence during the prescribed five minutes allowed for the doomed fish thoroughly to digest his repast, nor will all the impatience of his companions, to whom this pause of expectation appears an age, induce him to abate one second of the accustomed "law." At length, replacing his watch in his fob with as much importance as if his hounds had just settled to their fox, he laconically observes, "Time, Joe! wind him up!" Forward I rush with the landing-net, dripping a shower-bath, in my hurry, on the very *piquante* summer toilette of Mrs. Montague Forbes—a piece of awkwardness which, with the proverbial sweet temper of a lady when *angling*, passes unnoticed and unreproved. Joe works his reel like the handle of a barrel-organ; the rod bends to a semicircle; an unexpected resistance threatens destruction to the whole fabric; the lady opines that "Mr. Bagshot has only hooked a weed, after all;" and, for a few moments we are at a dead lock.

"The brute is sulky," says Joe. (Would a biped be sulky to find a silver fork in his *omelette soufflée* ?) "We must wait till he moves."

Again there is a tumultuous rush under water. Joe draws him in warily and gradually; a white side appears for an instant above the surface; I make sundry ineffectual thrusts with the landing-net; the Squire swears; Mrs. Montague laughs; and everybody speaks at once. Luckily, the boat is anything but what is termed "crank;" so, notwithstanding all our endeavours, we cannot upset her; and, as the Squire snatches the net from my unskilful hand, amidst Joe's expostulations, and Mrs. Montague's entreaties to "be quick," I tumble over the neglected oars, and find myself prostrate in the bottom of the boat, alongside of an enormous, struggling monster, two feet and a-half in length, and fourteen pounds weight (angler's measure and computation), whose ghastly maw, grinning defiance with its double set of sharp-pointed teeth, stamps him carnivorous and cruel as his negro-fed prototype of the tropical ocean. Then, what exultation and satisfaction! what reciprocal compliments on our mutual skill, and expressions of wonder and admiration at the size of the fish! The Squire votes it high time for luncheon; and we propel the craft, not without difficulty, to a commodious landing place. The hamper is unpacked, the corks are drawn; with the green sward for our table-cloth, and the blue vault for our canopy, we revel like so many fairies at their elfin banquet; and when Mrs. Montague Forbes warbles forth, in a voice of which she has complete control, one of our plaintive old English ditties, even her brother acknowledges that "we should not have got on half so well without Nelly;" whilst I feel in my innermost heart that a wilderness like this, "with one such spirit as my minister," or, in other words, continual pic-nics in the society of the Nelly aforesaid, would be rapture indeed!

Thus the time glided pleasantly on; summer gave place to autumn, fishing and cricket to dog-breaking and partridge-shooting, without my seeming to note the length of my visit at the parsonage, or making another important discovery as to the influence of the neighbouring enslaver, whose society it was that made the days speed like hours, the weeks like days. A dream can scarcely be called such till the moment of waking renders us conscious of the illusion; and I might have lingered on in my friend Joe's house for months and years without ever taking myself to task as to *what* was the attraction that made the little west-country snuggery so delightful, had it not been for a sudden summons which called my landlord from his home, and rendered it impossible for me to remain longer in the house during the absence of its master. We had returned, the previous evening, from a delightful fishing excursion to a reservoir at some distance, where we had been more than usually successful, and as we drove home, full of plans for future amusements, and anticipation of additional field-sports, nothing was further from the ideas of either of us than the immediate separation of the pair. The post, however, takes no denial; and the very next morning Joe received a letter from a certain aunt of his, residing at Bath, summoning him immediately to her presence in that salubrious city, to manage some trivial matters that, to an invalid spinster, appeared of the very greatest importance.

The aunt was elderly and rich; Joe was her only near relation, and it would have been fatal to refuse. A neighbouring clergyman was happy to oblige so popular a character, by taking his professional duties for a time, and the only difficulty that presented itself to my friend, was what he called " behaving so badly to his guest." With his usual hospitality, he was anxious that I should remain installed at the parsonage till his return; but as his aunt's letter hinted an absence of some weeks would be necessary, this was an arrangement to which I could not consent. There was nothing for it, we thought, but a mutual start; and an early hour was fixed for our departure on the morrow, that we might travel together as far as our diverse routes—his for Bath and mine for London—would allow. This point settled, everything assumed a sadly leave-taking aspect; the parsonage looked prettier, the garden more blooming, and the path towards Topthorne Lodge more attractive than ever. The latter direction I sought in vain for an excuse to take; but with a nervous shyness that ought to have made me sensible of my danger, I studiously avoided making any proposal to Joe, as to the propriety of our paying our friends a farewell visit. Luncheon time arrived, and I was still as far as ever from my object, when Bagshot exclaimed, as if the thought had suddenly struck him over his glass of sherry, "I had almost forgotten, Nogo; upon my word we ought to call on Topthorne and his sister before we start." As may be supposed, I was nothing loth, and in less than an hour we were ushered into Squire Topthorne's drawing-room.

"Master was at the kennel," the servant informed us, with that accurate knowledge of his employer's whereabout that a servant thinks it right to affect; "but Mrs. Forbes was in the drawing-room; would we step that way?"

We stepped into the drawing-room accordingly, where we found that graceful lady busied in arranging a whole wheelbarrow full of flowers which she had just brought in from the garden, in fragrant profusion. There she stood in the full glare of the sunshine, fresh and radiant as Flora herself. None of your darkened rooms, and sitting with the window at her back, so much affected by ladies of a certain age, whose bloom will not bear the scrutiny of what they call a "cross light." Widow though she was, and turned of forty, if she was a day, Mrs. Montague could still boast a complexion that might have vied with Hebe herself; and we are not to suppose that she was unconscious of this inestimable attraction, or loth to display it to the greatest advantage. Our greetings were brief and cordial, and the melancholy cause of our visit explained.

"Going away?" said the fair widow, and I could have sworn she turned a shade paler as she spoke; "and so soon! We shall miss you both very much. You will quite forget the west, Mr. Nogo, when you get back to London;" and the look which accompanied this remark brought my heart into my mouth.

What I should have replied I know not, doubtless something very incoherent and nonsensical; but fortunately for my presence of mind, the Squire at that moment swaggered into the room. Rough and uncouth as he was, want of hospitality could never be laid to Mr. Topthorne's charge; and ere our errand was well explained, I had received and accepted a cordial invitation to spend the remainder of what he called "my summer vacation" at the lodge.

"You'll dine with us to-day, Bagshot," said he, in his usual abrupt and off-hand manner: "Nogo needn't go back at all. I'll send the trap down for your things; and in the mean time, if you'll come with me, you shall see the hounds fed."

There are some men whom nobody ever thinks of contradicting, who settle everything for others as well as themselves; and who, by a certain "brusquerie" of manner and decision in trifles gain an ascendancy over their fellow-creatures that real abilities often fail to obtain. Such was Topthorne. I never could find out that he had more acuteness, more judgment, or more determination than his neighbours; and yet, was there a knotty point to be solved—a difference of opinion amongst his brother magistrates as to the legality of a committal without evidence, or a dispute between his fellow-sportsmen upon the respective merits of their dogs and horses—he was always respected as an authority, and referred to as an arbitrator. In the hunting-field, as I afterwards discovered, he was looked upon as a second Solomon. If Topthorne said the hounds "never went any pace," vain was the evidence of scattered riders and sobbing steeds—of panting hounds, who, having raced their victim through a burst that turned him up in the open at the end of two-and-twenty minutes, now lapped and bayed alternately round the gallant fox who sealed his testimony to the pace with his blood. Vain, even, was the unanswerable evidence of the "compasses" applied to that depreciating Ordnance map, on whose surface the deeds of modern Nimrods dwindle into contempt—the achievement that over "the mahogany" swells into an exploit worthy of the days o chivalry, becomes, when subjected to this uncompromising test, a mere "constitutional canter," unworthy of the name of a run. But talking equestrians, foxes' brushes, and surveyors' measurements, were all equally futile in the opinion of the Pippingdon Hunt when opposed to the fiat of their Master; and he must have been, indeed, a bold man who would have ventured to appeal to the testimony of his own eyesight against the assumed knowledge of the dictatorial Squire. True, he did not ride particularly forward; and his style of going being what they call in Yorkshire "not very venturesome," he was generally upon the skirts of a quick thing, his presence at the end of which was more due to his knowledge of the country than the use he had made of his horse. But then he could tell you what hound was leading during every part of the run; and from your ignorance of the names of the pack, to say nothing of the extra eye required for individualizing that streaming body which it requires all your energies and intellects to keep in view, your own natural orbits being fully employed in choosing your ground and scanning your fences—with these drawbacks, I say, although in Leicestershire phrase you may have "had the best of it every yard," I defy you to contradict him. In a word, to give him his due, he was unapproachable: his ear, never at fault, told him in an instant the direction his hounds were taking; and when sound failed to guide him, he seemed to have an intuitive knowledge of the intentions of his fox. Though a moderate rider, he was doubtless a thorough sportsman; perhaps all the more so from his want of that "dash" which, however indispensable to the hound, is a qualification not so desirable in the impatient throng mounted and assembled to pursue that sagacious animal, and whose headlong gallantry, merciful by mistake, saves the life of many a fox, as it destroys the equanimity of many a master.

But to return to the Squire. For my own part I would much rather have remained in the cool, fragrant drawing-room, doing the agreeable to his handsome sister, than have accompanied him to the odours of a boiling-house, and the fiery ordeal of those scorched flags, which paved his gloomy kennel. But I never dreamed of resistance: as the Squire said, so must it be; and with a rueful glance at the widow, and an envious look at Joe, whose immediate attention was required by some parish business, I followed my leader up the shady winding path, which led to the low detached buildings honoured by the residence of the Pippingdon Hounds; and conspicuous like all other kennels for a huge and hideous weathercock, which from June to January, probably out of compliment to the time-honoured "Billesdon Coplow run," pointed without deviation due north-east! "There's music for you," said Topthorne, as an unearthly yowling proclaimed the vicinity of his darlings; "to a sportsman like yourself, hounds are more interesting at this time of year than in December. I think I can show you a rare entry;" and trudging past a paddock, in which an equine skeleton was awaiting his doom—though what there would be to eat upon him when slaughtered, excited my curiosity—we arrived at the kennel door garnished with innumerable noses, which the Squire called "masks," heretofore owned by the gallant foxes of the west; and further guarded, with superstitious care, by the witch-defying horse-shoe. "Mind that bitch, she has got a litter," said the Squire, as an ill-favoured old vixen, with one eye, came snuffing round the calves of my legs, but ill-protected by a pair of thin summer trousers. "Go home, Venus," he added; and Venus, not liking me on a closer inspection, was content to depart without perpetrating an assault, just as the factotum of the establishment thrust his shock head through the kennel door, and disappeared again like lightning, to furnish us with

the customary long coats and heavy-thonged whips, necessary
defences against undue familiarity or unprovoked aggression.
"Ike," as this worthy's baptismal appellation of "Isaac"
was universally abbreviated, deserves a few words of notice
as an original in his way, and a servant of that accommodating kind which is, unfortunately, seldom to be met with
in crack establishments. He was originally a denizen of
middle earth, being, as he himself said, " bred and born down
a coal-mine;" but had attracted the Squire's attention by his
irrepressible fondness for the chase, and the enthusiastic
manner in which he acted on foot as an amateur whipper-in.
A vacancy occurring, he was put into the establishment, and
by degrees became the most useful and influential personage
about the place. Kennel huntsman, feeder, first and second
whip—all these multifarious duties were fulfilled by "Ike;"
and with the assistance of one boy, as idle a young dog as
ever went unpunished, he represented the whole staff, which
with the Pytchley or Quorn would consist of at least five individuals. In the field his utility was no less apparent, and
true to the destiny of his kind, he "played many parts."
When the Squire was "to the front," "Ike" shone conspicuous as the quickest of "first whips." When, as often
happened, the servant was "there," and the master only
"thereabouts," he slipped with ease into the character of a
huntsman, occasionally rating the astonished pack to his own
holloa, and in that capacity showed a knowledge of the craft
unsurpassed by many of far higher pretensions than this
natural and self-taught sportsman. He was ever thinking of
his hounds, never of his horse, and was a living instance,
with an unbroken neck, of the powers enjoyed by that animal
when not hampered by the assistance of his rider. To say
that "Ike" was a good horseman would be absurd; to call
him a bad one would be unfair. The fact is, he was *no horseman at all*. With a short broad-shouldered figure, and a pair
of sturdy bow-legs, encased in the "drabbest" of cords and
brownest of "tops," he sat anywhere and everywhere upon
his saddle that happened to be most convenient at the mo-

ment; and, thus liberally disposing his weight (by no means a trifling one), he seemed to think he had done all that was required as his share in the partnership. His "bridle-hand" was formed entirely on the principle of "non-intervention;" and no horse could go on pulling at him, as he never gave him an opportunity by taking hold of his head. His rein was usually loose on his horse's withers, and in this form he rode at every description of fence in a cramped and awkward country. His nerve, of course, was undeniable; and, to give an idea of it, I may mention an instance which occurred when he was drawing a gorse covert with his hounds, on a violent four-year-old, which the Squire had entrusted to him to "make." The young one naturally disliking the prickly covert through which he was forced, went on "bucking" and jumping in a manner that would have unseated many horsemen, and destroyed the equanimity of most. Not so with "Ike." He sat perfectly unconcerned, "yoaxing" and cheering his hounds, and scarcely deigning to touch his bridle-rein or pay the slightest attention to the four-year-old, till, in the course of his vagaries, the latter found himself directly above the shaft of a worked-out coal-pit, half concealed amongst the gorse; and, taking the bit between his teeth, he cleared it at a bound. The horse jumped a considerable distance; but, on alighting, detached some of the brick with his hind legs, the crumbling portions of which, as they rattled into the "profound," struck terror into the hearts of those who witnessed the awful feat. How did "Ike" acknowledge his escape? Turning the young one round, as if he was merely giving him a lesson in leaping at a common fence, he exclaimed, "Is *that* the slovenly way you do it? You *theatrical* beggar, I'll teach you better manners than that!" and ramming both spurs into his sides, he *jumped it again!*

Such was the character whom I now saw for the first time on my introduction to the Pippingdon Hounds.

CHAPTER XIX.

My hounds are bred out of the Spartan kind—
So flew'd, so sanded; and their heads are hung
With ears that sweep away the morning dew;
Crook kneed and dew-lapped, like Thessalian bulls;
Slow in pursuit, but matched in mouth like bells—
Each under each. A cry more tuneable
Was never halloa'd to, nor cheered with horn.
Midsummer Night's Dream.

As the kennel-door opened, and I stepped into the savoury precincts of Mr. Topthorne's hunting establishment, my first feeling was one of thankfulness to that prudence and foresight, which had supplied me with a long-skirted upper garment, something like a weather-beaten dressing-gown, and a formidable weapon for repressive measures, in the shape of a most efficient hunting-whip; not the light, cane-shafted, silver-mounted gimcrack with which the dandy "customer" of "the shires" condescends to open those propitious hand-gates, which make his ox-feeding and blackthorn-fenced country practicable to man and horse, but a huge and ponderous weapon, iron-handled, and heavy-thonged, with a punishing power that can cut "old Benedict" into ribbons, and a crack like the report of a pistol. Nor was my gratitude for such protection misplaced, for no sooner had the Squire put his foot over the threshold of their habitation than an immediate rush of four-and-twenty couple of working hounds, mostly dogs, square of head, and large of limb, deep, long, thick-throated, and tough-skinned, threatened to carry us clean off our legs into the middle of the coming hunting season. "Get over, Trueboy! Have a care, Bellman! Back, hounds! back!" accompanied by a sweep of Ike's professional hunting-whip, modified the first eager demonstrations of his favourites, and gave the master space to descant upon the different ornaments of his kennel. Topthorne, though on ordinary occasions a man of few words, had a surprising flow of eloquence upon the one subject which most deeply interested him, and, under the impression that he had got hold of a brother enthusiast, he now opened out voluminously.

"The lot you see here, Nogo, are the whole of my working hounds, twenty-four couple of dogs and bitches, and they come out three days a-week, and a bye-day when required. 'Plenty of flesh, and plenty of work,' is my motto. 'Well-clothed ribs, empty bellies, blood and whipcord;' and, though I say it, that should not, no hounds in England can carry a better head when working, or come home fresher after a heavy, tiring day. Put 'em over, Ike; how long does it want to feeding-time?"

Ike consults a huge warming-pan, which he drags up by a tiny key from the recesses of his brown cords, and correcting its report by a solar observation, replies—

"About an hour and a-half, zur!"

So that I am evidently in for it! The Squire's face brightens as he remarks—

"We shall have plenty of time to draft the young ones 'by litters,' and then the whole of them one by one." (What a prospect for a summer's afternoon!) "It is so seldom I find a man that really *cares for hounds*, that it is quite a pleasure to get a sportsman like yourself into the kennel; so we will go through them regularly," proceeds the unrelenting Squire; and, disarmed by this undeserved compliment, I am compelled to submit, and with suppressed yawns and feigned interest I go through the enforced ordeal.

First we have "Reveller," and "Rantipole," and "Ruby," by the Duke of Beaufort's "Ragman," out of "Our Red-rose." And the great sprawling brutes, combining the playfulness of puppyism with the weight of maturity, disturb me in a brown study about the widow, by nearly knocking me down. After a minute inspection, this "promising litter" are dismissed to give place to "Galloper" and "Ganymede," by

Mr. Horlock's " Boudsman," out of " Gertrude ;" and as there is a doubt as to which of these great white monsters is to be kept, they are submitted to a close survey for the establishment of their claims to superiority. " Galloper " is a little " throaty," but then he is the larger limbed of the two, against which " Ganymede " is declared to be the image of old " Gertrude " about the head (who must have been an exceedingly forbidding, not to say ferocious-looking animal), and I remark that Ike inclines, if anything, towards the canine cup-bearer. The Squire at last appeals to me, and, taking the chance of the servant being in all probability a better judge than the master, I unhesitatingly declare in favour of " Ganymede." By degrees we get through the entry, and arrive at the drafts. Here I find it somewhat difficult to preserve my assumed character as a judge of the animal, for even to my inexperienced eye it is evident that the symmetry and appearance of these " pickings from other packs " will not counteract the latent evil qualities for which they have left their respective homes ; however, it is always safe to abuse a draft, if such abuse be properly tempered, by comparison with the receiving establishment; and when I condemn a lame, crooked-legged, overgrown brute, called " Watchman," as only fit to be hanged, the Squire and Ike, with admiration pourtrayed upon their countenances, sentence him forthwith. I know not how long I could have kept up the deception, but I confess to have been overjoyed when the time for release came without my ignorance of the subject being discovered by the Squire. I thought once or twice I could perceive a look of comic malice on Ike's rough features as he asked my opinion about this puppy or that bitch ; but if he had any suspicions of my imposture he kept them to himself, and when feeding time arrived, and I stood complacently at the troughs, and suffered my boots to be trodden on, and my lower habiliments soiled by the slobbering gluttons, as they unwillingly relinquished their hasty meal, I could not but see that I was winning golden opinions from my enthusiastic host. He put his arm within mine as we re-

P

turned to the house; and when the dressing bell rang, and I proceeded with more than usual care to make my evening toilet, my head was dizzy, and my ears rang with a confused jumble of "Champion" and "Marygold," "Wanton" and "Wilful," "Guardsman" and "Graceless," "legs and feet," "backs and loins," "capital timber," "famous in his back ribs," "deep about his heart," and "a lengthy lashing-looking young hound."

As I descended the stairs, in hopes of a five minutes' *tête-à-tête* with Mrs. Montague Forbes ere the dinner-bell should summon us to table, I had an opportunity of judging of the former tastes and pursuits of the Topthornes, by the different pictures and articles of curiosity which adorned the hall and landing-place. Sportsmen they seemed to have been one and all, to judge from the pictorial subjects and other trophies which covered the walls. Uncouth representations of Newmarket in the olden time, ere Frank Grant and Landseer were born, before the pencil of an Alken and the brush of a Herring had done justice to the make and shape of the noblest of animals, displayed a series of wooden-legged rocking-horses, with short square tails, apparently just taken from the plough, to be ridden in military style, at a slow canter, by individuals in cocked hats, periwigs, and jack-boots. How unlike the "run in for the Derby," which in the present day attracts its crowd of theoretic sportsmen at every print shop window! Interspersed with these purchases of some turf-affecting ancestor was a variety of smaller portraits, showing how the favourite hunter, in his snaffle-bridle, was used to jump his gates standing, in the presence of a numerous pack of hounds running over a flower-enamelled sward, that suggested the month of June as being in those good old times the most favourable season for the chase. Here and there was a full-length representation of a former Topthorne, long since demised, delineated with a lofty disregard for drawing, and a bold taste in colours, as attired in bright-yellow breeches, brown top boots, a grass-green coat, and a flowing peruke. Even the ladies of the family, the ancestral housewives, who had fulfilled their destiny of " suckling Topthornes and chronicling small beer," seemed to have been ambitious of being handed down to posterity in a manner befitting the wives and mothers of a race of Nimrods; and for one that was clad as a long-waisted shepherdess, holding a posy of flowers to her bosom, there must have been half a dozen attired in Spanish hats and buxom riding-habits.

Beneath these family pictures, glass-cases contained representations of the different beasts of chase, on which the originals of the portraits had during their lifetime exercised their prowess. There they were cunningly stuffed to ape real life and infinitely better resemblances of nature than the specimens of the limner's art. Pied badgers were plodding on, in their sidelong canter; and lithe, twisting otters grinning up at you with their death-snarl of defiance. An amiable-looking fox, with bright brown eyes, appeared to be caressing a prostrate pheasant, whose plumage was fresh and radiant, as if he had just fluttered away his life by the side of some leafless spinny; whilst harmless hares, in the old conventional attitudes, the one eating, the other sitting up, gazed at you with a placid expression of listless wonder, far different from the startled glance with which the last you killed regarded your retriever after you had tailored her by shooting " too far behind."

Such and such-like were the decorations of the staircase, down which I now descended into a comfortable and well-carpeted hall, not too large for a sitting-room, and in which the Squire kept his guns, fishing-rods, landing-nets, hunting-whips, sticks, umbrellas, hats, gloves, and camp-stools—everything, in short, which could be wanted at a moment's notice; and the fire-place of which was the general rendezvous of every one staying in the house previous to all expeditions of sport or amusement. The different apartments, dining-room, drawing-room, and billiard-room, all opened into the hall, and vied in comfort and snugness with that centre of the whole. Library there was none; nor did the Squire's tastes and habits render such an addition to his occupations by any means necessary.

In his own sanctum he possessed "Beckford," "Colonel Cooke," "White's Farriery," "Burn's Justice," and "Colonel Hawker's Advice to Young Sportsmen;" and with this wealth of literature he was completely satisfied. His sister, who subscribed to the circulating library at Weatherley, generally had two or three new novels in the drawing-room, and I never yet heard any of the visitors complain of want of books.

The outside of Topthorne Lodge was in accordance with its inner arrangements: no pretensions to architectural style or ornamental appearance, but everything sacrificed—no bad plan in a country house—to thorough comfort and convenience. It dated from the Elizabethan era, but in all probability scarcely any part of the original fabric which stood in "the golden days of good Queen Bess" was now left entire. Different proprietors had improved, added, taken away, and altered, according to their several ideas of necessity and comfort; so that the Lodge, as it was called, in consequence of some ancient rights of forestry which it conferred upon its occupant, was now a long, low, irregular pile of building, with winding staircases, and quaint ins-and-outs—an exterior that was in admirable keeping with the thoroughly English scenery, the towering oaks and broad meadows, that surrounded its walls; and an interior in which any gentleman not gifted with the bump of locality would be safe to lose himself at least twice a-day, during the first week of his domiciliation, in its puzzling passages and corresponding galleries.

Trusting to chance and a stray servant to conduct me to the drawing-room, I pursued my way leisurely from my own chamber, alternately making my remarks on surrounding objects, and glancing down with no small satisfaction on the suit of sables, in which, with a white tie, it is considered decorous to appear amongst your fellow-creatures at feeding time.

"Could we but see ourselves as others see us" would be, like most faculties which are wisely denied us, a very disagreeable acquisition. As it is, each man is satisfied that he has in himself some peculiarity of attraction which his neighbours must eventually discover. Did you ever know a big, bloated, bagman-looking fellow, with a face like a furnace, and a frame like an ox, that did not delude himself into the idea that he was "a remarkably fine man?" or, on the other hand, was there ever a puny, half-grown, wasted, bilious-looking figure, that did not console itself with the conviction that it bore the impress of patrician birth and gentleman-like breeding on its attenuated proportions? I presume I am no wiser than my neighbours. Certainly, taking Jack Raffleton or Segundo as the type of male beauty—and I never heard it denied by any one that both are peculiarly handsome men— my face and form, which are as different as possible from either of them, must be far removed from the standard of perfection to which we are all anxious to approach. I was an ugly boy at school, but I am much altered since then— possibly for the better; and altogether I am content to take the opinion of my tailor, who says I have a "*genteel figure for a surtout*," and whom I am fain to believe, although he can never complete a coat for me without a dozen alterations, and was once heard to say, with regard to a pair of leathers (my property), that drove him out of all patience by their obstinacy, " We can make *breeches*, sir; but we cannot really make *legs!* "

However, on the evening in question, I felt that if Mrs. Montague Forbes' opinion of my "*tout ensemble*" was anything like that which I myself entertained, her fate was sealed. The widow must succumb, and surrender at discretion. Accordingly, I marched boldly to the attack. I took her in to dinner (I was the only visitor), I drank wine with her, and talked and flirted, and told second-hand London stories —as good as new in the west; and when the time came for her to leave her brother and myself to our bottle of old port, her look, as she rustled out of the room, said plainly as words could speak—"Don't stay prosing here about your horses, but come as quick as you can to coffee and music in the drawing-room."

Old port twenty years in bottle is a fluid which may safely stand upon its own merits, without fear of neglect; and it is astonishing how its influence adds to the conversational powers of your companion, not only by conferring eloquence upon his periods, but by soothing you into a state of complacency highly advantageous to a listener. A gentleman who can talk to you for an hour without ceasing, upon the merits and pedigrees of his hounds, interspersed with problematical anecdotes of their sagacity, and diffuse commentaries on the nature and uncertainty of scent, would hardly be considered an amusing companion, if lending his assistance to the consumption of a decanter full of toast and water, or a jug of iced lemonade; but let him fill his glass to the brim with the dry, full-flavoured, ruby stream which, he assures you, in parenthesis, has been in his cellar since he came of age—not forgetting at the same time to push the bottle across the table with an injunction "to help yourself" —let him smack his lips as he sets down his empty goblet, and look as if he was going to ring the bell, and order "the other bottle," and you feel convinced that his eloquence is equal to that of Cicero or Demosthenes, and are ready and willing to undergo the ordeal of another story longer than the last, upon the understanding that it shall be accompanied by a fresh supply of that liquid alchemy which "turns his words to gold." So was it with the Squire: he had got a listener upon the only subject he loved to talk about, and he made good use of him.

Ere the second bottle was done, I could have passed a very fair examination on the system of kennel management in the Pippingdon establishment, and could have told to a fraction how much meal they consumed in a week, and how many pounds of horseflesh each of these interesting animals stowed away as his own proper share in a twelvemonth. What a relief it was to swagger into the drawing-room, and make love to the widow! to drink the coffee she poured out with her own fair hands, and to feel established at once as one of the family, when the Squire, according to custom, went fast asleep in his high-backed chair, and I rendered my valuable assistance in the winding-off of a skein of much-tangled silk, assuming the imposing attitude of a bear dancing on its hind legs, and holding out my paws for the reception of the confusing web! If not the most commodious, this is certainly the most agreeable method of preparing silk for immediate use. But alas for the resources of the human mind!—the conversational powers of a gentleman are most unfairly taxed when he finds himself the only visitor amongst a family party, and as of course they have got nothing to say to each other, when he finds he is called upon to supply topics and small-talk for all. I had exhausted most of my conversation at the dinner-table, and although now in the enviable situation of commanding the widow's ear, I really had nothing to say. We got through "the weather," and "her garden," very fast—the fading roses, the lovely walks, the surrounding scenery, and the quaint old house—when my good genius prompted me to ask a question seldom, in so old a building, replied to in the negative—

"Have you a haunted room here?"

"Do you believe in ghosts?" was the counter-interrogative, "for, if you do, I won't tell you the story—it is too alarming!"

Of course I expressed my utter incredulity in those unwelcome visitants, and with but little persuasion Mrs. Montague proceeded to relate the following legend connected with the Topthorne family in the olden time. The hour and scene were well calculated to do justice to a ghost-story: one of the lamps had gone out, and the room was in that state of semi-obscurity which is so much more gloomy than actual darkness; the rising wind sighed in the trees around the house; the Squire, fast asleep in his chair, breathed audibly without disturbing us by a snore; and Mrs. Montague, with her drooping ringlets and large serious eyes, told her story in those low, eager tones which go straight to the listener's heart; and thus it ran :—

"Many years ago, during the reign of Charles the Second, and when the gloomy and rigid manners of the Protectorate had given place to the roistering habits of the new *régime*, an ancestor of ours, one Miles Topthorne, was the proprietor of the Lodge. Miles had served with the Cavaliers in the Civil Wars, and had added to the natural profligacy of his disposition the habits of recklessness so much affected by that party. There is a picture of him in the hall—a handsome, dissipated-looking man, with a bad expression of countenance, to which the artist has done ample justice. He was no better than he looked: he broke his wife's heart, and drove his daughter from her home by the disgraceful orgies in which he took delight; and even at this distance of time, the Lodge has scarcely recovered the bad character it bore throughout the surrounding country, for vice and debauchery. Amongst other perilous amusements, it was his delight to rise at midnight from his revels, accompanied by his graceless companions, and hunt the deer with hound and horn throughout the surrounding forest, during the hours of darkness, scaring the solitary cottages that he passed, and making the ignorant peasants believe in him as a supernatural being, something akin to the Wild Huntsman of German romance. There is a chasm within a few miles of here, that is called 'Topthorne's Leap' to this day; and the common people believe that 'Mad Miles,' as they called him, accomplished the dangerous feat of clearing the precipice by moonlight. It was supposed—and the legend is so handed down to the present time—that 'Mad Miles' was not unaccompanied by supernatural assistance in these perilous expeditions. Stories were afloat of his having been seen preceded by a shadowy form on a black horse; and wherever his spirit-leader rode, there was Miles bound to follow, and thence he still emerged unhurt. Boon companions, who had accompanied him on these wild flights, had been known, on their return weary and exhausted with the midnight chase, to declare that they had seen Miles and 'another' far before them in the moonlight, when they had abandoned the unsuccessful pursuit, and to inquire of each other, with blank visages, as to which of their number had so far distanced his competitors. The answers were never satisfactory; but then, to be sure, men who hunt in the dark after supper, are not likely to give a very clear account of their proceedings. But, unfortunately, the Topthorne of that day did not confine his vagaries to these moonlight rides. He was the terror of all whose families could boast of beauty, and who valued their good name. His assignations with the damsels of the surrounding district have given the name of 'Lover's Oak' to a huge old tree at the further end of what is now the park; and, amongst others in whose ears he poured his tale of treachery and falsehood, was Alice Torwood, daughter of his sub-forester (for Miles, like his fathers, was keeper of the forest), and commonly called 'The Lily of the Lea.' His advances were long received with scorn and horror by the high-minded maiden; but the cavalier, accustomed to consult only his own ungoverned passions, thought little of using force where persuasion was of no avail, and 'The Lily' was carried off at midnight from her father's house. She was brought to the Lodge a raving maniac. Tied upon his powerful horse, behind her captor, who shall describe the horrors of that dark, desperate gallop! In her incoherent lamentations, she raved of a demon-form that had pursued her on a fiery black horse; of a frightful chasm, over which Miles had urged his steed, to escape from his unearthly companion; of rivers of blood, through which they had waded—and sure enough, when she arrived at the Lodge, her dress, as well as that of Miles, was stained with gore; and of fearful conflicts between her captor and the demon, waged at intervals, when the latter's superior speed enabled him to come up with the flying couple. But her words were merely regarded as the ravings of madness; and although a young forester of the district, formerly attached to Alice, was found dead in the forest, with a sabre thrust through his heart, no inquiry, in those unsettled times, was made into the business, and Miles Topthorne, unsuspected and unpunished, pursued his former career of unbridled licence and profligacy. In the mean time, 'The Lily' remained a close captive in one of the rooms above-stairs. Inquiries were made in every direction by her family, but no clue was ever obtained as to her whereabout; and the agony of her father, in his uncertainty as to what had become of his darling, was perhaps preferable to the knowledge of her actual fate—out of her mind, and a prisoner in the house of such a man as Miles Topthorne. But the unaccountable part of the story is to come. 'Mad Miles' was brought home one morning, after a midnight gallop, with a broken neck; nor was this a catastrophe that should have created any surprise, but, on that very night, 'The Lily' had disappeared from her prison-room, nor was she ever afterwards heard of. She may, with the cunning peculiar to maniacs, have eluded the vigilance of those employed to watch her, and, when once out of the house, have precipitated herself into one of the many ponds or streams which abound in this neighbourhood. But, be it as it may, no traces of 'The Lily' have ever yet been discovered; and many a peasant vowed that, on that fatal night, he was woke from his sleep by the shrill blasts of a horn, mingled with piercing screams from a woman's voice, and, rushing to the window, he caught a glimpse of a hurrying cavalier, with a white figure behind him, galloping through the forest in the moonlight, and closely pursued by a shadowy form of unearthly proportions, mounted upon a huge and fiery black horse. Since then, the room that 'The Lily' occupied is supposed to be visited at full moon by sundry shrieks, groans, and mutterings; and one of our housemaids left, a few years ago, in consequence of meeting, as she declared, a white, transparent figure on the very threshold of the apartment: we now call it the Pink Dressing-room, and it opens into the Blue Bed-room—the one which you occupy. As you do not believe in ghosts, I have told you the story. Be good enough to light me a hand-candle. Good-night, Mr. Nogo, and pleasant dreams to you!"

CHAPTER XX.

A heavy summons lies like lead upon me,
And yet I cannot sleep.
Macbeth.

Dan.—He is indeed a horse, and all other jades you may call— beasts.
Con.—Indeed, my Lord, it is a most absolute and excellent horse.
King Henry the Fifth.

HORACE recommends the sleepless Roman to swim thrice across the Tiber, and ere he seek his couch to drench his frame with wine—a classical way of rendering what we in the vernacular term "passing a wet evening." And doubtless this was good advice to the luxurious denizen of the Imperial City, unaccustomed to take sufficient exercise, and imbibing in his revels only the pure unadulterated produce of his sunny and vine-clad hills. We gather from history that the masters of the world were claret drinkers; the size of their drinking-cups, the frequency of their toasts, their aversion to "heel-taps," which we infer from their recorded habit of striking the brim of each up-turned goblet against the thumb-nail, to show what thorough justice had been done to its contents—all these little social and convivial practices prove beyond a doubt that had "black-strap" been the particular "vanity" imbibed in such profusion, there would have been few instances of a senator *walking* to his couch; and "as drunk as Julius Cæsar," instead of being, as it now is, a pleasant and classical metaphor betokening helpless inebriety, would have stood recorded, in sad if not in sober earnest, as an undoubted historical fact. Now the "other bottle" of strong port, acting upon a frame already diluted with sundry glasses of dry champagne and "curious" Madeira, doubtless produces a slumber which, if if it were only long in proportion to its depth, would be refreshing to the last degree; but unfortunately ere "the cock's shrill clarion or the echoing horn" has proclaimed the approach of day, an unwelcome fit of vigilance overtakes the prostrate Bacchanalian, and with parched throat and aching brow he tosses to and fro upon his couch, too restless to relapse into slumber, and yet in a most unfit condition to be up and doing.

Mrs. Montague's ghost story was buzzing in my ears when I sought my dormitory. I certainly wound up my watch, though I have no distinct recollection of extinguishing my candle; *therefore* I cannot have been the least under the influence of Bacchus: no, it was probably the salad—salad never *does* agree with me—or the coffee might have been too strong; but it clearly was not the wine that caused me to awake about three o'clock in the morning, very much heated, rather nervous, and extremely indisposed to go to sleep again.

The full moon was pouring her beams into my chamber through a chink in the shutters, and the clock in the passage, whose every tick had for some time been irritating my overstrung nerves, gave its three silvery strokes, and then went on with its aggravating "one, two," louder than before, when to my infinite discomposure I fancied I heard a slight scream in a woman's voice. My first impulse was to put my head under the bed-clothes; but making an effort to master this not very valorous instinct, I sat up and listened! Who, that has ever gone through this performance in the middle of the night, will deny that it is, to say the least of it, the most uncomfortable method of passing the time usually devoted to repose? how the slightest sound appears magnified to an alarming degree—how every horror, of which the news-

papers are always full, becomes present to the mind at once
—how the boards of hitherto silent passages and deserted
rooms crack, as though trodden stealthily, by ghost or robber,
of no fragile weight—how the feeling of apprehension merges
into irritation, and *vice versâ*, till you hardly know whether
you are most alarmed or provoked, and how in the midst of
all these misgivings you generally drop insensibly into a
disturbed slumber, from which you wake next morning, at an
hour when you ought to be dressed, unrefreshed and very
much ashamed of yourself. Such is the usual conclusion of
a broken night's rest; but when you have been credibly informed, from lips on which you place implicit reliance, that
you are actually next door to a haunted chamber, Morpheus
is more chary of his favours: and never at high noon did I
feel more thoroughly broad awake than during the weary
hours of the first night I spent at Topthorne Lodge.

Again that stifled scream—again that light and stealthy
foot-fall passing my very door. Flesh and blood could
stand it no longer; and in sheer desperation I jumped wildly
out of bed and rushed into the passage, with a sort of morbid
impulse, that bid me face the worst at once, and get it over.

Cold crept the night air around my defenceless limbs; for
my garment was scant, and the draughts which pervaded the
old house were pitiless; but the bodily discomfort I experienced was nothing, compared to the mental chill that shot
through my very marrow, when at the further end of the long
gloomy passage I distinctly saw a white transparent-looking
figure vanish through one of those swinging green doors, so
especially adapted for the exits and entrances of ghosts.
Had I not been the solitary occupant of "the Visitors' Wing"
—had there been another denizen of that haunted locality to
rush to his chamber door in superstitious terror, I rather
think I should have frightened *him*, as I stood in the cold
moonlight paralyzed with horror—my mouth open, my hair
on end, my snowy drapery floating in the night breeze, and
my eyes fixed with a stony glare on the disappearing spectre.
But alas! I had no companion to encourage me with his

bodily presence. I was alone—all alone now; for the ghost was gone: and much discomfited under the combined feelings of shame, fear, and a half suspicion that the whole might be a trick to impose upon my credulity, I again sought my couch; and at length, when the cheerful dawn made its appearance, and the "early birds" were twittering gladly to meet the approach of day, I found courage to resign myself to a heavy slumber, from which I did not awake till the sound of a great bell tolling somewhere in the neighbourhood of my bed-room announced that breakfast would be ready in that short half-hour, which argues a toilette either completed with wonderful dexterity, or else curtailed of some of its most essential forms.

The Squire said I looked "seedy;" the widow hoped I had slept well, and not been visited by the "Lily of the Lea;" and breakfast passed over without any further remark on the disturbance of the night, which appeared not to have aroused my host or hostess.

Bolder in the daylight, and ashamed of my alarm, I thought it best to say nothing of my unwelcome visitor, though I confess that for an instant the unchivalrous thought crossed my mind, that if this sort of thing was to go on *every* night, not even the charms of Mrs. Montague Forbes' society during the day could compensate for such a life of terror; and I had better frame some excuse that might withdraw me from the dangerous neighbourhood of Topthorne Lodge and the romantic regions of the west. But the widow smiled as widows only can, and day after day saw me lingering on, a welcome guest at the rough Squire's table, a willing captive to the attractions of his sister. Occasionally as I lay awake in the Blue-room, I fancied I could hear *a* footstep stealing gently along the passage; but after a brief struggle with my pride, I generally buried my head beneath the bed-clothes, and emerged again hot and breathless, when I imagined the apparition must have passed away; and whether it was the old port, or the country air, or more probably the healthy out-of-doors life I was leading, I know not; but I found that altogether I slept passably well, and my quarters agreed with me amazingly.

Day after day glided away, and found me still a visitor at the Lodge. Friends came and went, and seemed to consider me as one of the family. Partridges got wild, pheasant-shooting began, cub-hunting became less and less gothic in its hours, and instead of six o'clock, I used to mount the Squire's roughest pony, always very much at my service, and hie to the fast mellowing woods at half-past nine.

I like cub-hunting: it is a sort of earnest of the delights about to be produced by the coming season; and if, as moralists tell us, the charm of pleasure lies chiefly in its anticipation, how much greater must be the satisfaction of the chase (particularly as you need not ride over the fences) when every day brings it nearer and nearer to its perfection, than when the drying winds of spring have parched the soil, the gaps been made up, stiff and plashed, and as high as a man's chin, and everything, from the staring coats of your hounds to the battered legs of your hunter, warns you that the end of your favourite sport is near at hand!

Well, November was approaching, and still I was at the Topthorne's. No intelligence arrived from Bagshot, and to the Squire's pressing invitation to remain until his return, and begin "the season" in the west, what could I reply but a grateful affirmative? And yet it all seemed like a dream—what with shooting, and fishing, and flirting; pic-nics, when the weather was fine; driving with Mrs. Montague in her pretty pony-carriage with its quiet pony (for Mrs. M. was too timid to mount a horse, gentle creature!) when it was doubtful; and playing at battledore and shuttlecock with her when it was rainy; the time glided by in peaceful happiness—all the more insidious for its tranquillity. Reader! have you ever played battledore and shuttlecock across a billiard-table, with maid, wife, or widow—especially the latter? If you never have, take my advice and don't try—" Where ignorance is bliss 'tis folly to be wise!" And should you wish to escape the common doom of your sex—to live and die unfettered by the matrimonial tether, unscathed by Hymen's torch; unimprisoned within his magic ring; a free man from tears and *trousseaux*, gauze and gossips, bother and bride-cake —then take your diversion at bowls with the parson; at skittles with the gamekeeper; ay! even at *écarté* with the Frenchman; but don't play battledore and shuttlecock with a lady. Need I add how the danger is enhanced when the said lady, in addition to her opportunities of fascination as an inhabitant of the same dwelling with yourself, is possessed of a rounded figure and a beautiful arm, shown to their greatest advantage as she strikes the winged mischief-maker high into air; a fresh complexion, deepened into a rosy hue by the exercise and *the pursuit*; and long sunny ringlets that droop over the prostrate shuttlecock, in playful despair, as she picks it up with a ringing laugh at "her own stupidity," and declares it is "so provoking we *cannot* keep it up above a hundred and twenty!" Such was my lot; and strange to say I wilfully shut my eyes to the danger, and still played on. I have often wondered whether the late Mr. Montague Forbes was an adept at this game, and whether this was the method adopted to capture that austere and puritanical gentleman (for such I have been given to understand was his character): probably if not so, some other equally efficient snare was prepared, and the bait—like that of a sagacious keeper—was adapted to the nature of the vermin to be entrapped. Well, as I have already said, the time slipped on merrily enough, and that important epoch, the first Monday in November, was rapidly approaching. I had decided to remain with the Squire at least till Christmas, and abandoning all visions of distinction in "the shires"—all ambition of shining amongst the daring dandies from Melton, or effecting a brilliant escape from the crowd of infuriated centaurs who periodically override the Pytchley Hounds, I had resolved to go deeply into the science of the thing, and have a good spell of wild hunting in a wild country with Squire Topthorne and the Pippingdon Hounds. The master was delighted, as masters always are with the compliment implied by a desertion of other hunting establishments in favour of their own, and kindly offered to put me in the way of obtaining the material for enjoyment, in the shape of two good useful nags, at the lowest possible expenditure.

"Maggs is the only fellow to deal with," said the Squire: "I bought old 'Blunderbuss' of Maggs. I'll tell you what, Nogo—we'll go over to 'the Paddocks' the day after tomorrow, and see what he has got."

When the Squire said a thing should be done, I always remarked that done it was; and accordingly a soft, mellow morning towards the close of October saw Topthorne and myself leisurely progressing in his sister's pony-carriage towards the picturesque abode of the west-country horse-dealer. Mrs. Forbes's old pony was a favourite, and not used to be hurried; so we had ample time to enjoy the beautiful scenery through which we passed. How unlike, in its romantic confusion of hill and dale, wood, water, and open moor, to the flat surface, the large grass enclosures, and the trim regular hedgerows, which I had been taught to associate in my mind with the enjoyment of the chase. It was a scene to have enraptured Poussin; though old Goosey would probably have passed it by in disgust, for he could scarcely have made the same remark upon its merits with which he replied to the inquiries of his last kind-hearted and liberal master, as to what he thought of the wonders of the metropolis. From his attic in Piccadilly he had looked with a sportsman's eye over the surrounding expanse, and although he had come up from Leicestershire for the express purpose of seeing all that was most worth seeing in the great centre of civilization, his characteristic answer of "Take leave to say, Sir R., there seems a good deal of grass in the place!" shows what was the subject that, even in the modern Babylon, lay nearest to the veteran's heart. But the country through which the old pony dragged us so leisurely was as unlike the pastures of Ranksborough as the surface of the Green Park. Here we skirted a rugged copse, hanging its rich autumnal foliage over the lane we followed; there we forded a rivulet brawling down from a bluff and rocky slope, which almost deserved the name of a mountain. At every turn in the road we came upon some fresh object of varied beauty; and at length, embosomed in a secluded valley, through the level sward of which a tempting trout-stream stole silently along, we arrived at a quaint old-fashioned public-house, bearing the somewhat unaccountable title of "The Goat in Boots," and adorned with a cunning representation of that animal in such unusual attire —whence, after sundry coercive measures to prevail upon the unwilling pony to pass that well-known resort, a few hundred yards brought us up to the unpretending line of stabling, and comfortable though lowly dwelling known as "The Paddocks, Tiverley," and much frequented by the Pippingdon sportsmen in their dealings with Mr. Maggs.

The arrival of even our modest equipage created an immediate commotion in the establishment; and with a sort of "Guard, turnout!" alacrity, the myrmidons of Mr. Maggs became instantaneously on the alert, as though one and all scented a customer. A red-armed damsel, brandishing a frying-pan, peeped forth from the kitchen; a stunted ostler, with bandy legs and one eye, received the reins from the Squire with a kind of silent reverence that showed his veneration for the office of a master of hounds, and patted the pony as if it were an old acquaintance; while the proprietor himself, emerging from a loose box, with a straw in his mouth, and a bustling air of giving many directions at once, peculiar to horse-dealers, masters of hotels, and other functionaries whose time hangs heavy on their hands, lifted his hat in rapid succession to his visitors, marking by the tone of his different greetings, "Good morning, Squire!" and "Your servant, sir!" the different estimation in which he held a chance customer, and an old patron.

"Will you walk round the stables this morning, gentlemen?" says Mr. Maggs, in an off-hand sort of manner, as if we had *not* come for that especial purpose. "Naylus!" (a west-country abbreviation for Cornelius) "open that box! Horses look ill at this time of year; but it is *beauti*ful weather, certainly, for the country. Have you had much sport with the gun, Squire?"

And thus Mr. Maggs runs on, as if it were imperative on him to find conversation for his customers, as well as hunters; and with the further view of putting off as much as possible the transaction of actual business till after luncheon. The Squire is a good judge of a horse, as Maggs well knows; and accordingly, although he cannot resist the usual practice of showing us every brute in the stable before we arrive at "the plums," the enforced inspection is gone through in half the time it would have taken had I been there alone; and after passing in review one or two weedy, long-tailed five-year-olds, an overgrown bay horse with curbs, and a broken-down steeple-chaser, none of which are worth the trouble of having out, we are introduced to a grey of very promising appearance, and contemplate him for some minutes in mute admiration. After you have ascertained that a horse is quiet in the stable, felt his crest, passed your hand down his legs, and picked up his foot, into which you glance as you might look at your watch, and from which you derive about as much information, there is always an awkward pause, during which the customer is at a loss what he ought to say or do next. Now is the time for the dealer; and now Mr. Maggs begins—

"You don't see many shoulders like those, Squire!" (observe, the grey is a good-shaped horse, but his shoulder is the worst point about him)—"they can't help riding pleasant when they're made like him! feel his legs, Mr. Nogo—*famous* legs and feet, and some rare hocks and thighs those, Squire, to help him through the dirt! But I never take notice of make and shape. Give me performances, says I: let me see a horse perform, Mr. Nogo, and I estimate his value by what he does in the field. Now I sent that horse last week with 'Naylus,' to meet Mr. Wildrake's hounds cub-hunting; and I says to 'Naylus' says I—you keep with the hounds. Well, they ran from Torwood Vale to Wild-Overton—and the Squire knows what that is—and 'Naylus' he never left them

There was only three of them would have the Tiverley Brook —no, I beg pardon, Mr. Nogo, I'm telling you a lie—there was five charged it, but only three got over; 'Naylus' he led the field upon the grey: Mr. Wildrake's huntsman followed him, and wanted his master to buy the horse; but I kept him for the Squire here to see. I think there's few like him in any country, but I *may* be deceived. Will you see him out, Squire?"

And "Naylus" is forthwith summoned to saddle the grey, whilst we pass on to the next box, containing a strong useful brown horse, short in his legs, and with all the appearance of a hunter. Here we have nearly the same "recitative," varied with the different exploits performed by this sober-looking animal in timber-jumping, which appears to be his forte, and in the indulgence of which taste the heroic "Naylus" is related to have ridden him over a complicated double post-and-rail, no later than the end of last season, which had previously been the terror of all the neighbouring hunts. The brown horse, after an observation of mine, derogatory to his beauty (for he has a large plain head), and which Mr. Maggs passes over in silent contempt, is likewise ordered to be saddled; and in the mean time the dealer courteously entreats us to "step in and take a little refreshment;" without which no transaction in the way of business is ever supposed to be able to proceed.

A comfortable parlour hung round with sporting prints, a slice of pork pie washed down by a glass of sparkling home-brewed ale, the newest of bread, the freshest of butter, and the raciest of cheese, the whole put to rights by a small glass of undeniable white brandy, prepare one to look upon all sublunary matters—quadrupeds or otherwise—with an indulgent and favourable eye; nor when you have offered your hospitable host a capital cigar, and lit another yourself, do you find that its wreathing fumes at all discompose or decrease this charitable frame of mind. Both the Squire and myself liked the grey horse a good deal better when we saw him out; and as the short-legged "Naylus" trotted, cantered, and galloped him here and there, he really looked, under his pigmy burden, a fine powerful animal.

"Take him over those rails, 'Naylus,'" said Mr. Maggs in an off-hand manner; and "Naylus," nothing daunted, turned him at a fair sized timber fence, bounding the soft level meadow in which he was careering. Like most horse-dealers' men, "Naylus" possessed better nerves than hands; but the grey, though held in a grasp like a vice, and urged upon the off side by a single spur, jumped his fence cleverly, and landed in the field beyond in undeniable form. Back comes "Naylus" over the hedge, and again the horse does what is required of him tractably and well. He "reins up" where we are standing, arches his neck, snorts as though he liked the fun, and I begin to covet him. The Squire lays his leg over him, and gallops round the field, and I like him better and better. Mr. Maggs does not interfere with the favourable impression by any ill-timed remarks, but merely says, "Would you like to feel his action, Mr. Nogo?" and much as I hate an unknown "mount," I too have a taste of the grey. With stirrups the wrong length, and a confused mass of hard, thick reins in my hands, I cannot make him go unpleasantly; and as I return to where Maggs and his man are standing, and hear the former remark, as if he did not know I was within hearing, "Evidently a workman, 'Naylus.' I should say a gent, from Leicestershire!" I decide upon buying the grey "*coûte qui coûte.*" Elevated by the luncheon, the brandy, and the gallop, I proceed forthwith to mount the brown horse, who is now brought out to sustain his character, and as he is very fresh, and the saddle not yet warm to his back, narrowly escape getting kicked off for my rashness. However, a sharp canter round the field makes us acquainted, and with a lively faith in Mr. Maggs's representations of his jumping powers, and a lurking ambition to show these west-country sportsmen the capabilities of a "gent, from Leicestershire," I turn the brown horse's great fiddle-head, not without trepidation, at the rails. He faces them boldly enough; but at the last moment stops dead-short, and refuses with, as I suspect, a touch of temper. The Squire laughs, and I feel in honour bound to ride him at them again, with an inward anticipation of a fall, and a confirmed disgust for "larking." I give him another chance: again he stops short, but thinking better of it at the last moment wriggles his fore-hand over, and clears the remaining portion of his frame with a lash of his powerful hind-quarters, that sends me clean over his head, to alight on the broad of my back in the splashing water-meadow. I get up rueful, crestfallen, and irritated, but not the least hurt; whilst the brown horse careers round the field with streaming rein and tail on high, in undisguised exultation at his liberty. There is nothing for it but to buy him as well as the other, to show that I *can* ride him; and after a good deal of desultory conversation, a glass of hot brandy and water, much haggling as to price, many compliments from Mr. Maggs, and a curious arrangement entered into, by which a certain sum is specified as the price of a certain article, and a certain per-centage on that sum returned *for luck!* I re-enter the Squire's pony-carriage a richer man in the amount of my personalities by one grey and one brown gelding, warranted sound in wind and limb; and a poorer one in my funded property by the sum of one hundred and seventy-five pounds—the price of the quadrupeds aforesaid; besides one golden sovereign bestowed as a free gift on the one-eyed Cornelius, and requested by that enterprising functionary wholly and entirely *for luck!*

CHAPTER XXI.

" Yelled on the view, the opening pack,
Rock, glen, and cavern paid them back ;
To many a mingled sound at once
The awakened mountain gave response—
An hundred dogs bayed deep and strong,
Clattered an hundred steeds along."
Lady of the Lake.

My old friend Jack Raffleton, in his hunting days, used to avow that the happiest moment in his life was when he said to his servant, " Call me to-morrow morning at half-past seven ; and let the hacks be at the door by nine." Mr. Jorrocks, that most immortal of Nimrods, dearly loved the ride to cover, " the mud on his top-boots, and the smell of the morning h'air." Whilst many an aspiring sportsman, I verily believe, prizes beyond all other hours of the day, that moment of relief in which he dismounts from his jaded hunter, and hies to his long-wished for " dressing-gown and slippers," and the welcome embrace of his " too easy-chair."

But none of these authorities, however much they may disagree as to the exact period which brings them their greatest amount of felicity in connection with the chase, will venture to deny the charm of that most sociable of meals—a hunting-breakfast; not the uncomfortable repast taken in the dark, with a fork in one hand and a button-hook in the other, by the hurried citizen, who makes " the express" his covert-hack, and who knows not what it is to start for his destination in " The Vale " at a later hour than six A.M. : not the modicum of milk and soda-water which, with half a devilled kidney, forms the sole support of the dissipated youth, whose two thorough-bred hacks must be " told out " between Melton and Keythorpe, because their "wide-awake" master played whist this morning till two, and smoked till four: no, the hunting-breakfast I mean is that at which a party of quiet steady-going sportsmen meet at some picturesque old country house, with clear heads, rosy faces, and sharpened appetites; men whose affection for hunting vies (and it is saying a good deal) with their regard for their dinners; who know the points of a hound, the line of a fox, and every gap in the fences within twenty miles—such a breakfast, in short, as we sat down to, in the comfortable morning-room of Topthorne Lodge, on the Squire's first hunting day in November.

At the top of the table, half hidden by the urn, the long sunny tresses of Mrs. Montague Forbes drooped over the tea which she knew so well how to sweeten to *my* taste; need I add that, late or early, a place was reserved for *me* at her right hand? Old Mr. Shaftoe and his wife were staying at the Lodge; and sundry jolly squires and substantial magistrates, rejoicing for the most part in roomy cords and stout black boots, had dropped in to partake of the morning meal. The hounds were to meet on the lawn, and all were full of hilarity and anticipation.

I thought the lady glanced admiringly at my attire as I made my appearance, clad with the strictest attention to costume, in well-cleaned leathers and deserving "tops;" and even the Squire, although stoutly repudiating dandyism, nodded his approval of my "get-up."

Breakfast progresses—the eggs disappear, and the ham wanes rapidly. The post arrives, and the squires one and all exhibit that rabid eagerness for the newspaper, which in middle-aged country gentlemen supersedes all other considerations. I am deep in my second cup of tea, and becoming gradually absorbed in a reverie as to the probable merits of my new purchase, the gallant grey, whom I am about to ride with hounds for the first time, when Mrs. Montague's eager exclamation of "a letter from Bagshot! and what do you think?" startles us all into attention.

"You'll never guess, John," she continues; "you'll be so

surprised, Mr. Nogo—Bagshot is *going to be married!* and, of all people in the world, to cousin Kate!"

In my ignorance of the fascinating relation who, under the cognomen of "cousin Kate" has subjugated my old friend, I address some unmeaning congratulations to the excited lady, and her somewhat indifferent brother; but the torrent of feminine eloquence, once let loose by so prolific a subject as a wedding, rushes on unchecked.

"Such a short acquaintance—quite love at first sight, Mr. Nogo—and she seems so much attached to him. They are to be married immediately, and he will bring his bride here at once. What a nice clergyman's wife she will make, and so pretty; but there are few girls like Kate Cotherstone! Shall I give you some more tea, Mr. Nogo? you have upset your last cup all over your"—here Mrs. Montague checked herself, and, fortunately for me, distracted the attention of the company from my manifest confusion.

I never was so completely taken aback—could I believe my ears? "Kate Cotherstone going to be married to Bagshot!" I inwardly ejaculated; "and a cousin of these people, with whom I am on terms of such intimacy—this *is* a go! And coming here almost immediately; but perhaps it may not be *my* Kate Cotherstone," and with this slender consolation I summoned up courage to make further inquiries of my delighted hostess.

"Did you never meet the Cotherstones?" she proceeded; "he is a *great sportsman*" (very like it, thought I); "and she is a most good-humoured pleasant woman—a cousin of ours. They used to have a charming little villa in Windsor Forest; but they have been abroad lately. I am sure you would like them so much: and as for Kate, she would captivate you altogether," added the widow, with a glance of triumphant malice and conscious success in her mischievous blue eye.

The truth was now completely revealed. A villa at Windsor, and a tour on the continent, left no doubt as to the identity of that dangerous family, and stammering out some incoherent remark, as to "having met them once at Ascot," I took advantage of the Squire's impatience, which was now waxing highly irritable, to make my escape to the lawn, where the hounds were already assembled, and there, in the fresh morning air, endeavoured to regain that composure which this startling and unwelcome intelligence had so completely put to flight.

What to do I knew not. In the first place, notwithstanding all that was past and gone, notwithstanding the fascination exercised over me by Mrs. Montague Forbes, I was still sufficiently sore from the feelings I had so lately entertained for the too charming Kate, not to relish the idea of meeting her as the bride of another, and that other my old friend Joe Bagshot.

In the next place, this was hardly a connection that would be advantageous to that worthy and respectable divine; and was it not my duty to warn him, before it was too late, of all that I knew concerning this very enterprising family? But then, if they were indeed people to be avoided (and no one had better reason to think so than myself), what was to become of sundry day-dreams gilded by the widow's smile, in which I had lately indulged? If *my* friend was to be dissuaded from marrying Kate on account of her connections, how could *I* consistently enter into an alliance with her mother's first cousin? And if such a proceeding was to be immediately dismissed as out of the question, was I not in honour bound to leave Topthorne Lodge immediately, and at once break off an acquaintance—to call it by no softer name —fraught with such dangers and inconveniences? This, however, would destroy all my arrangements for the autumn, and put me to great personal discomfort—always with me a primary consideration; besides, I doubted my own stoicism if once it should come to bidding the widow farewell, to say nothing of the difficulty I should find in parrying the Squire's direct questions, and his friends' roundabout inquiries, concerning my speedy departure. There was no Jack Raffleton to advise me : I never had enough energy to act entirely for myself in a doubtful case; so adopting my favourite plan of being guided by circumstances—like those doctors, who, leaving Nature to herself, suffer her to kill the patient in her own way—resolved to take no decided course, but to wait philosophically for such events as should duly arrive upon the stream of Time.

It was now necessary to turn my attention to the business of the day, as the Squire was already mounted on his famous horse "Blunderbuss," and, with his hounds around him, two or three of whom I recognized as my tormentors in the kennel, was all anxiety to begin. Whilst he is drawing his own laurels, shrubbery, flower-garden, and washing-green, with a small patch of gorse on the hill, in which the butler sees a fox every morning, and which, as a matter of course, is invariably drawn blank, I may find time to describe the assemblage of sportsmen who now meet my view, and who, I am given to understand, comprise the *élite* of the Pippingdon Hunt.

To begin with the Squire and his stud. The equestrian was probably as unlike the famous *squire* of Leicestershire notoriety, as "Blunderbuss" was to "Ashton," which, if the description I have had from eye-witnesses of the latter clipper may be relied on, was a difference sufficiently obvious to the most careless observer. But yet Jack Topthorne, as his familiars called him, was a varmint-looking fellow enough : despite his stained coat, with its abominable collar, despite his drab cords, cloth tops, huge hunting-cap, uncouth gestures, and ungainly seat, there was a game flash in his eye that looked like "killing :" and I fancied that it was indeed bad scenting weather when the Pippingdon hounds were shor· of "blood." Though unmistakeably "rough," the Squire looked "ready," and appeared what he was—a thorough practical sportsman. As for "Blunderbuss," a greater brute I never wish to see: with a large, ugly head, lop ears, a sleepy eye, and a white face, he had not one single beauty to make amends for his mealy bay coat—of all colours, to my fancy, the most unsightly; and yet, though a cross-made horse, he had some good working points about him, but even these were disfigured by the shortest tail I ever saw upon a hunter. This was a crotchet of his master's, for which I was quite prepared by a conversation I chanced to overhear in the Squire's dressing-room, a few weeks previously. A new purchase had lately come home; and, contrary to his usual practice, "master" had bought him from "character," without a personal inspection. Accordingly, no sooner had the animal entered its future quarters than the groom hurried to "master" with a report of the fresh arrival. The Squire was dressing for dinner, with his door locked; but I plainly heard the following colloquy carried on from either side of the unopened barrier:

Squire: "Well, Ike" (for that functionary united the office of stud-groom to his other avocations), "what sort of a looking horse is he?"

Ike: "Loikely, zur; but uncommon low in flesh he be."

Squire: "Mash him to-morrow, and physic the next day. And, Ike, what sort of a tail has he?"

Ike: "Shortest dock I ever see anywheres—longest hair I ever see *here.*"

Squire: "Very well; cut his tail off square with the dock —that'll do, Ike."

After this, my surprise was greater to behold Blunderbuss with any vertebral termination at all, than with the short four inches that spasmodically answered every application of his master's spurs.

As was the Squire, so were his field, modified, certainly, in particular instances, but still one and all of the "drab and ditch-water" school—heavy-thonged hunting-whips (a "cut-and-thrust" punisher is an abomination unknown here), short tails, and snaffle-bridles, with a general family resemblance in their jolly complexions, which I could only attribute to their getting their port from the same wine-merchant, and drinking it in equally liberal quantities. They seemed to know one another well, and the country, if possible, better, and were chiefly men of a certain age, on which, as on their old jokes and time-honoured anecdotes, they rather seemed to pride themselves.

Why is it that at every fixture in every country, not excepting the so-called fast "shires," for one man under thirty you shall find a dozen above forty amongst those who comprise the field? It is as unaccountable as the accompanying fact, that hunting—far from being on the wane, as those who bewail the absence of "young ones coming on" would fain lead us to suppose—is becoming, year by year, a more popular amusement; somewhat, it must be confessed, to the detriment of sport, and greatly to the danger of "forward riders" and "tail hounds," but still a satisfactory reflection to the true lovers of the glorious pursuit. It may be that the young ones now-a-days are rather pinched for money—it may be that the old ones undoubtedly last longer than was the case with the preceding generation, and when the governor and the heir of entail each keeps a stud, it is rather a case of "burning the candle at both ends;" but whatever may be the cause, the Pippingdon Hunt was by no means singular in the proportion it showed of "the prime of life" *versus* the glorious spring-time of delicious twenty-one. Besides these veterans in their scarlets and collars, there was a parson of course; and although unassuming, quiet, and gentlemanlike in his appearance, as is invariably the case with his profession, he was obviously the fastest of the lot. As I took off my hat to return the bow with which Mr. Rockly honoured my introduction to him, and ran my eye over his lathy figure, graceful seat, and long, low, well-bred chestnut horse, I could not help thinking if there is any truth in appearances, *you* are a first-flight man anywhere and everywhere, be it in a steeple-chasing "scrimmage" from Shankton Holt or the Coplow, be it in a sobbing fifty minutes over the Vale of Belvoir after a thaw, or be it in a long wild foxhunting run, over moor and mountain, "bank and brae," ragged copse and brawling river, from such a rough, straggling, picturesque woodland as we are even now about to draw.

" Yooi in, Bellman and Bonnylass !—stand still, Blunderbuss!" says the Squire in a breath, as he forces the bay horse to take up his position on the side of a bank, and, standing erect in his stirrups, contemplates his hounds, bustling through the still leafy underwood. "Ike," on a five-year-old, has already clapped on to a certain corner, without thinking it necessary to wait to be *told* to do his duty; and there he sits like a statue, looking all ways at once, and eagerly watching for a view: not that he will holloa if he gets one, as long as there is a hound able to speak to the scent: no, the Squire stands no holloaing, and woe be to the man, servant or gentleman, that gets those square sagacious heads up from their proper occupation.

The hounds are drawing the covert well, and with a certain busy keenness that betokens a scent. The Squire gets into a ride, terminating in the only hand-gate in the country, and fumbles hurriedly for his watch, as old Bustler, snuffing eagerly under his horse's nose, throws up his enormous head, and with a deep prolonged note, like that of some triple-tongued Cerberus, proclaims a find! There is no swell, hard-riding, first whip, to rouse the echoes and scare the wood-nymphs with his loud-cracking thong and unnecessary injunction to "get together," addressed to a pack who are straining every nerve in their efforts to score to the cry. "Ike" is at the further end of the covert, at least half a mile off, and the Squire's horn is left undisturbed in its case.

The hounds have every advantage, for the field are close packed in the lane, like so many herrings in a barrel, and the fastest horse out would scarce get round the wood in time to head the fox. Now they are running gloriously, throwing a chorus around them that beats the keys of a pianoforte for variety, and what musicians call "expression." We gallop up the lane, parallel with the line, squelching through the puddles, and flinging the dirt in one another's faces, like so many maniacs. See, "Ike" has a view, with his cap in the air; but the well-trained scout is as mute as a mouse.

It is evident our fox is away; and the lessening chorus of the deep-mouthed pack announces that they too must have reached the open. The squires wax frantic: standing in their stirrups and grinning with excitement, they make superhuman efforts to "get forward," and the "breadth of beam" cased in its drab-cord covering, and revealed by many a pair of fluttering crimson tails, shows how right are these ponderous equestrians in holding their nags hard by the head. Mr. Rockly and the chestnut turn short out of the "ruck," and disappear over an awkward stile to the left; but although this is undoubtedly the most direct way to hounds, I can neither pull up in time to follow him, nor have I sufficient confidence in the grey to charge such an ugly impediment. I gallop on accordingly with the tide. We turn the corner of the wood, dash over a solitary cottage garden, skirt an orchard, squeeze through a gap in a high bank of hazels beyond, and emerge upon the open moor. What a line! what a country! not a fence in the whole of it! and such galloping ground—a soft elastic sward of tufted grass and heather, that carries a scent totally unknown to less favoured localities, and with room enough to "blow" an Eclipse at the rate we are going. Far ahead of us, rising the opposite hill, stream the lengthening pack, actually *tailing* from pace; but one and all owning the scent. "Ike" is shaking his reins alongside of them; and Parson Rockly, leaning well forward over the wiry chestnut's shoulders, is creeping gradually up to his place. We shall never catch them like this, in fact they are perceptibly gaining upon us even now; but in hunting, every day proves the converse of the old coaching aphorism, "what the big 'uns do by strength, the little 'uns do by cunning"—in the field, where the light weights get by speed, the heavy weights get by sagacity; and just as the hounds disappear over the crest of the hill, the heaviest and rosiest of my companions shoot off at a tangent down a half-obliterated cart-track to the right. Like sheep after the bellwether, we follow his hoof-marks, and for a considerable period, during which we never slacken our speed, we might, as far as hunting goes, as well be galloping up Rotten Row, for all we see of the chase. Once our pilot pulls up short, takes off his hat, wipes his beaded brow, and listens for an instant. I catch the distant melody on the breeze— down goes the hat with a cram, up he gets in his stirrups, and away again faster than before. We round the shoulder of a hill, and come upon a picturesque and copse-clothed dingle, where we find the hounds at fault, and strenuously endeavouring to recover the scent. "Ike" is sitting quietly on the five-year-old (who looks a good deal blown), waiting with praiseworthy patience till they shall have made their own cast. Parson Rockly has leaped off the chestnut, and is turning his horse's head towards the breeze with an expression of intense enjoyment on his countenance; and the hounds spreading like a fan, are feathering and snuffing for the scent, conscious that they will be undisturbed till they have quite done with it. I look round for the Squire, and behold him nearly a mile further down the dell, ready to come to his hounds should they require his assistance. How he got there no one can tell; but with a sort of instinctive knowledge of the line of a fox, he had arrived at the very spot where his hounds, on recovering the scent, afterwards crossed the brawling streamlet that divided the ravine. "Ike" was preparing to lift them, when "Rantipole" proclaimed that they required no such assistance; and stooping together to their work, they hunted merrily on, down the banks of the stream, into a more inclosed and habitable-looking country.

And now began the humours of the chase. Hitherto it had been all plain sailing, the fastest galloper and the best-winded horse had the advantage; but the ground upon which we now entered was a deep holding plough, with only an occasional grass field, enclosed by high rotten banks and "pleached" fences; while the lanes were few and far between, and the gates occasionally locked. Of all breaches of confidence, that of locking a gate is the most unpardonable; and, if anything can add to the heinousness of such duplicity, it is the further outrage of turning downwards the upper staple on which it revolves, thereby rendering it impossible to obtain a commodious egress by lifting the gate off its hinges. Alas! that such "a dodge" should have reached the unsophisticated west. Under these circumstances ride we *must*; but it takes a considerable time for a string of cautious gentlemen to follow each other, in due and well-timed rotation, over a series of double fences; and, although the hounds are only *hunting*, not *running*, I soon find that my view of the sport becomes again limited to the cords and coat-tails aforesaid. Every now and then I catch a glimpse of the parson "doubling" a high, awkward fence, in masterly style, two or three fields a-head of me; whilst, occasionally, I can see "Ike" shaking his elbows and running in his spurs, as he hustles the young one at some large and uncertain impediment; but there is plenty of occupation nearer home. Our corpulent pilot, warmed by the work and excited by his hitherto unparalleled success, rides boldly at the weakest place in a straggling treacherous sort of hedge, and comes upon his head in an artfully-concealed ditch. After this he discreetly abandons the post of honour, and at each succeeding obstacle there is a ludicrous politeness displayed by the field in their unwillingness to go first. Then what "come ups" are heard, as a stout gentleman, perched on the summit of a bank, to which he has arrived by a series of cautious advances, is startled by the unwelcome discovery of a second yawning ditch as a trap for the unwary, into the abyss of which he is convinced nothing saves him from being precipitated but the fast hold he has of his horse's head and the unmerciful "job" he inflicts on the docile animal. At last it gets to "leading over;" when luckily, just as the chance of again seeing hounds is becoming more hopeless than ever, a level green lane, running straight as a line for miles, greets our delighted eyes. It is a continuation of Watling-street, or Leeming-lane, or Amen-corner, for aught I know; but never before did I feel so thoroughly grateful to the conquerors of the world as when that old Roman road hove in sight. There is an ugly fence between us and the wished-for highway, which, as "a gent from Leicestershire," I find I am generally expected to negotiate first; and, with a vivid idea of a fall, I harden my heart and go straight at the obstacle. The grey does it so well, and lands so cleverly in the lane, that I feel quite ashamed of not having ridden him more forward; but am consoled by the consciousness of having been surrounded throughout by the *élite* of the Pippingdon men. I see a red coat clattering along on the same friendly road a few hundred yards in front of me, and, as I gradually overhaul the owner, I discover it is the Squire, whose hounds are running through a farm-yard a couple of fields to the right. As I near him he pulls out his watch, and giving old Blunderbuss a "refresher" with both spurs, he exclaims, "An hour and ten minutes, Nogo! he is running for his life." Sure enough the conclusion seems near at hand: the hounds are dashing up one hedgerow and down another, with bristles up and sterns down, as though they were maddening for his blood. All at once up go their heads; and, after a vain effort to recover the line, they stand looking about them in helpless bewilderment. There is a woodland, a field to our right, and the earths are open at Mellerton, two miles further on. The Squire's mind is made up in an instant; thrusting his tired horse through a gap in the fence, which I should never have perceived, with one blast of his horn he gets his hounds round him, and *casts them back*. Probably he thinks his fox much too hot to seek the woodland, and that had he persevered in making his point for Mellerton we should not have checked. The event proves the Squire was right. He had lain down in the ditch behind us, and the hounds had overrun the scent for a field and a-half. How they take it up in that orchard: ha! yonder he steals, below the fence, towards the gate; they view him as he crawls under its bars, and, tumbling over one another with the rush of a

cataract, they precipitate their two-and-twenty couple of bodies on that gallant little morsel of draggled fur. Who-whoop! who-whoop! resounds in every key—Iko tumbles from his horse amongst his darlings; Topthorne's face beams with delight; Parson Rockly wishes the Master joy of "so gallant a fox and fine a run;" and the rest of the field who, thanks to the Roman road, are mostly forthcoming, burst out into a Babel-like chorus of congratulation and applause. The pilot, heated up to boiling pitch, makes it an hour and twenty-five minutes by his watch; but as he did not come up till some little time after the conclusion, it is probable that although *his* run may have been of that duration, *ours* was not quite so long: the Squire's description of it in the following words is most likely to be correct—
"Not a bad run for the provinces, I think you must allow, Mr. Nogo; eleven miles from point to point, over a fine wild country, with but two trifling checks, and done in an hour and seventeen minutes."

CHAPTER XXII.

> Dined, o'er our claret we talk o'er the merit
> Of every choice spirit that rode in the run;
> But here the crowd, sir, can talk just as loud, sir,
> As those who were forward, enjoying the fun.
> *Hunting Song.*

> Do you pity him? No: he deserves no pity.
> Wilt thou love such a woman? What! to make thee an
> Instrument, and play false strains upon thee?—not
> To be endured. *As You Like It.*

TIME—half-past eight o'clock at night; scene—a snug dining-room, a blazing fire, and a horse-shoe table, on the polished surface of which the massive cut-glass decanters, sparkling with old port, that glows like liquid rubies in the firelight, are making their rapid and welcome rounds. The dinner has been excellent, the company agreeable, Mrs. Montague and the ladies have just retired, and we stretch our legs under Jack Topthorne's mahogany with that delightful sense of repose and comfort which those alone experience whose exercise in the open air has been pushed up to the point at which fatigue commences, but has stopped short of actual "distress." How loose and easy are the thin sable "continuations," to limbs that have been encased since morning in the uncompromising buckskins of the fox-hunter! how grateful the soft, well-cushioned chair, to a frame that has been pounding for some eight or nine hours on the unyielding pigskin, perchance with low cantle, and flaps devoid of stuffing or support! How, as the mind looks back through a halo of enthusiasm on the events of the day, do the difficulties and mischances of the chase wane, in proportion to the waning decanters, whilst its exploits and its triumphs stand out in bold and glorious relief! "Breathes there the man" that cannot at least go, "over the mahogany" —whose nerves are not braced (for the time) to that pitch at which ox-fences are a privilege and a delight, whilst wood and water, in the shape of stiles and brooks, as negotiated in countless succession by his "little bay horse," furnish themes for the pleader's eloquence and the poet's fire?

The after-dinner autobiography of an equestrian is usually a surprising display of self deception and infatuation. Then how general is the epidemic, attacking equally the old and the young, the bold and the timid; the "customer" who has all day "had the best of it," and who may to-morrow attempt perhaps a third of what he vows to-night, and the sceptical veteran, whom nothing but a continuous line of gates, and an unusually lucky turn, has enabled to scramble up in time to see the finish of to-day! "How well your grey horse carried you, Mr. Nogo!" says my next-door neighbour, whom I had remarked in the morning as the stoutest man I ever saw riding a cob: "you went like a bird, sir: *I was close to you the whole time!*" "What a beautiful turn the hounds made in the bottom, Topthorne, just before we came to the brook," says another, anxious to draw the attention of the company to the solitary exploit which he has persuaded himself he accomplished—" by-the-by, how did you get over? I thought it was a wide place, so I took old Golumpus hard by the head, and he did it beautifully in a fly." I remember no brook, but I suppose there must have been something of the kind, as I was in company with the last speaker from the moment we found, and I do not see why my grey horse should not obtain as much credit from *his* master as falls to the share of the unsuspecting Golumpus. So, taking courage from the chorus around me, I too begin to talk of the events of the day; and half unconsciously, half led on by the force of example, I fear I YARN most unmercifully as to the feats, past, present, and future, of which I boast myself capable.

The run of the morning, undoubtedly a good one, goes on increasing with every fresh version, till it swells into a performance totally unparalleled in ancient or modern history; and when my health, as a stranger, has been proposed by the most enthusiastic magnate present, the scarlet in whose visage vies with that of his gorgeous attire, the full-dress evening costume of the Pippingdon Hunt, I hesitate not, in my reply, to assure the Squire and his applauding guests that " I never saw such hounds, I never saw such horses, I never saw such a country, and never—no, never—in the whole course of my hunting experience, did I see such a run as that which we have enjoyed together on this eventful day —a run, sir, unequalled in the annals of the chase, and reflecting immortal honour on the toast I am about to take the liberty of proposing—Health and prosperity to my friend, if he will allow me to call him so, my friend John Topthorne, and the Pippingdon Hunt! With all the honours, gentlemen!" "Capital!" " Bravo !" ("Gammon!" *sotto voce*, from the Squire.) " Topthorne, your health ! no heel-taps ! More port! Hip, hip, hurrah!" And the enthusiasm of the Pippingdonians finds vent in a burst of shouting which startles the ladies in the drawing-room, and wakes an alarm in the very kennel, a good quarter of a mile from the house.

Are these the shouting bacchanalians, that glide so stealthily into the adjoining room, where the ladies are assembled over their tea and needlework, seasoned by that mysterious conversation which none of the male sex has ever yet been known to overhear? Is there an instance on record of the earliest arrival from the dining-room ever yet finding the graceful bevy otherwise than sunk in profound silence, and apparently each totally absorbed in her own tea, her own embroidery, or her own thoughts? Are such habits of speechless meditation natural to the sex, or at any time usual with that conversational race? I have been informed that the contrary is the case, and that the organs of female speech are seldom, if ever, still, but on occasions such as these. What can we conclude? That there are mysteries into which we must not seek to pry; that there are subjects on which we must be content to remain in ignorance; and that the freezing stillness which pervades the cheerful-looking apartment in which tea awaits us is but the reaction consequent upon a burst of simultaneous eloquence, roused by some subject on which the enchanting conclave are solemnly bound to maintain, in the presence of the hostile sex, an unbroken and Masonic silence.

Nevertheless, emboldened by port and encouraged by smiles, we break the formidable line. The seniors, who are conscious of having exceeded their usual moderation with the bottle, assume an additional air of gravity and decorum, to cover the unwonted joviality within, not always successfully, for a bland smile, with occasionally a stifled chuckle, attests the enlivening effects of Topthorne's cellar even on the most pompous of the veterans; whilst some of the younger members wax unusually confidential to their fair neighbours, and embark upon long stories, in which, to judge by the inquiring looks of the puzzled listener, the point seems continually to elude their mental grasp. Still, one and all appear to enjoy themselves.

Tea succeeds coffee, and music follows the departure of tea. There is shilling whist for those who like it; and the click of billiard-balls from the adjoining room announces that well-lighted apartment to have its share of occupants. A snug flirtation is going on at the pianoforte, between a bachelor squire—at this period of the evening sufficiently malleable—and a not very juvenile young lady, in a most Parisian *toilette*, and with her hair very nicely done. The softening squire leans over her music-book, but what he says is completely drowned to other ears by the swelling *refrain* of the " Marche des Croates," which, as I happen to admire the air, I know she has played at least five times over. Probably, like many other of those *tête-à-têtes*, which the world calls flirtations, if we could overhear their conversation, we should find it was quite as uninteresting as that of old Mrs. Shaftoe and her neighbour—a bland, pleasant-looking matron—on the sofa, who are deep in the merits of the former's youngest grandchild, and the defects, culinary and otherwise, of a certain kitchen-maid, who came to the latter from Castle Bowshot. Every one is occupied, and Mrs. Montague only is alone. I drop into a vacant chair by her side; and, whilst the Croatian March keeps grinding on at the pianoforte, and the old ladies at my elbow ring the changes upon measles, teething, hooping-cough, and board-wages, I spend another evening of delicious enjoyment, that sends me to bed once more, asking myself, as I wind up my watch, " How is this to end ? She certainly is a very nice woman; but what is to come of it ?"

* * * * *

It is proverbially "a long lane that has no turning;" and what with my own indecision how to act, my disinclination to take any step that might alter the extremely pleasant footing on which I found myself at the Lodge, and the rough Squire's hospitable disposition, gratified beyond measure by a long and unceremonious visit, I might have remained as a sort of tolerated hanger-on and family friend of my entertainers till we had all grown old together, without any question being asked as to my intentions, or any hint hazarded as to my departure. But as the stream, which, swollen to a torrent, bears away before it all opposition, tearing up the very rock from its earth-fast foundation, may yet, when rippling lazily down its summer bed, be turned from its course by the minutest pebble, so doth the human mind, albeit so invincible if inspired by a worthy object and directed to a noble aim, become, when uninfluenced by such higher considerations, the prey of the most trifling circumstance. "What great events from trivial causes spring!" and how little did I think that the accident of my meeting a good-looking, middle-aged lady at an archery-meeting, and afterwards joining her robust brother in the sports of the field, would exercise the influence which it eventually did upon the career and the comfort of the unconscious Tilbury Nogo! Certainly, I was overcome by a concatenation of circumstances: it was not *one* pebble that turned *me*, but a whole heap of them; and, after all we are willing to persuade ourselves that we are but tools in the hands of Fate—a doctrine which saves the undecided man a large proportion of trouble, and the unsuccessful one a good deal of self-reproach.

Well, I "took no note of time," as I stayed on at the Lodge. Three days in the week I devoted to the study of the chase with the "Pippingdon," and found myself becoming daily more conversant with woodcraft, more cunning in the art of smuggling over a country without the painful and perilous necessity of jumping large fences; the other three "lawful days," as they are called by our Calvinistic neighbours in the north, were consumed in various sporting pursuits, all connected with the destruction of game and vermin, all studied and effected by the Squire with the ardour of an enthusiast, and the skill of a professor.

Amongst other devices for wearing through the shortening hours of a November day, there is one much in request amongst those who particularly plume themselves on their keenness as sportsmen, or who absolutely require the stimulus of severe exercise to counteract the labour imposed on the digestive organs by their gigantic performances at dinner-time. This amusement, if such it can be called, is playfully termed "shooting wild partridges," whereas it has always appeared to me that the verb " hunting" would convey a far more correct idea of the mode in which these feathered " will-o'-the-wisps" are persecuted. To stagger all day long under a heavy double-barrelled gun, deafening in report, and wide in bore, so as to insure that extensive range the necessity of which is implied by the very words "November shooting"—to walk at that painful stretch of muscle and sinew, which would hail a jog-trot as an inexpressible relief—to be blown without getting warmth, and tired without achieving success—to enter an extensive stubble, bare as your own lately shaved chin, with the monosyllable "mark" upon your lips, and to leave its bleak and disappointing acres with undischarged weapon, and the same exclamation, now guttural from despair, still gurgling in your throat—to scramble through quickset hedges, and climb up and down precipitous banks, in hopes of getting a shot, and to be forced to console yourself for torn clothes and lacerated person by the suggestion " that they *must* be gone to them turnips," said turnips being two miles off as the crow flies, and in a contrary direction from home—to tie up your disgusted dogs, and resolve manfully upon walking up your game, which the vigilant coveys suffer you to do at a distance of several hundred yards—and finally, shaking from fatigue and sulky from disappointment, to miss the only fair shot you have had all day—"this may indeed be sport," as was once remarked by an observant philosopher, "but you can hardly call it pleasure." Nevertheless, experience makes even fools wise, and after a few such unsatisfactory days, a few such unsuccessful walks as those I have described, the Squire and I hit upon a method of circumventing these flighty denizens of the stubbles, that saved us both considerably in wind and limb, and that, if it did not fill the bag as rapidly as it should have done, was at least productive of a very liberal consumption of powder and shot.

Our plan was this: Despising, with one antiquated exception, the aid of the pointer-kennel, our first destination was the stable, from whence we selected a certain raking-looking four-year old, whose instruction as a hunter was about to commence; then, of course, we had to find "Ike," as nothing could ever be done on the demesne of Topthorne without the assistance of that original. A snaffle-bridle was put in the young one's mouth, "Ike" swung himself into the saddle, and we proceeded to business. Choosing a large and thick field of turnips at the back of a certain farm called Wild-wood, and directing all our operations to that green oasis as an eventual rallying-point, "Ike" was despatched to scour the surrounding stubbles, and as much as possible to drive the birds towards our selected turnips, when such a conversation as this would ensue between the huntsman-gamekeeper and his laconic employer:—

Squire: "Ike, beat that large oat-stubble."

Ike: "How be I to get there, zur? will'ee have un crawl over the dyke, or be I to deliver un *through* the stile?"

Squire: "Teach him the timber."

And without more ado, the undaunted "Ike" would gather his reins up in a bunch, ply his solitary spur—for on these occasions, under the idea, I presume, that he was only *half* equestrian, he never wore more than one—and despite of slippery ground, unbending ash, bad take-off, and very likely a determined refusal, would arrive at the other side *somehow*, in company with the four-year old; for even if they fell, they always seemed to get up together. Such was the tuition of the Squire's hunters; and in this manner he combined, as he said, instruction with amusement.

Whilst our domestic Centaur was pursuing his solitary steeple-chase, we would ensconce ourselves in some sheltering ravine, or under some concealing spinny, and occasionally get a delightful "rocketing" shot at an unwary covey that might fly over our lurking-place on its way to the distant turnips; and when at length the country had been sufficiently scoured, and the partridges driven to that treacherous covert, we used to enter the dripping "swedes," and prepare for action.

Here "Ike" was more than ever in his glory—one steady old pointer being set at liberty on these occasions, our ally conceived that the sport now partook of the nature of hunting, and his excitement was of course proportionate. When the old dog, looking cautiously around him, and lifting one paw after the other, as if the wet contact was most disagreeable to him (which I believe to have been the case), crouched gradually up to his game, and straightened his short stumpy tail, to all the inflexibility of an undoubted point, "Ike's" enthusiasm knew no bounds. Standing up in his stirrups, and waving his cap down to his horse's knees, he would exclaim, "Yooi! over Ponto! have at 'em there, good dog! yooi! rustle 'em up!" and then, suddenly recollecting himself, would take his words up sharp, with a stammering "I mean, toho! down charge! you brute, and be hanged to you!" After which, as we shot and bagged our game, he relapsed completely into the keeper. In this manner, if we had not a great deal of sport, we were sure of a certain share of amusement; and as the season wore on, and the birds got wilder and wilder, we more and more affected these laughable expeditions.

One blustering afternoon, as the Squire and I were concluding a more than usually successful day's sport, in the well-known vicinity of Wilton Cowslips, we descried a stalwart figure hastening towards us, over the adjoining field, which elicited from each of us the simultaneous exclamation of "The Benedict, by all that's wonderful!" and "Bagshot for a hundred!" and sure enough, as he drew near, 't was none other than our lately-married friend. The greeting was cordial—nay, boisterous; and congratulations, good wishes, questions and replies were bandied to and fro with heartfelt sincerity.

"You'll come into the vicarage, Squire, and be introduced to Mrs. Bagshot; you must stop at your old quarters, and renew your acquaintance with an old friend, my dear Nogo," said the hospitable parson; and in another five minutes we were all three walking arm-in-arm up the gravel walk that led to the rustic porch of that well-known dwelling, never before regarded with the painful interest with which to one of the party it was now invested. How my heart beat! how I envied the Squire his careless demeanour and robust unconsciousness! *She* was but Mrs. Bagshot to him—a new neighbour, and nothing more. What was she to me? another minute would show—there is but a satin-wood door between my agitated self and her who was once the hope of my heart, the mistress of my destiny. The door opens—the furniture of the apartment seems whirling round me, the floor and ceiling are heaving and swimming before my eyes, for my brain is reeling as I stand once again in the presence of Kate Cotherstone!

Not the least altered—not a shadow of difference between the Rev. Mrs. Bagshot, and the dangerous Kate of Ascot Heath and Windsor Forest: the black waving hair had lost none of its crispness; the malicious playful glance shot bright as ever from under those jetty eyelashes; the arch smile, curving her Grecian lip, and disclosing the pearly teeth within, went straight to my heart as in the days of old; the shapely figure had retained all its rounded graces, and the dress was, as usual, perfection. It was Kate herself; and when she came up to me, and put her hand within mine, uniting the cordial greeting due to an old friend, with the most perfect self-possession and *sang froid*, in a manner that none but a woman, and a very clever woman to boot, could have effected, I felt, I am ashamed to say, as much her slave as ever. Of course this was all nonsense: it needed but little reflection to remind me that she was now the bride of my old and valued friend; and even had this not been the case, after all that had taken place, it would have been quite impossible for us ever again to resume our former intimacy. Whilst the Squire was making the agreeable to his new and charming neighbour—for even he was fascinated by the enchantress, and in his uncouth efforts to please reminded me of a bear dancing on its hind legs—I had time to recollect myself, and to press upon Joe, as in duty bound, the usual congratulations which ignorant bachelors offer so warmly to the friend who has gallantly preceded them in the momentous plunge.

In our hurried conversation, I gathered from the delighted bridegroom that his journey to Bath had been the immediate cause of all I now saw before me. A short acquaintance, commencing at a ball, and cemented by one or two tea-drinkings, had convinced him that life without Miss Cotherstone would be a blank indeed—*that* was the piece of furniture, without which the Parsonage was incomplete—*that* was the smile to which it would be so heavenly to return, after clerical duties, or fatiguing field-sports; and, in short, "Joe," for the first time in his life, was completely captivated. As usual, the difference of disposition and character between the two riveted the chain only more firmly. My friend, with his fine manly open heart, his ignorance of guile and deceit—which amounted almost to the simplicity of a child—his trustful nature and unsophisticated candour, was safe to marry a thorough-going woman of the world.

Could I blame him? could I, of all people, be astonished at his infatuation? Ere long he made his proposals to Kate in due form—papa and mamma were abroad; but it took little time to obtain their cordial consent (nor did this surprise me), and the female relative with whom the fair "fiancée" was staying lost no opportunity of impressing upon her admirer that he was indeed a fortunate man.

Joe's aunt behaved like a trump, as he said himself,—like the Queen of Trumps: and she, too, was so fascinated by the little witch, that in addition to the handsome present, standing in her venerable name in the Three per Cent. Consols, with which she complimented her nephew on the morning of his nuptials, she likewise presented his bride with a valuable set of diamonds—none of your paste, but real genuine sparklers, that had remained safely locked up in the custody of the old lady's bankers for the last fifty years.

"We have now been married a fortnight," added Joe, his face beaming with delight, and looking a proper man to win the fancy of any young lady; "and we have not a secret in the world from each other" (Good gracious! I thought, I wonder whether she has told him all about me). "If you wish for happiness, my dear Nogo, follow my example; I never knew what it was really to enjoy life till I found Mrs. Bagshot sitting down to breakfast on the opposite side of the table every day, as a matter of course."

The Squire was by this time making a courteous farewell to the cousin who was to him almost a stranger, and it was now my turn to wish the new Mrs. Bagshot good-bye. Again that cordial shake of the hand, again that half-careless, half-meaning glance, that seemed to say, "let by-gones be by-gones"—it was evident that she thought the less said about our previous acquaintance the better; but I had a right to expect some little embarrassment, some slight half-indicated expression of interest in one for whom she had formerly confessed she entertained a decided regard; but no, it was—"Good-bye, Mr. Nogo; I trust you will complete your visit here before you leave the country, and not suffer me to frighten you away from your old bachelor quarters," and she smiled in my face as if I had been her grandfather.

"They are an inexplicable race," thought I to myself, as I followed the delighted Squire to the garden-gate; "and this is a chapter in their history that I may puzzle over in vain: the old mythologist was right when he made the Sphinx a lady!"

Reader, have you ever experienced the luxury of being an ill-used man? If you have not, depend upon it you are ignorant of one of the most engrossing sensations known to the human organization. A man without a grievance is like a kettle half-filled, or rather a kettle merely filled with cold water; but let him only consider himself unfairly treated, let him brood and hatch his grievance till it prevades his system, and straightway he frets, and seethes, and simmers, till at last he boils over in a perfect ecstacy of self-condolence.

As I walked silently alongside the Squire, on our homeward journey, I felt ill-used; I knew not why— I felt dissatisfied with all the characters of the drama in which I had lately taken part, and, above all, with myself. My companion was neither loquacious himself, nor tolerant of loquacity in others, so I had no one to whom I could unbosom myself; and as I kept chafing over Kate's indifference, which piqued me to the core, and at the same time despising my own folly for caring two straws about it—as what could it signify to me?—I gradually worked my feelings up to that state in which a man finds he is ready for any action, no matter how foolish, that takes him from *himself*. In such a mood the sympathy of a female friend is likely to prove dangerous in the extreme, and to such peril was it my fate unwittingly to expose myself.

As we entered the shrubberies that surrounded Topthorne Lodge, I caught sight of a light-coloured dress fluttering in the breeze before us, which could only belong to the widow, and declining the Squire's invitation to "kennel" with more decision than I could usually find courage for, I pushed on to overtake and walk home with Mrs. Montague, partly in the hope of unburdening my mind by a detail of our afternoon visit, partly with a lurking feeling of triumphant vanity in the thought that here at least I could command an interest in one sympathizing breast—that in those blue eyes I should read no malicious sarcasm, no cold forgetfulness.

It had been dusk an hour ere the dressing-bell summoned us into the house. Backwards and forwards, to and fro, up and down those winding walks and well kept shrubberies, had we walked and talked, and hinted and hesitated, and lingered, often trenching upon the topic which I believe was nearest both our hearts, and yet the fatal words were unspoken. Grateful to my wounded vanity was the healing salve of Mrs. Montague's implied admiration—triumphant reflection to think that it was in my own power to show

Mrs. Bagshot that *she* was not the only person who could forget: and besides such considerations, the widow's smiles, to do her justice, were sufficiently intoxicating in themselves to make a wiser man than me forget prudence, foresight, and everything but the companion by his side. Yet when I went to dress for dinner I was still a free man—the last meshes of the net were unwoven—the spell was incomplete—I had not passed the Rubicon, but by Jove I had been uncommonly close to its brink.

CHAPTER XXIII.

Lo you, here she comes!—this is her
Very guise—and upon my life fast asleep.
Observe her; stand close.
Macbeth.

In slumber, I prithee how is it
That souls are oft taking the air,
And paying each other a visit,
While bodies are—Heaven knows where?
Moore.

I HAVE already said, that pleasant as were the days which passed on so smoothly at Topthorne Lodge, the hours of darkness were those in the diurnal twenty-four which were spent least to the satisfaction of my somewhat nervous temperament. Not only did the supernatural horrors of "the Lily of the Lea" haunt my nightly dreams, but the more substantial terrors of midnight assassins, and burglarious entries into peaceful dwelling-houses, as vividly painted in the daily columns of the morning journals, kept me awake for many an uncomfortable hour, in a most unenviable state of morbid apprehension.

"The Forest" was a thinly populated district, and proportionably ill supplied with rural police. Poaching on a grand scale had from time immemorial been the characteristic crime of the country; but of late a series of burglaries, not always unaccompanied by violence, had been effected upon lone farm-houses and detached mansions. The larder at Castle Bowshot had been stripped of its savoury contents; Farmer Veal had lost a dozen of currant wine and a side of bacon, ingeniously abstracted by removing a lattice from the cheese-room; whilst old Mrs. Swanshot, on looking under her bed, as had been, during a long and well-spent life, her nightly custom, had found the usual prospect afforded by that dusky locality varied by the lurking figure of a stealthy marauder, certainly a thief—possibly an assassin—coiled up, as the old lady herself said, evidently for no good purpose. With a courage and coolness that proved indisputably the truth of the well-known French military maxim, " *C'est le cœur qui fait le grenadier*," this resolute old woman pulled her unwelcome visitor out by the heels, and as she dragged him from his ambush, greeted him with the following pithy salutation:—

" Now I've got you, I shall not let you go—you're the man I've been looking for for forty years, and here you are at last!"

All these events were decidedly of an uncomfortable tendency; and I'm not sure which of the two catastrophes I regarded with the greatest horror—a visit from the "Spectre-Lily," whom I had now heard so often passing my door, that I believed as firmly in her existence as in my own identity, or a personal collision with some bodily desperado; my only attacking weapon a short brass poker, my only defensive armour a thin cotton shirt.

After such a day of agitation as that which beheld my first interview with Kate in her new capacity, and my long and confidential walk with Mrs. Montague Forbes, it is no wonder that the broken slumbers which visited my pillow were short and unrefreshing to my excited system. Disturbed and pantomimic dreams, in which confused and changing scenes and figures crowded themselves inexplicably on my brain, were succeeded by an attack of obstinate wakefulness, that no change of position, no amount of tossing and turning, could overcome or modify. It was a mild winter's night, such a night as precedes "a fine hunting morning," and the soft south-west wind sighed mournfully round the house, as it drove the heavy vapour-laden clouds gently athwart the struggling moonbeams; now partially veiling, now totally obscuring her light. It was a night for an adventure of love or war, but no night to be lying wide awake on a restless bed. That cursed clock—how it ticks! I shall ask Topthorne to stop it—I know his sister will, if I only mention it. Ah! I might do worse than come to an understanding at once with her; and that little jilt Kate—how it would pique her! and serve her right. Well, it is no use, but I suppose I must try to get to sleep again.

Such were the dispirited thoughts that half rose in broken murmurs to my lips, when—horror! curdling my blood and freezing my marrow—came the well-known stealthy step along the passage, that too surely heralded the unearthly approach of "The Lily." A cold perspiration broke out on my forehead, my damp hair stood on end, and my sense of hearing became sharpened to a degree painfully acute. What is this? a low continuous grating sound, as if it were outside the house, below my window, and I could almost fancy I caught the tones of a smothered whisper. For a period that to me seems an age, but in all probability is a short five minutes, I sit up in bed, and strain every nerve into the one office of listening. Hark! a slight crash, a low tinkling sound as of broken glass—horror upon horror! the window must surely have been forced; and there are thieves at this moment entering the house! All the ghosts in Acheron are a joke to this ghastly reality: the awful scene I have so often contemplated in fancy has arrived at last; and what am I to do?—lie trembling here whilst the house is robbed and its inmates murdered, to be discovered and have my throat cut after all? or make a dash for the Squire's bed-room, and perhaps in those dark passages come into personal collision with the armed ruffians, who are even now parading the ground floor? Stay here I cannot—no; sum-

moning all my feelings of honour, all my sense of shame to
my assistance, I resolve to rush incontinently to the Squire,
devote my person to the defence of his hearth, and die like a
man in the breach.

Alas that it should be out of my power to meet my fate in
the plural of that warlike substantive!—my continuations
have been taken down to be brushed, and with naked limbs
and unslippered feet I speed along the cold passage on my
way to my landlord's dormitory. As I pass an unshuttered
window, that looks out to the front of the house, a sort of
morbid fascination impels me to stop my frantic career and
gaze upon the invading force. To my surprise and confusion
I behold two men speeding away over the lawn in the moonlight, apparently in agonies of terror; and I can distinctly
hear their wild thrilling cries of "The Ghost!" "The
Ghost!" as they disappear over the Ha-ha, which divides the
smooth and shaven turf from the wild glades of the undulating park. By this time the house is alarmed—doors bang
in all directions—a confusion of voices pervades the night
air, in which the shrill organ of female inquiry is predominant; and the Squire, clad in a rusty dressing-gown, and
armed with an iron-headed hunting-whip—in his opinion,
for the Squire is a resolute fellow, a weapon efficient enough
to disperse an army of housebreakers—comes stalking down
the passage, and announces to his terrified domestics that
there is no danger: an attempt has been made to enter the
house, but the villains have been scared, as he concludes, by
a fancied discovery, and we may all go to bed again. With
hospitable commiseration for my scanty garments and shivering condition, my anxious host hurries me, with many thanks
for my intended assistance, back to my own dormitory, and
as he entreats me to seek my couch as quickly as possible, he
enters the room at my side; the shutters are unclosed, and
the moonbeams streaming in, almost with the light of day:
I start back in re-awakened horror, with an exclamation of
" The Lily of the Lea" frozen upon my lips, for a white
figure stands as if rooted to the floor, in the centre of the

apartment, and surveys us with a fixed, stony, and unearthly gaze. Ere the Squire's furious execration of "Nelly! by all that's——" has thundered in mine ears, the truth flashes upon me in overwhelming confusion; for the white figure staggers backward as we approach; the eyes suddenly kindling into light, roll upon us with dilated horror, and as she sinks into an arm-chair, Mrs. Montague Forbes (for Mrs. Montague Forbes it is) bursts into a paroxysm of weeping, and covers her face with both hands in an irrepressible agony of shame.

* * * * *

Here was a pretty kettle of fish! as is said to have been observed by the celebrated wizard Michael Scott, when, after a successful day on Tweed side, he was startled to find the contents of his panniers turned into grotesque imps, and miniature salamanders, by one of those mocking fiends that were ever at the magician's elbow. I had now succeeded in wedging myself into as uncomfortable a fix as ever yet curtailed the freedom of a harmless bachelor! On all sides I was surrounded by difficulties and dilemmas; there was but one way out of it, and that might be described in vulgar Saxon as "out of the frying-pan into the fire." How was I to face the Squire at breakfast? and how was poor Mrs. Montague Forbes to face me? Of course her brother would be furious and vindictive, deaf to reason, and bent on avenging the insult which he naturally concluded I had offered to his household gods and genealogical tree. Of course he would scout the idea of his sister's being an incurable sleep-walker; and remain incredulous to the fact of her feeling infinitely more horrified than himself at the ambiguous predicament in which this involuntary affliction—for an affliction it is—had placed her. Of course I should be taxed with all the breaches of trust and ungrateful returns for confiding hospitality that had stained the code of honour since that very improper flirtation which eventually led to the siege of Troy. Of course there was but one appeal, and that must be answered at a short twelve yards, before breakfast, and face to face with what Irish gentlemen call "a peacemaker" at full cock. The way my hand shook, as I contemplated this possibility whilst shaving, was not calculated to inspire me with confidence as to the result of such an "ordeal by battle." Then, even if these desperate measures should not be resorted to, was there not a civil power that might be brought to bear on my unlucky head? I had heard of many cases of what Mr. Weller calls "conviction for breach" successfully adjudicated *against* the defendant, with far less grounds for an eloquent barrister to go upon than those which might be skilfully adapted to the comprehension of an intelligent jury, as sufficient reason for mulcting my personal property to a large amount, much to the satisfaction of the distressed victim and the pecuniary benefit of the gentlemen of the long robe. No, I could not bear to be brought before the public in such a manner as this. Some men do not care three straws about notoriety, in fact they rather like it, however questionable may be the means by which it is acquired; but to a shy and sensitive man like myself, the very heading of that unblushing newspaper report, "Forbes *versus* Nogo—Breach of promise of marriage," would be enough to drive the patient out of his senses. Such a method of revenge would be nearly as effective as the more probable retaliation I had to dread from a personal encounter with the pugnacious Squire. And then, had I no softening feelings for the agitation and distress which the events of the past night would cause to poor Mrs. Montague? Should I be deaf to her entreaties, and callous to her tears, if it should come to an interview, which was not impossible? Was it not an extremely hard case upon her, that her own character should be sullied, and the peace of her family destroyed, by the pardonable trespass of an unconscious somnambulist? For I saw at a glance how it had all happened; there could be no doubt whatever of the facts of the case. It was evident that the restless widow was an habitual sleep-walker; like Lady Macbeth, it was her custom nightly to patrol the dark staircases and moon-lit passages of Topthorne Lodge; and doubtless the time-honoured tradition of the "Lily of the

Lea" had prevented the scared servants from either ascertaining the identity of the apparition, or making their peripatetic mistress aware of her inconvenient habit. This would at once account for the stealthy footsteps and alarming sounds that had broken my rest for so many weeks; and the only extraordinary circumstance was, that the catastrophe had not occurred sooner. On the night in question, an attempt had clearly been made to break into the Lodge by some daring ruffians in the neighbourhood. I had been alarmed by the clumsy manner in which they took out the necessary pane, and the fall of the glass on a sort of skirting of pebbles which surrounded the house. It is probable that the somnambulist had looked out of one of the passage windows, all of which were unshuttered, and that the startled burglars, much to their horror, found themselves all at once face to face with a white spectral-looking figure, in the unearthly moonlight. The tradition of "The Lily" was known far and wide over the district, and the country people one and all firmly believed that Topthorne Lodge "was a haunted house." No wonder the rascals were frightened; and this accounted for the tumultuous flight of which I was a witness from that very window. In the mean time, however, the supposed ghost must have passed my chamber, in its nightly course; when I rushed out to alarm the Squire, I naturally left my door ajar, and the sleepwalker on her return, with the instinct peculiar to that malady, as naturally wandered into the unsecured apartment. Our sudden entrance awoke her roughly, which I have been told is even dangerous for a person in that state; but when the consciousness of her position, and first feeling of her sex, the unfitness of her costume, burst upon her, no wonder the shame-stricken lady was ready to sink into the earth. But would the Squire believe all this? Here was a question to which, often and often as I turned it over in my own mind, I could give no satisfactory answer. Yet was there one way, and that a mode of proceeding to which I was not half disinclined, that would soothe the feelings of his sister, propitiate the unruly Squire, and gratify the vanity, though it might add to the responsibilities, of the agitated individual who was now revolving all these knotty points in his mind as he proceeded with an irregular and protracted toilette. Why should I not marry the widow? She is handsome (she looked uncommonly well in white, even amidst all the distresses and peculiarities of her position last night), she is sensible, she is good-tempered, and, above all, she is partial to me. Ah, that little egotistical monosyllable; half the attachments that are formed are based upon the supposed good taste and discrimination of the other party, in his or her fancied preference for ourselves. Then this is no crude idea that has now for the first time arisen in my mind : I have been long revolving, though half insensibly, the possibility of such a conclusion to our rapidly progressing acquaintance. I suppose I must marry some day, and why not now? I wonder what Jack Raffleton will think, and what Segundo will say! And then Kate, now Mrs. Bagshot, what a disappointment to her, to know that I have been meditating this long before she contrived to capture poor Joe! The last reflection was a clincher! but with it came a whole host of misgivings as to the irrevocable step which I was considering; visions of bachelor amusements, Greenwich dinners, midnight cards, "the morning slumber, and the evening wine"—all these to be given up and repudiated at once and for ever; then the long winter evenings, when a *tête-à-tête* with Mrs. Montague might have become a very sober, not to say sad enjoyment; the domestic details, the bores of housekeeping, the annoyances of servants—all these visions of the future floated through my brain, and sorely marred my resolution as to the exploit I was meditating; balanced, however, on the other hand, by many and favourable considerations. What dreadful tortures does he impose upon himself, who is incapable of making up his mind! Better be the most wrong-headed blunderer that ever rushed blindfold into a difficulty, than that victim of every apprehension, that contemptible slave to every circumstance—an undecided man!

Need I say how it was to end? We breakfasted that very morning a united family party. The Squire, whatever may have been *his* intentions had I not declared *mine*, was less gruff than usual, and seemed, to do him justice, really pleased with the arrangement by which we were to become relations. Mrs. Montague, with a shaking hand, a fixed red spot on each cheek, and a glance of quiet triumph in her blue eye, whenever the long-fringed lid was for an instant raised, looked to perfection the pleased yet agitated bride-elect (recollect, it was her second appearance in that character); whilst I felt, as I suppose every other man does who is going to be married, conscious that I ought to be very happy, and that I was very much surprised, half delighted, and half frightened at the magnitude of the undertaking on which I had embarked, and the whole extent of which now dawned upon me for the first time, and firmly resolved that, as there was no retreat, the only thing was, to put a bold face upon the matter, and fight it out like a man.

* * * * * *

I pass over the intermediate time required to arrange lawyer's matters, disagree about "settlements," and—most important item of all—procure the *trousseau* of the bride; nor can I explain upon what principle it is that a lady, as soon as she has made up her generous mind to confer perfect happiness upon one of the baser sex, should instantly discover that the whole of her previous costume is totally unfit for wear, and that it is absolutely indispensable to procure a new "rig-out" from top to toe. Why those garments, the fascinations of which have materially assisted in gaining the victory, should be discarded as unworthy of participating in the triumph, I am at a loss to explain; but that such is the fact, I appeal to Swan and Edgar, Redmayne's, and Harding's—mammas who shop, and papas who pay. Equally inexplicable, unless we refer it to their partiality for "new clothes," is the extraordinary interest shown by one and all of the fair sex in the approaching nuptials of any individual of their number: no matter whether she is an intimate friend, an avowed enemy, or a total stranger ; the fact alone of her having made arrangements to lead one of the opposite party to the altar entitles her at once to the support and sympathy of the whole sex. Stout elderly women, of between fifty and sixty years of age, may be seen any morning in the vicinity of St. George's canvassing eagerly for places from whence to view the nuptials of any fashionable couple who may choose to be united in that aristocratic temple of Hymen. They will walk miles on foot, miss their dinners, and shed tears by the pailful, in the unaccountable interest they seem to take in the ceremony ; and yet, were you to give yourself the trouble of inquiring, I will venture to say you will find that not one in ten of these agitated spectators had ever either seen or heard of bride or bridegroom before.

It is not my intention to dwell upon the happy days preceding the final catastrophe about to be presided over by my old ally, Joe Bagshot. The congratulations of friends, more particularly those of the lady, the hints and inuendoes as to my good fortune in securing "such a treasure," the assurances that "I was indeed a lucky fellow," carried to an extent that, as the day drew near for my reaping the advantages of such favourable stars, made me feel painfully conscious of my own unworthiness of the blessings in store for me. The introduction of my *fiancée* to my own "collaterals," who I was quite sure would find fault with my choice, and the being "trotted out" for inspection and presentation to hers, who I was equally convinced would find fault with me ; the visits that had to be paid, and the letters that must be written ; the choosing of plate, tea-cups, mahogany bedsteads, coal-scuttles and domestic servants (in all of which the previous experience of the future Mrs. N. was really invaluable, and probably averted from me the fate of finishing my days in a lunatic asylum); the obtaining a commodious carriage, capable of conveying a large quantity of luggage (my great delight used to be, travelling with nothing but a carpet bag); and the fixing on a suitable residence, of course in the vicinity of my future lady's friends and acquaintances—all these necessary operations and arrangements would fill a folio to describe, as they would destroy the equanimity of a Socrates to undergo. Willingly do I pass from such harassing details to the *tête-à-tête* walks with Mrs. Montague, which it now became a rigorous matter of duty to perform, and which, truth to tell, were pleasant enough as we sauntered socially along, and made our plans for our future *ménage*.

I had for some time been wondering in my own mind what "Kate"—for by that name I still thought of my old flame—would say to the step which I had taken, and in what manner she would couch her congratulations the first time we should meet; nor were my conjectures destined to remain long unsolved. An early visit from the parsonage to the Lodge was forestalled by our meeting the clerical couple, in one of our ante-nuptial strolls, half-way between the two houses; and by this chance *rencontre* we avoided much of the stiffness and formality which, even among friends, is inseparable from a morning call of ceremonious congratulation. Mrs. Bagshot was looking her best, as I could not help remarking, although in duty bound to have eyes but for one; and as she took her cousin by both hands, and kissed her with that affectionate *empressement* which ladies are so fond of wasting upon each other, it would have required a close observer to detect the actual dislike which lurked under all this affected cordiality. I am not generally gifted with an eye that penetrates below the surface; but upon this occasion—perhaps because my senses were sharpened by the severity of the training I was undergoing—I could distinctly perceive that between the two ladies there was, to use a common expression, but "little love lost." How diffrent from the frank warmth of honest Joe's sincere congratulations! But when Kate turned her mischievous eyes upon me, and wished me joy with the frankness of an old friend, and that comic look of arch wickedness which was her principal fascination, and of which, in days gone by,

I had too keenly felt the power, I could not help thinking that, with all her inferiority in sense, conduct, and character, to the lady who was about to honour me with her hand, there never was in this world anything half so charming as Kate Cotherstone, now Mrs. Bagshot. "We always considered Mr. Nogo an irreclaimable old bachelor," the little vixen had the unblushing effrontery to say in my very face; "but the fascinations of the west, Mrs. Montague, have been too much for him. When is it *to be*, my dear? I should so like to see the *trousseau*—I hear it is perfectly magnificent." And the two ladies, having got upon that prolific subject, walked towards the Lodge, amidst a torrent of conversation turning upon the deceptive art of dressmaking, and seasoned with a little amicable sparring, and a few of those retorts with which, at periods of unusual excitement, the gentle beings love to season their discourse. Joe and I followed in their wake, soberly enough. I thought my old friend looked more subdued than usual; but as he had only been married about a month, of course his chains must have sat lightly, and it could not have been his new character that worried him. He did, however, hint to me, in the course of our conversation, that the old brown horse, so much admired in the field as between the shafts, was about to be sold; and that he was thinking of getting his duty done for a few months, and giving Kate *a little gaiety at Bath*. Oh, my prophetic soul! could I not foresee the gloomy future of my own destiny in the clouds which darkened the brow of my once so cheerful friend?

"It won't take long, sir; but somehow, I wish it was well over," remarked "The Muff of the Minories" to my unworthy self, on the morning of his eventful contest with the well-known "Brummagem Bouncer," for the particulars of which, couched in the flowery language of the "fancy," I must refer my readers to the columns of that eloquent periodical, *Bell's Life in London;* and, without for an instant presuming to compare the ceremony illumined by the sacred torch of Hymen with those antagonistic matches which, we learn from the authority of the classics, are presided over by Pollux, I am bound to confess that my waking feeling, on the eventful morning which ushered in my wedding-day, was very much akin to that of my former instructor in the science of self-defence. My head was in a whirl of confusion, consequent upon the number and variety of my necessary arrangements; my eyes were dazzled with the gorgeous and exceedingly unbecoming raiment in which, as is the custom of my country, I was about to face the ordeal; my ears were deafened with the continuous peal which clanged out from the church steeple of the adjoining village, *pour encourager les autres;* and the only clear impression on my bewildered brain was, a fervent wish that it was this time to morrow, or next week, or next year! To other and less-interested actors in the scene I must resign the task of describing the different details of the important ceremony —the merriment of friends; the gravity, not to say sadness, of the principal performers; the business-like air of the clergyman; the concealed commiseration of the beadle; and the sarcastic applause of the clerk. Flowers, I am told, were scattered in our path to and from the simple village church, ale flowed in hogsheads, and there was bride-cake enough to make all the school-children sick; but of these facts I did not become conscious till long afterwards. The Squire gave away his sister, Bagshot performed the service, the fatal words were spoken; and as I began to have a dim consciousness that Mrs. Montague Forbes had now become Mrs. Nogo, part and parcel of myself, I felt a horrid uncertainty as to the identity of the former owner of that patronymic—a ghastly doubt as to whether this was indeed still the same individual whom, for more years than it is necessary to specify, I had considered as my best and most indulgent friend.

CHAPTER XXIV.

Davy. Marry sir, thus—those precepts cannot bo served : and again, sir, shall we sow the headland with wheat?
Shallow. With red wheat, Davy.
Davy. Now, sir, a new link to the bucket must needs be had.—And, sir, do you mean to stop any of William's wages about the sack he lost the other day at Hinkley fair?

King Henry IV.

GLOWING hath ever been the poet's description of the simplicity of rustic life; and much hath plain English been swollen into stanzas, and distorted into rhyme, for the purpose of enlarging on the fable of the " town and country mouse." But paradoxical as it may appear, I am inclined to believe that those, who in theory are most enthusiastic in their admiration of a country life, are the very men, Londoners by destiny, and cockneys in grain, for whom the charms of such a vegetable existence are chiefly enhanced by the impossibility of their following out their Arcadian ideal, and with whom, as with the rest of us, in this discontented world, desire springs most intensely from separation. That poetical wag and polished satirist, who delighted the rank and fashion of ancient Rome with his life-like descriptions, as with his dancing numbers, and bequeathed the name of Horace to our later age, as a type of all that is amusing and agreeable to the man, albeit somewhat unpopular with the schoolboy, modestly expresses the summit of his dearest wishes to be a small farm, a few rods of wood, and a clear and rippling stream; while the very vividness with which, in a few lines, he places before us the sunny slope, the shady grove, and the refreshing waters, proves that in his yearning after the clear atmosphere, and the balmy breeze of the country, he was at heart essentially a cockney. But had the bard been destined to sit down for life under his arbutus trees, removed from the charms of his Augustan *coterie*, as from "the smoke, the riches, and the noise of Rome;" had he been compelled to earn an appetite for his garlic pottage, by the daily superintendence of his Sabine clodpoles, cleaving his Sabine clods; had his conversation with his neighbours been limited to the price of wheat, and his computation of time been reckoned by the yearly epochs of hay-making and harvest, we may fairly conclude that the sociable minstrel would have found such an existence a very poor exchange for the life, the fun, and the luxurious repasts of the capital, and would have left us many a terse and classical interpretation of that too well-known substantive which the French call *ennui*, and the English bore.

Well, I too have pined for a country life; I have got up on a fine morning, in London, when the sun, for want of anything better, was wasting his gilding on the chimney-pots; and I have longed for the smiling pastures, the breezy uplands, and the hill and dale of the open country—have thought that the summit of earthly happiness was to walk round the farm before breakfast, the *acmè* of human comfort to make your own butter and eat your own mutton; but it is a dangerous experiment for any man, whose youth has been passed in a metropolitan sphere of life, using the expression in its widest sense, and thereby including all the pleasures and amusements of Windsor, Ascot, Epsom, Melton—ay, even the Highlands of Scotland, which are enjoyed by London people, in a London manner—I say it is a dangerous experiment for a man educated in such a school to sit down for life in some quiet nook of a rural parish, and to suppose that because he has sometimes been bored with London, he is for that reason fitted to live entirely in the country. I have always fancied that to fill the situation effectively a man should have been bred a farmer; and although we see many noblemen and gentlemen, when they have done with the more stirring avocations of the court, the camp, and the senate, assuming the yellow gaiters and out-of-door habits of agricultural prosperity, I have never been given to understand that their cultivation of the soil is based upon a method either so convenient or so profitable as that of the honest yeoman, " whose farm on his honour's estate is the same that his grandfather tilled ;" or that, much as they may study its nature, and argue upon its minutiæ, they ever attain that success in the profession of our first parents, which they have achieved in the busier avocations of their early life. For my own part, sparingly as fortune has ever smiled upon my endeavours, I think my farming has been the worst speculation of all; nor can I be convinced that I was in my right senses when, having determined to settle permanently in the west, and as near as possible to Topthorne Lodge, I bought the small estate and commodious farm-house of Wild-wood, formerly the property of my friend Segundo, for which I paid fully one-third more than its marketable value, and on three hundred acres of which I determined, at my own risk, to put in practice my own ideas as to the tillage of the soil.

Behold me then settled in life ; married to the handsome widow, and, truth to say, somewhat proud of the feat ; inhabiting a comfortable though small and detached house, furnished by my wife's tact in a luxurious manner, and what people call comparatively at small expense, qualified as a magistrate, respected as a landowner, and, in short, learning to be a country gentleman, And now to begin a series of troubles and annoyances which, innocuously as they fall on the heads of some callous individuals, are to an indolent and sensitive man like barbed darts and venomed arrows. Morning, noon, and night, there was no leisure and no repose. Time hung heavily on my hands ; yet I had never an hour to myself. An out-of-door life was what I wanted to accomplish by my new pursuit ; yet every one connected with the farm would come and talk to me in my own sitting-room, " larding " the neat carpet with mud of every description of fertility. If I wished to shoot, my beat had to be regulated, not by the wildness of the birds and the lay of the ground, but by the necessity of diverging into this " close" to see if the fence had been mended, or splashing through that meadow to ascertain if the drains were running properly. Domestic details were bad enough; but the carelessness of the butcher, or the stupidity of the grocer, were as nothing compared to that which was done which should have been left undone, and never commenced which should have been completed, at that infernal farm.

Probably a diary of one of the many weary days at Wildwood will give my sympathising reader a better idea of rural felicity than all the lamentations which I could pour forth upon this plaintive theme. Imagine, in the first place, a pretty little house in a most picturesque situation, the building itself combining the attractiveness of a cottage with the conveniences of a mansion; imagine it fancifully furnished and thoroughly warmed, with good stabling and out-houses attached, and plenty of room for servants—that *sine quâ non* without which peace is not. Imagine a surrounding country, beautiful in all the undulating richness peculiar to the west; a manor fairly stocked with game, and a neighbourhood in which good dinners were plentiful as blackberries, and old port common as ditch-water; and conceive all these agreeable sundries being spoiled and alloyed by the proximity of that confounded three hundred acres of arable land.

But to return to the diary. Seven o'clock brings a summons to arise; and although an early hour for a bridegroom, it must be attended to, because "Jacob," my bailiff and factotum, has appointed to see me "fust thing i' th' marning," about giving the men their orders with regard to cutting an unnecessary drain to an unheard-of depth. I yawn my way to my dressing-room, where there is no fire, for the new housemaid is not an early riser, and "master" is too green at the trade to have yet become much of a disciplinarian. Lukewarm water produces a rugged shave, and enduing myself in dread-nought attire, I accompany "Jacob" through a drizzling rain to the "thirty acres," there to find two of the men cannot come because to-day happens to be "Weatherley revel," and for all the good I have done by my exertions

I might just as well have remained in bed. A second toilette fits me for breakfast, and I look forward to a comfortable and domestic meal, the novelty of having my tea made by Mrs. Nogo (I cannot quite bring myself to call her "Nelly") not having yet worn off. The widow, however, has had experience in the ways of the world, and one of the lessons which it has inculcated is never to hurry herself—above all in such an important ceremony as the toilette; so I am reduced to the painful alternative of beginning breakfast without her (in which case I shall appear churlish, and have my tea badly made), or of sitting down to the-day-before-yesterday's paper, already conned through, and last night fallen asleep over, to wait in patience for the arrival of my better half. Down she comes at length, very nicely dressed, but not feeling "very well," which I have already learned means being slightly out of sorts, and is a bad beginning for the day.

"My dear, I wish you would speak to James about that teapot; it is disgracefully cleaned, and nothing spoils servants so much as passing over these things."

James is the new footman, a six-foot magnifico, and I should just as soon think of reprimanding Julius Cæsar; but I dare say Mrs. N. will do it for me, and twice as effectually.

"You'll drive me to the Lodge, Til., after luncheon," adds my wife, in an accent I never quite like to disobey; and although I had meant to get a quiet afternoon's shooting, I express a ready compliance, and breakfast progresses comfortably; I am just going to have a second cup of tea when enter stately James, as though he were announcing a Duke, to say that "Farmer Veal" is waiting to see me in the study, as servants always persist in calling the apartment where "master" keeps his guns, &c.; and as the gentle Mrs. N. signifies "I had better speak to him at once and have done with it," I forego my other cup and hasten to an interview with the yeoman, having for its object the purchase of a certain quantity of what are termed "store-pigs." It is by this time getting towards noon, the hour at which I was once accustomed to enjoy the double luxury of a book and a cigar; but these "littering habits," as Mrs. N. calls them, I have now entirely abandoned for ever, and contenting myself with the unsatisfactory substitute of a tooth-pick, I accompany " Jacob " to the yard to inspect a new arrival in the shape of a famous short-horned bull, whom I have purchased at the price of a hunter, but whom I dare not approach with any of the familiarity with which I should handle the latter animal. "Jacob" thinks I paid too much money for him, in which opinion I cordially coincide, and the morning passes off in a series of fault-findings with inefficient bricklayers and dull labourers, who only seem to comprehend how much more profitable it is to work by "the day" than by "the foot." Luncheon, in which I detect more of yesterday's dinner than I could easily believe to have survived, is interrupted by the collector of rates and taxes (imposts which I fancy my predecessor Segundo never dreamed of paying), and that functionary seems disposed to visit upon the successor all the deficiencies incurred by the previous owner.

"Have you ordered the pony-carriage, Til.?" says Mrs. N.; and my multifarious occupations having prevented the morning visit to the stable, which I had always looked forward to as so principal a charm of a regular life, I am forced to confess that I have neglected to do so, and to swallow as best I may the involuntary exclamation of "Dear, how stupid!" which escapes from the lips that have so lately vowed "to love, honour, and obey." The filth of the straw-yard has made it necessary to adjourn once more to the dressing-room, before I am fit to enter a carriage of any description; and this time, with a pardonable anxiety to appear to advantage in the eyes of my late wedded wife, I get myself up with more than common care and smartness. Alas! the new Southdowns, placed in a secluded meadow at the back of the house, have one and all broke from their moorings in a state of timid insubordination ludicrous to contemplate; and I cannot resist lending my assistance to "Jacob" and his myrmidons, in reclaiming the woolly truants to their original bounds. Varnished boots harmonize but ill with a clay soil, and I am greeted "as a very untidy figure," when I at length take my seat in the pony-chaise *en route* for Topthorne Lodge. The Squire is not at home, having gone to shoot the outlying coverts, at Moorbank, whither had it not been for my farming avocations I was to have accompanied him, and where he is now peppering away in all the enjoyment of a capital day's sport; so there is nothing for it but to drive quietly home again. The pony suddenly falls lame, and at the same time a tempest of wind and rain, which has been brewing in the horizon during the whole afternoon, bursts upon us in pitiless fury, and as there is not a building for miles of our road, we are exposed to the whole violence of the storm. The umbrellas have been forgotten, of course, and we are drenched to the skin; Mrs. N's. *recherché* toilette, part of the lately acquired *trousseau*, being completely spoiled, and my sweet bride's silence, not to say reserve, becoming more profound with each succeeding gust. We reach Wild-wood at last, and here a dry suit of clothes, albeit endued in a smoky dressing-room, restore me to something approaching towards comfort, and I refrain from disturbing Mrs. N., in hopes that by the time dinner is announced she may have recovered her former gaiety and cheerfulness : that necessary meal is kept waiting, and the mutton irretrievably spoiled, by an enforced interview with one of my new tenants, who taking the opportunity of his return from Weatherley revel in a state of tipsy jocularity for the ill-timed interview with his landlord on matters of business, is good enough to favour me with his com,any for three-quarters of an hour, during which he discusses the weather, the ministry, Mrs. Nogo's health ; in short every thing in the world except the point at issue, and eventually takes his departure having effected no decided result except the ruin of my over-roasted joint. A quiet evening, a snooze over the " *Quarterly*," undisturbed by any music (for Mrs. Nogo confesses she has become " very idle about playing "), and a cup of tea at nine o'clock, would console me for the annoyances of the day, but that my rest is interrupted and my nerves shaken by the keeper bringing in a poacher whom he has taken at this untimely hour, and whom he seems to expect, in the double capacity of magistrate and proprietor, I shall transport on the spot. The evening is concluded by a perusal of the county paper, in which the account of a horrid burglary accompanied with violence, and perpetrated at a lone farm-house not twelve miles from where we live, sends me to bed not at all satisfied that the life of a country gentleman, residing on his own property and farming his own acres, is half such a course of unruffled prosperity as in my London career I had ever been taught to consider it.

Thus the days rolled on; and as I soon got more careless about the farm, and discovered that Mrs. Nogo, with all her charms, was subject to sundry weaknesses of her sex, such as "nervous attacks," "palpitations of the heart" when anything went wrong, and "lowness of spirits" when cheered by no other society than my own, I began to cast about for some amusing pursuit, which, while it took me abroad for the purpose of air and exercise, should at the same time furnish me with a little of that wholesome excitement to which I had all my life been accustomed. The Squire's hounds were generally so wide of my present residence, that one day a week with my brother-in-law was the most I could conveniently accomplish; and shooting, besides being comparatively a tame amusement, cannot last over the month of February. Suddenly the idea struck me, why should I not keep a pack of harriers? Like all new comers, I was as yet popular with the farmers; I had two or three moderately good horses, and one very clever pony. "Bill," the boy who did all the work of the stable, was quick and handy, and rode well: he might whip-in to me; I would hunt the hounds and blow the horn in my proper person. And already, in my mind's eye, the appointments of the Wild-wood hunt, or Mr. Nogo's harriers, took their honoured place at the bottom of the hunting column in *Bell's Life*. I hinted my intention to the Squire; and, unlike most masters of fox-hounds, he largely encouraged the idea, and liberally presented me with a most unsightly draft from his own kennel. Far and near the country was scoured for anything in the shape of a hound that was attainable for love or money : and blue-mottled beagles, lap-eared harriers, and now and then a great rough-coated southern "bellower," made their successive appearances in the make-shift kennel at Wild-wood farm. A green coat was built by the tailor at Weatherley, a couple of useful forty-pound nags purchased from the neighbouring farmers, a horn, which I could not blow, ordered from London ; and in a space of time so short that it astonished even my impatient self, I found the day had arrived on which I was to take the field for the first time in my new capacity of master and huntsman.

Much do I fear that the once-appreciated sport, so much lauded in the ancient ditty which affirms "that nothing can compare with the hunting of the hare," is now falling, if not into disuse, at least into a contempt which it does not deserve. In the present days of rapidity both in thought and movement, any amusement which does not partake of the boiling excitement so necessary to our modern youth, is at once condemned as "slow," an adjective that seems to comprise everything that is most despicable in the opinion of those who use it. To get upon a high-couraged, well-bred, and perfectly broken hunter; to ride him for twenty minutes at the rate of twenty miles an hour, after a pack of hounds that during the last half of that time have over-run the scent; to jump the stile that Rasper fell over, and face the brook that Brag refused; to take gates in his stride and doubles in his swing—such seem to be the ideas connected with hunting, in the mind of one of our rising generation of sportsmen. Hear him describe a run after dinner—that genial period when the true sentiments of the man rise to the surface as brightly as the *Château Margeaux* bubbles to the goblet's brim; and is not this very much the fashion in which he relates a day's sport, wherein the hounds seem to be the very last subject under consideration ? "Directly I heard the foot-people holloa him away from the opposite side, I went down and jumped that 'bottom' where Smasher got his horse cast last season, and by that means got a capital start away from the people, and a-head of the leading hounds. We had some queer fences, I can tell you; but luckily for me, I was riding old Flash-in-the-pan, 'and at the pace we were going' he thought nothing of them. Bumptious was a little a-head of me, but his horse refused the brook; and as I jumped it in my stride, I overhauled him." Here you put in a question as to what sort of head the hounds carried, what terms they were on with their fox, the assistance, if any, which they received from their huntsman; and for a moment you rate the fast one back to the line, but it is only for a moment. "Oh, the hounds!" he replies, as if he should not otherwise have mentioned them—"they ran like fury; it was all grass, and I believe up wind. I know the pace was so good I was blown when we got to the double-post and rails; but I broke the further one, and got over without a fall." And filling a large glass of claret, he gets back to his own deeds of daring and the incomparable prowess of Flash-in-the-pan. But exciting as all this is, and good fun as unquestionably it must be, we can scarcely call these steeple-chases after hounds by the name of hunting, or the vain-glorious promoters thereof by the title of sportsmen. Do they ever consider that if no one took more pains than themselves to master the arcana of that pursuit, to which, after all, they devote a large portion of their time; if master, huntsman, whips, hounds, &c., were "all for a gallop" and nothing else; if the head of the establishment were not cautious, and his myrmidons what our lively friend terms "slow," what would become of that reliance on each other, that equality in pace, and union in quickness, which enables a pack of hounds to show him such a breather as "winds up" his favourite hunter—thoroughbred one though he be—in less than a quarter of an hour? This brilliant display, like some gorgeous pantomime, has been prepared and "got up" with a degree of pains and trouble which only those who are "behind the scenes" can appreciate or calculate: and many an endless woodland, many a cold hunting "journey" can bear witness to the perseverance and discipline which eventually attain such popular results as " twenty-five minutes without a check over grass, six miles from point to point, and pulled him down in the middle of a sixty-acre field, a quarter of a mile from the main earths at Cold Harbour, which were open." Let us then not turn up our noses when the hounds put down theirs; let us not despise slow hunting; and, above all, the slow-hunting which is so characteristic of a pack of harriers. I have heard it said by men who have distinguished themselves in both pursuits, that the science and ingenuity required to kill "a good hare," are even greater than those which are necessary to give an account of a "bad fox;" and there is many a weather-beaten old dodger, in low-crowned hat and mahogany tops, mounted on some venerable "bo-kicker" with a snaffle bridle, who brings a degree of thoughtfulness and quick apprehension to bear on his long-eared, blue-mottled favourites, that would do honour to the fastest huntsman that ever rode over the most flying country of the much-admired "Shires."

Well, notwithstanding Mrs. Nogo's contempt for the whole performance, I got my hounds together, learned their names, drafted, fed, and encouraged them till they knew me as intimately and confided in me as entirely as the most sagacious retriever in Norfolk knows and confides in the tyrant in velveteen, whose heel he has followed since his puppyhood, and from whom no amount of seduction can tempt the faithful and much-enduring animal. It really was a pleasure on a fine scenting morning to ride one of my quiet steady-going horses to the kennel door, and witness the rush of my favourites as they came pouring out to meet me, jumping over each other's backs in their eagerness to share their master's approbation, and ever and anon throwing their deep mellow tongues; while they shook back their long pendant ears, as if to tell me how ready and willing they were for our mutual labour and amusement. It is needless to describe the difficulties I had to encounter, or the ignorance I was obliged to conceal, in my first attempts at hunting the wiliest animal of the chase; for in shrewd cunning and baffling subterfuge I conceive a hare to be infinitely more deceptive than a fox. In time my hounds became steady, and I began to *learn ;* and ere long a good scenting day and some opportune assistance from a farmer enabled me to decide upon the great superiority conceded at the dinner-table to a hare that has been *hunted* to death, over her sister peppered with No. 6, and afterwards mangled by a retriever at a battue. But satisfactory as was my success on this never-to-be-forgotten occasion, I had no one with whom to discuss my perplexities or to enjoy my triumphs.

Mrs. Nogo took, as she said *now,* " little interest in field-sports ;" the few farmers over whose land I rode were not people I could ask to dinner, and the Squire was so occupied with county business and the management of his own fox-hounds, that he had seldom leisure to pay me a visit, or to look at my harriers. Joe Bagshot, who was a priceless companion in the field or at the dinner-table, had sold the old brown horse, and was becoming, since his marriage, an *altered man;* whilst the country gentlemen and squirearchy lived mostly so wide of Wild-wood, as to make it impossible to keep up anything like constant intercourse. In this dearth of society, it occurred to me that I should be doing myself a favour, as well as conferring a kindness upon my *ci-devant* medical adviser, by inviting little Dr. Dott, that enthusiast in sporting and surgery, that Nimrod of the Pharmacopœia, to come down and stay with me a week or ten days, and enjoy in practice those amusements on which in theory he loved to expatiate. My horses were easy and temperate: even if *they* should be too much for the little doctor, a child might ride the pony. Yes, I would ask him down, mount him, take him over to the kennels at Topthorne, and send him home with anecdotes of the wild sports of the west, that should last him his lifetime, and make his wife and children stare with astonishment to hear the heroic deeds of the head of the family.

Leave was obtained from Mrs. Nogo, though not without

some slight demur, until it occurred to her that to have a "medical man in the house" would be such a comfort in her state of health; a note was despatched to London containing a pressing invitation, and full particulars as to the route by which my guest was to reach the farm. His reply to my letter, forwarded by return of post, so eagerly accepted my offer, that I really looked forward with the greatest pleasure to the arrival of my Esculapius; nor from my previous knowledge of the limited extent of his practice did my conscience smite me as to the harm his absence from London might inflict upon his interests. I sent a dog-cart to meet him at the station—for even in that remote district there was a railway, and consequently a station; and as Mrs. Nogo and myself sat over the drawing-room fire, and deferred ordering tea until the arrival of our guest, we amused ourselves with speculating on his surprise and delight at a mode of life so entirely differing from his usual habits; whilst we listened, not I am afraid without a slight degree of self-satisfaction, to the wintry wind that howled round the house, and drove the pattering rain against the windows, whilst we charitably hoped that "the waters might not be out" at the ford through which our expected guest must pass ere he could arrive at Wild-wood farm.

CHAPTER XXV.

> Oh! how they bustled round him,
> How merrily they found him;
> And how stealthily they wound him,
>   Through each dingle and each dell!
> Oh! how they sped together
> O'er the moor among the heather,
> Like birds of the same feather!
>   And their music like a bell.
>   *Original Hunting Song.*

> *Fool.*—Prythee, nuncle, be contented; this is
>   A naughty night to swim in.
>   *King Lear.*

A RING at the door-bell—a shuffling of feet—a banging of doors—and that peculiar vibration which, even in the most solidly-built house, heralds "an arrival"—announced that the Doctor had successfully braved the dangers and difficulties of open commons, treacherous fords, muddy lanes, and dubious cross-roads, in defiance of the darkness and the gale. As I rushed into the entrance-hall to greet my guest, he was in the act of "peeling:" nor could "Cheops" himself, though swathed in the multiplied paraphernalia of a "mummy," have rejoiced in a greater number of defensive garments than those which enveloped the careful wayfarer. Off they came: first an oil-skin travelling head-dress, attached, like the mailed hood of some warlike Templar, to a set of waterproof robes that might defy a deluge—then a red silk handkerchief, bound skilfully round the ear-flaps of a fur cap—then a gaudy-patterned shawl, which had preserved nose and mouth from contact with the elements—then a series of great coats, commencing with a sporting wrap-rascal, and concluding with the well-known black "Taglioni," which was considered a sufficiently professional costume for the metropolis—lower down, drab mud-boots, and india-rubber goloshes, challenged even the casualties of an upset and a pedestrian pilgrimage through the mud—till, skin after skin being cast off and laid aside, we came to the Doctor at last.

"Glad to see you looking so well, Mr. Nogo," was his cheerful reply to my greetings. "Ah! nothing like country air and exercise. This, sir, is indeed a delightful situation (it had been pitch dark for the last ten miles of the Doctor's journey)—so wild, so free, so completely the country. Charmed to be presented to Mrs. Nogo. No more reckless escapadoes now—an altered man, sir, an altered man. The wildest of us tame at last, I say to Mrs. Dott: but the spirit remains the same."

And, thus prattling on, the Doctor was ushered into the drawing-room, and set down to the tea-table, where I was agreeably surprised to find Mrs. Nogo was inclined to be extremely affable and condescending. Our good-humoured little guest was enchanted with all he saw and all he heard. The country cream was so rich—the country butter was so good—it was so pleasant to hear the wild wind howling round the house, uninterrupted by the muffin-man's bell, or the roll of the Kennington omnibus; but never shall I forget his delight when, on the retirement of Mrs. Nogo, I announced to him the arrangements I had made for the following day's sport, and the exciting intelligence that I had a "capital mount for him with my harriers."

"A thing I've pined for, for years, Mr. Nogo," exclaimed this theoretical Nimrod. "Fond as I am, sir, of shooting, and other field sports, I despise them all as compared with the chase. Destiny, sir, has made me a doctor; but Nature, Mr. Nogo—'pon my word, I sometimes think, Nature intended me for an Osbaldiston!"

And with this comfortable assurance my enthusiastic guest, refusing all offers of wine-and-water on the plea that he wished his nerves to be in tip-top order for the morrow, lit his bed-candle and retired to his chamber in that enviable state of anticipatory excitement which few of us are fortunate enough to experience after our schoolboy days have been numbered with the past.

Notwithstanding our ill-natured remarks upon it, what a climate after all is our own! John Bull thinks it his right to abuse incessantly two things which he considers his peculiar property; and those are, his ministry and his weather; yet if we can get him to reason—no easy task—he must confess, that in no other country are public affairs managed with so much regard to public good, and under no other skies does animal life, whether of man or beast, thrive so well, or attain so high a degree of perfection. "Variety is charming," and that charm no one can deny to the different kinds of weather which successively constitute an English summer's day; yet, with all its fickleness, all its changes, I doubt whether there is any other climate under the sun in which a person may be so many *hours* out-of-doors and taking exercise as in our own. Either it is too hot during one part of the year, or too cold during another, or there is a stillness which suffocates you, varied by a land-breeze that produces, you know not why, ague, malaria, disease, and death; whilst in England that very mutability which disappoints you of your excursion in the morning, produces in the afternoon an atmosphere such as you have figured to yourself surrounded our first parents in Paradise; whilst a night of wind, rain, and tempest, is succeeded by a soft, sunny, mild, winter's morning, breathing fragrance from saturated sward and dripping hawthorn, and reminding you, if a sportsman, of bounding steed and echoing hound, and the many fine runs you have seen and enjoyed, during that golden period of the foxhunter's calendar, the sport-producing month of February.

Such a morning greeted the Doctor and myself as we started—after a voluminous breakfast, to which I thought my guest did but scant justice—on our way to the meet. My hounds had gone on early. As we were to hunt in a wild moorland district several miles from the farm, and with a praiseworthy regard for his unaccustomed frame, and a due consideration of the "loss of leather" sustained by the sportsman who can only obtain "an occasional day," I thought it best to take the Doctor "on wheels" to the place of meeting, and thereby save him as large a portion as possible of that equestrian exercise which, when freely indulged in without proper preparation, makes "the rack of a too easy chair" anything but an ironical metaphor, or a poetic exaggeration. As we drove along through the fresh morning air, my companion was loud in his anticipations of sport, and his implied compliments to his own prowess in the field, though I thought I detected a shade of nervousness in the rapidity of his utterance and the many questions he put to me as to the temperate deportment of his "mount." The Doctor's costume, too, though doubtless well adapted to encounter the "moving accidents of flood and field," was hardly what we should call workmanlike in its general character and the way in which it was put on: drab cord trowsers, thrust into the recesses of large jack-boots, the latter appendages adorned with huge brass spurs, harmonized but ill with a black frock-coat and moleskin waistcoat; nor did the addition of a velvet hunting-cap, purchased for the occasion, at once confer upon the wearer that sporting air of distinction which he evidently desired to assume. However, the Doctor's dress was his own affair; it was my business, if possible, to show him a run: and when we drove up to our appointed "rendezvous"—a small clump of firs on a wide open common—and found hounds, horses, one or two well-mounted gentlemen, a country horse-breaker, and several farmers, grouped about in picturesque confusion, I began to feel that my reputation, too, was at stake as a master of hounds, and to experience a sort of nervous anxiety to show them a fine day's sport! The first thing, however, was to give the Doctor a fair start; and in order to do so, it was necessary to get him well established in the saddle. With this view my grey horse Blueskin, the soberest and most tractable animal in my stable, was sidled up to the step of the dog-cart, in order that the Doctor might get upon him, in true Melton fashion, without soiling the brilliancy of his jack-boots—a manœuvre which the grey resented by putting his ears back, tucking in his tail, and looking very much inclined to kick. Why is it that whenever you have been boasting of any peculiar excellence in your steed, he should invariably take the first opportunity of showing himself to be in a diametrically opposite humour to that for which you have been praising him? Why is it that no sooner are the words out of your lips, " This horse has never yet given me a fall," than down he goes neck-and-heels over a contemptible place at which a donkey would be ashamed to make a mistake? and that the docile animal, whom you have been recommending for his immoveable steadiness and general good conduct to carry a nervous lady or timid elderly gentleman, should, in the immediate presence of the disbelieving purchaser, think it necessary to squeal and gambol like the veriest two-year-old that ever ran unbroken in his paddock? As are other horses, so was Blueskin. Contrary to all previous experience, he was evidently in that disagreeable state which ladies call "frisky," and apologists "fresh;" and when I saw the awkward manner in which the Doctor climbed into the saddle, and gathered his reins up all of a heap, I confess I began to have misgivings as to the result.

"I say, he's—he's—very quiet, isn't he?" asked the breathless equestrian, as the horse sidled away amongst his old friends the hounds, snorting, shaking his head, and "reaching" at his bridle, in a manner which much discomposed the security of his rider's seat. "These large horses require a deal of holding," added he, half ashamed of his want of skill in the *manége*, as, with mounting colour, he knotted his reins and crammed his hat down upon his head in a "do-or-die" sort of fashion which was anything but suggestive of a pleasant excursion; but the Doctor was now in for it, and being a gallant little fellow at heart, there was a game sparkle in his eye that, with all his misgivings as to the result, showed he "meant mischief."

My attention, however, was soon taken up with the many and onerous duties of my position; and, after much consultation with the sporting agriculturists who constituted my field, we hastened to dispose ourselves over the surrounding country, and spread abroad in every direction, peeping into furrows and lashing turnip-tops, in the orthodox manner of performing that not very enlivening ceremony denominated "drawing for a hare."

The farmers were a capital set of fellows, thorough sportsmen one and all; the country, a wild district, with few resident landlords, and totally unpreserved. Coursing was a favourite amusement with the aboriginal inhabitants; and I have no doubt that whenever a poor man wanted a brace of partridges or a pheasant, he went to look for them without more ado. All this might be very pleasant, but, as may be supposed, was not conducive to the superabundance of game. At three o'clock in the afternoon we were still pursuing a fruitless search for the object of our chase without having experienced any excitement or amusement, save what may have been derived from the hapless "medico," who tumbled off Blueskin at two successive leaps; but, nothing daunted, resumed his precarious situation on " the pigskin," and, borrowing a penknife from the whipper-in, shortened his stirrup-leathers to an unheard of brevity, and with a fortitude worthy of a nobler cause, shook his feathers, and was "up and at it again!"

" There do be mostly a heer in Varmer Vowles's turmits," said the last of my attendant pedestrians, as he pointed to a small enclosure, bordering on the open moor, and signified his intention of " cutting it " if this final chance should prove a blank; and, indeed, by this time the hungriest of my field had departed for their comfortable homes, where the pudding was already being spoiled, and my retinue was reduced to the horse-breaker (who had no dinner to go to); the occupier of the turnips alluded to, on a stout black pony; the indefatigable Doctor, my boy " Bill," and myself. A wilder spot of ground could hardly be conceived than that on which we now found ourselves. The small enclosure we were entering bordered upon a steep narrow dingle, covered with small patches of gorse, which, scattered more and more thinly as the ground ascended, gave place at length to an expanse of open moorland, bounded as far as the eye could reach only by its own black skyline; a few groups of fir trees served to mark the extent of this undulating tract; and as the farmer got off his pony to remove a low sheep-hurdle (an operation the horse-breaker saved him the trouble of completing by knocking it all to shivers) he remarked: "The moorland heers be woundy stout 'uns," and opined the Squire (meaning me) would have enough to do in "catching on 'em, if so be as we was lucky enough to be concerned with an old Jack as knew the trade and was pretty stout of heart!"

The words are scarcely out of his lips when Woldsman and Jezebel, feathering down a furrow, throw their heads into the air, and burst forth in a melody which awakens a chorus of harmony from the rest of the pack. Ere I have time to collect my scattered ideas—ere I am conscious that the horse-breaker's four-year-old is rearing straight on-end, too frantic to be prevailed on to go one way or the other—that "Bill," having got them together with two cracks of his whip, is sticking his spurs in up to the rowels, and "setting-to" like a workman—that the strokes I hear, applied so vigorously and in such rapid succession, are from the stalwart farmer cudgelling his pony; and that Blueskin, having completely overpowered the Doctor, is now tearing away at the very outside pace which a somewhat slow horse can command—I find myself, I scarcely know how, across the dingle—through the gorse-bushes—all plain sailing before me—standing up in my stirrups, laying hold of the brown horse's great fiddle-head, and galloping for bare life after those streaming hounds, which, as they scour along over the level moor, heads up and sterns down, in the mute ecstacy of a burning scent, I can scarcely believe are my own steady, sedate, "tow-rowing," close-hunting, pack of harriers! The force of habit induces me to fumble for my horn; but I am not yet sufficiently skilled in music to combine a solo on that instrument with the Derby pace at which I am compelled to go along; and there are no stragglers to bring up—no, they are all forward, eleven couple of them, and racing over the heather like mad. We shall burst this hare in ten minutes—kill her and get home before dark. But where are my field? A deep holding patch of black half-boggy surface obliges me to reduce my pace, and I look around me at what I must necessarily call my companions in misfortune. The horse-breaker, his red neckcloth streaming in the wind, his knees up to his pommel, and his hands up to his chin, has got the four-year-old tolerably steadied by the unmerciful pace at which he has come, and is now gallantly holding his own in a style which I cannot help thinking "dealer's condition" will be unable to sustain. Bill, a precocious urchin for his years, who, when I hired him as a quiet lad to do odd jobs about the stable, had the impudence to enumerate his only two qualifications, as being able "to holler and ride," is slightly ahead of me, down wind of the hounds, and with his feather weight and every turn in his favour, going so much at his ease, that I determine to take that horse from him and ride him myself in future. The stout farmer, far in the rear, and utterly hopeless of ever seeing us again, is still licking the pony. Whilst Doctor Dott, who, since he has got a pull at Blueskin, has been riding behind me, line for line and foot for foot, so close that any mistake on the part of my horse must inevitably result in my instantaneous destruction by my pursuer, now comes up alongside, bathed in perspiration, and in a perfect ecstacy of delight.

"Capital horse, sir," says the Doctor; "what a line!— what a country!—what a moment!!"

But there is no time for congratulations, as the hounds, after a momentary check, have stooped again to the scent, and are running faster than ever. See, they top that ragged stone wall, which grins at us in uncompromising hideousness as we get nearer and nearer, and the unavoidable obstacle looms larger and larger; it stretches to the horizon on either side, and we must indeed "jump, or else go home." Bill flies it like a bird; the horse-breaker and the four-year-old follow him over, in a sort of complicated scramble. Now for it,

Doctor!—the little man is boiling with excitement, and goes at it forty mile an hour—Blueskin jumps it like a deer; but the hapless novice, describing a rapid parabola in the air, shoots over the astonished horse's head, and forms a spread-eagle on the resounding turf with a thump that makes my teeth feel loose in my head! Game to the last, he retains his hold of the bridle, and though dragged upwards of twenty yards by the impatient Blueskin, succeeds in stopping and remounting him without losing his place. The little man is a right good one after all, if he had only had practice. My horse gets over, but dislodges two or three stones, as though to give me a gentle hint that this sort of fun is not to go on all day; and welcome indeed is the check which takes place half a mile further on, and enables us to come up really with the hounds, and give a moment's breathing-space to our panting horses.

"Forward, lads—forward, sir!" says Bill, as the hounds, dashing once more to the front, begin work again as though there was to be no end to it. "No hare this, sir; my life on it we have got an old dog-fox before us, and *we'll* have his nose, my little darlings," adds the presumptuous youth, as he sticks *my* spurs into *my* horse, and rides to *my* hounds, as if he were a peer of the realm. Sure enough, the line is still forward, and the pace still good. Blueskin is getting confoundedly blown; the horse-breaker, it is evident, cannot last ten minutes longer; and the merry harriers, not adapted either by breeding or condition for this sort of rapid and protracted locomotion, are tailing most woefully; the dwarf fox-hounds, particularly two insubordinate puppies lately drafted from Squire Topthorne's, are racing away at head; the legitimate harriers, throwing their occasional tongues as if to claim some participation in the sport, are moiling on as they best can, in a tolerably compact body; whilst the southern-crossed and beagle-bred line-hunters, scattered for miles upon our track, are limping and yowling in the rear. Once we turn as if for the low country, and I confess my hopes are aroused that we may soon be about to conclude the performance; but no! a sharp turn *up wind* brings us back more decidedly upon the moor, and I can see no reason in the world why we should not go on till to-morrow evening. Meanwhile, grief and persuasion are the order of the day for the quadrupeds. The last farewell look which I cast at the horse-breaker shows that pitiless worthy standing on his own short legs, ruefully contemplating the hapless four-year-old, who, with head and tail erect, nostril distended, and his feet resolutely planted as widely as possible from each other towards the four points of the compass, offers a flagrant example of that helpless state which metaphorical wags describe as being "done to a turn." Bill is going best. My horse is by no means comfortable, and seems to think a strong severe bit a delightful support to lean upon. Blueskin is lobbing on; but the pace at which he bustled away with the Doctor during the first burst has told tales, and I calculate another seven minutes ought about to finish *him*. The farmer has been told off a long time. We have been running an hour and twenty minutes, and it is getting dark.

What do I see?—another stone wall looming through the rapidly-increasing obscurity, and the hounds topping it like a cataract. No power on earth shall induce me to follow that dare-devil Bill in his mad career; and, cautiously dismounting, I establish a gap, through which the still-excited Doctor and myself drag our jaded steeds. How quickly it gets dark! As we remount, and, with much exertion, "boil up" a sort of apology for a canter, Bill and the leading hounds are completely out of sight. Here and there a white speck, fleeting along through the gloom, shows where some champion of the kennel is vainly struggling to resume his place amongst his forward comrades; whilst "Tumbler" and "Tuberose," their great square heads drooping to the earth as they labour along at my horse's heels, look piteously up at me, as though to say, "What could induce a respectable, steady-going pack of harriers to embark upon such a harum-scarum performance as the present?" For long we have lost sight of the main body, and been guided in our course only by the rapidly-failing cry of the hounds still in chase. At length this last auxiliary deserts us, and we pull up in sheer despair; for it is now pitch-dark, and the surface of the moor, at no time much to be depended upon, is not to be traversed on horseback except by daylight. The situation is not without its romance; but the facts are extremely uncomfortable—not to say disheartening. The Doctor's figure looms like some phantom horseman by my side; and although I cannot distinguish his face, the joyous rapidity of his utterance, the triumphant swagger of his tone, betoken that he at all events is entirely satisfied with his heroic achievements and his day's amusement.

"What a run, Mr. Nogo! quite unparalleled, sir, I should conceive. Famous horse, this—never *was* so carried. How far may we be from Wild-wood?—you know the road, of course." Alas! I was obliged to confess my total ignorance, not only of the country in which we now found ourselves, and the distance we were from our dinner, but likewise of the whole bearings of this thinly-inhabited district, and of any the most remote chance there was that we should obtain shelter for the night. This was a damper even for the Doctor's enthusiasm; but the excitement had not yet subsided, and he bore it gallantly enough, considering his state of soreness and fatigue. Alas! he was destined to experience a more effectual cooler ere the conclusion of his adventures.

"I think we are on a track," said I, peering over my horse's head, as I fancied his feet rung on somewhat harder soil.

"Shall I get down and feel?" replied my companion, willing at any risk to obtain a change of position.

As the Doctor staggered down from the saddle, the sky lifted a little, and enabled us to distinguish a long low line of dark objects that might possibly be farm buildings; and I even fancied I discovered something like a glimmer of light, as it were from a casement, in the indistinct mass.

"All right," said the Doctor, stepping cautiously on, in front of his horse, as I called his attention to the probable refuge; "and here there seems to be a road—a white chalk road—if we could but get down this bank to it. What a comfort, a good hard road!" added he, as the indistinct bundle, which I knew to be his figure, disappeared totally from my sight; and Blueskin, tired as he was, started back with a loud snort. In another second a tremendous splash, followed by a succession of plunges and spattering,

> Just like unto a trundling mop,
> Or a wild goose at play,

from my alarmed and totally-immersed comrade, convinced me that the Doctor's good hard road was a wide brook, a navigable canal, or some other deceptive form of the comfortless and limpid element.

"Help!" sputtered the Doctor as he came to the surface, where, despite of my most strenuous endeavours, I found it impossible to distinguish him. "Help! Mr. Nogo! I shall be drowned!—what a conclusion!" and, leaving the horses to their fate, I scrambled down the bank, and found my unfortunate friend standing up to his shoulders in water —for though the brook was of no great depth, it must be remembered that neither was the Doctor a man of colossal proportions—and totally unable, even with all the assistance I could render him, to extricate himself from his dangerous and uncomfortable position. A faint moon, struggling through the stormy sky, looked down in pitiless indifference on the clear cold surface of the stream, relieved by our two struggling figures (for I was hauling at the Doctor with might and main); whilst a thick bush of alders and an old pollard willow, standing out against the fitful, stormy sky, gave a desolate and hopeless appearance to the scene. What was to be done? haul as I would I could not get him out; and the poor little man, what with cold and apprehension, was fast becoming more and more helpless. In this dilemma, it occurred to me that I had better begin to "holloa" with might and main, and at least take the chance of those buildings being inhabited which I felt confident I had seen. Accordingly I began to roar out, at the utmost pitch of my voice, the alarming cry of "Murder!—Help!— Murder!" accompanied, though in feebler tones, by the failing soprano of the chattering Doctor. Ere long I had the satisfaction of seeing lights distinctly glimmering at no great distance, and in the direction where I had before supposed there stood an inhabited house; and, as we redoubled our cries and exclamations, we were cheered by the tones of a gruff voice shouting, in accents of mingled anger and anxiety, "Where be ye?—we're a-coming!—Here, Giles! Tummas!" till a few more exclamations from the exhausted Doctor brought a powerful auxiliary to our rescue in the shape of a sturdy west-country farmer, accompanied by two ploughmen and a lantern; who, after much difficulty in finding out our actual position, and a somewhat prolonged dialogue exchanged between the rescuers on the bank and the sufferers in the bed of the stream—for in my efforts to extricate the Doctor I had myself got in up to my waist— succeeded in hauling us by main strength to "*terra firma*," where, with natural curiosity, he proceeded to inquire how we came into our present plight, and what train of events had produced the very unusual spectacle of two dismounted gentlemen, clad in hunting costume, standing waist-deep in water, towards the commencement of a dark and stormy winter's night.

"Glad to see ye, Squire Nogo," said the hospitable yeoman, as he strode before us towards his farm, greedily listening to an explanation—"Glad to see ye, even in such a plight as yon. My men'll find your horses, I'll warrant, and hounds as well; and, meanwhile, you're heartily welcome —and you too, sir." With which words, he ushered us into his ample, clean-looking kitchen, where a blazing fire, lighting up all the etceteras of that most comfortable apartment, vividly suggested to us the kindred ideas of supper, warmth, and accommodation, which but a few minutes before had seemed so utterly hopeless and unattainable. The host was in earnest, the hostess active, and the visitors nothing loath to be comforted; and when, an hour afterwards, I stretched my legs beneath the farmer's mahogany, in his best parlour, and surveyed myself in a suit of his homely clothing, "a world too wide" for my less robust proportions, I forgot my hounds, I forgot Bill, I forgot Mrs. Nogo, and mixing myself a steaming glass of hot gin-and-water—no bad conclusion to a plentiful repast of cold boiled beef, hot eggs and bacon, the richest of home-made butter and cheese, and the strongest of home-brewed ale—I pledged my jolly host with a lively perception of that merriest of all "symposiums," an accidental jollification—that greatest of all luxuries, rest after labour, ease after anxiety, internal warmth after external cold—in fine, pleasure after pain.

As for the Doctor, to use a common but forcible expression, there was "no holding him." Enveloped—I may say lost—in the farmer's clothing, nothing much more ridiculous can be conceived than the little man, holding his half-emptied tumbler to his eye, and pledging his delighted host with an enthusiasm hardly warranted even by such an occasion as the present. Cæsar after Actium, Napoleon after Austerlitz, Wellington after Waterloo, were but faint examples to typify that hero which the Doctor felt himself in his own person. What was it to him that the harriers were probably lost? that Bill was undoubtedly, at that moment, bivouacking with a tired horse on the open moor? that he himself would unquestionably be crippled for a fortnight by his day's work, and, in all likelihood, rheumatic for life, from his evening's immersion? What was that? Had he not gone a run? Had he not ridden, to his own satisfaction, in what would hereafter take its place in the annals of the country as "Squire Nogo's day with a wild fox?" Had he not jumped a veritable hunter over a real stone wall? and was he not sitting in a strange farm-house, the actual impersonation of one of Alken's successful sportsmen, who, having tired his horse and worn out his clothes, is dependent for shelter and costume upon the first stranger that may take pity on his forlorn condition? All this the Doctor felt; and, to give him his due, he acted the character well. As the gin-bottle waned, and fresh kettles of hot water steamed upon the hob, so did the still-commencing relation of the medico's exploits trench more and more upon the marvellous—border more and more on the sublime. With a vividness of description, not to be brought out by any liquid save "hot with," brewed by the orator to his own peculiar fancy, he recounted his adventures and his success. How he had mastered the grey horse—"a hunter that nothing but a workman could ride;" how he had viewed the hounds away, and told "Bill" he was sure "it was to be a run;" how he had *led the field* over the five-foot wall! and distinguished himself when even Mr. Nogo's horse was beat! how he had preserved his presence of mind when on the point of destruction in " the river at the back of the house, sir;" and how nothing but his extraordinary proficiency in swimming "had preserved him from an untimely death"— all this he told again, with a delight that, much as it amused our open-mouthed host, it was impossible for him not to share; and when, towards eight o'clock at night, "Bill' made his appearance with the lost hounds and the head and brush of the game fox, that they had gallantly accounted for, some twenty minutes after we had declined the chase, and that they had eaten in the dark, with no other witness than my undeniable young whipper-in, whose presence at the finish seemed little short of miraculous, the Doctor, whose triumph wanted but this culminating *finale*, embraced us all round, with tears in his eyes, and, falling prostrate on the ground, was carried off to his dormitory, a Bacchanalian Nimrod, feebly struggling with his potations, and to the last endeavouring to describe to us how well he had been going all day, and the exact method in which Blueskin had jumped the wall, &c.

Luckily for my hounds, Bill, though not knowing the least where he was, had hit upon a cart-track, which after many circumvolutions, at last led him through the darkness to the very farm-house we were occupying; and by ten o'clock men, hounds, and horses, snug and warm for the night, were enjoying that repose which an unusually severe day renders so grateful to man and beast. The last toast proposed by our hospitable entertainer, after we had disposed of the Doctor, was, "Success to fox-hunting!" and I sought my welcome couch with the stentorian refrain of his jolly song, "Tally-ho the hounds, sir!" ringing in my ears. Nor was it without many a kind invitation to return, and many a hearty good wish, that he allowed us to commence our homeward journey on the morrow, jaded, stiff, and weary, but triumphant notwithstanding; though I am bound to confess that the Doctor had a splitting headache, and I myself was not without misgivings as to the sort of reception which, after "being absent without leave all night," I should experience from Mrs. Nogo.

CHAPTER XXVII.

They reached the hotel; forth streamed from the front-door
A tide of well-clad waiters and around
The mob stood. *Don Juan.*

    And laughed, and blushed, and oft did say
    Her pretty oath by yea and nay
    She could not, would not, durst not play.
    At length, upon the harp, with glee,
    Mingled with arch simplicity,
    A soft, yet lively air she rung,
    While thus the wily lady sung.
                    Marmion.

I KNEW how it would be. "Such conduct," as Mrs. Nogo remarked, "must never be repeated. Was it to be borne that, not satisfied with neglecting her by day, in the pursuit of those field-sports which rendered me so fatigued in the evening that a hog would have been a livelier, and less snoring companion for the drawing room—not content with lavishing my energies, and wasting my substance in these ridiculous attempts at achieving fame as a sportsman— attempts which met with invariable failure and derision, I should likewise *make a practice* of leaving my home at daybreak, and regardless of the terror I inflicted on the weak nerves of my delicate spouse, spend the night in carousing with boon companions at some disreputable farmer's, and return the following day glorying in, rather than ashamed of, such an utter subversion of all marital duties, and domestic subordination ?"

Such is an abbreviated summary of the lecture which Mrs. Nogo thought proper to inflict as a slight castigation for my misdemeanours, on the eventful day that witnessed the triumph of my gallant little pack, and the first and last appearance of enthusiastic Doctor Dott in the hunting-field. But alas! this was not all. So good an opportunity of at once assuming the reins of government was not lost on the female diplomatist at the head of the home department. The agitation of mind endured for my sake (how could I resist such an *argumentum ad hominem ?*) very naturally brought on one of those organic affections of the nerves, which, I need not call on the heads of families to bear me witness, so mysteriously baffle constitutional vigour and professional skill. Little Doctor Dott shook his head as though conscious that he too was in the scrape; while he avowed his utter inability to minister relief to this inexplicable affliction. Aware that he had participated in its origin, he felt so uneasy in the immediate presence of the sufferer, that he implored me to allow him to curtail his visit, and return forthwith to the bosom of his family, and that London practice, which he always thought it necessary to extol as "equal to that of the late Sir Henry Halford—a weight of responsibility, Mr. Nogo, that few shoulders could bear."

"But, at least," said I, "before you go, Doctor, set my

mind at ease by recommending some beneficial treatment for Mrs. Nogo, as I am exceedingly anxious about her state of health."

"Not the slightest cause for alarm, my dear sir," was the reply. "Between ourselves, in professional confidence, Mrs. Nogo is as well as you or I; but—" (and here the Doctor laid his finger to his nose, and looked unutterable things) "your good lady will never get better here. She has taken a dislike to the place, sir; and consequently it disagrees with her. Take her away, Mr. Nogo; take her to Leamington, Cheltenham, Malvern, Bath—anywhere you think you can command a certain amount of gaiety and amusement, and I am prepared to stake my reputation as a physician, that she is quite recovered in a fortnight."

Such was the farewell advice of my kind-hearted friend, as I packed him up in the dog-cart on his return to the metropolis; and when I thought it over in my own mind, and found with what avidity the idea was seized upon by my wife, I resolved—though sorely against my inclination—upon quitting Wild-wood, selling the harriers, breaking up the establishment, and leaving the farm to take care of itself—a method that, at least, could not pay *worse* than the present one. No sooner had this course been decided on, than I had reason to admire Doctor Dott's professional foresight, in the immediate improvement which took place in my wife's health; and by the time our arrangements for departure were concluded, and Bath—that city of precipices—fixed upon as our temporary residence, she was so well, that for the life of me I could not perceive any reason why we should go away at all. However, it was too late to repent. The farm-house was shut up, the furniture put away and covered, the stables deserted and desolate, with here and there a melancholy pitchfork propping the open door of some comfortless loosebox—for I had sent on the three horses I determined to keep, that I might get a little hunting during my banishment. The kennels were cleaned and emptied; the very garden looked like a wilderness; and as the woman "left in possession," with soapy arms, and coarse apron curiously folded round her skirt, made her farewell curtsey, and shut the front-door upon our departing carriage, I threw myself into the corner of the vehicle, and for the first time in my life felt very much disposed to quarrel with Mrs. Nogo, for the unfeeling state of high spirits in which she left her home.

What a contrast was it, after a few hours of travelling, to rattle up to the door of the White Rose Hotel, where we had determined to take up our abode until we could procure a suitable residence in the valetudinarian city of Bath! How the post-boy, conscious of the dignity in which these railroad days is attached to a real travelling-carriage and appendages, boiled up his merriest canter, to stop dead-short with a jerk that nearly sent my nose through the front-window! How the magnificent proportions of "James" and his cauliflower head struck dumb the throng of idlers, who are always ready to witness the descent of a private individual from his carriage! How the landlord attended Mrs. Nogo into his house, with a deference usually reserved for princesses of the blood; while the head-waiter—a privileged and plethoric individual in black silk shorts and gold knee-buckles—asked after my brother-in-law, Mr. Topthorne, and "hoped I had enjoyed good sport with my 'ounds!" How the ostlers and attendants without, and the chambermaid and boots within, all seemed to know me personally as a friend, and to revere me immeasurably as a superior; and how I hugged myself in the conviction that although I might have driven up to the door of the Clarendon, nor found that the name of Nogo commanded attention from one regardless functionary of that metropolitan establishment, yet my arrival at the "White Rose Hotel," Bath, was heralded with all the honours, and attended with all the distinctions due to a visitor whose stay was likely to be prolonged to an indefinite length, and whose bill would bear due proportion, multiplying its items and increasing in its volume, as the termination of his sojourn was further and further postponed!

"The bill of fare, sir—this morning's paper—list of

visitors in Bath—and card of appointments of the hounds!" wheezed the fat waiter, as he entered our sitting-room with all these important documents in his hands.

"Like to see your apartments, ma'am?" added an elderly and smartly-dressed female, who had evidently made a capital race with the waiter up-stairs, and only been beaten on the post.

"I trust you will find the suite of rooms I have prepared comfortable," continued the landlord, as, following on the heels of his myrmidons, he conducted us through a labyrinth of passages, and across spacious and stately halls, to the comfortable dormitories prepared for our reception.

And here I leave Mrs. Nogo, in her glory, to arrange with James about bringing up cap-boxes, parcels, and imperials, and, with her own Abigail and all the chambermaids, to discuss warming, airing, and unpacking, whilst I flee from the inextricable confusion to consult with my first friend, the fat waiter, as to ordering dinner, and afterwards to refresh my agitated mind with a stroll through the town.

"There is no solitude like solitude in a crowd;" but at the same time, few things are more amusing than to find oneself suddenly dropped among a set of people, to all of whom one is unknown, and to be able as an *unobserved observer* to watch the habits, and study the peculiarities of these unconscious fellow-creatures. I knew nobody in Bath, and nobody knew me; and as I turned down Milsom-street, at that hour in the afternoon the fashionable resort of all the distinguished individuals whose names I had perused in the Visitors' List at the "White Rose," I felt the same sort of interest in remarking on the customs and manners of the aborigines, as if I had been a visitor in Paris, a stranger in St. Petersburgh, a wayfarer in Warsaw, or a missionary swaggering down the principal promenade of that enlightened capital which rejoices in the residence of His Majesty the King of Congo. Nor was I destined to remain long without exercise of my perceptive faculties. Groups of "fashionables" thronged the street on either side, and, like the figures in a *spectacle* "got up regardless of expense" by the spirited lessee of a minor theatre, I remarked that those who challenged my admiration as they sauntered down the street on this side, failed not in due rotation to reappear, slowly toiling up the steep ascent of the opposite pavement, again to pass before my eyes, now beginning to recognize their respective toilettes on their downward career, and so on *ad infinitum*, in what could not but appear to me a circular course of labour in vain.

Ere I had been thus occupied for half on hour, I began to make acquaintance with the forms and features of the well-dressed individuals thus continually passing in review before me, and to speculate on the different characters and pursuits of these indefatigable promenaders. Here I beheld, with an admiration not wholly unmingled with awe, the *passée* beauty, for whose failing charms, alas! even the healing waters of King Bladud, recommended in sheer despair by the "family physician," must prove a hopeless remedy. In vain to o'erlay that parchment skin with paint, and plaster it with cosmetics; in vain to conceal that grizzled "crop" beneath those dark flowing ringlets, shorn from some guilty head, whose very beauty, perhaps, was the primary cause of the female convict's disgrace and punishment; as she minces down Milsom-street, in shoes a "world too tight" for those lame and swollen feet, not all the charms of "manner," not all the hypocrisy of "dress," can conceal the unwelcome fact that the toast of long-forgotten revellers, the "flower" of days gone by, has shrivelled into an ugly old woman at last; but see with tottering step and bow of the old school (alas that its flexibility should be so damaged by chronic rheumatism!) a contemporary Damon staggers up to this antiquated Phyllis, and in croaking tones they exchange greetings and inquiries, mutual compliments, and welcome bits of scandal, with an eagerness and a concern which prove how anxious they still are to retain their slippery foot-hold in society—how they are still gasping and struggling to stem "the tide, nor leave the world which leaveth them." And now a fine old admiral, frank of countenance and bluff of bearing, but whose limbs, alas! " the bullets and the gout " have rendered incapable of supporting his jolly frame, is wheeled up in an invalid's chair, which, much to the danger of the toes of an inattentive public, he persists in steering himself, and joins these faded fashionables, to whom he forms a pleasing and instructive contrast. The living stream thus stemmed for an instant, rapidly accumulates its volume of idlers, and ere long the pavement is blocked up by the gossiping throng. A tall, handsome girl, with bright sunny ringlets (such an one—so thinks ancient Phyllis— as she herself was not *so very* long ago!), chaperoned by a stout lady, who is doubtless the mamma, forms an additional attraction to the group, and accounts by her presence for the number of young gentlemen who swell the conclave, and offer to the curious in costume an interesting study indeed. Various are their garments; and of a cut and texture seldom seen, save amongst their own immediate set. But the prevailing taste appears to be a habit in which the wearer, without the slightest inconvenience to himself, is prepared to jump into the saddle, and ride to London at a moment's notice. The noble animal, the horse, furnishes with his accoutrements the favourite ornaments of these his adorers. As the ladies of ancient Rome caused their jewels to be shaped into such talismanic forms as were best appreciated by those virtuous matrons, so does young England, in its outward adornment, affect an equine style of decoration, which shall argue a corresponding taste within ; and whilst a turquoise horseshoe fastens the folds of a cambric bosom, picked out with Derby winners, the snaffle connects his button-holes, the curb-chain secures his watch, and the top of his walking-stick is dignified with a representation (wrought in the precious metal) of that quadruped to whom certain cynics will opine the owner is but a first cousin once removed.

What a relief to discover the honest, handsome countenance, to recognize the manly simplicity of dress which distinguishes my friend Joe Bagshot, amongst this bevy of second-rate dandies! His greeting is kind and cordial, as usual; he links his arm within mine, and soon in our multitude of confidences and inquiries we forget faded belles, superannuated bucks, mutilated warriors, juvenile tigers, Milsom-street, Bath, and all but our own concerns and our own proceedings.

"Kate will be so glad to hear you have arrived!" says my friend; "come to us to-morrow evening at half-past eight. She has a sort of quiet 'at-home' in our small house. I cannot ask you to dinner, old fellow, for our cook gave up her place yesterday, because Kate objected to her wearing her hair in long ringlets: only don't say I told you so; but drop in to-morrow night, any time before twelve, and bring Mrs. Nogo with you."

And with these words—it being now lamplight—my friend took leave of me on the steps of the "White Rose," and betook himself to his own home, and the society of his wife, who, I could not help suspecting, was a helpmate by no means adapted for my frank-hearted old schoolfellow.

The whole of the ensuing day we spent in what Mrs. Nogo terms "settling"—a mysterious evolution, of which it is difficult to describe the nature or the details. My own share of the performances was limited to an inspection of my stud, who had arrived the day before by the road, under the immediate custody of Bill, and had performed their journey with the usual loss of condition and filling of legs, inseparable from a cavalry movement. Whilst I was feeling sinews and spanning joints, terribly swelled by that unnecessary punishment the animal inflicts on his own person, in what grooms term "hitting hisself," I had to listen to a tissue of complaints from my master-of-the-horse, as to the accommodation provided for himself and his charge. Of course the water was hard, the oats kiln-dried, the hay musty, the stable too low, ill-ventilated yet full of draughts, and "no servant in Bath could keep a horse's coat down in such a dog-kennel as this here." Then his own dormitory let in the rain, and did not keep out the cold, and "was not fit for a pig, let alone a Christian, to sleep in;" and it was not without the exercise of a good deal of patience, and the making of sundry promises of an alleviating tendency, that I effected an escape from my grumbling whipper-in.

A solitary walk to Lansdowne, for the sake of the fresh air, of which I obtained a sufficient quantum from the north-east, made me vote Bath the coldest place in England, and served to while away the afternoon till dinner-time, before which I had received a gentle hint from Mrs. Nogo, it would be unnecessary for me to present myself, as I should only be "in the way," and interfere with the essential ceremony of "settling," which could not be concluded till that hour.

I have already confessed in these pages that I am an indolent man: shall I expose myself to the reader's contempt by likewise allowing that, without being exactly an "epicure," I am capable of appreciating and enjoying the good things of this world, when brought to perfection by a skilful practitioner in the art of cookery?

"I understand, Mr. Gibbon," said his anxious hostess to the illustrious historian, "that you are a great *gourmand?*"

"Pardon me, madam—I am only a great glutton!" was the discerning reply of him whose pen has rescued from oblivion the costly dishes of a Domitian, the luxurious banquets of a Nero.

But without going quite so far as the candid confession of Mr. Gibbon, I am willing to concede that there are few corporeal enjoyments in this world superior to that of a good dinner, followed by a bottle of good wine, and all this properly consumed in agreeable society, and, if in winter, by a cheerful fire; but a *sine quâ non* to the whole comfort of such an arrangement is, that digestion, which avowedly goes on best in a state of perfect repose, should not be interfered with by any labour or exertion whatever, whether of body or mind, and that the active duties of the day having been disposed of, the patient should be allowed to remain a certain number of hours undisturbed in his easy-chair, and only exchange that

x

recumbent attitude for the more complete repose of his welcome couch. With these feelings, and these inclinations, can anything have been more disagreeable to me than the necessity of performing the duties of the toilette after dinner? To wash the post-prandial face in cold water—to imprison in starch and patent leather the well-fed frame, to whose swelling proportions a dressing-gown and slippers would be the most acceptable and appropriate costume—to exchange the cozy fireside, and the embraces of a roomy arm-chair, for the cold interior of a damp fly, and standing-room amongst a crowd of people whom one don't know—and above all, to do this without the satisfaction of growling, and with a smiling face, as though it were one of the greatest pleasures of life to be thoroughly uncomfortable: if this is not domestic martyrdom, I should like to have a satisfactory definition of that very general infliction.

But, luckily, Bagshot's temporary home is but a few streets from the "White Rose;" and ere the jingling wretched fly has discomposed the muslin folds of Mrs. Nogo's well-chosen toilette, or shaken out one ringlet of her rich soft hair—and truth to say, I am somewhat proud of Mrs. N.'s taste in dress, and her magnificent "*chevelure;*" in fact, I cannot conceal from myself the fact, which I think *she* has not yet discovered, that she looks "best of an evening"—we arrive at the place of our destination, and are admitted by a sober clerical-looking personage in black, hired for the occasion, who consigns us to the care of a pretty waiting-maid, in a wondrously-becoming cap, by whose dexterous assistance Mrs. Nogo is relieved of her ermine cloak and coverings, whilst I tie up travelling-cap and overcoat into a shapeless mass, and consign them to a heap of similar entanglements, with small hopes cf ever seeing my property again. The house is small, though commodious; and ere I have settled myself well into my neckcloth, and got a tight kid glove partly on my left hand, I find myself following my better-half into Mrs. Bagshot's pretty little drawing-room, and, as I shake hands with my smiling hostess, admiring for the hundredth time the nameless fascination of her manner, and the admirable taste of her "get-up."

I confess myself to be a shy man—one of those unhappy individuals who, with a constant hankering after the pleasures of society, suffer torments only known to the diffident, under the gaze of their fellow-creatures, and dissemble with Spartan fortitude the pain inflicted on them by the casual observations which well-meaning neighbours address to those who are so obviously ill-at-ease with themselves. At a London party an immediate refuge presents itself in the vortex of the crowd, who, jammed together in a half-suffocated mass, neither know nor care for any other consideration than the facility of obtaining "the carriage," in order to go through the same martyrdom elsewhere. But here, in Bath, no such protection was afforded by the contracted circle that comprised the *élite* of that city; and small as was Mrs. Bagshot's drawing-room, it was not half full. Mrs. Nogo, who suffered as little from bashfulness as any other lady of a certain age (and it is curious to observe at how early a period the fair sex outgrow this weakness), was soon comfortably established as the centre of a small group of admirers—evidently old acquaintances; and chiefly of high military and naval rank, as indeed, from the obvious length of their services, they deserved to be. My friend Joe was busy making the agreeable to an elderly lady, adorned with a curious superstructure on her head, who, I concluded, was either his aunt, or an intimate friend of that important relative; and I had ample leisure, as I sipped the cup of weak tea offered me by the temporary butler—whose countenance I have since recognized at all the entertainments I have attended in Bath—to take a good look at the different individuals thought worthy to comprise one of pretty Mrs. Bagshot's "at homes." It speaks volumes for the tact and cleverness of the *ci-devant* "Kate Cotherstone," that short as had been her residence in this exclusive city, she had contrived to render her abode the resort of all who considered themselves "the best people" in its varied society; and an admission to one of her parties gave the fortunate visitor an immediate footing amongst the local fashionables whom I now had an opportunity of studying in their natural element. The mass appeared chiefly to consist of persons—both ladies and gentlemen—considerably past the middle period of life, and with few exceptions, suffering from some bodily infirmity, the concealment of which afforded them a never-failing occupation. The gradations of rank, too, seemed to be known and observed with a degree of exactitude totally unprecedented in my previous experience of the law of precedence; although Burke or De Brett would hardly have recognized the claim to distinction put forward by the wife of a captain on half-pay, or the widow of a minor-canon. There were, however, two grand exceptions to the general run of commoners constituting this assemblage, in the persons of a dowager viscountess, and an earl's younger son; and the deference with which poor old deaf Lady Ricketts was listened to, and the Honourable Lionel Legerdemain toadied, were instructive proofs of the respect in which England still holds the illustrious ornaments of her aristocracy. The sufferings of poor Lady Ricketts from intermittent paralysis prevented her being anything more than a passive recipient of the general homage she commanded; but Mr. Legerdemain's popularity did him, indeed, the greatest credit, inasmuch as there must have been some admirable though hidden virtues concealed beneath so unprepossessing an exterior, to render that short, thin, dirty, and vulgar-looking man the centre of an admiring crowd. Badly dressed, not half washed, and more than half drunk, he was relating to a listening circle that day's run with the stag-hounds; the chief merit of the performance being the fact that he had ridden nearly a hundred miles on the road, exclusive of hunting, since breakfast —and this feat, perhaps, in a measure accounted for his seedy appearance.

" 'Main, my boy!" said a good-looking, fresh-coloured young gentleman, who seemed to derive much reflected honour from the familiar abbreviative,—" 'Main, my fine fellow! what did you do to-day with *The Buck*?"

"Ran ten minutes, and broke my horse's back," replies 'Main, who is evidently a man of few words.

"I'll mount you to-morrow with the Duke," good-naturedly suggests the pitying inquirer, who is basking in that time of life when the loss of a horse is the greatest conceivable affliction.

"Wouldn't give a thank-you for fox-hunting!" is the somewhat uncourteous reply, which, however, elicits a burst of applause from the attendant circle; and the young one, rather disconcerted, walks off to pay his court to Mrs. Bagshot, whilst 'Main confidentially whispers to a red-faced Irishman, with whom he seems most intimate, that "he shall go and smoke a weed at Joe's, and try for a drain, as this thing's mortal slow," and the honourable himself "curious thirsty." The baffled young gentleman who rejoices in the high-sounding appellation of Constantine, joined to the less ambitious patronymic of Slopes, is rather a favourite amongst the Bath ladies, being tolerably well-off, always exceedingly correct in dress, of fresh colour and curly hair, with a guileless expression of countenance, reminding one irresistibly of a sheep, and is extremely well received as he edges his way amongst sofas and ottomans to Mrs. Bagshot's side. Oh! Kate! Kate!—still as great a flirt as ever! Even in the absence of higher game, to think it worth your while to waste your artillery upon this harmless boy! Ere he has exchanged three words with you, I can see by the nervous manner in which he shrinks from your eye, by the pinker colour that mounts to his chubby, unwhiskered cheek, as your thrilling tones fall upon his ear, that Constantine Slopes is a "gone 'coon!" The old story, Kate—you ought to be ashamed of yourself! "Sport to you, but death to him!" Mr. Slopes, probably for want of anything better to say, hazards a stammering request that "Mrs. Bagshot will give us a little music;" and the clergyman's lady, calm, radiant, and collected, sits down to the piano-forte, protected in flanks and rear by two post-captains and a Commander-of-the-Bath, *vis-à-vis* to a general officer with one leg, whose infirmity obliges him to remain seated, and assisted by Mr. Constantine Slopes, who hangs over the fair performer, and turns the leaves of her music-book, with an *empressement* that forcibly reminds me of days not long gone by, when I was as great a fool, as infatuated a victim, as that simple young man. Who shall account for the fascination exercised by some women upon all who approach their sphere? The peculiar power of the rattlesnake, whose eye is said to lure the conscious victim unresistingly to its doom, and the attractive properties possessed by certain ladies, and by them used with equal recklessness and cruelty, are two arrangements of Nature which make me a believer in "Mesmerism;" and I am convinced that Mrs. Bagshot possessed fully more than her share of the magnetic influence. What else could it have been that, ere she had run her fingers over the keys with her own peculiar touch, half through one of those complicated preludes she executed so brilliantly, drew me irresistibly towards the piano-forte from the other end of the room, and brought me, open-mouthed, to gaze and listen spell-bound by the enchantress, forgetful of the presence of my own legitimate Mrs. Nogo, the proximity of Joe—who, by the way, hated music—and all, but those sounds which bore me back upon the wings of harmony to the shades of Windsor, the green alleys of Virginia Water, the villa at Ascot, and the dreamy follies of the past?

Then, as if the music, accompanied by the half-reproachful glances shot at me from beneath those long eyelashes, was not enough, Kate must needs complete the charm—thereto, I acknowledge, incited by the supplication of Mr. Constantine Slopes—by warbling forth one of those plaintive ditties which people who are not "by way of" singing, sometimes execute so beautifully and so touchingly. With just enough accompaniment to melt the tones gradually away; with just enough expression not to mar the plaintive simplicity of the sentiment: and with looks of pitiful tenderness that might have thawed St. Anthony into a sighing Strephon, and that *did* make me very uncomfortable, and caused young Constantine Slopes to shake like an aspen-leaf, she drew from the responsive chords a soul-stirring harmony as she poured forth her plantive wail for

"THE DAYS WHEN WE MET.

"There is mirth in the sunshine, there's peace in the shade,
There's the fragrance of June on the flower;
There is love in the whisper that steals through the glade—
But the sunshine may pale, and the roses may fade,
And the skies may be dark in an hour;
And the heart may grow weary—the brain may forget—
And the loved one be changed since the days when we met.

"There is morning to hope for, when darkness is past;
There's a dawn that shall smile into day;
Though the winter be chill, and unsparing the blast,
Yet the flow'ret shall bloom in its spring-time at last,
And the bird carol forth from the spray.
But the heart hath no morrow, when its sunlight is set,
And its music is hushed since the days when we met.

"Will you seek for a blossom when the tree is laid low?
Will you look to find life in decay?
Is there joy in despair? is there laughter in woe?
Can you ask me to smile through the tear-drops that flow
For the hopes which have faded away?
No! the cheek shall be pale, and the eyelash be wet,
While I mourn all alone for the days when we met."

Amidst the applause that succeeded to the "voice of the charmer," I caught a glance from Mrs. Nogo which somewhat moderated the fervour of my approval, and a peremptory order to "see about the carriage!" sent me into the dark street to grope up and down for the fly which had brought us, and which, according to agreement, was to be ready to take us back. The interval having been whiled away by the driver in the consumption of exciscable commodities, we were not long on our homeward journey, and were soon arranged for the night in our comfortable dormitory at the "White Rose."

Shall I confess that as I laid my head on the connubial pillow, the still-present "refrain" of "The Days when we Met" was yet ringing in my ears, undrowned by the confidential discussion that took place, ere I was suffered to taste repose, relative to the merits and foibles of *my* old friend Mrs. Bagshot.

CHAPTER XXVII.

"Let me not live," quoth he,
"After my fame lacks oil, to be the snuff
Of younger spirits, whose apprehensive senses
All but new things disclaim, whose judgments are
Mere fathers of their garments."
All's Well that Ends Well.

Farewell! with him alone may rest the pain,
If such there were—with *you*, the moral of his strain.
Childe Harold.

LIFE is a strange medley. As I sit here in lonely grandeur, the sole inhabitant of that great desert which constitutes the principal dining-room of "The Munchausen Club," I can scarce believe that the middle-aged member, whose bristling whiskers and incipient crow's feet I can too plainly discern in yonder unflattering mirror, is the same Tilbury Nogo who, but a few short years before, bounded up the steps of this exclusive caravanserai with all the buoyant elasticity of youth, and swaggered through its halls, in the pleasing consciousness that "the world was all before him, where to choose." The very waiter seems to glance increduously at the country-made boots and ill-fitting attire of a gentleman whom, it argues now no vanity to say, he remembers once the most particular in his *chaussure*—the most scrupulously correct in his attire. Well may he look as much astonished as a waiter is capable of looking—for these functionaries, like the chairs and tables with which they are chiefly associated, never grow old. For them the spring-tide and winter of life are not. Who ever recollects to have seen a waiter either in the bloom of youth or the decrepitude of old age? If he should be short-winded and gouty, your father remembers him afflicted with these inconveniences when he himself was a young man. If he is light, wiry, and active—light, wiry, and active he will remain, when you are tottering upon crutches, or writhing on a water-bed. Leave England, to seek your fortune at the antipodes; pursue your search after the fleeting jade from pole to pole; and when half a lifetime has elapsed, return to London, bankrupt at least in health and constitution, and so altered as not to be recognized by the very cousin with whom you have been brought up from a boy, walk into that club in which the wholsome rule, that "members abroad are not liable for their yearly subscriptions," has induced you to keep your name, and the same waiter, apparently in the same attire, offers you the evening paper, with the same flourish that used to call a smile to your countenance twenty years ago; and for a moment the magic of association makes you feel as young as that evergreen attendant. Look at him: he is neither bent nor wasted, neither wrinkled nor grey; he always looked like a waiter, and he looks just as like a waiter now as he did before you went abroad. What is his secret? and can he be induced to part with it for love or money? Perhaps he has no family cares—Ah! the daily epistle from Mrs. Nogo, which the rogue presents on a silver salver, with a careless air that is enviable to a degree.

"Waiter, bring me a large glass of sherry and a biscuit."
"Glass of sherry, sir—yes, sir. Biscuit, sir—yes, sir."

And now to see what information my news-loving lady can give me from Bath, where we still hold our head-quarters, and are considered, I rather flatter myself, what the purser's wife in "Peter Simple" calls the "Smiths, of London"—"quite the topping people of the place." She still crosses her letters word for word, and line for line; and her hand, though faint and ladylike in appearance, gets more illegible every day. I wonder if I shall have to come to glasses at last! however, with the assistance of alternate sips at the goblet of sherry, I manage to decipher the contents, which a respect for the confidence of conjugal correspondence prevents me giving *verbatim*, but by which I am glad to learn that "the cockatoo and the white mice are well, though the bullfinch has broken his leg!" (The reader will infer, from the importance of these pets, that my establishment is unblessed with a nursery.) " The mastiff puppy, as yet nameless, has been lost, and recovered at an enormous sacrifice; and Toko —a long-eared, useless spaniel—has been bitten by the butcher's dog. My own two hunters have the influenza, and one of the carriage-horses is lame "—which bulletin concludes the domestic details of this daily report. The remainder of the epistle, like its predecessors, is full of that ever-increasing intelligence which men call news, and gods scandal, and for the growth of which the climate of Bath appears peculiarly favourable. From its perusal I learn that the Honourable Lionel Legerdemain has been concerned in some most equivocal proceedings on the turf, and that it is doubtful whether even his exalted rank will enable him to retain his position in the immaculate society of Bath; that old Admiral Dolphin is paralytic, and poor Lady Ricketts dead; and young Graceless—formerly of the Guards—has behaved shamefully to her niece; that venerable Miss Dido, supposed to be the most inveterate of spinsters, had been seen at ten o'clock at night walking with a man in a cloak, who, Mrs. Nogo's maid thought, was the postmaster at the corner, but whom Mrs. Champfront likewise saw and declares to be Louis Napoléon; that people did more and more extraordinary things every day; and that she, Mrs. Nogo, did not know what the world would come to at last, etc., etc. The letter concluded with an earnest hope that my business in London would soon be brought to a close, and was further elongated by a postscript, to the effect that " she had just seen young Constantine Slopes driving four-in-hand down Lansdowne-place; and people received him just the same as ever; though what had become of *that* Mrs. Bagshot, she had not an idea—only it would be extremely painful considering the relationship and all, if accident should ever bring them together." This last piece of intelligence set me ruminating upon the many changes that had taken place since my own marriage—our first establishment at Wild-wood; the exploits of little Doctor Dott with the harriers; our removal to Bath, and the delightful *réunions* at Bagshot's house, of which Kate—the now-never-to-be-mentioned Kate—had been the ornament and the charm. Few were the years that had elapsed; and yet how far apart were the different individuals that had constituted those pleasant assemblages! My own wife a confirmed invalid, never leaving the vicinity of her physician; my brother-in-law Topthorne, who had given up his hounds, relapsing into a sort of yeoman—never seeing a visitor, never associating with his equals, fast losing the manners and habits of a gentleman; poor Segundo fallen into the hanger-on of a sporting patron, who was himself obliged to reside at Boulogne, and living from hand to mouth in a foreign country—as truth to tell, he was tolerably accustomed to living at home. Jack Raffleton, my early friend—the wildest of them all in his hot youth—was the only one of the lot whose after-career seemed prosperous and successful. But Jack, in all his escapades, was not only a thorough gentleman himself, but scrupulous only to associate with gentlemen; and this it was which invariably proved a safety-buoy to my volatile companion. Military distinction and a good appointment were doing their best for him in India; and the golden opinions which he gathered in command seemed equal to the popularity he had formerly enjoyed in a subordinate capacity. There was some comfort in knowing that Jack was getting on well. But poor Joe Bagshot! how could I bear to think of him— the merry, kind-hearted, manly, athletic Joe—now living in weary solitude at his vicarage, going through his daily round of parochial duties, in a subdued, broken-hearted frame of mind, for which those duties alone appeared to possess the slightest interest. No more cricket, no more archery, no more joyful gatherings and active sports for that morose and altered man! They tell me his herculean frame is shrunk and wasted, and that premature old age has furrowed his open brow, and silvered the waving clusters of his nut-brown hair. Since the morning she left him with young Constantine Slopes—and her infatuation for that uninteresting youth is as unaccountable as the admiration she was capable of inspiring in such a mind as her husband's—Joe had never been seen to smile. A strong moral sense of his duties, and the responsibilities of his calling, prevented my friend from taking such vengeance as human opinion esteems only just for the greatest injury that man can inflict on man; and those alone can appreciate the struggle it must have cost him to forego the reprisals which society enforces, who know as well as I do his gallant, fearless spirit—his high and sensitive feelings of what the world calls honour. Poor Joe Bagshot! time will deaden the acuteness of the pang, but time will never be able to restore that image whose place is now desolate in your heart! the sunshine will never look as bright to you again in this world: but take comfort, old friend! no one knows better than yourself that the end of all is not here: were it so, yours would indeed be a cheerless lot. Nor are my own reflections on the past untinged by that bitter drop which has turned your cup to gall. Knowing as I did the heartlessness and vanity of Kate Cotherstone's character—having myself so narrowly escaped shipwreck on the Circean rock—ought I not to have warned you ere it was too late? ought I not to have interposed between the moth and the candle—the frank, open-hearted country clergyman, and the wily, finished coquette? She married but to obtain a certain position in society: she left you, without a struggle, the instant a more brilliant career appeared to open itself before her: and I hear the young dandies, as they dawdle in here for their late luncheons, discussing, in their careless, hap-hazard manner, the wit, the tact, the accomplishments, and the beauty of Mrs. Bagshot, as she still dares to call herself; her interesting widowhood (that is now the *rôle*), her wonderful equestrian skill, her extraordinary taste, and the furniture of her house near Chesham-place.

Oh, sin! oh, sorrow! and oh, womankind!

How this taste for moralizing grows upon one! I conclude

it is one of the prosy habits which too surely accompany the approach of maturity—that reflective period when man, having arrived at the culminating point of his career, gazes down, as it were from an eminence, on the prospect both before and behind him, but pauses chiefly to admire the landscape which he has already traversed, and prefers to dwell, not without exaggeration, on the past toils and triumphs of the half-completed journey, rather than look forward into the dim uncertainty of the future.

As I look back upon the follies and the failures of my irrevocable youth, it seems to me that, were it possible to turn back the wheel—had I the privilege of again living over those golden days which shall return no more—in no single instance should I act exactly as I have done; there has not been one occasion on which I should commit the same absurdities in the same manner. Whether the vagaries of a staid middle-aged gentleman, when submitted to the test of common sense, are less unaccountable than those of impetuous, impulsive boyhood, I leave to the attentive observer of human nature to determine. All I know is, that, like the retrospective octogenarian, who summed up his whole reflections on existence with the conclusion that, " if he had to live his time over again, he would eat more and drink less," I am convinced that, though my follies might be equal in quantity, they would be essentially different in quality; though the madness were as apparent, the method would be by no means the same.

Like many a wiser and better man, I have been the victim of an unworthy ambition—not the noble infirmity which urges the aspirer to be great—not the heaven-born sentiment which impels him to be good; but the paltry and unmanly thirst for frivolous distinction, which, originating in vanity, finds its end in disappointment and disgust. Not satisfied to take the sports and amusements of life as I found them, it has been my desire to raise for myself a kind of spurious fame for proficiency in pursuits which, after all, deserve but to be the pastime of an idle hour; and even this worthless distinction I have failed to attain. When the man who had spent a lifetime in learning to balance peas on the point of a needle, was brought before Alexander, the conqueror of the world ordered him the appropriate recompense of a packet of needles and a bushel of peas. Alas! my proficiency has not even deserved the Macedonian's sarcastic guerdon. Money, time, and perseverance have been wasted, and I cannot balance the pea on the needle after all. In vain have my stud eaten their heads off at Melton, and I myself gone to the height of personal inconvenience, not to say bodily peril, to achieve a first-flight character on the grass. Can I lay my hand on my heart, and tax my memory with one single instance on which, after hounds had been running hard for ten minutes, I was present in the same field with them? I have ridden a two-hundred-guinea hunter, and been pounded by young Graceless on a forty-pound hack! I have placed my horse's head at Lord Rapid's tail, and vowing to stick to him throughout the day, have lost him in three fields. No! High Leicestershire was no arena for my prowess; and hopeless as was my success in the pastures, the turf was even worse. What availed it to elbow my way into the waving mass which constitutes the Ring at Epsom; or to swagger, with open betting-book, and pencil daintily fitted between my front teeth, down the sunny slopes at Ascot? The "make-and-shape" backer jumped at the odds I offered against his favourite, and showed his judgment by the form in which his selection swept past the goal an easy winner, and "the only horse I stood to lose by in the race;" or the better-informed leg, with his liberal investment against the Flyer that broke down this morning, gave me another opportunity of what is playfully termed " paying and looking pleasant." Shooting, deer-stalking, sparring, cricket, hare-hunting, rowing, fishing, etc., not forgetting my first and only appearance as a jockey at Weatherley—I have had a turn at them all—and if this be what is meant by "sowing wild oats," I can only say that in my case the crop has failed to pay the expenses of cultivation. My trip into the west of

England, though in itself the accident of an accident—the consequence of a *fracas* in which I had no business to be concerned—was in its effect not the least important of my vagaries; and that, too, originating in my ambition to obtain a certain share of fame as a sportsman in that out-of-the-way locality. Of my visit to Squire Topthorne, I confess there did spring some very decided consequences; but with my conviction that, in the words of Shakspeare, " your marriage comes by destiny," I forbear to make any reflections on that unavoidable catastrophe. And what has been the result of thus wasting the golden, the irretrievable years of early manhood—that important period in which alone can be laid the foundations for a future superstructure of utility and self-content, if not of distinction and renown—an edifice to which success in the more trifling pursuits of life should be but as the carving which decorates its pillars, the ornamental work which softens the severer grandeur of the whole?

A brief period of hollow excitement, constantly embittered by dissatisfaction and disappointment; a consciousness of time misspent and opportunities thrown away; something very nearly akin to remorse for the irremediable past; and above all, the degrading conviction that though age is steadily and surely stealing on, wisdom is still as far distant as ever, and the experience which makes " even fools wise " has in my own case been entirely thrown away.

" Could we but see ourselves as others see us," how different would be the estimate we should place on our characters! how much less often should we hear it remarked of such an one, " that it would be well to buy him at the world's price, and sell him at his own." Were it possible to look into the hearts of those with whom we associate, and there read the opinions they really entertain of ourselves, the lesson, though totally upsetting the whole organization of society, would prove as instructive as it would unquestionably be disagreeable. Perhaps in London we have better opportunities than elsewhere of arriving, if we are not completely blinded by self-conceit, at our true value amongst our fellow-creatures. The young men of the present day are not prone, without some very cogent reasons, to conceal the unflattering opinion they seem to entertain of every one but themselves; and certainly that insincerity which would fain disguise the truth, simply because it is disagreeable, is not the failing of the age we live in. As I sit here in a window of "The Munchausen," and gaze upon the boundless prospect afforded by the opposite side of Pall-Mall, I study the manners and customs of the future promise of Great Britain, with a melancholy conviction that I am no longer one of themselves. Truth, however, compels me to state that the few years which confer upon me what is ironically termed "the advantage" of them, totally fail to command that deference which, we are told, was in Lacedæmon the invariable tribute paid to old age. But little of the Spartan, save his courage, is to be traced in the Anglo-Saxon of the present day; and how that young gentleman now breakfasting on mulligatawny and old Madeira, at four P.M., would turn up his nose at black broth! But to return to my moralizing reflections on that position in society which I have failed to attain—that very youth who, because I have not the honour of his acquaintance, thinks it right to gaze upon me with a supercilious stare, as though I were some curious piece of upholstery badly covered, may perhaps chance to ask the waiter the name of that rural-looking gentleman who occupied the table next to our youth's protracted breakfast. "Nogo!"—ah! twenty-one summers have shed their sunshine on his clustering locks, but he has never heard of Mr. Nogo, and *therefore*, with a power of reasoning, a grasp of induction that does honour to his intellect, he concludes Mr. Nogo *must* be a snob! So much for the charitable opinions entertained on my behalf by those who cannot boast the advantage of my intimacy. Now for the deferential homage I am to expect from those who can. In swaggers young Graceless—a great man at "The Munchausen," and though, as I happen to know, and as a reference to the "Army List" would bear me witness, no longer so *very* young as a slight figure and whiskers carefully shaved to the roots would lead the fair sex to suppose—yet by dint of buoyant spirits, consummate impudence, and unfailing tact, an authority amongst the juveniles whose oracles there is no gainsaying.

"What, Nogo—my antediluvian!" says the irreverent joker, as he pats me on the back with a cordiality which the London man can afford in empty February, but which dries up to an imperceptible nod and whispered "How-d'ye-do?" in crowded June; "I didn't know you were alive—but how old you are looking, and how fat!" glancing down with unconcealed satisfaction at his whipping-post of a frame. "Well, I'm glad to see you. If you are going along Piccadilly, come as far as Tatt's with me: Camarine's horses are to be sold, and I want to take the odds to a pony against "Bareface."

The old feeling steals upon me: I link my arm in that of young Graceless, and ere I reach Hyde Park Corner the ruminations of the preceding half-hour have been forgotten; Bath, Mrs. Nogo, domestic responsibilities, the increasing corpulency, the irretrievable decade, are as though they were not. Tattersall greets me with a nod that would seem to infer he had seen me every day for a fortnight; and the ancient ambition, the foolish itching for sporting notoriety breaks out again as strong as ever. There is a chesnut mare of Lord Camarine's (a nobleman declining hunting for the best of all reasons, that his difficulties have forced him abroad), loudly celebrated by report for her capabilities as a fencer. What an animal, on which to acquire distinction as a bruising rider in the hunting-field! Who is that gentleman, who ought to know better, bidding in hundreds for this patent-safety conveyance, originally purchased for forty pounds by the dealer, who let "Camarine" have her as a favour at five hundred? "There is no fool like an old one!" that gentleman is Mr. Tilbury Nogo! Going! going! gone! It matters little whether the costly purchase was destined to become his property, or that of some one obstinately deter-

Y

mined to become even a greater fool than himself. Here let him take his leave of the patient reader, earnestly hoping that these few random sketches of his adventures, if they have failed to amuse, may at least have the credit of doing their best to warn that weary sufferer of the way in which he should not go—to point out to him the degrading annoyances, the petty vexations, that hover around the ill-omened path of an Unsuccessful Man.

SCOTLAND AND THE MOORS.

BY

TILBURY NOGO, ESQ.

SCOTLAND AND THE MOORS.

CHAPTER I.

Backward, backward let me wander,
To the noble northern land—
Oh, my heart is sad and weary, &c.
Aytoun's Lays.

IT is no use dilating on the miseries of London in August—every one, with the exception of an eccentric correspondent of the facetious Mr. *Punch*, seems agreed upon that point; and as my own opinion in this respect marches with the times, I had at an early period in the summer made my arrangements to breathe the mountain air, and breast the heathery "braes" of the north. Long before the middle of July I found myself repeating "The Lays of the Scottish Cavaliers;" and "Scrope on Deer-stalking," "The Moor and the Loch," Mr. St. John's delightful excursions and adventures in the neighbourhood of the mighty Findhorn, and every other work connected with "the hills," formed the staple of my studies, and the subject of my thoughts. How I despised the blue-book, and contemned all balls but the Caledonian! how I adored the Puritani and the Lucia (mind I had never been across the border); I even went so far as to learn the Highland fling, up two flight of stairs, in a London lodging-house, in the dog-days, the step-accompanying bag-pipes causing the two respectable Quakers below to give immediate notice to quit, and driving an elderly gentleman, supposed at times to be rather flighty, smack into a lunatic asylum, where he is at this moment living on linseed tea and a vegetable diet. All this and more must be laid to the account of the Waverley mania; and right glad was I when the two companions with whom I had taken a moor far in the north announced themselves ready to start, and, as the ladies say, "fixed the day."

The night of the 7th of August was determined upon to embark on board a Scotch steamer at Blackwall; the quantity of dogs (of which more anon), keepers, provisions, Fortnum and Mason's best, and other paraphernalia, making it advisable to proceed, *en masse*, over "the briny," instead of the infinitely shorter, though more confusing method, of the tea-kettle from Euston-square. Need I add that a dinner at Greenwich was the inevitable ante-consequence of our voyage? Of course we dined at the Trafalgar, and in one of that best inn's best rooms did we three—Beeswing, King Cob (so called from an old university nickname), and the "humble individual now addressing you"—eat a dinner in the face of an afternoon sun, that Lucullus might have envied, and Heliogabalus himself could hardly have outdone. Oh, for the pen of Dr. Kitchener! oh for the ἔπεα πτερόνετα of Christopher North—not Christopher under canvas, but Christopher over the mahogany—to emblazon on the golden page of history that gorgeous repast, from its turtle thick and thin—its champagne, sweet and dry—its thousands of specimens of fishes—its millions of animalculæ miscalled whitebait, and devoured with brown bread and butter—its Scotch pigeons—its tendrons de veau—its five magnificent courses leading gradually on to a haunch of venison, and sloping off again through the gradations of a regular dinner of five more, to a cool bottle of claret (by the way, the least thing too cool), a cup of coffee, a glass of white brandy, and a cigar that came from "old Varginny a long time ago," through whose mazy wreaths we contemplated, as at a distance, the action we had been engaged in, and looked back with a calm and virtuous satisfaction on the prodigies we had performed.

The conversation going to the steamer was decidedly dramatic, and was carried on in the eastern fashion, by symbols and signs, rather than by the usual method of interchanging ideas amongst gentlemen. The transition was, I believe, performed in a boat; Beeswing, who had travelled in many lands, being under the impression that he was navigating the Bosphorus, and being much disturbed with the idea of introducing two friends on board a Queen's ship, the quarter-deck of which he appeared convinced he was momentarily approaching. King Cob, who was amiable and accommodating to an incredible degree, was most eager to pull—an exercise from which I with some difficulty dissuaded him, as I was myself anxious to solve a problem which had for some time puzzled me, namely, how many oars we had rowing us, and whether the stroke, a sturdy little waterman with an inflamed nose, was possessed of one eye or four.

"Not knowing the captain," said Beeswing, "and there being no admiral on the station"—what more difficulties he would have enumerated, or to what conclusion this train of reasoning was likely to lead, can never be ascertained, his reflections being here cut short by a bump and a sort of unpleasant heave, accompanied by a rushing sound of water, the tension of a boat-hook, and some valuable assistance under the arms from two powerful individuals. In another moment I was standing on a spacious deck, from whence I could see the lights from the shore reflected on the river till it seemed impossible to distinguish the real from the illusive; and then feeling conscious that the system was somewhat over stimulated, I had the sense to retire to my berth, leaving Beeswing fast asleep on one of the horse-hair sofas in the saloon, and King Cob engaged in a most violent argument with a presbyterian divine, on the free kirk, the currency question, Puseyism, tithes, and the General Assembly, the worthy ecclesiastic appearing to be somewhat bewildered by the suddenness and volubility with which my friend jumped from one subject to another, and the inflexible obstinacy which he displayed upon them all.

Certainly the sensation of waking at sea has a charm peculiar to itself: even through the sickness, the jolting, the smells, and all the miseries of a steamer, there is a freshness in the dancing wave that to me pays for it all. You hear sounds of horror; your boots are not where you put them when you went to bed, and your carpet-bag and hat-box have walked as nearly as possible to the door of your cabin; you share the dressing-room of an asthmatic gentleman, who is groaning and creaking above you: you hear cups and saucers rattling, and feel most unpleasantly convinced that you have no appetite for breakfast; you are aware of the miseries to be gone through before you can even appear upon deck; that shaving is an impossibility, and dressing a series of gymnastics; all your habits, cleanly, comfortable, and coddling, are thoroughly broken through and set aside; yet only open one half inch of the port-hole of your cabin, and when you see the green wave dashing up in the sunshine, and flinging its spray playfully into your face, when you feel the salt breeze cooling while it braces your aching brow, and perhaps catch a glimpse of the white wing of a sea-gull, as he dips into the glancing water, you will confess that there is an additional pleasure in life that you knew not of; and the wish to be on deck, and to inhale the pure and freshening breeze, will become a longing that can only be satisfied by enjoyment.

So it was with me, as I dived and tumbled about my cabin, collecting the necessary articles of dress, unblacked boots, unbrushed clothes, tumbled neckcloth, &c., &c. Beeswing, like the immortal Major Monsoon, preferred making out the first twenty-four hours of squeamishness in bed, and beguiling the lingering hours with hot brandy-and-water; but King Cob, who must have been possessed of the real *pectus robur et æs triplex* of Horace, and who knew not the meaning of sickness or indisposition, by land or sea, was already bustling about the ship, talking to the passengers, hurrying the steward, and promoting the speedy arrival of breakfast by all the means in his power. Him I joined, envying his rosy countenance and sparkling eye, as with trembling limbs and tottering steps I came to anchor on a green settee, and began to "derive great benefit from the sea air."

The voyage altogether was certainly "good fun." Every one knows the eastern coast of Britain too well to have patience with a description of it; but there is a deal of beauty and wildness : witness the cliffs about Flamborough Head, along that sea-board of the German Ocean ; and when we got over our little squeamishness, found our appetites, and began to appreciate the merits of bottled porter and hot whisky toddy, there was much to amuse, if not to interest us. The perpetual eating and drinking, under the especial auspices of King Cob (I must once for all apologize for distinguishing my worthy friend only by his *nom-de-guerre*), assisted by the "meenister," astonished my weak mind more than anything. Not only did we breakfast at half-past eight, lunch at half-past twelve, dine at half-past three, drink tea at half-past six, and sup at half-past nine ; but a grill was always forthcoming, if necessary, about eleven ; and it appeared as if the sickness which pervaded the greater part of the ship between decks was merely a necessary effort of Nature to counteract the perpetual stuffing that went on in the saloon. One of our evenings, I think the first one, was peculiarly sociable ; the party (for there were but few passengers, and most of them were still recumbent) consisting of Beeswing, who had just risen—time half-past ten, P.M. ; the minister ; a Mr. Spoony, *en route* for the Highlands with his family ; King Cob, concocting "a devil ;" and myself. A short cross sea was just getting up, and the steamer expostulating, as steamers do, with the most heart-rending sobs and groans, and an occasional lurch, that made one seize one's tumbler and burn one's fingers involuntarily. The minister was drinking " hot stopping," made particularly "stiff," and we were talking mesmerism, clairvoyance, law, physic, and divinity ; in short, what' ver came uppermost.

"You must allow," said Beeswing, who was deep in magnetism, and a great stickler for the influence, "that there is an affinity between every two human beings, even between every two living animals, that can only be accounted for upon this principle. If I yawn, you yawn (I see nothing to laugh at, Cob!). If you grant me this, you must allow that there is a certain sympathy irrespective of the will of either, between any two given individuals. This is the point I start from; and I conceive everything apparently incredible, which we hear as an operation of magnetism, is simply a modification, or rather a continuation, of this principle—your second sight, sir, in the Highlands, on which I doubt not you place implicit reliance."

"No, sir; no," said the worthy divine : "I can *not* just say I am in my ain self convinced of that faculty as desairving of credence. There was an auld wife in my parish of Auchnakilty, west of Strath-bonnart, that was fain to mak' me believe she was possessed of shupernatural powers; but whesky, sir, whesky was at the bottom o't; and since the breaking up and destruction of the sma' stills, sir, over the greater pairt of the Hielands, I have observed that the second sight has declined in a manner proportionately; tho' it is not for me, sir, to give an opeenion as to the causes thereof."

"Bravo, doctor!" said Mr. Spoony, who, like myself, had never been over the Border, and whose clerical neighbour might be a dean or a bishop for aught he knew; "but I am sorry to hear that the 'still' trade is so far on the decline. I was in hopes that we were not to be much troubled with law beyond the Highland line, and I have been particular to take some shooting in Aberdeenshire, as being a good deal to the north of the Tay, which I take to be the line of demarcation between the Highlands and the Lowlands."

"For the maitter o' that, sir," said the minister, "ye will find there are lowlands in Aberdeenshire as well as in Fife; though when ye get up Dee-side, towards the Castleton of Braemar, ye find yerself surrounded by an awfu' hash of hills; and I'm told the muir-fowl are uncommon rife about

Ballater, tho' being no sportsman myself, sir, I cannot just take upon me to say; but as for law, sir, we hae mair lawyers, ay, and keen skilful men they air, baith in Edinbro' and Aiberdeen, than we can find work for them to do. The Scottish bar, sir, stands high in the profession; and I am myself acquent with an instance whaur the skeelful defence of a counsel, though it failed to convince the jury, was powerful enough to impress upon the mind of the prisoner that he could *not* have committed the crime for which he was tried, and which he had himself confessed, and that he was about to suffer on an unjust and one-sided verdict."

" Clever lawyer that, sir," said Cob, who had just ordered a grill; " I should like to hear the particulars."

" Weel, sir," said the reverend, " it was an aggravated case of murder; and the prisoner, a man of middle age, had himself pleaded guilty to the charge. Mr. Hepburn, now Lord Cockermouth, a lord of session, ye will understand, defended the panel, as we tairm it; and he made sic an awfu' powerful and persuasive speech, demolishing the evidence for the prosecution piecemeal, and holding up his client to be sic an honest, douce, meek, and mercifu' man, that the prisoner himself behoved to weep and take on till he was satisfied it was *not* possible that he could have committed the crime they charged him with; and who was more surprised than he, when the jury, who, providentially for the ends of justice, were a dour plain-dealing set of men, found him 'guilty,' and he was condemned accordingly to be hanged by the neck on the 28th of the month; while Mr. Hepburn set down to prepare for his next case, like a man who had performed his duty with credit to himself, and satisfaction to all concerned. Weel, the puir creature, as he was removed from the dock, passed close to where his counsel was seated, and says he, 'I'm dooting, Mr. Hepburn, that a didna get justice the day?' 'No,' says Mr. Hepburn, as he lookit up from his papers, 'no, but ye'll get it on the 28th.' It was uncommonly neat, sir," was the divine's concluding remark, as he finished his story and his tumbler—an opinion in which all except Mr. Spoony, who was asleep, cordially joined. The powers of speech and redundancy of anecdote being slightly fostered by the strength of his potations, and the *vires acquirit eundo* principle being most true in conversation, he went on to relate to us another anecdote connected with this distinguished lawyer.

"Lord Cockermouth was as good in cross-examining of witnesses as in every other pairt of his profession. I was in court upon one occasion when his lordship's colleague was endeavouring to prove the general ignorance and stupidity of a particular individual, in a case connected with the lease of a farm, thro' the evidence of the witness, a hard-headed Lowland farmer, and intimate friend of the individual whose want of general intelligence it was advisable to establish. 'Well, my good man,' began the cross-examining counsel, 'how long have you known Mr. Mac-Tod?' 'Oo' a've been acquent wi' him may be fifty year.' 'Do you consider him an intelligent man?' 'What's your wull?' 'I say, do you consider him a well-informed man, and one capable of understanding or arranging a difficult matter to his own advantage?' 'A dinna ken.' 'Well, but do you think he is a man of general capacity?' 'A could not say.' 'What I mean is this, my good man: you have known Mr. Mac-Tod for several years, should you say now that he was what you would call an intellectual man?' ''Am no just clear that 'am understanding what y'ere sayin, sir.' 'Allow me,' said Mr. Hepburn to his brother lawyer, 'allow me to try what I can do with this witness;' and accordingly with a good-humoured air and much in his own dialect, he began—'Are ye weel acquent wi' Archie Mac-Tod?' 'Ay, am I; 'am weel acquent wi' him.' 'How lang is't since ye first became acquent wi' him?' 'Hoot! 'ave kent him syne we were bairns at the schule thegither.' 'Is there anything intill him!' 'Hoot! there's just naething at a' intill him but what he puts in wi' the spune.' The evidence was conclusive as to the capacity of Mr. Mac-Tod, and the case progressed accordingly."

We so much applauded the worthy minister at the conclusion of this last story, and were getting on so comfortably under the joint influence of supper, toddy, and small talk, that we never remarked the wind had freshened, and consequently the swell increased, till our attention was attracted to the uncomfortable fact by a wail from the ladies' cabin, and a faint soprano, which whispered, "Stewardess!" *crescendo*, "Stewardess!!" "Yes, mam." "A little more"—I did not quite catch the end of the sentence; but by the tinkling of a teaspoon and the apparent necessity of hot water, it was probably some cordial which had before proved beneficial. It seemed to have succeeded in this instance; for the same voice, apparently much refreshed, was again heard to articulate, " Stewardess, whereabouts are we now?" a question I recollected to have heard at short intervals ever since we left the Nore. "Just getting into 'the Deeps,' mam, at the mouth of the Humber," was the alarming reply. "The deeps! oh, good gracious!" "The deeps—how dreadful!" "Stewardess, ask the captain if there is much danger." "Frightful—the deeps!"—in every key, from matron's bass to maiden's treble, amongst which I recognized the baritone of an ancient Swiss governess, the only lady who had that day appeared at dinner; but who, I have reason to fear, suffered for it afterwards. The stewardess, who eventually obtained the office of matron in a lunatic asylum by way of retiring into an easier situation, was most assiduous in her praiseworthy endeavours to calm the terrors of her lady passengers, and amongst other comforting and imaginative remarks, assured them that the captain said the wind would be sure to go down at twelve o'clock—a promise which appeared to afford the greatest consolation, and which I gave her the more credit for inventing, as it then wanted just five minutes of midnight, and the skipper himself had for the last two hours taken advantage of the comparatively favourable weather, by what sailors call "caulking it," on one of the saloon sofas.

I was in the act of retiring for the night, when Mr.

Spoony, who had been comfortably asleep in his chair, was summoned to attend upon his *sposa*. As I believe he might not venture beyond the door of the ladies' cabin, and consequently the whole of his conversation must have been carried on while standing sentry outside, I did not envy him when I woke some two hours afterwards, and heard him tumbling about for a light, and rolling backwards and forwards to his cabin, he having been then only just dismissed upon the repeated assurance that the ship was not gone overboard, and that there was no apparent likelihood of destruction before dawn on the morrow.

The following day nearly all had recovered their health and good humour, and the voyage proceeded with its usual routine of pacing the deck, smoking (in the forecastle), eating, drinking, arguing, and sleeping, varied only by the amusement we derived from the self-devotion of a Highland piper, returning with his chief to his native hills, and who persevered, in defiance of the most violent sea-sickness, in playing the pibroch which had marshalled his feudal superior to dinner for years, and which the faithful retainer, notwithstanding many interruptions, persisted in completing. It was, too, ludicrous to see the swelling gait and turkey-cock appearance so necessary to enhance a solo upon that national instrument, exchanged for the pale dejected looks of a vassal doing homage unto Neptune, exacted every five minutes, and always at the moment when the "gathering air," getting faster and fiercer, seemed to imply that scores of kilted warriors were tramping their "quick step" to the notes of the sickening minstrel. Notwithstanding all these little events, the whole thing began to get tedious long before we arrived; and I believe it would be difficult to say which of us was most delighted when, steaming up one of those noble estuaries that embellish the N.E. coast of Scotland, we arrived at our place of disembarkation, men, dogs, and guns, all in good order, and tolerably ready for work.

Little time did we put off in seeing curiosities or visiting lions, whilst completing the few arrangements necessary before our fresh departure for "our lodge." Our lodge—what a wild-sounding name, and at the same time what ideas of snugness and comfort suggest themselves at the word! Every squire can have a shooting-box; and it calls to your mind nothing but dust, turnips, partridges, and an occasional hen-pheasant. But a lodge! an Indian warrior has his lodge; and when we talk of it in connection with Glen-anything, we involuntarily associate the idea with grouse, black game, *the chance* of a red-deer at least, peat, mountain dew, and the glorious air of the hills. Impatient were we to get there; never were cartridges, fishing-tackle, and two or three plaids, bought in such a hurry; and scarcely could we refrain from a school-boy's "huzza!" when, late on a glorious summer evening, just about crimson sunset, we came to the front view of our future Highland home. There it lay, white and clean, about a mile from us; a loch—or rather lochy, for it was of the smallest dimensions—within twenty yards of the door; a few birch trees on a green knoll behind it, enabling your eye to form some idea of the mighty mountain at its back; and a small plot of corn covering about two acres, flanked by a dusky peat-stack, and enclosed by a low stone-wall. It got darker and darker as we approached, and we saw but little of our future haunts before bed-time. Everything was arranged in anticipation of our arrival; and when we had inspected kennels, sleeping rooms, &c., &c., we were glad enough to betake ourselves to bed. The last thing I did was to open my window, and gaze into the darkness, trying to picture to myself the outline that would greet my waking eyesight in the morning, and fancying that even then it was possible there might be a wandering red-deer within point-blank distance of my dressing-case.

CHAPTER II.

> It's up Glenbarchan's braes I gaed,
> And o'er the bent of Kittle-braid,
> An' mony a weary cast I made
>   To cuittle the muir-fowl's tail.
> If up a bonny black-cock should spring,
> To whistle him down wi' a slug in his wing,
> And strap him on to my lunzie string,
>   Right seldom would I fail.

GLORIOUS to the emancipated Londoner is the waking on the 12th of August. Tried friends, good dogs, and guns that mock at distance, a well-preserved moor, a picturesque country, and above all, that Highland air which acts like a cordial upon the frame and spirits, making a Falstaff feel as elastic as an Auriol, and induing the pigmy that steers the winner of the Clearwell with the muscular power and self-relying vigour of Ajax the son of Telamon.

"Beeswing, are you getting up? breakfast is ordered at seven. Bravo, Cob! the monarch has actually thrown his royal line over the glassy surface of Loch Cleinich, and already the merry trouts, small, sweet, and ruddy, are fulfilling their destinies in the frying-pan. Beeswing, pray get up."

"My dear fellow, I *am* up, only I can't speak when I'm shaving. Send up Big Sandy; I must arrange about the beats for to-day, as I am the only one of the party who has ever been here before; and if I gave you your own way, *you* would be off deer-stalking, without glass, gilly, or knowledge of any kind whatever; and Cob, with his antics, would disturb the whole ground before luncheon-time, and leave all the best places half-hunted. Come in, Sandy."

Enter Sandy, or Big Sandy as he was usually called — as fine a specimen of a hillman as you shall see between Strathearn and John-o'-Groat's; tall, muscular, square shouldered, and clean made, he would have stood for the portrait of a catheran as well as any proscribed M'Gregor of them all; but Sandy, honest man, was a quiet, decent, kirk-going fellow, who never harmed man or beast in his life beyond the roving hawk or other vermin he trapped so successfully, and whose only weaknesses, if weaknesses they might be called, were a wonderful inclination for tobacco in all its branches, and a slight tendency to take the other sup of the whisky which marks the line between decidedly drunk and provisionally sober.

"Well, Sandy, it's to be a fine day; the mist is clearing, and it seems to be coming down from the tops, which is always a good sign. We ought to get a good bag to-day, from what you told us last night about the birds."

"Oh, yes, ye will get a fine bag the day; and I am thinking it will hold to be a fine day. Yes—there is a good sprinkling of birds in Glen Mivart, and there are many more broods than I remember to have seen amongst the tops into Craig Altyre, and," added Sandy, with a considerate glance at me, "if Mr. Nogo was to take the lower beat of the Moss of Struanach it would not be that steep walking for him, and he would have a fine chance for a blackcock in the corrie where we louse the dogs."

"That's all right, Beeswing. Heavens! how I should like to kill a blackcock! Next to a red-deer, I think I had rather whistle down a fine old blackcock than anything on the face of the earth."

"Well, you can take that beat if you like; you and the King might shoot together, as there ought to be work for two guns, and have Sandy with you; and I will take the upper part of Struanach and the tops beyond the big moss, and take the English keeper with me, as I know the ground. But I hope Cob will not be offended at my requesting his jager to take off those light yellow gaiters, which I fear will much impede his action 'up the hill.' Well, then, that is settled ; so now for breakfast."

And to breakfast we accordingly did ample justice, not without a due vote of thanks to the angler for the first course of our voluminous repast.

As I lit my cigar and lounged over the window of our dining-parlour previous to starting, I thought to myself that hardly even the pencil of Landseer or Frank Grant could have done justice to the scene before me. Imagine a loch of about a mile in length by a third of that distance in breadth, sleeping calmly in the shadow of a glorious black-looking mountain, whose august head was still shrouded in the mist, and whose height, left to the imagination, appeared immeasurable ; the ripple on the nearer shore was all that caught the gleam of the morning sun, but a cultivated strath to my left was bathed in his golden light; the corn was yellowing in patches, and the trees which studded its surface lost nothing of their effect from their stunted growth in such gigantic scenery, where the oaks of Royal Windsor itself would have been but as pigmies in the embrace of that mountain-pass. To my right, hill was heaped upon hill in magnificent confusion; each gaudy tint and variety of light and shade at length resolving itself into that indescribable greyish-blue of a distance that seemed to melt into the summer sky. In the foreground—and here Grant would have been in ecstasies and Landseer in his element— two shaggy ponies, accoutred with panniers, and loaded with plaids, spare ammunition, luncheon, and all other necessaries, held by two heather-legged gillies (alas ! not kilted), and an ancient shepherd in a plaid, and lowland bonnet, lighting his morning pipe. Sandy was still consulting with Beeswing in the lodge, but six handsome pointers and a venerable retriever were scattered over the greensward ; and Mop, the roughest and most insinuating terrier that ever sat on end and begged for biscuit, couching lion-like across the door, with his head between his paws, completed the detail of this Highland picture.

But out comes Cob, in *the shortest* trousers tied at the knees for getting "up the hill"—an operation he never performs without much lamentation, sobbing, and sighing, and many a halt and face-about to enjoy the scenery. Out he comes, shouldering a long double-barrelled *chef-d'œuvre* of the house of Lancaster, and woe to the wing that shows itself above the heather within distance of those deadly tubes. A better shot, a keener sportsman, or a jollier companion never walked. Out he comes, his good-humoured face lighted up with merriment, his jolly sides shaking from the effects of a repartee with which he has just favoured Beeswing; and with a joke for the gillies and a pat for the dogs, he begins to describe to me the intricacies of the path by which we are to arrive at our beat, and having persuaded me that walking is by far the safest way of getting there, proceeds deliberately to mount the pony, and make himself agreeable from the saddle whilst I trudge by his side. In this form we journeyed about a couple of miles, till a turn in the path brought us in view of a mountain stream, stealing down the most sheltered of corries and terminating in the most picturesque of waterfalls. Here Sandy, who had preserved an unbroken silence for the last half-hour, suggested that we should "louse the dogs," as he called it; and forthwith he set at liberty two as handsome pointers as you would wish to shoot over, rejoicing in the names of Port and Kedger, whilst we anxious sportsmen proceeded to load, shoulder, and prepare for action.

Away they go, forty mile an hour, up the hill-side, as if they meant to put its brow between themselves and all restraint; back again, down to the very burn that washes the corrie, to and fro they range; they can go like fox-hounds, and yet how perfectly they are under control! I do like to see the dash of two very high-bred pointers who have not been shot over in a low country, and whose range has never been broken by the "ware fence" discipline so necessary for partridge-shooting. But look, Kedger is down, perfect the attitude, but wanting the eager straining look of a dog when game is close before him, as I find to my cost after striding breathlessly up to him. He is only backing, but Cob points towards the fern which is growing rank and high some two hundred yards below me, and down I go again, cocking both barrels and shaking with excitement. It is Port who has got them, and the game must be close before him. What a moment! but no, his stern moves, and on he crawls, down upon his belly like a stalker as he is; his stern stiffens, but still he moves on, putting one foot before the other like a cat, and as noiselessly as the gossamer that floats above him. Again he stops, and this time his stern is like a bar of iron, and the whole dog is endued with that indescribable, and to me I confess somewhat ludicrous appearance, which distinguishes the pointer when close upon his game. I steal a look at Cob, who replies with a wink. That instant up they get; whir! whir! flap! flap! flap! a brood of black-game, accompanied by their venerable mother, the old grey-hen. Cob probably never moved a muscle; I fired both barrels; alas! the matronly bird fell a victim to my second shot: "down charge" went Port licking his lips, and down went Kedger a long way above us, with his head in the air; Sandy merely remarked, "There is mair grey-fowl before the dogs;" it was not till I had loaded and put my caps on, that I bethought me of my iniquity. Black-game before the 19th, and to slay the old grey-hen! Well, never 'mind—it was Sandy's fault for bringing me here and promising me the chance of a blackcock, which Cob, after he had enjoyed his laugh, told me the honest fellow invariably did with a neophyte. The fact is, he was not very particular about times and seasons himself, and he had so often remarked the keenness about black-game peculiar to beginners, that he brought them here to shoot one as a "bonne-bouche" out of pure civility. "No fines here," said Cob; and as he spoke, cock! cock! cock! whirr! up got an old cock grouse behind him, laughing, as it would seem, prematurely at his anticipated escape. Kedger had passed over him, but my partner's gun was up in an instant, and whack he came, a plumper, rebounding from the heather with the force of his downfall ; a fine old bird he was, wonderfully black for the time of year, and his beak like iron. We voted him a patriarch of the hills, and decided to send him away in the boxes—not to eat him. This was the first grouse I had seen killed, so no wonder I examined him minutely. "Hold up, good dogs ; how hot the sun is! but we shall get a breeze when we have got over this ' face ;' " and "on we goes again."

*　　　*　　　*　　　*

A delightful morning's shooting we had. I was pretty successful for an inferior shot, and my partner as deadly as usual. The fact is, grouse-shooting early in the season is highly complimentary to one's prowess ; the birds are a good size, and consequently a fairish mark ; they generally get up at about the right distance, and there are no hedges, trees, or people at work to make it necessary to rap them down at any particular moment; the consequence is, that a slow poking shot may fill his bag with great certainty and satisfaction. But wait till brown October closes his mellow career, when the oak coppice is red and tan-coloured, and the heads of Ben Cruachan, Ben Mohr, or Ben Wyvis are whitening with snow ; then the old cocks skim whirring away, two feet above the heather, and fifty yards from the gun at the nearest, whilst the bare and exposed places are covered with game in packs that never wait to be looked at. True must be his eye, and quickly must he pitch his gun and shoot, who would walk home triumphant with his eight or ten brace at this period of the year ; and more enjoyment has he for his toil in bagging that gallant few, than if he had slaughtered hecatombs on the 12th, or depopulated the preserves of the whole county of Norfolk.

Toiling over all sorts of ground under an August sun is doubtless as exhausting to the inward man as it is fatiguing to the outward one. We had settled to meet at luncheon, when, according to a time-honoured custom, one hour was always devoted to refreshment, repose, and the sedative of "sublime tobacco." Beeswing's ground lay so that the extremity of his beat was close upon the spring where we had arranged to lunch. And as, enveloped in our plaids, we threw ourselves upon the heather in all the enjoyment of rest after labour (the poor man's luxury, entailing no regrets and burdened with no tax), we heard a shot fired a little way from us, and ere we had unpacked our eatables, Beeswing made his appearance, evidently ready to take his share of whatever was going on.

"Well, old fellow, what have you done?"

"Thirteen brace and a-half, one snipe, and one rabbit. And you?"

"We have had a capital morning's sport, and have not been over the best of our ground yet; twenty-one brace of grouse, five hares, and a grey-hen. Nogo shot uncommonly well, so that the grey-hen hadn't a chance."

"It was my first appearance," I modestly suggested, "and I could not be expected to be steady from riot."

"Never mind," said Beeswing, alluding to an old story of poor Goosey, when "a gent" rode on to one of his hounds and killed him; "it's a poor concern that can't afford one a-day. Put the whisky-flask into the spring to cool. Sandy, get me a game-bag to sit upon. Now then, caterer Cob, what have you provided for luncheon?"

I have been at many a mid-day feast, wedding-breakfasts, *déjeûners*, pic-nics, and all; but never did I enjoy anything so much as our simple meal by that mountain spring; the water was like crystal, and tasted positively sweet; and after nature was satisfied, it was too luxurious to smoke recumbent, gazing with half-shut eyes upon one of the fairest scenes in bonny Scotland.

"Sandy, what is the name of this spring?"

Sandy's respectful reply I cannot put into orthography, for the Gaelic word was unattainable by my Saxon ear; but it signified, as he condescended to translate it, The spring of the corrie of the Glen of the Fairies.

"Yes, that is just the meaning of it in English—The spring of the corrie of the Glen of the Fairies:" and truly it was worthy of the Elfin land. Beeswing, who is a Gaelic scholar and a sort of a poet to boot, volunteered us a metrical version of the tradition which gave to the glen its fairy title. He wanted to tell it us first in Gaelic, but I think even he was abashed at the idea of Sandy's criticisms on his pronunciation; and as I remarked to him that the original would not benefit either of *us* very much, he tipped us his own doggrel, as King Cob expressed it, in the following words :—

THE FAIRIES' SPRING.

They have stolen the child from his father's hand,
    He is gone from his mother's knee ;
They have borne him away to the Fairy-land,
To ride in the van of their elfin-band,
    For a babe of the Cross was he.
Kind father, meek mother, ye seek him in vain ;
You never shall look on your darling again.

To the mountain side, where the flowers grew wild.
    He would wander forth to play ;
And the fairies had seen that winsome child,
With his golden curls and blue eyes mild,
    And his simple childish way.
And the Elf-king met him ; " Come hither," said he,
" Come ride to the land of the fairies with me."

He thought not once of his mother's woe—
    He forgot his father's home ;
For they gave him a steed like the driven snow,
And he smiled as they led him down below,
    Through the middle of earth to roam.
And they showed him their treasures of jewels and gold,
And they welcomed the boy, for they loved him of old.

But the child soon pined for his mother's care,
    And he pined for the light of day ;
He pined for the freshening mountain air,
And his blue eyes ached with the dazzling glare
    Of their cavern's magic ray.
For the sign of the Cross had been pressed on his brow,
And he might not be thrall to the fairy-folk now.

> But few that have lived with the elfin race
>   May revisit earth again;
> No more shall he smile in his mother's face,
> For his spirit has flown to its heavenly place—
>   With the fairies it could not remain;
> Though deeply they loved him, and hopeless and wild
> Was the elfin's grief for the Christian child.
>
> They buried him down in a cavern lone,
>   Deep, deep in the mountain's womb:
> And their tears welled up through the hard grey stone
> To the earth above, as they made their moan
>   O'er the infant's early tomb.
> And sweet to the thirsting lips of men
> Is the Spring of Tears in the Fairies' Glen.

"I believe it to be an invention of your own, Beeswing."

"You shall have Sandy's version in Gaelic if you are incredulous; but we must be on the moor again; so fill powder-horns and shot-pouches, out with the two young dogs, and '*en avant, messieurs;*' but first, one small libation of the pure dew of the mountain; it will taste like 'liqueur' after cooling in that icy spring."

"How we shall walk after it!"

> "Nunc est bibendum, nunc pede libero
>   Pulsanda tellus."

"Sandy, your health."

"Here is better sport still, gentlemen."

And the young dogs being uncoupled, my partner and I are again on foot and bent upon destruction—somewhat stiff, 'tis true, but much invigorated in body and mind by our repast.

We toiled on, as is usual in shooting, some part of the day, for two hours or so, with but indifferent success; and here, I may remark, how often I have heard surmises as to the whereabouts of grouse during a portion of the day. You shall go on a moor, where on the 11th your keeper found a brood in every moss-hag, and you shall find that at one period or another of your day's sport generally during the early part of the afternoon, you keep stamping on over every description of ground without firing a shot, till surprise fades into disappointment, and disappointment degenerates into disgust. You are presently rewarded, when the birds begin to feed, by coming in upon them in multitudes; but where they get to during the "dark hour"—whether they retire to dress for dinner, or what becomes of them—passes our knowledge of the craft altogether. So it was with us. Two mortal hours had we of this pursuit of moor-fowl under difficulties, varied certainly by one brood getting up considerably out of shot, and the consequent committal and punishment of one of the young dogs, who, tired of snuffling all over the hill-side without finding, testified his joy at the presence of game by pursuing them open-mouthed and putting up another brace who might have sat till now but for his exertions. This glaring offence having been properly taken notice of, Sandy called my attention to a deep zig-zag mark upon the heather about eight or ten yards long, and terminating as abruptly as it commenced; a large rock, apparently split, lay midway, and this he informed me was the work of lightning in the previous week: there was something awful in the visible handiwork of the destroyer thus traced upon nature's boldest features; the brow of the mountain thus seared and riven by the thunderbolt called up an idea of its immeasurable force verging upon the supernatural. Everything is now accounted for upon scientific principles, and it is quite right that it should be so, and that the human mind should know and understand its power over the very elements. We have tamed the lightning on our wires as we have bound the giant steam upon our railways; we have made the one a porter and the other a postman. Yet for all that, there is something to me in a thunderstorm beyond a mere chemical combination of certain fluids; and the child who cowers in holy awe at that voice from heaven has more of my sympathies than the sagacious "Franklin" flying his kite into the thunder-cloud, and drawing off from its lightning-charged batteries whatever quantity of the electric fluid he required for present use.

These remarks I did not make to Sandy, who would not have understood them, or to King Cob, who would have laughed at them; so I kept them to myself, and my meditations were soon disturbed by the improvement which showed itself in our sport. The sun was getting low, and the birds were on the move as feeding-time approached. "Bang, bang!" "Down charge!" "To-ho!" and the rest of it, was now the order of the day; and we picked up a capital bag by the time we got to the end of our ground. The last moss we shot was full of hags, and impossible to be traversed by a pony, or indeed by any animal but a tolerably active pedestrian; the moss or bog being very soft and treacherous, and the little knolls of sound ground—*Scotticè*, "hags"—being at that exact distance apart which tempted the ambitious sportsman to a leap, not always a successful one. Here, though nearly dark, we got some capital shooting; and when we turned out our bag on the track where we met the pony, and which was the conclusion of our beat, Hesperus, or whatever the star was that had just made its appearance, twinkled down upon forty-five brace of grouse, seven hares, a couple and a half of snipe, one teal, and my grey-hen. Six mountain-miles had we to trudge home in the dark, and no pony to ride, this time; but, after such a day's sport, who would feel beat? And then the relief of getting upon a road, no matter what sort of one, after moiling all day up and down hill, working back, shoulders, loins, and lungs, is *faute de mieux* the next thing to an arm-chair; so we lit our cigars, and steamed away merrily, beguiling the distance with many a pleasant jest and oft-told tale.

"Ye will see where there is a grey rock above yon knowe, *wast* of the birches—no, ye will not see the grey rock, but ye will see a bare place in the heather. Aweel," began Sandy, between the puffs of the shortest and blackest of cutty-pipes, which seemed to grow to his teeth; and forthwith he related to us a plaintive tale, which, tragical as was its termination, was somewhat spoiled in the sentiment to his hearers by the language in which it was couched, being translated into the "other tongue," as Sandy called it, out of the metaphorical dialect of Ossian; but the substance of his story was melancholy enough. It appears that when Sandy was a "bit laddie," as he called it, there were two brothers of the name of Connell living in the Glen: stout, active hill-men were they both, and employed in looking after the game, destroying the vermin, and keeping down the rabbits. John—or "Dark John," as they called him— the eldest, was a wild, headstrong, good-humoured fellow, with but little of the proverbial caution of his nation, and a tendency to fun and frolic, of which even an Irishman need not have been ashamed. There was not his equal in the Strath at putting the stone, tossing the "caber," dancing the Highland fling, and all the other accomplishments of a mountaineer; whilst Angus, the younger one, was of a more reflective turn of mind, and delighted in passing his hours alone upon the hill, or wandering by the loch. He was supposed to know most concerning the habits of deer, to be the wariest stalker, and the best fisherman of all the inhabitants of the Strath; and a good-looking, quiet lad he was, with a degree of determination and pluck concealed beneath his mild exterior that a stranger would hardly have given him credit for. In fact, Sandy, who knew them both, was of opinion that, where "heart," as he called it, was wanted—signifying courage—Angus was more "to lippen to" (*Anglicè*, to be depended on) than his boisterous brother. The fair sex were not so very plentiful in the glen, and most of the specimens were somewhat tough, smoke-dried, and stricken in years; but Agnes, the daughter of old Peter Cameron, the publican, needed not such foils as the ancient crones about her to be reckoned the flower of the whole country-side. At kirk and market Agnes was the acknowledged beauty, and as good as she was bonny. Many a lad, both up and down the glen, was sighing for Agnes: but she never so much as looked over her shoulder at one of them: and although a lassie that knew her most intimately affirmed, as she told

Sandy, that dark John Connell was the fortunate suitor, it was certain that no one had ever seen her bestow the slightest mark of her favour on the jovial forester, nor had that worthy himself ever been heard to boast that Agnes would come to his whistle, as he called it—a note which, by his own account, caused half the lasses in broad Scotland to come trooping over moss and heather in his wake. Nevertheless, Dark John was the man; and in vain did the gentle Angus, whose heart had been long given to this mountain-daisy, woo and strive to win her in his homely way. Who can explain the wayward causes of a woman's fancy? John, who was not much given to the softer emotions, liked the lass well enough, as he himself said, and it is certain that he respected her more than the rest of her sex; but as for the sort of passionate love which she had conceived for him, and which poor Angus suffered for her, he had it not to give. Things went on in this way, somewhat after the fashion of Stone's popular picture of "Cross Purposes," till poor Angus, wearied with his unsuccessful suit, heart-sick and desolate, determined to "take the shilling," and strive to forget his love and his native glens in the columns of the gallant —th Highlanders, then quartered in a town some thirty miles over the hills from his abode. It was during the heat of the war; and there was no fear of a stalwart, clean-limbed youth like poor Angus being refused. Everything was settled for his departure; and one fine morning in October, the embryo soldier started off on his career, accompanied by his brother, to see him over the first few miles of his journey. They were the best of friends, those two; not even the affection borne by the one for her who loved the other, had been able to sow dissension between the brothers; and often had the elder, in his rough, good-humoured way, endeavoured to dissuade Angus from his purpose of enlisting. They started, accordingly, like true Highlanders, "shoulder to shoulder" —Angus more cheerful than he had been for months, and John, with his gun poised on his broad shoulder, and his brother's bundle in his hand, careless, merry, and swaggering as usual. Sandy saw them as they passed his bothy. Alas! he never saw either of them again alive. The following morning, he went through the knoll of birches he had pointed out to me, to look at his traps; and his attention was arrested by some hoodie-crows circling and wheeling in the air over an object in the heather some distance ahead of him. He walked on, thinking it might be a dead sheep, or some stricken stag who had staggered there from the forest with his death-wound. Imagine how his blood curdled when he came upon the body of Dark John lying stiff and stark, with his gun by his side! The whole charge had passed through his broad chest, in a wound you might have put your hand in, and he had been dead several hours. Sandy carried him on his back to his father's house; and as an over-ruling Providence willed it, the first person he met was Agnes Cameron, as he toiled down the path with his ghastly burden. Often has he prayed that never again might he hear such a scream as burst from that poor girl's throat. It was too much for a woman to bear; and when at length Sandy succeeded in getting some assistance, they carried her home a raving maniac. With the wildest gestures, she denounced Angus as the murderer of his brother—"her John, Dark John, the loved of her heart." She would share his grave—was he not her own? And then, with bursts of fearful laughter, she spoke of him as still alive, merry, and dancing at their wedding; and called to her father, and the minister, and her neighbours, to see how happy she was. Happy, poor girl! before another autumn shed its leaves, she was at rest in her grave; and many an eye was wet, and many a cheek pale, amongst the kind-hearted mountaineers who bore her to her last home. Many were the different opinions in the glen as to the cause of poor John Connell's death; but he who could alone have cleared it up was drowned some two months afterwards, in embarking for foreign service; and the simple and primitive inhabitants of the glen had no means of knowing whether Angus had ever been made aware of his brother's death, or whether he knew too well that brother's fate, and sank into the ocean stained with a brother's blood. I must say for Sandy that he put the more charitable construction upon the facts, and seemed to look upon the catastrophe as an accident that must have happened after the brothers had parted, as it proved, for ever.

Ere the story was concluded, we were long past the spot that Sandy had first pointed out to us; and before we had done discussing the details of the tragedy, the lights were twinkling in the lodge in front of us; and thus ended my first day's sport in the Highlands of Scotland.

CHAPTER III.

> Bold Robin Hood was a forester good,
> As ever drew bow in a merry green wood,
> And the wild deer we'll follow, we'll follow,
> The wild deer we'll follow.
> *Old English Glee.*

> Then let the stricken deer go weep,
> The hart ungalled play,
> For some must watch while others sleep;
> Thus wags the world away.
> SHAKESPERE.

"I CAN'T see them, Beeswing. How many are there?"

"You are looking a mile too far; carry your eye over the burn; have you got the upright stone above that bare place? now then, a little to the right of that."

Following these directions with a hand not over steady, I caught a glimpse of a moving object in the field of my "Dolland," and then after dancing the horizon up and down in my glass a good deal, I got fairly steadied on the objects I wished to study; two, three, all stags; another getting up, a hind evidently; and moving the prospect a little further to the right, I made out two or three more of the weaker sex, apparently somewhat restless, and feeding only at intervals, one head out of the lot being always in the air. I turned to Beeswing, eager to be at them; but to my surprise, and somewhat to my disgust, he had calmly sat down upon the heather with his glass shut up, and the air of a man who did not mean moving yet awhile, at all events. I looked at the forester who that day was to be the guide of my destiny. He was quietly lighting his pipe with his back to us, and appeared to concentrate all his energies on that soothing task.

"Well," I said, rather impatiently, "why can't we get at these fellows? they are not very far, and nothing can be easier than to get into that broken ground and stalk them."

"*Festiná lente*, my good fellow?" was Beeswing's sagacious reply; "those hinds are very restless; I fancy there must be more deer that we cannot see that have the wind of us; *they* have probably moved, and our friends opposite can see them. Now, M'Cormick, who is, as you say, a man of few words, when he has finished his pipe will crawl forward to yonder brow, whence he will get what he calls a fine view down the glen, and when he comes back we shall know better what to do. In the mean time we are as well here as anywhere, and if you like to smoke you may puff away with a good conscience and this consolatory reflection, that if the deer can wind the tobacco they can wind you, and the latter odour is the most likely to disturb them of the two."

Whilst James M'Cormick, the forester, is crawling to the brow aforesaid, and ruminating there upon his stomach, I will explain how an humble individual like myself came to be enjoying the princely sport of deer-stalking in one of the finest forests in Scotland.

One Sunday, early in September, we had attended our parish church as usual—an excellent habit, which except from stress of weather we never broke through, although the distance was an honest seven miles from the lodge. Coming

out of the kirk we met a hospitable chieftain whom Beeswing
and myself had both known in the south, and whose stalwart
frame I have seen carried in no mean place over the grassy
hills of Leicestershire, which probably appear a dead flat to
a Highlander. With all the hospitality of his nation, and
the kindness peculiar to himself, he begged us to come over
to him and kill stags, shoot grouse and roe-deer, drink
claret, and eat venison for as long as we could make it convenient to stay. Our engagements prevented our availing
ourselves of his invitation that week, and his own unavoidable absence from home prevented our now doing justice to
his hospitality, save as far as the forest was concerned, and
in that he had insisted we should have a day at any rate.
Accordingly that morning Beeswing and I, accompanied by
the faithful Sandy and one of the ponies, had started at early
dawn for the forest, and after seeing the mist clear away,
and speculating on the beauty of the sunrise, had it not been
so shrouded, we arrived at the trysting place, where we
found our silent friend, James M'Cormick, the chieftain's
principal forester, smoking the pipe of contemplation on the
rock of silence. No Indian warrior could be more stoically
immovable than this "*shallager*" of the north; I think,
during the whole day, the words that passed his lips might
have been counted on my fingers; and his second in command, a hard-featured personage with a grey eye, grey hair,
grey whiskers, grey clothes, and a grey pipe, seemed to
emulate the discretion of his chief. I afterwards found that
the tongue of the latter gentleman was to be loosened by an
occasional sip from my flask, but all the whisky of Loch-
nagar would not have oiled M'Cormick into rhetorical trim.
After the most respectful greetings on our part, and a Gaelic
salutation from Sandy, replied to by the great man in a guttural monosyllable, we proceeded to our work. First of all
we walked up a steep hill at a very merry pace, following
our silent guide in Indian file; and after we were sufficiently
blown to render such a proceeding most acceptable, we called
a halt, and the wizard, looking sagaciously about him,

plucked a handful of heather blossoms and threw them into the air to ascertain how the wind blew. This appeared a sufficient reason for walking down the hill again and half way up another, when, to my delight, we turned aside into a corrie and stopped once more. Here the same natural dog-vane was again made use of, but this time the blossoms floated the wrong way, and we were accordingly led in the same cautious manner right up an almost precipitous ascent at the same pace as before—I should say a good five miles an hour. How blown I was! and when I had panted myself into a recovery, and addressed a polite observation to M'Cormick relative to the fineness of the weather, if I remember aright, the look of contempt with which my observation was received by the Gael effectually prevented my making any further advances towards his confidence, and I made up my mind that, come what might, unbroken silence and implicit obedience were to be the order of the day. One or two more halts only led to one or two more breathers, and I was not sorry when a cairn of stones, evidently put up for the purpose on the brow of a wide descent, and commanding an uninterrupted view of the mountain opposite, promised us a resting place. Here it was that we caught our first view of the deer before mentioned, and here we waited patiently till our oracular guide should have completed his survey and decided upon his plan of operations.

It appeared that the rest of the deer, which we thought might have winded us, were too far "wast" to have been influenced by our presence, and our friends opposite continuing to feed on most contentedly, it was decided that we should proceed to circumvent them at any rate; but there was a stag in the other parcel which M'Cormick had seen, that the chief was most anxious to get, from the peculiarity of his head: he had no antlers but the two brow ones, his horns being totally devoid of points, and, when seen sideways, like those of an antelope. The forester had recognized him in an instant, and as he was a large heavy deer it was advisable to get him. After a low conversation in Gaelic, in which Sandy was called in to council, it was arranged that James M'Cormick should take charge of Mr. Nogo, and endeavour to bring him within killing distance of the original parcel, in which there were two very fine stags; whilst Beeswing, attended by the grey man and Sandy, was to do his "possible" towards bringing home the singular head which was destined to decorate the chieftain's halls. This decision having been come to, I was forcibly divested of my rifle (a double-barrel that only wanted to be held straight like the rest of them), and after a brief farewell to Becswing I was marched off in the custody of M'Cormick, apparently in the contrary direction to that in which my destined victims lay.

It appears to me that the pleasures of deer-stalking would be materially enhanced by some slight insight into the principles on which the sport is conducted, or, if I may so call it, into the "rules of the game." Here I was striding away after a little round-shouldered Highlander, turning when he turned, crouching when he crouched, and running, leaping, crawling, and wading, like the shadow of my conductor, who all the time seemed to imply by his manner that I was the same sort of incumbrance to him that a kettle proverbially is when attached to a dog's tail; and all this without my having the slightest idea where I was going, what we were striving to do, or how all these mysterious evolutions were to bring us any nearer the object of our "chasse." I can conceive that to go out by yourself to look for deer, and then to stalk and bring down the "fattest i' the forest" by your own unaided sagacity, must be one of the greatest and most exciting of all triumphs connected with "*gun-sporting.*" I do know one gentleman who is in the habit of "stalking for himself," but he is a man endued with talents that fall to the lot of few; and unequalled as he is in his profession, he is almost as distinguished in the deer forest, the hunting field, or the river. He "kens the wiles of dun deer-stalking" as well as Donald Caird himself; but I believe that to the generality of sportsmen the extremely accurate knowledge required of every inch of a large extent of ground is the insuperable difficulty, a knowledge seldom gained but by one who has been brought up in the forest, and hence the necessity for a leader or dry-nurse in this most popular sport. But in the mean time down goes M'Cormick as if he had been shot, with a wave of his hand much like that with which Sandy signalizes Kedger to "back," and readily as that well-drilled pointer I imitate his motions. Once he looks round, and in the face which I see under his arm, there beams forth at length something like a spark of excitement. What a catching thing that same excitement is! I feel my heart begin to beat and my hand to shake, though *my* prospect is bounded by the nail-studded soles of M'Cormick's shoes. "Doon, doon; bide you there;" and with head bent low towards the heather, and a half-nervous inclination to laugh, I lie impatient, watching the proceedings of the artist. Carefully, warily, and cat-like, he crawls to where the heather is growing thick and bushy, some fifteen yards ahead of me. Often stops he, and stealthily creeps on to the wished-for spot; once he looks back at his charge, but though shaking with impatience I lie quiet as a mouse. Now pushing the tufts of heather aside, his body prone upon the earth, he raises his head an inch, an inch and a-half; then watches, gazing motionless, as if turned to stone. Once only I saw an involuntary motion of the hand towards the glass; but no, it would make too much noise, and they are probably so near that it is not worth while to use the telescope. Will he never come back? At length he has looked his fill, and cautiously and stealthily as before he crawls first backwards, then sideways, crablike, but ever noiselessly, to the spot where he has left me. With one finger he beckons, and I follow. Serpentlike is the advance, as before. Well might Falstaff say that "eight yards of uneven ground were three-score miles and ten" to him, for in those few yards how many ideas came rushing through my brain! the few seconds it took to accomplish them seemed like hours. And now we reach the reconnoitring-spot; and drawing me alongside of him, M'Cormick places the rifle, long since uncased, in my trembling hands, with the short and pithy injunction, "Tak time!"—words that should be written in letters of gold. My brain is in a whirl, but I have sense enough left to know I had better have a good view of them before I think of firing, and I part the heather with my hands to take my first look at a red-deer on such intimate terms. What a glorious fellow, feeding unsuspiciously, broadside on to me, and not seventy yards off! He looks as big as a cow, and much lighter in colour than I had fancied from seeing deer at a distance, and through a glass. Surely I shall not miss him. Somehow I feel cooler now, and stretch back my arm for my rifle; though I never heard the click, Sandy has given it me cocked. How silent everything is! I can hear my own breathing and my heart beating. Not another sound in the waste about me. Firmly I press the butt to my shoulder, and remembering Purdy's oft-told directions, I cover him scientifically, beginning at the knee, and so up the fore-leg to the shoulder; but no, it will not do, the sight of my rifle is dancing up and down, now over his back, now under his belly. I fear a hand, at no time over steady, is now shaking like an aspen leaf. "Tak time!" I think of that watch-word, and determine to be deadly. I will give myself two or three minutes to recover, and remain in readiness with my rifle to my shoulder; but see, he raises his head; in another moment he may move to a less favourable position. Again the sight travels from the knee to behind the shoulder; again I feel that I am too hurried, but this time mortal finger will bear the suspense no longer, and the trigger is drawn. Crack! it is over. Can that be the *thud* I have heard deer-stalkers describe—the hollow dead sound of the well-directed ball? I fear not, for see, they are dancing away towards the hill, apparently not going very fast, pitching and lurching along much at their ease and not at all as if they were frightened. My fellow is in the rear; can he be wounded and lagging behind? no, he joins the others, and now they all turn to the right, and re-crossing a small burn appear to be coming back to us. M'Cormick, who has been looking through his glass with a satisfied air that ought to have convinced me I had made a clean miss, the next best thing at all times to a " clean shot," shuts up his glass in a twinkling, loads my rifle in double quick time, and without a word of explanation, but almost imperceptibly signing to me to follow, dashes away over the moor, making furious running in a diagonal direction up the hill, bounding over the mosses like a tennis-ball, whilst I labour breathlessly in his rear, eyes watering, head swimming, and knees shaking, but inwardly trusting that all these exertions may in some way lead to the retrieval of my character as a sportsman. How I got up that hill, or how I contrived to wait upon the sinewy little Highlander in that severe race, I have never been able to conceive. Fortunately my rifle was a heavy double-barrelled one, and as *he* carried the fire-arms, it may be that the weight brought us somewhat together. However, this forced handicap at length came to an end; and when I threw myself prostrate by my leader, where he had quietly sat himself down and was pressing the caps more firmly on my rifle, I found that, strategist as he was, he had conducted me to a pass up which his sagacity and experience informed him our deer were almost certain to make; and not only these, but also a large herd that had been disturbed by the flight of their friends, and who incontinently made for this well-known passage. Long before they appeared I heard them coming; quicker and louder was the tramp; I even heard them blowing like so many over-driven sheep, and at last up the steep they charged "*en masse.*" The run in for the Great Yorkshire Handicap would have hardly made more noise. I picked out a big one in obedience to Sandy's "Noo, noo;" but whether the pace deceived me, or the excitement was too much for me, I know not; I have only reason to believe that the billet appropriated to my bullet was drawn upon mother earth. The second barrel, however, was more fortunate; as, although a regard for truth forces me to confess, I fired into "the brown of them," it lodged just behind the shoulder of a very fair-sized, decent sort of stag—by no means one of the finest, but an average sort of fellow, that weighed some twelve stone after he was "*gralloched.*" Poor fellow! I thought of Jaques and his "dappled fool"—a disrespectful epithet for so noble an animal—as he tried in vain to stagger on with the rest of the herd. Soon he stopped, sickening; and ere the rifle was again loaded, he was prostrate in the heather, kicking convulsively on his back.

It was a moment of triumph, when M'Cormick, running up to the dead deer, putting his knife in his throat—a piece of carving which I declined the honour of performing —proceeded to gralloch him *secundum artem*, and pronounced him a "fine fat beastie," whilst I smoked a cigar by his side, and persuaded myself I had killed him most artistically. His head was his worst part, numbering but few points; however, he would doubtless have had a very fine one in a year or two, had he been spared, as M'Cormick remarked for my consolation. Triumphant as I was, I could not help feeling something akin to remorse at what I had done— this morning bounding over the moor in vigour and beauty, and now stretched upon the heather "a slovenly unhandsome corse." So it ever is; an alloy must be mixed with all earthly pleasures, and in shooting more especially: it is difficult to say what *is* the moment of enjoyment, though the fascination of the pursuit on the whole is undeniable.

"Well, M'Cormick, another sup from the flask, and then we shall be better able to decide upon our future proceedings."

A long and unsuccessful stalk, spoilt by putting up an envious old cock-grouse just as we were getting within shot, brought us nearly to the twilight hour, and darkness had closed upon the mountains ere we reached the forester's lodge, where we met Beeswing and his companions glorying in the downfall of two fine stags; the one a royal one, the other the antelope-headed hart that had been coveted so long. An enthusiast in stalking, as in all other sports, I had better give a detail of his adventures in his own words, which served to beguile our long and wearisome journey home, performed in the primitive fashion usually called "ride and tie."

"After I left you," said Beeswing, "the parcel of deer that we had made up our mind to circumvent shifted their position, and, moving up the hill to some very rugged ground, gave us a capital opportunity of coming in above them, and so getting more easily within shot. After a council of war and a good look at the ground, we determined to move cautiously down the burn that you remember remarking, then along the wood at the bottom of the glen, and so, by a wide circuit over the tops, keep our advantage of the wind, and make a pretty sure, though a long and tedious stalk. Accordingly, down the course of the burn we went, creeping on our hands and knees, and occasionally stopping and taking a look through the glasses to see that the deer had not moved. All was most favourable, the wind was quite steady from the same quarter as before, and the deer appeared to have no idea of changing their ground. At last we reached the river at the bottom of the glen, and, after fording it, proceeded to walk in a more comfortable attitude through those magnificent old firs that fringe the water all the way down its course. You, who are fond of scenery, would have been delighted with it. All round us the giant fir-trees were standing in every kind of position, rugged and magnificent as the mountain that overtopped them. Beneath our feet the river was brawling and rippling its course towards the western loch; and whenever we got a glimpse of the far distance through a vista in the dark pine wood, our view was shut in by the 'monarch of mountains,' rearing its conical-shaped head towards the heavens, and blue as the summer sky into which he seemed to melt. I confess I walked along so absorbed in the wild charms of the scene, that deer-stalking was the last thing I thought about, and I got into the realms of fancy as far as the Rocky Mountains and the peaks of the Himalayas (in both of which ranges, as in many other places, I have wasted my time), till I was recalled to the business in hand by a whisper from the cautious Sandy to the grey man, which, when rendered into the Saxon, signified that it was quite possible to come upon deer in the wood, and that the gentleman (meaning me) had been 'here before.' This significant hint was not lost upon grey Donald, and our order of march was resumed with the caution so necessary where deer are concerned, and which we had all laid aside for a time, to enjoy the luxury of straightening our backs and stretching our limbs after our transit down the burn. As the wood got thicker we moved more stealthily, and I remarked in one or two mossy places the tracks of deer, evidently quite fresh, and from one of the prints on a sandy spot at the water's edge, it was evident that a large heavy deer had been there this morning. I was sure we all drew the same conclusion, though not a word or sign did we exchange; but I thought the grey man's caution was redoubled, and Sandy kept turning a piece of heather round his brown fingers, as he always does under strong excitement. Suddenly Donald stopped, and ere he could turn to me, the same object brought me down upon my marrow-bones in a twinkling. There in front of us, not sixty yards off, and fast asleep, lay a magnificent dark-coloured stag, with a royal head to all appearance, and not a sentry near him in the shape of hind or companion. We could see his great brown side and one of his horns; but from where we lay, it was impossible to cover a vital place. Without exchanging a syllable, Donald and I simultaneously pointed to a soft boggy place about twenty yards below us, where we should be more under cover, and probably be able to get a better view of him, while at the same time we should increase the distance but little. You may suppose that extreme caution was required to shift our ambush, and once during the operation he lifted his head; like Medusa's, it turned us for the moment to stone, and ere I had time to count his points, for I could see him quite plain through some scrubby juniper, he sank to sleep again. Well, we got to our lair at last; and when we arrived there, we found that he had shifted his attitude again, so that his back was to us, and as long as his head was down it would be impossible to *account for him*. There was nothing for it but patience; we were in the best possible position should he get up, and we dared not risk another move for fear of disturbing him, more particularly as we could not be certain that there were no other deer in his vicinity. I contrived to look at my watch, and you may imagine how long the time must have appeared when I tell you that we waited there quite an hour—what a nap he must have had! I had determined in my own mind not to give him longer than that, and there I lay, rifle cocked and finger on the trigger, biding my time. Very few events happened to beguile the weary minutes: once a couple of wild ducks soared over our heads high up in the sky, and once I fancied I caught the sound of the trampling of deer, but faint and indistinct, and producing no effect on my sleepy friend. A passing cloud gave us the benefit of its contents, but we bore its wrath even more philosophically than Socrates did his ducking from Xanthippe, and soon the sun shone bright as ever again. At last, time was up, and I determined, come what might, to rouse my royal victim. Cautiously and slowly I covered the spot where his head *should be*, and, when I had secured my range, gave a long shrill whistle, such as I have heard accompany the vociferous demand for music shouted by the Olympic gods of modern times: as I anticipated, up went his head to listen, the back of it between the horns completing the straight line of which I had got the first two points with the sight and notch of my rifle. That instant I pressed the trigger, and with a bound into the air the glorious fellow turned over and lay motionless upon his last resting-place. We gralloched him on the spot, and left him there to be brought home this evening. His head was a particularly fine one—royal, having twelve points, and the three topmost forming a cup on each side quite '*en règle*.' His antlers were magnificent, spreading almost into a semicircle, and, in short, one of the finest heads I ever saw. We poured an appropriate libation, in the shape of a dram, down each of our throats; and whilst the disembowelling process went on, I found the grey man became much more communicative. It appears that he knew me by name, having been employed in a large and well-known forest where I used to stalk a good deal, though I had never actually been out with him; and amongst other matters connected with deer, he told me one curious fact, which proves how strong the vital principle must be in the wild animal:—

"His former noble master—whose coronet should have borne the heather-blossom proper, interlaced with its own strawberry leaves, so fond was he of 'the hill,' and so untiring and successful a deer-stalker—had shot a fine stag through the heart, one day at the commencement of the season. On opening him the duke's bullet was found, as might have been expected, having passed right through the heart and caused instantaneous death; but, *mirabile dictu*, another ball was likewise discovered actually embedded in the fleshy part of that vital region, which from its appearance must have been there a considerable time. Whether the deer had actually been shot in the spot where the bullet was found, or whether it had worked its way gradually from a wound in some other part of the body, it is impossible to say; but I believe this is the only instance of an animal surviving the contact of a foreign substance, such as lead, with its heart.

"Well, this being entirely an extra performance, and a piece of unlooked-for good fortune, I gave my auxiliaries an additional sup, and we then proceeded to stalk the original herd that we had seen from 'the cairn.' We had, of course, to take a fresh observation, and found that they had again moved, and were apparently somewhat restless; the consequence was that we had a most severe stalk. Once, when we were getting near them, they moved across a corrie in a manner that obliged us to enter upon a new system of operation. Another time the wind changed, and we had to begin over again, thinking ourselves lucky that they did not discover us; at last we got well above them, and into some pretty good ground, that bid fair to bring us within distance unobserved. Everything was propitious, and we had advanced to, as near as I could guess, about one hundred and fifty yards from them, when we distinctly heard them move. It was impossible to say what had disturbed them, but disturbed they certainly were, and the only thing to be done was to rush forward to the brow that we were making for, and take the chance of a wild shot. A hundred yards did it, and never in my life did I go such a pace—up hill too. When I got to the brow they were lurching away over a moss, some three hundred yards below; but, '*fortunati nimium,*' one fat heavy fellow had loitered behind the herd, and had stopped to rub his horns against a scraggy dead tree that stood out in the foreground—there never was such a piece of luck: it was the antelope head. Down I squatted upon the heather, got a rest upon my knee, took lots of elevation, for I had hardly time to put up my second sight; and blown as I was, I shot him right through the heart—'more by good luck than good management'—but I was delighted to get him, and I think altogether this has been one of the most satisfactory days at deer that I have ever enjoyed."

THE END.

www.ingramcontent.com/pod-product-compliance
Lightning Source LLC
Chambersburg PA
CBHW020318240426
43673CB00039B/851